CONSTITUTIONAL
DEMOCRACY

CONSTITUTIONAL DEMOCRACY

by
János Kis

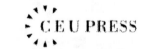

CEU PRESS

Central European University
Budapest New York

©2003 by János Kis
English translation © by Zoltán Miklósi in 2003

First published in Hungarian as
ALKOTMÁNYOS DEMOKRÁCIA – Három Tanulmány
in 2000 by INDOK, Budapest

English edition published in 2003 by

Central European University Press

An imprint of the
Central European University Share Company
Nádor utca 11, H-1051 Budapest, Hungary
Tel: +36-1-327-3138 or 327-3000
Fax: +36-1-327-3183
E-mail: ceupress@ceu.hu
Website: www.ceupress.com

400 West 59th Street, New York NY 10019, USA
Tel: +1-212-547-6932
Fax: +1-212-548-4607
E-mail: mgreenwald@sorosny.org

Translated by Zoltán Miklósi

ISBN 963 9241 28 8 cloth
ISBN 963 9241 32 6 paperback

Library of Congress Cataloging-in-Publication Data
Kis, János, 1943–
  [Alkotmányos demokrácia. English]
  Constitutional democracy / by János Kis; translated by Zoltán Miklósi.
  p. cm.
  Includes bibliographical references and index.
  ISBN 963-9241-28-8 (hardcover) – ISBN 963-9241-32-6 (pbk.)
  1. Democracy. 2. Liberalism. 3. Constitutional courts–Hungary. I. Title.
JC423.K53713 2002
321.8–dc21

                                                    2002014606

Preprint by Attributum Stúdió, Budapest
Printed in Hungary by Akadémiai Nyomda, Martonvásár

Table of Contents

CONSTITUTIONAL REVIEW

1. Introduction

2. Interpreting the constitution

3. Striking down legislation

THE LEGACY
OF THE FIRST HUNGARIAN
CONSTITUTIONAL COURT

1. The interpretive practice of the Constitutional Court

2. Summary and a glance to the Future

Introduction

Let me begin with a terminological question. The title of this book is "Constitutional Democracy". That of one of its studies is "Liberal Democracy". What does the different choice of words refer to?

Liberalism is a set of political values and principles: values such as liberty and equality, and principles such as everyone's right to make sovereign decisions about their own lives. The term "democracy", too, when combined with the adjective "liberal", refers to political values and principles, to everyone's equal right to participate in the conduct of public affairs, to collective self-governance, and so forth. Thus, to talk about liberal democracy is to articulate normative ideas, aims to be pursued and restraints to be observed.

Constitutional democracy usually refers to a set of political institutions. A regime is called democratic if members of the legislature are selected through periodically held elections, if the vast majority of the nation's adult population has the right to vote as well as to run for offices, if the electorate may choose between a number of competing candidates, if lawmaking is the prerogative of elected representatives, and so on. In a constitutional regime, the provisions regulating the legislative process itself cannot be amended through the normal procedures of the legislation but certain special procedural requirements must be satisfied.[1] Thus, "democracy", when combined with the adjective "constitutional", refers to a specific arrangement of political institutions.[2]

In the world Hungary is aspiring to join, constitutional democracy enjoys widespread acceptance. Let us assume that it is unanimously accepted.[3] Should this be the case, one should still be able to offer reasons for preferring constitutional democracy to all other possible political regimes. It, like every other institutional arrangement, or indeed the mere existence of political institutions, is in need of justification.

The values and principles of liberal democracy present us with ideals and requirements that can furnish reasons for preferring constitutional democracy. There are other strategies of justification available, too; not all proponents of constitutional democracy are at the same time liberal democrats. Conservatives, while maintaining that the masses are in need of guidance by the elites, may nevertheless hold that it is preferable for various different elite groups to change each other in government, and may favor the practice of periodically held elections for securing the alternation of elites.[4] At the same time, they may emphasize the importance of political traditions being changed only in a piecemeal, organic fashion, and may value constitutionalism as a guardian of historical continuity.[5] Technocrats may argue that a representative system provides better chances overall than its alternatives for experts to gain access to power, while claiming that constitutional constraints tend to rationalize macroeconomic policy.[6] Individual rights, political equality and the values do not play a discernible role in these approaches (or are rejected outright as delusions). For liberal democrats, on the other hand, these values have a foundational role; they favor constitutional democracy because it removes more obstacles from the course of realizing liberty, equality, collective self-government and political participation than its rivals.

Any justification must satisfy two requirements. First, it has to show that the values and principles it invokes are attractive and worthy of being pursued, and that they cohere with one another as well as with our fundamental convictions about how things are in general (i.e. what we think about human nature, the sources and motivating force of morality, the laws of social stratification, or the relation between individual and collective goals on the one hand and the available resources on the other). That is, it has to show that its values and principles mutually reinforce and elucidate rather than exclude one another, and that they are consistent with our general beliefs about social reality. If humans are essentially irrational, being in need of the guidance of tradition and authority, as old-style conservatism claimed them to be, then liberty is a mixed blessing. If individual liberty and collective self-government are, though both in principle valuable, in profound conflict with each other, then one cannot satisfy their requirements simultaneously. The first step of justification must involve, then, a demonstration that our values and principles are really worthy of being pursued, that they mutually support one another, and that they are compatible with our ordinary beliefs. Such unified systems of values and principles constitute the normative political theories, i.e. liberalism and its rivals.[7]

The political theory that is the best in this sense can justify the political regime that it privileges. Liberalism makes the claim of offering the best justification for constitutional democracy.

However, it is only a necessary but not yet a sufficient condition for justifying an institutional order that the best political theory should privilege it against all other conceivable arrangements. There are political theories whose requirements could be met only by otherworldly, utopian regimes. The liberalism of the mid-twentieth century, having been formed, as it was, in response to the spread of totalitarian ideas, popularized the belief that there is a direct link between utopian thinking and practical politics drifting towards totalitarian dictatorship.[8] I doubt if there is such a relationship; in any case, the mechanisms of this putative connection still await reconstruction. In fact, utopias may perform an important critical function in social thinking; they may highlight undesirable features of the existing regimes, may help to uncover their sources and to set a direction for the advocates of change.[9] A political theory, however, cannot rest content with this much. A theory whose requirements are satisfied only by some utopian regime can only be of a rather limited use. For a theory to be able to orient political action an institutional realization is needed that is compatible with the constraints of the real world. That is, it must be able to maintain prolonged existence and to accomplish its goals without the fundamental facts of social existence being mysteriously removed (thus, for instance, without the scarcity of resources being overcome by universal abundance).

This implies, on the other hand, that it is not only the theory that justifies the institutional arrangement privileged by it, but the privileged institutional order, too, contributes to the justification of the theory itself. If one succeeds in showing that constitutional democracy is the best available institutional realization of liberal values and principles, and that the liberal theory offers the best available reasons for preferring constitutional democratic institutions, then what one has achieved is not merely a justification of constitutional democracy, but also a justification of liberalism.

In the first phase of the inquiry, the nature and specific order of institutions do not surface; in this "pre-institutional" phase, the subject matter of the discussion is the relation between values, principles and beliefs about social reality. In the second round, on the other hand, institutions are being confronted with our normative conception.

Yet the confrontation cannot be confined to evaluating institutions against the standards of our normative conception. Nor does it suffice to provide additional reinforcement for our principles by demonstrating their institutional practicability. Confrontation with institutions inevitably raises new questions for theory, for it may occur that even the best institutional arrangement is unable to simultaneously realize such values that were shown to cohere with each other at the "pre-institutional" level of analysis. Then, the assessment of the theory is reopened.

My book addresses difficulties of this latter nature. It does not discuss whether, for instance, the values of individual rights and of collective self-government are *in themselves* mutually supplementary to and reinforce one another. I discuss, rather, the question as to how it bears on what one should think about liberal theories that their values and principles are–like any other political values and principles–not practicable immediately, but only through the medium of institutions. I will address three major difficulties.

The first of these concerns the principle of *economizing on virtue*. It is an idea inherent in liberalism since its inception that social institutions may function effectively only if people tend to observe their rules even in the absence of permanent supervision. Institutions must be designed in a way that under ordinary circumstances almost everybody be sufficiently motivated to abide by them. Thus, it is not prudent to coordinate social action through institutions that rely, for the observance of their rules, on the motivating force of extraordinary virtues; being virtuous is not something altogether alien from most people, yet it does not belong among the motivations that tend to become dominant under all circumstances. Predictably functioning institutions must entail systems of rules that people may find it reasonable to observe even if they are not unusually virtuous; even if, in the limiting case, they are not moved by anything other than self-interest. The early liberals formulated this thesis first in relation to the market, yet they were quick to extend it to politics. Be that as it may, in the sphere of politics the principle of the economy of virtue gives rise to serious difficulties. In the economy, at least under the ideal conditions of perfect competition, it may be acceptable that everyone observes only their own interests, the countless individual decisions being coordinated by the market in a way that the outcome be the greatest possible good of all. By contrast, one of the subject matters of politics is precisely the stipulation of those rules that steer individual decisions in the economy and elsewhere, and which system of rules is to be preferable over others depends on how the public interest is to be (collectively) interpreted. Politics can avoid neither discussing what the common good is nor making decisions that depend on interpretations of the common good. If it nevertheless tries to do so, and refers the individuals as citizens to their private interests, democracy comes into conflict with its point. Politics will be divided between, on the one hand, Institution Designers who know what the common good consists in and shape the rules of politics accordingly, and, on the other hand, the majority of citizens from

whom the common good is concealed and who are manipulated by the Designers, through their private interests, to make the desirable decisions. The
first study in this book, "The Common Good and Civic Virtue", addresses
this difficulty. It discusses how the liberal principle of the economy of virtue
could be made compatible with a conception of democratic politics that may
be attractive to liberals.

The second difficulty I address may be put in the following way. Liberalism requires, on the one hand, the protection of individual rights and, on
the other hand, that all individuals participate in political decisions as equals.
It appears, however, that the protection of rights and democratic equality
are not compatible; if people are equal as voters, the majority may decide
whatever violation of rights it deems practical. If, by contrast, rights are
granted special protection, democratic equality is infringed upon. Traditionally, this objection is presented as indicating a direct conflict between liberal and democratic principles, as though these two sets of values originated
in two different and distinct sources, with their eventual clash being inevitable, since their respective definitions do not take into account the other. In
this form, the argument is untenable. Any satisfactory theory of liberalism
must be able to show how democratic values proceed from fundamental liberal values; for liberal theories, democratic values are not external facts but
applications of liberal principles to the special problem of collective decision
and deliberation. That is exactly why it is not an infringement on democratic values, but an indication of the boundaries of their legitimate scope, when
a liberal theory states in what sort of situations is it acceptable to make
democratic decisions and what belongs to the exclusive authority of individuals and their voluntary associations. The "pre-institutional" phase of
inquiry, therefore, need not detect a conflict between individual rights and
democratic equality. Yet the difficulty is a real one, even though it is usually located inaccurately. Its real location is in the domain of institutions. The
issue of the limits of collective decisions is a controversial one and, thus, it
requires a collective decision. If that decision, in turn, is bound by special
procedural requirements to secure the victory of liberal principles, the principle of democratic equality may be violated. If, on the other hand, the polity rejects all constitutional restraints on the collective decision making process, the liberal rights themselves may suffer. The second study in this book,
"Liberal Democracy", is for the most part devoted to identifying and resolving this difficulty.

The third difficulty is directly linked to the one just mentioned.
Constitutional restraints are of no use if the legislation can make valid laws

with a simple majority, without respect to the higher-order provisions incorporated in the constitution. In order that the constitution be a set of enforceable legal provisions rather than a collection of mere good wishes, it is necessary that there be such an organ that safeguards the observance of constitutional regulations and strikes down unconstitutional legislation. This organ—in Europe typically the constitutional court—has such a competence that seems to conflict with the basic principles of democracy. The main arguments supporting this contention are usually presented in the following way. First, in a democracy, only elected representatives may amend the constitution, and while constitutional review often amounts to constitution making, the judges are not elected representatives. Second, even though in a democracy the body of elected representatives may delegate authority to other bodies, they can do so only on the condition that the thus authorized organs act within the boundaries set by the laws given to them by the representatives, and are not allowed to revise these. By contrast, the authority of the constitutional court is a delegated one, yet it includes the power of striking down legislation. I cursorily take notice of these objections at the end of "Liberal Democracy" and address them in detail in the longest study of this book, titled "Constitutional Review". This study also makes an attempt to outline a theory of constitutional arbitration which is coherent with the conception of constitutional democracy proposed here. The fourth study included in this volume applies the most important insights of this theory to the practice of the first Constitutional Court of the Hungarian Republic created in 1989.

This extension indicates that even though the present book discusses theoretical problems that are worthy of consideration in their own right the context of raising these problems is practical. The studies collected in this volume reflect political debates provoked by the transition from communism to democracy in the fatherland of the author, Hungary. Nevertheless, I will in general refrain from making the practical conclusions explicit; for reasons of genre, the four studies for the most part only *show* rather than *say* them.

* * *

This book was born at the Political Science Department of the Central European University. I discussed each of its pieces with a number of my colleagues here. I received inspiring remarks about an earlier version of "The Common Good and Civic Virtue" from Loránd Ambrus-Lakatos, Iván Csaba and Gábor Tóka. "Liberal Democracy" owes a lot to Ferenc Huoranszki's criticism and to my conversations with Iván Csaba, Róbert Gál and Tamás Meszerics. It was the latter colleagues, too, with whom I discussed the most difficult questions of the second and third chapters of the study on "Constitutional Review". This study also owes a great deal to András Bragyova and to the debate I conducted with Nenad Dimitrijevic about his manuscript "Constitutional Democracy, or How to Prevent the Rule of the People". I am much indebted to all of them. Special thanks are due to Andrew Arato, who subjected the Hungarian version of my studies to thoroughgoing criticism. Following his remarks I have substantially rewritten the sections on popular sovereignty and on collective self-binding.

I also thank Csaba Tordai for taking care of the manuscript and István Musza for his assistance in collecting the material.

The first version of "The Common Good and Civic Virtue" was published in the 1998/2 issue of *Világosság*. "Liberal Democracy" was first read at the symposium dedicated to the memory of László Csontos, and it is also included in the volume containing the material of that conference [Róbert Iván Gál and Zoltán Szántó (ed.), *Cselekvéselmélet és társadalomkutatás* (Osiris: Budapest, 2002)]. "Review" was first published in the 1999/3, and 1999/4 issues of *Fundamentum*. "The Legacy of the First Hungarian Constitutional Court" appeared in the 1/2000 issue of the same review.

Budapest, July 28, 2000   *The Author*

NOTES

1 A democracy is obviously constitutional if it has a written constitution whose amendment rule contains special provisions. Yet it may be constitutional even in the absence of a written constitution, provided that there are unwritten constitutional customs that may not be overridden by a simple act of the legislative majority.

2 Our terminological usage would be more transparent, should we make a distinction between P-democracy and I-democracy, with the former referring to democratic principles and values, while the latter to democratic institutions. Yet I would like to avoid an overly technical use of language, thus I adhere to the same term in both cases, while trying to avoid equivocations by contextually clarifying the actual referent of the term "democracy".

3 This is far from being the case. There are some who, while favoring democracy, reject all constitutional constraints on the legislation as contrary to democratic principles. Others even reject legislation through representatives and admit only the direct exercise of the legislative power as truly democratic. Yet others claim that there is no democracy until the private sphere (eminently the sphere of labor) is exempted from the authority of democratic decision making. And of course there are those who

oppose democracy in principle, who prefer some of the traditional versions of authoritarian rule or total dictatorship, or, on the contrary, favor a social order without a state, that is, anarchy. Such views, however, fall outside the current political consensus, albeit for different reasons.

4 Cf. S. M. Lipset, *Political Man* (Garden City: Anchor Books NJ, 1963).

5 Cf. M. Oakeshott, "On Being Conservative". In: *Rationalism in Politics and Other Essays* (London: Methuen, 1962).

6 On the rationality of economic constitutionalism, see J. M. Buchanan "Law and the Invisible Hand". Buchanan, *Freedom in Constitutional Contract* (Texas: A&M University Press, 1977), pp. 25–39.

7 I wrote "liberalism" rather than "liberal democracy", for I take it that liberal and democratic values do not originate in two distinct sources but constitute a single unified theory. True, democracy has liberal as well as non-liberal justifications (such as the populist one that regards the people as a collective subject, and equates democracy with the rule of the thus conceived people), but these differ from one another not in combining the same democratic values with different complementary values but in tracing back democratic values and principles to, and interpreting them in the light of, divergent more fundamental values and principles. A theory of liberal democracy is, if successful, nothing but comprehensive and unified theory of liberalism.

8 Cf. F. A. Hayek, *The Road to Serfdom* (Chicago: University Press, 1944). K. Popper, *The Open Society and Its Enemies I-II* (London: Routledge, 1945, and Princeton: University Press, 1962).

9 Ferenc Huoranszki makes a similar though not identical claim in his book: *Filozófia és Utópia* (Budapest: Osiris, 1999).

THE COMMON GOOD
AND CIVIC VIRTUE

1. Liberalism
and republicanism

Liberalism came to dominate political philosophy in the early 19th century. From hindsight, it long appeared as though it had dominated the two preceding centuries as well. Fresh developments in the history of ideas have shown, by contrast, that this image is false. During the centuries of its inception, liberalism had to share its theoretical influence with a rival trend of thought that is now called republicanism.[1]

The republican doctrine constituted a specific interpretation of the political tradition of Antiquity. Its central thought was furnished by two theses: first, the aim of any political community is to promote the common good; second, the primary condition for realizing the common good is that the actions of individuals should be motivated by civic virtue. The republican authors took civic virtue to consist in those personal traits which the majority of citizens must possess in order that their state be capable of realizing the common good, that is, that it be internally stable and flourishing and externally independent. First and foremost, they thought civic virtue to involve a readiness to participate in public affairs and to subordinate private interests to the interests of the community.

Early liberalism may be read as a critique of these republican theses. It claimed, on the one hand, that nothing can be good or bad unless it can be shown to be good or bad for individual persons. When claiming that something is good (or bad), one must be able to show that the existence of that thing is good (or bad) for at least one living—or future—human being. Thus, one can talk about the common good only in a derivative fashion; in the sense, that is, that something is good for every member of a community, or that it is good for some of its members while it is not bad for any one; or that even though it is good for some and bad for others, the goods outweigh the bads and the distribution of harms and benefits is not unfair to anyone. Let us call this the thesis of *ethical individualism*.[2]

Ethical individualism entails that goods cannot be experienced by one person for another one (one cannot enjoy a good novel for one's beloved partner, no matter how much she would like to enrich the body of his literary experiences), nor can the capacity of experiencing such states be acquired for another person (one cannot learn to ride a bicycle for one's child, no matter how clumsy it may be), nor can an action be performed for some other person (one cannot act as a responsible teacher instead of one's friend, no matter how important it is for one that he be one). Individuals take charge of their lives, they possess the ultimate authority when adopting, revising and pursuing their personal mode of life, and they bear the ultimate responsibility for their lives being meaningful and good. This claim has further important consequences.

First, any acceptable political arrangement must provide the greatest possible liberty for the individual, so that he can seek and promote his own good, and this liberty must be protected by rights to prevent illegitimate invasions by others. Call this the thesis of *negative liberty*.[3]

Second, even though participating in public affairs belongs to the aims that give meaning to a life, it inevitably has to compete with other aims for the scarce resources of time and energy of the individuals. And while in the private domain the decision of an individual who is in possession of her freedom is of decisive importance, in the public domain it is only one among countless other such decisions; its influence on the outcome is, thus, almost negligible. It follows, therefore, that the time devoted to private affairs is much more valuable for the individual than the time spent on public affairs. Thus, such a political arrangement is required that can guarantee the greatest possible liberty for everyone, without at the same time having to demand their permanent, unwinking and selfless political activism. A political order seeking to satisfy the requirements of ethical individualism must allow its citizens, should they so desire, not to participate in public affairs more than what is needed for the periodical reelection of their leaders, and to leave politics to their representatives in the periods between elections. Call this the thesis of *limited political readiness*.[4]

Finally, the proper functioning of a polity must be independent not only from everyone's readiness to devote all their time to participating in public affairs. It should no more depend on the citizens' readiness to subordinate their private goals to the interests of the community whenever they make decisions. Institutional rules must be so specified as to provide individuals with self-regarding incentives to observe them in most of the typical situations, self-interest being a safer, more reliable motive than identification with the interest of others. Such rules are needed, therefore, that yield the greatest possible common good while allowing each individual to be guided by self-interest. Call this (together with the contention that a good polity order does not require the permanent, vigilant public activism of its citizens) the thesis of the *economizing on virtue*.[5]

The thesis of ethical individualism challenges the republican principle of the primacy of common good. The thesis of negative liberty, along with the thesis of the economizing on virtue, challenges the idea of politics based on civic virtue.

Republicanism was in the descent, while liberalism was on the rise. By the early nineteenth century, the contest was unambiguously decided in favor of liberal thought.

In the last third of the twentieth century, however, the controversy once thought to be closed for good has been unexpectedly reopened. The reconsideration of the place of the republican tradition within the history of ideas itself was related to the new controversy. Western democracies are plagued by *malaise*; politicians and politics are losing authority, and there are increasing doubts about the capacity of representative democracy to adjust government decisions to the will of the voters. The new republicans blame the victory of liberalism two centuries ago for the symptoms of decline of these days. The reinvigoration of democracy requires a break with the classical principles of liberalism, they hold. One must return to the tradition of *res publica* that relies on strong political participation and personal sacrifice— on the primacy of the common good and on civic virtue.[6]

The message of new republicanism is for the most part critical; it does not provide a program for transforming democratic institutions. Thus, it is not entirely clear whether today's republicans seek a general rejection of liberalism or only its thoroughgoing revision.

The republican critique of liberalism has surfaced in Hungarian political thought as well after 1989. In the case of Hungarian republicans, however, the question of their relation to liberalism can be easily decided. The Hungarian republicans are liberals. While they unequivocally state their profound misgivings regarding the picture liberalism draws about the public domain and the workings of democracy, they nevertheless want to maintain liberalism's commitment to individual liberty and the protection of privacy. They are not considering the abolition of the representative and constitutional framework of democracy, either. Yet they are profoundly dissatisfied with the way constitutional democracy is operating in the third Hungarian republic. And they maintain that the political outlook of liberalism is either one of the causes of this predicament or at the very least it hinders a genuine confrontation with that predicament. The situation can be remedied only through a radical theoretical revision of liberalism, so they claim. Hungarian republicans propose exactly this—a republican "correction" of liberalism.[7]

But what does a "correction" of liberalism mean? The new republicans talk quite a bit about the need of modern democracies to raise citizens who are mindful of public affairs and willing to participate in them. They talk less about how the workings of a democratic polity that relies on substantial civic participation should be imagined. It is clear what the republicans think is wrong with the liberal conception of representative democracy. It is less clear what kind of alternatives they propose.

My present study has two goals. First, I would like to clarify what a conception of democratic politics which is still liberal but which is nevertheless corrected in the republican spirit would look like. Second, I examine what is tenable and what is untenable in the republican critique of liberalism. To achieve that, it is necessary that we make possible a comparison between the classical liberal conception of democratic politics and its republican rivals. I shall begin with the latter task.

Jean-Jacques Rousseau is the one classical republican author who formulated the single most developed theoretical model for understanding democratic decision making. In what follows, I will try to summarize this model and contrast it with the classical liberal model of democratic decision making, first expounded by Jeremy Bentham and his disciple, James Mill. However, I will not present these models in the versions found in their first exponents, but will rather discuss the improved modern versions that originate in them.[8] Thus, the Bentham–Mill model will be divorced from hedonistic utilitarianism. In a similar vein, the Rousseauean model will be divorced from the belief that the laws of a representative democracy rule over their subjects as alien powers, exactly like in any despotic system, and so that the people must itself be its own legislator.[9] Likewise, I drop the Rousseauean contention that voting is a cognitive act whereby the majority of votes actually reveals the truth about the common good (or rather about the "general will" directed at the common good). In what follows, I will refer to the former as the *preference-aggregating* model, while to the latter as the *ethical* model.

The models presented here give a very rudimentary picture of democratic politics. Detailed descriptions of political institutions or of organized political groups do not figure in them. They make observations only about the motivations of individual participants of politics, about the objects and the manner of their decisions, and about the outcome of the aggregation of the multitude of individual decisions.

A last remark should be made before plunging into the subject. My study takes the theses of ethical individualism, negative liberty and limited political readiness for granted, and examines how the thesis of economizing on virtue is to be judged in their light. The theses of ethical individualism and negative liberty formulate moral principles of a foundational role, while the thesis of limited political readiness enters into the discussion at a later stage, where the fundamental moral questions have already been settled. Ethical individualism can be taken as settled; the idea of negative liberty needs slight corrections; the thought of limited political readiness rests on valid observations, yet the early liberals failed to harmonize the latter with a further, equally valid claim, to the effect that political participation belongs among the privileged values of human life. These details, however, are beyond the scope of this study. In what follows, I will concentrate on the thesis of economizing on virtue.

2. The preference-aggregating model

The preference-aggregating model conceives democratic politics after the image of the market. Voters play here a role analogous to that played by consumers; they seek their share in the goods distributed by politics. Political programs among which voters may choose represent the supply. Not unlike decisions of consumption, voters' decisions are governed by self-interest. Citizens rank the offered programs according to the benefit they may expect for themselves and for their immediate families from their realization. They give preference to the program from which they expect the largest private gain. Their votes reveal the demand that the totality of individuals who possess the right to vote have for the programs supplied.

In the preference-aggregating model, politicians are akin to businessmen on the market. The difference is that politicians try to maximize electoral votes rather than profits expressible in terms of money. Of course, like business profit, votes are not valuable in themselves but as a means of what may be achieved through them. Votes decide who will occupy various representative positions. The model does not rely on the assumption that politicians are guided by an urge to promote elevated goals by performing their offices. It takes them to strive for power to attain personal gains (whatever such gains may consist in). This, however, involves no disadvantage to the outcome of the political process. A selfish politician is no worse than a selfless one, provided that he is able to act rationally. If so, his decisions will end up promoting the greatest good of the community, just as the self-interested decisions of market agents combine to yield the largest possible common benefit. The politician who will finally succeed among his rivals is the one whose program offers the greatest personal advantage for the greatest number of citizens. The proper functioning of democracy, in the preference-aggregating model, is safeguarded precisely by the fact that everybody acts self-interestedly, without needing to exercise extraordinary virtues.

Like the market itself, democratic politics, according to this model, understands the demand represented by individual preferences as given. It does not evaluate preferences but rather simply aggregates them, no matter what their content may be, and adjusts collective decisions to the thus calculated outcome. The outcome of voting depends solely on the actual preferences of the voters; as to what the outcome *should have been like* (had the majority recognized its real interests or had it taken into account independent moral considerations) does not influence the result.

Therefore, the preference-aggregating model cannot define the common good in any other way than as the sum of the goods privileged by the totality of preferences revealed through voting. It does not and could not accommodate the idea of any common good that would be distinct from and could be confronted with the latter. In the assumptions of this model, the goal of democratic politics is to select and realize that specific set among the possible sets of goods producible and distributable by politics that was preferred by the largest number of voters against other such sets of goods. All other considerations are beyond its scope.[10]

Finally, the primary goal of the preference-aggregating model is explanation and prediction. It relies on two sorts of data: the preferences of the voters and those running for office on the one hand, and the fundamental rules of the electoral system, on the other. Based on such data, it tries to predict who will be the winner, or whether the system will be able to guarantee a relatively frequent change of leadership, and so forth. Yet beyond explanation and prediction, the model also furnishes normative criteria for evaluating the workings of representative democracy. It claims that filling the most important offices by election and reelection produces the available maximum of the common good.

In this model, the common good is identified with the set of goods privileged by the totality of preferences of the individuals constituting the state. Furthermore, it is supposed that a representative democracy maximizes the preferences of the community, because only those have a chance to get to power and retain it whose program and capacity for governing is judged to be the best by the majority.

Unless voting rights are sufficiently universal, the majority of voters do not represent the majority of those living in the territory of a given state. Thus, one of the normative implications of such a theory is that suffrage must be as nearly general as possible.[11]

The main tenets of the preference-aggregating model are relatively well known; thus, they could be summarized briefly. The ethical model, on the other hand, requires a more detailed discussion.

3. The ethical model: the responsible voter

The ethical model rejects the market analogy. It does not necessarily reject the market itself; that is, it does not necessarily reject the idea that the market lets the individuals pursue their private interests and treats their preferences as given. It allows to take that to be acceptable in the market, where everyone decides for oneself and only for oneself. If there are such decisions that it is better for them to be made independently, each for oneself, then the institution of the market is ethically defensible. The question then becomes what it is reasonable to let market mechanisms decide, and what needs to be retained for different forms of cooperation—such as democratic politics. In any event, the analogy of the market ceases to be valid in the domain of collective decisions—or so the ethical model believes. In case of voting, individuals are not choosing simply for themselves. They do so for all.

Therefore, the question voters have to decide is not merely which program is best for them and for their families. They must decide in favor of that which is best for the community as a whole, in favor of the program that might be expected to make the community economically successful, culturally flourishing and socially just, and so on. This is the vantage point of the ethical model.

Let us call *communal preferences* the ranking individuals make when they order—with a view to the community as a whole—the states of affairs attainable as a result of political decisions. Let us assume that every voter forms her communal preferences and everyone votes exclusively on the basis of communal preferences. Theoretically, this assumption is compatible with the preference-aggregating model, for the form of the latter is neutral with respect to the content of individual preferences. Thus, if communal preferences replace the voters' private preferences, the preference-aggregating model will show that the common good is identical with the sum of communal preferences as indicated by the outcome of the vote. To put it differently, the common good is that which the majority prefers for the community. The next contention of the ethical model to be examined rejects this thesis. What is good for the community does not depend solely on the desires of the individuals who constitute it, but also on factual truths and value judgments that make these desires reasonable. The common good is not that which we happen to collectively prefer; to the contrary, one has reason to prefer for one's community that which is the common good. If it is true that it is favorable for Hungary to provide government subsidies to small farms (because it makes the territorial, professional and income distribution of the society more equal, while allowing the national economy to flourish, for example), we have a good reason to prefer redistribution directed towards agriculture and its small units. If, on the other hand, our beliefs are false, we have to revise our preferences.

True, self-regarding preferences depend no less than communal preferences on the truth of a number of underlying beliefs. When we make market decisions, our goal is not to obtain a set of goods we *believe* (maybe wrongly) to be more valuable for us than their alternatives. To the contrary, we would like to obtain that set of goods which is *actually* the most valuable. It is not indifferent for us whether our decisions are guided by informed preferences or not, or whether we are positively deceived.

Our preferences are, thus, not brute facts; neither the ones informing our decisions for the community, nor the ones guiding our private decisions. There is an important difference between the two kinds of decisions, though. When we decide for ourselves, we take responsibility for the rightness of the decision only for ourselves and to ourselves. Others may criticize our decisions and point out that it would be more reasonable for us to decide in a different way—yet the decision we take for ourselves is not supposed to give rise to resentment and moral criticism on their part. On the other hand, if we decide for others—for the community—our decision is subject to moral assessment. We are responsible for choosing for the community that which it is reasonable for us to prefer for it. This is the third thesis of the ethical model.

Even if our decision affects others as well, this circumstance appears to be offset by the fact that we are making a decision together with others. In a well-ordered liberal state (usually) no one interferes with the decisions that concern only the agent. Thus, the agent alone is responsible for the outcome of a typical private act. With collective decisions, this is not the case, except under extraordinary circumstances. Let us imagine that before the last voter casts her ballot, the votes tie. In that case, the ballot of the last voter is a decisive one. It is as though she were the only one to vote, like in the case of a private act. However, the probability of the other votes being evenly distributed is inversely related to the size of the electorate, and decreases sharply. Likewise, the personal responsibility of each voter for collective decisions decreases in the same proportion.

One might be tempted to think, therefore, that since the impact of each individual ballot is so tiny, it does not make much of a difference whether it accords with the common good or not; it is in any case inconsequential. We may vote in accordance with whatever communal preference we may see fit—or even completely selfishly or arbitrarily.

This thought, however, does not follow from the fact that it is unlikely that our vote will be a decisive one. Assume that acquiring and processing the information underlying our communal preferences is totally costless; in any one moment, we are perfectly well informed without investing time, money or energy into acquiring the necessary information. If such were the case, we would have to adjust our vote to the best-warranted factual statements and value judgments, even though we knew that it is most unlikely for our vote to be a decisive one. For still, it *may* turn out to be decisive.

In fact, acquiring the necessary information has costs; therefore, we may not be expected to cast our vote in the possession of the most reliable knowledge. It may be acceptable to economize on the resources we wish to devote to gathering and processing information. One need not be mindful of every single detail of different party programs. It may be sufficient to select our party by relying on simple, easily recognizable symbols. A devoted Christian will vote for a Christian party. A secular humanist will vote for a liberal party. We may expect that in a sufficiently large number of cases our party will represent the policy we would favor (or its closest proxy), should we familiarize ourselves thoroughly with each detail. We need to invest more energy into gathering political information only if our chosen party begins to act conspicuously "wrongly". This much follows from the fact that the personal responsibility for the outcome of the elections is distributed among millions of voters. It does not follow that we may in good faith disregard what we take to be true about the likely political conduct of various parties.

Yet is it really the case that voters need to consider the alternatives on offer with a view to the other members of the community as well? Why could they not each decide only with an eye to their own good (and that of their family), and the many self-interested decisions add up to yield the common good, as happens on a well-regulated market?

We have four reasons to reject this hypothesis. One is brought to attention by the preference-aggregating model itself. Self-interested decisions may produce the greatest good of the community only if nobody can displace the costs of their decisions onto someone else. If the market cannot make the producer pay for environmental damages, for instance, the outcome will not be either optimal or fair. Likewise, the production of public goods may be below the optimum, too.

Second, there are advantages and disadvantages not attributable to the decisions of particular individuals. One might be responsible for one's absolute position, but not for one's position relative to that of the others. And there are many advantages and disadvantages (such as genetic talents and handicaps, for example) that are beyond the control of anybody. Initial differences between individuals due to impersonal factors may seriously distort the effect of market mechanisms. (Just think of the job competition between healthy and physically handicapped people.)

Third, communal decisions are not only about which possible program is to be realized and whose preferences are to be thereby satisfied. Preferences are not fixed, and their changes are not insensitive as to which of the competing political programs is being finally realized. Long-term preferences are not influenced by the realization of short-term goals. There are political goals, however, whose effects are sufficiently long-term that their realization is able to influence even the most durable of our preferences. When voters make decisions about such goals, they have to take a stance not only on the question of what would satisfy the given preferences. An even more important question concerns the direction in which these preferences should be changed. Assume it is predictable that if Hungary joins the European Union, it will become increasingly the norm for the highly educated members of the next generations to spend much of their lives abroad. Should this be the case, the ones voting for or against joining the European Union will decide, among other things, about whether the attachment of a substantial portion of Hungarian citizens to their country should be allowed to change or should remain the same. Assume someone votes against the change. What does she protect with her vote? Surely not her own personal interests, for what occurs 50 or 100 years after her death cannot affect her situation. Or maybe she protects her distant descendants' interests? It depends on what one means by the interests of the unborn. If one means by it that which they will *actually* prefer, then the answer must be negative. For she votes for staying outside the Union precisely because she expects that if the cause of joining it will prevail, future generations will prefer cosmopolitan mobility as against local rootedness—and this is precisely what she wants to prevent. The aim of her decision is not the emergence of whatever circumstances that serve best the unpredictable preferences of future generations; rather, she wants that which she herself believes should be the norm for future generations.

Fourth, such decisions as for instance joining the EU will have an impact not only on the preferences of the as yet unborn but also on those who will be born to begin with. Such decisions alter a large number of conditions that may influence which couples will be formed and when. Should Hungary join the EU, our offspring will not be the same persons as the ones who would populate our country if we were to stay outside the Union. Thus, we cannot meaningfully maintain that the same people will have a better (or worse) life after 50 or 100 years if the enlargement takes place (or not). All we can say is that future generations with better (or worse) lives will be born.[12]

In a word, even if we accept that the market legitimately takes the voters' preferences as given, politics cannot accept them as such.

If this is indeed the case, the object of decisions is different in the ethical model than it is in the preference-aggregating model. In the latter, votes express preferences. In the former, they reveal what the voters believe the common good to be. An expression of preferences need not commit voters to the view that everyone else should prefer that which they do. A statement about the common good, on the other hand, lets the others know what it is that each of them should endorse. Even though expressed preferences may happen to converge, there is no requirement that they do so. A statement about the common good, on the other hand, does contain the requirement of convergence. The goal of the preference-aggregating model is to realize the best available compromise among competing interests. The goal of the ethical model is not compromise but consensus. This is the fourth distinctive claim of the model.

Finally, it is not among the functions of democratic voting in the ethical model to aggregate the common good, as it were, from a sea of individual preferences. In case the voters vote in accordance with the requirements of the ethical model, the program of the winner will not be one that maximizes the personal preferences of the greatest number of voters but the one that is believed to approximate best the common good by the majority of votes. Reaching agreement about the common good is not identical with determining the common good through aggregation and subtraction. This is the fifth distinctive claim.

4. The ethical model: the relation between private and communal preferences

We have seen that in the ethical model voters may not rest content with ranking the offered alternatives according to their own interests only; they have to take into account the interests of the community as well. However, we have not examined yet the way they should relate the two orderings in making their decisions.

The preference-aggregating model suggests the following solution. Voters do not simply order their private and communal preferences separately, but order the two rankings with regard to one another as well. This makes it possible for them to decide in each case which is the better; the alternatives they prefer for themselves or the ones they judge to be the best for the community. If they attribute more value to the realization of their communal preferences, it is reasonable for them to vote for the sacrifice of their private preferences. If they rank the realization of their private preferences higher, it is reasonable for them to vote so that politics sacrifice their communal preferences.

The ethical model rejects this solution. It cannot do otherwise, since it is among its original hypotheses that voters bear moral responsibility for promoting, by way of casting their votes, the common good; what the common good is, in turn, is independent of their preferences. These two claims together entail a negative consequence to the effect that the solution offered by the preference-aggregating model is wrong. But what positive consequence follows from it?

One may be naturally tempted to think that the ethical model requires of the voters to give strict priority to the common good over their personal interests. That is, it seems to demand that they consider their personal interests only if the alternatives on offer are equally good or bad with respect to the common good. However, such a consequence does not follow from the ethical model. It would follow from it only if the model were combined with a substantive morality that requires the individual always to choose what is best impersonally, never allowing her to give special weight to her personal projects and commitments. This position is called ethical rigorism. Exponents of the ethical model of democratic politics need not, however, be at the same time ethical rigorists as well.

When one tries to evaluate the ethical model, it is reasonable to consider it in its most acceptable form. Therefore, in what follows I will take it that while some moral requirements exclude weighing them against the personal losses one might incur when adhering to them (e.g. no amount of material loss could possibly justify killing an innocent person), certain other requirements may allow for such weighing (there is such economic harm that no one may be obliged to undertake to help the needy[13]). On the other hand, I will take it that the evaluation of possible reasons for exemption is not a question external to morality; it is moral considerations themselves that specify the range of personal losses one may invoke when defending one's less-than-moral conduct.

Assume that two individuals' situations are is identical in every respect. Still, one of them dutifully validates her ticket whenever she gets on the bus, while the other does so only if a conductor approaches her. No doubt, the moral prohibition against exploiting others is more important to the former than to the latter. Now let us assume that the prohibition is so important for the former that she would never ride free, while it is so less important to the latter that only the risk of getting caught would stop her from free riding. We would not say that if such is the case, one of them does it well to validate her ticket all the time, while the other does it well to do so only if necessary. This would amount to denying all normative significance to moral requirements. To justify the free rider's conduct, we must find reasons for her deviation from the norm that are judged respectable and sufficient by morality itself.

If we accept that voting is a moral decision, and that voters are responsible for their votes—and the ethical model does exactly this—then the above observation will hold for the voters' conduct as well. Assume that the central issue of an election is whether higher education should remain free or become charged by tuition. And imagine a poor couple with many children who may admit that it would be better for the community as a whole to introduce the charge. Yet they know that should this happen, they will not be able to send their children to university. Such a couple probably has acceptable reasons to vote for retaining free higher education. Those parents with many children, by contrast, who live in abundance and will continue to live well even after the introduction of tuition fees act wrongly—according to the ethical model—if they acknowledge the communal disadvantages of free higher education and still vote for retaining the existing situation.

Supplemented with this claim, the ethical model proposes the following requirements for the voters. In case of a conflict between one's communal and personal preferences, one should decide the issue of their priority by considering what sort of personal interests count as respectable reasons for disregarding one's communal preferences in the light of the right conception of the common good. Voters who are ready to make it dependent upon the requirements of the common good as to what sort of situations allow for their giving primacy to their personal interests and what sort of situations do not admit so do satisfy the requirements of civic virtue. Nothing more may be demanded.

5. The ethical model: public debate and voting

Earlier, I have written that making a statement on the common good implies the claim that others should share the same view. In case an agreement is actually reached, the vote will be unanimous. The coincidence of votes, however, is not a source of the agreement: it only registers it. A convergence of views is reached through different channels. It might have a number of sources, such as adjustment to the majority opinion, manipulation, conformism, the rapprochement of lifestyles, and so forth. The ethical model, on the other hand, privileges one of the many possible causes of convergence, i.e. rational discussion. It claims that the agreement reached is acceptable only if it can be reached in unforced public discussion where no one is prevented from publicly expressing her objections and the prevalent view survives criticism.[14] The ethical model expects citizens to reach an agreement not just in *any* possible beliefs but only in beliefs that may be defended in rational discussion.

In a word, the ethical model grants pride of place to *public debates*.[15] This is what is supposed to transform a group of people into a *justificatory community*. Those who accept each other as partners in discussing what the common good is take it that they all participate in a joint ethical project directed at identifying the principles of their shared life. Although they may not agree about what the right principles are or what goals it is reasonable for them to pursue in common, they nevertheless agree that they are accountable to one another for their views and for the practical consequences of their views, that is, that they have to justify their position. Their disagreements may give rise to profound cleavages and group them into hostile camps. Yet recognizing the need for justification makes them part of the same community. Conversely, one who acts towards others as though she had no obligation to justify her views to them in fact declares herself not sharing community with these people.[16]

If public discussion has such a central role in the ethical model of democratic politics, does voting retain any important contribution at all? In the preference-aggregating model, voting is necessary because the resources that may be distributed through politics are scarce and the competing options are not realizable simultaneously. It is not possible for everybody to reach all of his or her political goals at the same time, thus it is not possible for everyone to prefer the same option. The ethical model, on the other hand, does not conceive of voting as a solution to a distribution problem. Truth is not a sort of good whose possession excludes others from having access to it. One person's recognizing it does not diminish (in actual fact, it increases) other people's chance of sharing in it. And the aim of discussion is exactly this: to reach an agreement.

Thus, it may appear as though the only reason the ethical model has for retaining the procedure of voting is its need to determine, from time to time, whether the desired identity of views has been reached yet or not. The discussion must be reopened as long as there are dissenting votes; each voter must have a veto right. The only valid decision is decision by unanimity.

This would assume, however, that the public debates preceding a vote may go on interminably and that information gathering has no costs. These are implausible assumptions; no realistic model of the political process may rely on them. By contrast, if one assumes scarcity of time and information, one must also accept that collective decisions are typically controversial. The evidence marshaled for or against any position is typically insufficient to compel unanimity. Each participant may consider the objections made against her position with the utmost attention and may still think in good faith that she has no reason to abandon it.[17] This is one of the reasons why voting is necessary in the ethical model as well.

Another reason is this. From time to time, every community has to choose between goods which it has sufficient reason to value but insufficient reason to rank against each other. We may find both theatergoing and body-building valuable. Yet if we are faced with a choice between the two, it is not clear whether we can offer good reasons for all for *preferring* going to the theater rather than to the gym. More specifically, we may not necessarily find reasons that are independent from people's personal endowments. One person may prefer theater performances while the other may prefer working out, and while the one may possess the endowments necessary for the reception of a performance, the other may have more of the bodily endowments, and so on. In such circumstances, the ethical model does not require a unanimous vote even under ideal conditions. Assume that a city local government has the necessary financial means to build either a gym or a theater but not to build both. Neither of these preferences is unjustifiable. Yet the choice between the two may not be sufficiently justified; it will ultimately remain an expression of will. The peculiar, irreplaceable character of individual democratic communities is partly shaped by the choices they have made in the course of their history between equally valuable but simultaneously unrealizable options and by the way such decisions have accumulated and have constrained subsequent changes into specific directions.

Finally, the ethical model may not abandon voting because—as we have seen at the end of the last section—the common good does not require that the people relinquish their personal interests in every single instance. Even though the voters may agree on which specific decision is most conducive to the common good, they may still have respectable reasons for voting against the alternative privileged by the common good. Thus, the divergence of interests may produce a divergence of votes even though there is actually a complete consensus about what the common good requires. In such cases the vote reveals whether that which is taken to be the common good is realizable without such sacrifices that could not be reasonably expected.[18]

By now, we have all the necessary information to compare the two models.

6. On the relation of the two models

What the ethical model does is first and foremost to highlight the deficiencies of the criteria of evaluation furnished by the preference-aggregating model. Its main normative claim is that it is not sufficient to judge democratic voting by the sole measure of efficiency in satisfying the contingent multitude of (individual) preferences. The common good is not simply that which the majority actually prefers but rather that which it is *reasonable* for it to prefer.

At the same time, the model shows that people's motives do not render it impossible for democratic decision making to realize the thus conceived common good. It makes three important descriptive claims about the motivation of voters that go beyond the original assumptions of the preference-aggregating model. First, when people make their decisions about the political alternatives on offer, what they take into account is not merely their self-regarding preferences; their decisions are influenced by their communal preferences as well. Second, preferences are not external parameters for the political process but are alterable, internal variables. Second, most preferences depend on beliefs about the world and on value judgments, and may alter in response to the changes in those beliefs and judgments. Furthermore, *rational discussion* is the privileged way for the adjustment of beliefs and value judgments.

The preference-aggregating model as summarized in Section 2 above is a model of democratic *decision making*; the processes of deliberation preceding the decision fall outside its scope. When voting occurs, the preferences have already been fixed and their ranking is already given. Thus, only the first among the specific assumptions of the ethical model (the one rejecting self-interest as having an exclusive role in motivation) is directly related to what the preference-aggregating model is concerned with. The other two assumptions urge for an extension of the scope of inquiry. They emphasize that restricting our attention to the voters' decisions, to the exclusion of the processes that shape our preferences that in their turn inform our decisions, radically impoverishes our conception of democratic politics.

This is an important point and, in what follows, I will say a bit more about it. Before that, however, I want to point out a fundamental deficiency in the ethical model.

I have claimed above that the ethical model shows why the actual motivations of people do not render it impossible that the results of democratic decision making do indeed approximate the ethically understood common good. Yet for it to be a serious rival for the preference-aggregating model it has to show more than just this. I mentioned that the preference-aggregating model is primarily an explanatory-predictive one. True, it furnishes substantive criteria of evaluation as well (it claims that decision to be the best one that maximizes the preferences of the greatest number of people) and thus it is able to make normative judgments. But it does not rely on the expectation that the participants of the political process adjust their choices to its value judgments. It claims that the democratic electoral system will put that party (or individual candidate) to power whose program maximizes the preferences of the greatest number of voters, *no matter what* those preferences may actually be.

The ethical model condemns this weak (merely efficiency-based) criterion as unsatisfactory. On the one hand, this is a strength of the model: it brings within the focus of the discussion considerations that are relevant for the understanding of democratic politics. On the other hand, this enlargement of focus puts a considerable burden of proof on the model. Since in this model the outcome of democratic voting does not necessarily coincide with the common good, and since the extent to which it approximates the common good depends on the preferences at the moment of voting, the ethical model cannot accept just any preferences as the input of communal decisions. It has to subject the voters' preferences to normative constraints. It claims, for instance, that voters may be expected to adjust their communal preferences to beliefs about the world that may in good faith be taken to be true. Or it claims that in a conflict between personal and communal preferences, voters may be expected to decide which ones to give priority to by considering whether reasons for ranking their private preferences above the communal ones are morally respectable. A collective decision may be judged to be a good one depending on the number of voters deciding virtuously.

The ethical model may compete with the preference-aggregating one only if it can show that the interaction between the voters' preferences and the institutional rules typically produces virtuous decisions. The summary of the model outlined here does not contain anything to this effect, and the summary is—I believe—a fair one. One may either acknowledge that invoking civic virtues has no more than an exhortatory or inspirational role in the ethical model, or one has to amend it.

We are now in a position to confront our proper problem: Is the program of the Hungarian republicans workable; is the "correction" of liberalism in a republican spirit a realistic aim?

7. Liberalism and the descriptive claims of the ethical model

Should the fundamental theses of the liberal theory be found to be contradictory with the descriptive assumption of the ethical model, the program of "correction" would be bound to fail; one would have to choose between liberalism and the ethical model. Therefore, we have to see first whether or not liberalism is compatible with these assumptions.

Let us begin with the thesis that—at least in the sphere of politics—individual decisions are not governed solely by self-regarding preferences. No doubt Jeremy Bentham, the father of the preference-aggregating model, believed that people are driven almost exclusively by selfish motives.[19] Furthermore, many of the modern proponents of the model share Bentham's hypothesis.[20] It is well known, too, that critics of liberalism tend to identify it with the hypothesis of *Homo oeconomicus*.[21] However, this hypothesis is not even necessary for the preference-aggregating model itself. We have just seen that from the point of view of the criteria of evaluation of this model, the content of individual preferences is indifferent. No matter whether the voters are egoists or altruists, the outcome of democratic voting will be the maximization of the preferences of the greatest number of voters, and this is alone what is relevant for the model.[22] As far as the anthropological assumptions of liberal theories in general are concerned, on the other hand, the latter are simply not reducible to the hypothesis of universal selfishness.

It was Adam Smith who first developed in a mature form the thesis that institutions, or at least market institutions, must treat individuals as though they were driven by nothing else but their self-interest. "It is not from the benevolence of the butcher, the brewer or the baker that we expect our dinner, but from their regard to their own interest. We address ourselves, not to their humanity, but to their self-love", read his celebrated statement in the first pages of the *Wealth of Nations*.[23] The explanation for this, however, resides not in that in Smith's views humans are altogether selfish creatures who have no sympathy for anyone but themselves and their families. The same Adam Smith clearly distinguished his position from that of egoism in his *Theory of Moral Sentiments.* Following David Hume, he proceeded here from the assumption that sympathy with others (the inclination, that is, to feel pleasure by others' pleasure and pain by others' pain) belongs among the natural sentiments of human beings. True, such secondary pleasures and pains are weaker, and thus so is their motivating force as well. So, even though most people are ready to make sacrifices for the suffering and the needy and to promote the happiness of the many, this readiness has its limits. The interests of the larger community or of distant strangers will be given priority over our own interests and that of our immediate family only as long as the loss is limited. People differ in where to draw the line, yet very few make considerable sacrifices regularly. They are endowed with a certain generosity, yet this generosity is usually limited. Adam Smith's and the other early liberals' conception about the conditions of the proper functioning of the market follow from this anthropological assumption rather than from the thesis of *Homo oeconomicus,* and it was this assumption that was later applied by Bentham and the elder Mill to democratic politics. Institutions must rely on such motives that work with high predictability rather than on such whose operation is unpredictable. The market is an efficient institution because it would maximize the common good even if human individuals were governed by exclusively selfish considerations in their decisions, not because it is actually true that human beings are consistent egoists.

Now, what about the claim that no matter what individual preferences may be, they must be accepted as given?

It appears as though this thesis had a more direct relation with the fundamental tenets of liberal democracy than the hypothesis of universal selfishness. As we have seen in the introduction, liberalism is committed to the position of ethical individualism, and ethical individualism entails that individuals should take charge of their lives, that they have the ultimate authority over their way of life and that their ultimate responsibility for leading a meaningful and good life is owed to themselves. For this reason, liberals tend to reject paternalism, that is, they reject subjecting a competent person to coercion aiming to promote her own best interests.[24] Furthermore, in interpreting democratic decision making, liberals take it that only the actual expression of will by the voters confers force on a decision; it is the decision *actually* made by the voters, rather than the one they *should have* made, that possesses validity. It comes naturally to understand this claim as an extension of the anti-paternalistic thesis to the realm of communal decisions. This seems to involve that liberal anti-paternalism entails that, for the aims of democratic decision making, only actual preferences matter.

The anti-paternalistic thesis, however, has two different readings. In the strong reading, it is *exclusively* her actual preferences that have a bearing on what is good for an individual; it is *exclusively* the actual preferences of its members that have a bearing on what is good for a community. In the weaker reading, actual preferences have a *privileged* significance for the good of an individual; the actual preferences of the members of a community have a *privileged* significance for the common good.

If it is the case, as we accepted earlier, that for it to be reasonable for an individual to pursue some goal it is not sufficient that she *believes* that goal to be valuable but it also has to be *in fact* valuable, then only the weaker can be acceptable. Now the weaker reading, as distinguished from the stronger one, plays an important role among the premises of liberal political theory.

An autonomous agent understands her life as being decisively shaped by her own choices. Her autonomy, however, implies more than just freedom to choose. One who makes a very large number of choices, but allows her preferences to take shape in a contingent manner and blindly follows those that she happens to have, does not yet shape her life in an autonomous manner. Shaping our lives autonomously includes that we are ready to subject our preferences to judgments and to act upon those preferences that prove to be worthy of following in the light of the values we have reason to adopt. We do not say that our life is one of our own choosing if we always choose that which we happen to desire most at the moment; we only say so if our choices translate a *conception of a good life*, that we identify with even upon careful consideration. Thus, an autonomous agent inevitably makes a distinction between that which she happens to prefer and that which she should prefer. Such a distinction entails the possibility of being mistaken when adopting a preference; it may occur that what we genuinely desire is not what we believe to be desiring or that what we desire is in fact not worthy of being desired by us. An autonomous agent does not attribute authority to that which she happens to desire *in itself*; she attributes authority to it because she believes the assumptions underlying it to be true.

Liberalism is committed to such an interpretation of individual and common goods that involves the possibility that a person is right or wrong about what her own good is and communities are right or wrong about what the common good is.

Now, the validity of democratic decisions is independent of whether they are based on true or false beliefs. Elected representatives have a mandate to make laws, regardless of the question whether it was reasonable for the majority to give a mandate to them. It may appear that the distinction between actual and reasonable preferences is an important one only in the domain of individual-regarding preferences, but not in the case of community-regarding ones. This could only be the case, however, if humans were different in their individual and in their communal decisions; that is, if when making decisions about their own lives, they were trying to pursue preferences reinforced by true beliefs, while when making decisions together with others for the community, they were willing to pursue whatever preferences they might actually have. But we have no reason for such a splitting of human beings.[25]

Suppose a voter casts his ballot for a certain party because he believes it to be an advocate of isolationism. Should it dawn on him that he had been wrong about isolationism, he would have no reason left to vote for that party. And since he is making a decision for the whole community rather than simply for himself, sticking with his old commitments would not only be unreasonable but morally wrong. As voters we are responsible for voting for the alternative that is, to the best of our knowledge, the best one.[26]

Yet if it matters for each individual voter, severally, that the party they vote for represents a program they have reason to believe to be the best among all the feasible programs on offer (rather than only to appear to do so), then this must matter for the voters as a collective decision making entity, too. But the outcome of the vote is indifferent towards the appropriateness of the collective choice. The electoral system allows for a separation of the validity of the vote from its correctness.

Does it follow that democracy as a political regime is of dubious normative credentials? This conclusion would be hasty, or so I believe. Democracy must satisfy two separate standards: it must assure that the ultimate political decisions are made by those who will be constrained by those decisions, and it must assure that the ultimate decision makers make the right choices. There is no assurance that the second requirement always obtains: we are finite and fallible beings both individually and as a community. But democracy can meet the first requirement in such a way that, at the same time, allows for the electorate to revise its wrong decisions. In so far as it incorporates mechanisms that urge the voters to gather information and give them opportunities to repeat and correct their earlier decisions, democracy is a defensible political system.[27]

Moreover, liberal theories are not bound by the peculiar claim of the preference-aggregating model to the effect that the common good is constituted by an aggregation of individual preferences. Liberalism is committed to the principle of ethical individualism, not to the idea of preference aggregation. No doubt, ethical individualism entails that nothing can be good for a community unless it can be shown to be good for particular individuals. Yet it does not follow from this that the common good amounts to a sum of the (actual) individual preferences.

Finally, liberalism is not hostile in principle to the thought that collective decisions must observe certain moral requirements. The existence of such requirements is central to liberalism, for it seeks to protect the fundamental moral interests of individuals against unbound collective decisions. It is a basic feature of the liberal conception of democracy that democratic decisions may be regarded as legitimate only if they respect fundamental rights. This requirement is not stated as a prudential rule but as a moral demand; the inviolability of rights is part and parcel of the treatment that is due to a human being; the government has to observe these rights and make everybody observe them not because such conduct is instrumental to bringing about collective benefits but because it is morally required in itself.

Now, the traditional strategy of liberalism consists in limiting collective decisions by incorporating fundamental rights into the constitution, by requiring special majorities for amending the constitution, and by entrusting non-elected bodies with overseeing that majority decisions do not violate constitutional rights. All this would make it appear that the moral requirements that really matter for liberalism are being put by liberal theory beyond the scope of democratic politics, that the protection of fundamental rights consists in removing them from the jurisdiction of democratic decisions, thus exempting the community from considering the nature, scope and normative force of these rights. But this is not so.

True, in constitutional democracies the moral requirements of politics are partly built into its institutional constraints. Whether such constraints may be justified and whether they are compatible with the ideal of democracy is a separate problem. I will discuss this at a later point in this book.[28] At this point I merely want to show that institutional constraints do not insulate the enforcement of liberal principles from the democratic political process.

First of all, the majority has room for making attempts to test the judgment of the guardians of the constitution; for example, rather than abandoning the rules deemed unconstitutional they may proceed to amend them until they pass the test. Second, the constitution itself may be amended, should the required majority be obtained. Third, the rules regulating the way constitutional provisions may be amended are themselves the outcome of political decisions. Finally, the guardians of the constitution are not demigods standing above the democratic political process; they are not elected by a Society of the Doctors of Natural Right from among their own ranks; they constitute a body whose authorization is a part of the democratic political process, its members being appointed by elected officials. In a word, the moral requirements protecting the status of human individuals have pride of place in the liberal conception of democracy; the making, amending and applying of the rules that translate these moral requirements into institutional constraints is part and parcel of democratic politics no less than the decision making processes that go on within them.

To sum up, liberalism is not committed to those features of the preference-aggregating model that are rightly criticized by the republicans; thus, the project of a republican "correction" of liberal political theory is not necessarily doomed to fail. When the new republicans who want to be liberals try to incorporate the perspective of the common good in the theory of democracy, they propose an intellectual reform that is coherent with the basic tenets of the liberal tradition. But we have yet to face the question as to what is the case with civic virtue.

8. Virtue in politics

There is no work left for moral sentiments in Adam Smith's theory of the market. In the world of laissez-faire, the outcome is the realization of the maximum of common good, even if each person pursues her own interests. But such a removal of moral requirements is tied to unrealistically strong conditions. Some of these were discussed explicitly by Smith himself, others being made explicit by later economic theory.

Here are some of these conditions; every market actor must be perfectly well informed, and the acquisition and processing of information must be costless; no one should be able to influence the size of the aggregate demand and supply, or the market prices; no one should be able to incur such costs on others that he has not paid for; all goods and services should be such that no one could have access to them unless he had paid the price for them, and so forth. Unless these conditions jointly obtain, individuals are not exempted from observing moral requirements.

Thus, the "really existing" market does not remove the burden of moral reflection from individuals.[29] Furthermore, democratic politics may not remove it even among ideal conditions. Why this is so was already shown in the discussion of the ethical model. First, whatever the majority may decide, it does not have to compensate the losers in the case the program it supported triumphs; majority decisions always carry external costs shifted onto other people. Second, some decisions are not about whose preferences the government should satisfy but about whose preferences should become the dominant preferences—that is, about what it is right to prefer. Finally, since our preferences depend on beliefs and value judgments, it is not only unattainable but also unreasonable for participants of democratic politics to be exempted from the obligation of moral reflection. I want to develop this latter claim in some detail.

Suppose the preference-aggregating model works perfectly well; every voter follows her own preferences and yet the collective decision tackles the common good. Should this be the case, the smooth functioning of the model does not require that the voters know and approve of the common good that is the outcome of the multitude of individual decisions. But of course those who design the institutions must know the common good and seek its realization. This asymmetry makes the choices of citizens mere means in carrying out the aims of the (benevolent) Designers. The system would *manipulate* voters into promoting their own aggregate good. This conception is not altogether alien from Jeremy Bentham and his Fabian socialist followers. But it is incompatible with the conception of liberal democracy. In that conception, voters are the ultimate subjects of politics. It is not sufficient that the outcome of the political processes be good in itself. It is also necessary that the outcome be selected in such a process that urges and encourages the voters to participate in reflecting on what is the common good and to cast their ballot according to their own judgment.

Thus, if we approve of democracy as liberals, we have independent reasons for preferring such a model in which periodically held elections occur amidst widespread, vigorous and rational public discussions. An ideal picture of representative democracy must be able to show that the preferences of the voters are not shaped contingently, as it were, but partly in response to a collective deliberation about the reasons that underlie these preferences. And it also must be able to say something about what makes collective deliberation widespread, vigorous and rational. This is the only way to ensure that the outcome of political decisions will be transparent for the totality of participants rather than to the Designers only, and that it will be at least in part their own collective making—not the consequence of the workings of some manipulating and alien (though benevolent) power.

If so, then not even the best ordered of democratic politics can dispense with counting on the individual moral motivations of the participants. No liberal theory of democracy can do without the hypothesis of civic virtue.

With this claim we have arrived to the soft point of the ethical model; if it is the case that the realization of the common good requires that virtue be involved in the citizens' decisions, we must ask what makes it plausible that people will be sufficiently virtuous.

The core of the problem is that virtuous conduct carries costs. That which has no costs for the individual does not require virtue (even though it may be morally appropriate). A virtuous person does what morality requires her to do because she recognizes that her personal loss does not constitute a sufficient justification for acting differently. The larger the costs she is willing to pay for pursuing the demands of morality the more virtuous her decision is. Now there are two ways to ensure that virtue comes into play whenever needed.

The first is that society educates its members to be maximally virtuous. Genuine democrats are always ready to decide in favor of the common good, no matter how high the price may turn out to be. This solution would fit classical republicanism. The second option is to devise such rules as to diminish the costs of virtuous conduct. In a well-ordered society, the price of virtue is not higher than that which is reasonably expectable from individuals. This solution would fit classical liberalism.

The difference between the liberal and the republican solutions lies not in that republicans esteem virtue highly, while liberals necessarily reject it. The root of the discrepancy is to be traced back to what the two theories hold about the sufficient conditions of successful institutional operation. All institutions provide rules for individual conduct. They cannot tolerably approximate their goals unless a sufficiently large number of people are motivated to typically abide by them. (If nobody pays their taxes, there is no point for the government in making estimates about the amount of revenues that would be at their disposal *should it be the case* that the citizens pay their taxes in due course.) The question then turns out to be: what sort of motivations is it reasonable for a community to rely on when designing its institutions?

As we could see the liberal answer is this: institutions should rely on such motives that come into play predictably and are decisive. Human beings are driven by a mix of motivations, including self-interest, sympathy for others, commitment to values, and so on. Yet the workings of these motives are not equally predictable. Early liberals expressed this fact in a simple dichotomy: self-interest is a reliable motivation, while the rest is not.[30] We have many reasons for rejecting this dichotomy. These are, first, certain normative considerations: political institutions are in need of moral justification, and the justification itself must possess some motivating force—that is, if the moral justification of an institutional order does not appeal to the people acting within its rules, the order is unjustifiable. Second, descriptive claims about people's motivations also urge us to dismiss the dichotomy. It is simply not the case that self-interest is the exclusive basis of predictable expectations in a well-ordered society. Modern liberalism takes it that moral motivation is among the assumptions of political institutions, provided that the price to be paid for observing moral requirements is not too high. A liberal institutional order may safely assume that a sufficiently large number of its citizens will be ready to make sacrifices for the common good, provided that the costs of virtuous conduct remain within tolerable limits.[31]

Rules that require too much from individuals must be rejected. If the gap between the consequences of the required actions and the consequences of the actions that the agents would prefer in the absence of moral concerns opens very wide, rule breaking becomes the rule; and if, in turn, people see that whoever is able to act contrary to the laws and displace his part of the costs of sustaining society to others does indeed act so, it will become exceedingly difficult to conceive the society they live in as a community.

9. The politics of virtue and personal autonomy

In his influential work called *A Theory of Justice*, John Rawls makes a distinction between ideal and non-ideal theory. He calls a theory ideal if it makes ideal assumptions about circumstances and conduct, if it assumes, for instance, strict compliance with the requirements of morality. A non-ideal theory, by contrast, takes it into account that such ideal assumptions are not satisfied in the real world. Thus, non-ideal theory assumes partial compliance, i.e., it assumes that, even though most people are motivated to do what is morally right, they tend to give priority to non-moral considerations even in the absence of admissible reasons, should the costs of morally right conduct be too high.

The argument outlined in the previous section belongs to the realm of non-ideal theory. It assumes that even though morality is among the motivations of human beings, it may be predictably relied on only to the extent that the price of morally right conduct is not very high. Let us now assume, by contrast, that everybody is ready fully to comply with morality. Is the principle of economizing on virtue tenable under such conditions?

This question does not merely ask whether economizing on virtue is needed under ideal circumstances. The problem lies much deeper. The classical liberal position drives a wedge between self-interest and moral motivation. It stipulates that complying with morality's requirement is not in the interest of the individual, and vice versa. It is not clear whether such a distinction can hold for ideally motivated people. The interest of an individual is all that which is good for that individual. The individual decides well if he decides in favor of the action privileged by the best reasons. Should moral reasons be stronger than the competing ones, it would be reasonable for him to decide in accordance with the moral reasons. The choice in accordance with the moral reasons is good for the chooser—this is the best thing he could choose under the circumstances. In the case of ideally motivated persons, thus, deciding in compliance with morality does not require them to be virtuous, because it is a decision demanded by their best interests.[32]

It seems as though it is only under the assumptions of a non-ideal theory that self-interests appear as distinct from moral interests. Non-ideal theory is, then, a response to the facts of imperfect human rationality. Among the assumptions of ideal theory, the place reserved for virtue is taken by rational choice. The question is whether this is really the case. Can individual interests and the concerns of morality be distinguished? Can there be a conflict between them, in the world of ideal theory?

This problem has an aspect that is directly relevant for our subject matter. Liberalism deems a political system acceptable only if it makes, at least in principle, the autonomous shaping of one's own life available to everyone. In a society in which virtue requires enormous sacrifices, only those few could be secure to lead an autonomous life who choose the pursuit of the common good as their life plan anyway. For the rest, the possibility of being both virtuous and pursuig their own life plan might not be given.

For what does it mean for virtuous conduct to have a high price? It means that that which one has to forsake is really valuable to one. And what is it that we value highly? That which has a significant contribution to the way of life we have chosen for ourselves. It is no great loss to sacrifice something that is peripheral from the point of view of our life plan. On the other hand, if virtue urges us to regularly forsake that which we value greatly for its contribution to our life, it makes it impossible for us to lead our own lives.[33]

This claim has nothing to do with the problem of whether private or communal preferences constitute the center of one's life. Should the price of virtue be too high, it could destroy life plans moved primarily by altruistic motives as much as self-centered ones. It is sufficient for a life plan to be destroyed by the claims of virtue that the activities making it up, though directed at others, be different from the ones required by the common good.

Imagine a person with many different talents. He would make a great environmental or an equally outstanding music critic. In his country, the cause of environment protection is neglected. The talents of our man are badly needed. High-level music criticism, too, would enrich the life of the country, yet the need for the contribution of this particular man is much less urgent than in the domain of environment protection. It would be better for the community if he were to invest his talents in the latter field. Yet his true passion is for music criticism. He values both the flourishing of musical life and the improvement of the state of the environment. But his personal ambition is to have his fingerprint on the first, not the second.

Assume that this person has been long preparing for writing a huge Mozart monograph when the cause of environment protection gains urgency. If he switches to environmentalism, the book will never be completed and all his preparations will be lost. Yet he is still ready to make the sacrifice. He seeks an employment with the environmental authority and becomes an outstanding specialist of the ecology of rivers. We might believe that the loss to autonomy our man is suffering is only transient. The demands of the common good damage the integrity of his life plan, indeed, but the damage must not be a permanent one[34]. But the same conflict that made our man abandon music for the sake of environment protection might reappear again. Suppose he gets under the grip of the project of river ecology and finds an interest in the related theoretical problems. He is thinking about authoring a book on revitalizing extinct river fauna. Yet by the time he gets there, the cause of protecting the environment does not appear so pressing anymore. In the meantime, the decline of the country's population has reached dramatic proportions. Unless the process can be arrested aging will take dangerous dimensions, and the generations of active jobholders will find it increasingly difficult to support the pensioners. This person may be required to switch to become a demographer...

His life will lack what one might call an internal coherence; his decisions about the future will always be divorced from his earlier decisions, his projects never reach fruition, his commitments will be left without consequences.

Judging individual life plans from the perspective of the common good amounts to assessing their consequences, i.e., the state of affairs they help bring about. From the vantage point of the community, the best activities are those promoting the best state of affairs. From the vantage point of the individual, however, it is not sufficient that carrying out a life plan gives rise to valuable consequences. What matters for the agent herself is not only the value produced by different alternative pursuits but also which pursuits she could derive satisfaction from, and could identify with as her own. The two sets of criteria do not necessarily privilege one and the same activity. They may come into conflict with one another.

It should be noticed that both sets of criteria are of an ethical nature. The first is concerned with the ranking of different states of affairs from the point of view of the community, and with the kind of activities this communal ranking privileges. The second is concerned with what the recognition of individual autonomy requires from us individually and collectively. Virtue and self-interest may part company in this approach because the communal value of different activities need not coincide with their personal value.

The common good requires the realization of that one alternative which is most valuable to the communal approach. It requires from the individual that she decide in favor of the activities best fitted for attaining the alternative that is best impersonally. That decision, however, need not be the best one for the agent. It may damage her personal autonomy. If personal autonomy is to be a fundamental ethical value, its recognition should set limits for the pursuit of the common good.

In ideal conditions, political institutions coordinate individual decisions for the advancement of the common good while taking for granted that the choice that is best for an individual may legitimately depart from one privileged by the common good.[35]

The above case tacitly assumes that though the environmental and demographic situations are bad indeed, they do not threaten with an immediate catastrophe. In cases of emergency, morality may make huge demands on the individuals, capable of overriding all considerations of the integrity of a life plan. When such a case emerges, one has to act as the moment requires, without deliberating on the dimensions of personal loss. It is notable that in such situations the readiness to make sacrifices is also more visible than in ordinary circumstances.

However, a morality one can live with should not treat cases of catastrophe as the standard for ordinary circumstances. And so it should not encourage the establishment of institutions that rely, in normal times, on readiness for sacrifices characteristic of times of emergency. Other things being equal, a world with far more Mother Theresas living in our midst would no doubt be a better one. But a world in need of far more Mother Theresas is not one we should strive for.

To sum up, liberals have two separate reasons for approving of the principle of economizing on virtue. One belongs to the realm of non-ideal theory and rests on the assumption that the motivating power of moral norms is limited; most people are not ready to pay just any price for living up to the requirements of morality. The other reason belongs to the realm of ideal theory and claims that in ordinary circumstances virtue may not demand more from individuals than what is compatible with autonomously shaping their own lives. The two claims point in the same direction, though they need not privilege exactly the same solution. It is likely that non-ideal theory makes more concessions to private personal interests than ideal theory does. But we need not go into that issue.

10. Concluding remarks

Liberalism's commitment to the principles of ethical individualism, of liberty and rights, and of economizing on virtue is sustainable and worthy of being sustained. Its traditional conception of representative democracy, however, is in need of revision. Revision is necessitated by any defensible interpretation of the basic liberal principles themselves.

According to such a revised picture of democracy, the preferences of the citizens do not serve as external parameters for the political process; as they do not express brute desires but are dependent on (true or false) beliefs and value judgments they may be subjected to rational debate. An acceptable model of democracy must involve the idea of vigorous, widespread public deliberation. The moral dimension may not be removed from the view of the participants of the political process. It is neither possible nor desirable for democratic politics to leave everything to the motive force of non-moral considerations of self-interest.

Up to this point, claims attributable to republicanism are of help in re-thinking the traditional theory of liberal democracy. There is, however, an important issue on which the liberal correction of the republican outlook still holds. A well-ordered society should not rest on the assumption that people may be made virtuous beyond limits. This is no more less possible or desirable than the reduction of all motives to self-interest. Democratic institutions are supposed to pay respect to individual autonomy and this is not possible unless they are able to reduce the costs of virtuous conduct to human dimensions.

All of the above is about how liberalism should understand representative democracy. But the Hungarian republicans did not raise this theoretical question for itself. They took their cue from a diagnosis of the third Hungarian republic after 1989, and proposed a remedy by making an attempt at theoretical revision. They claim that post-1989 democratic politics has drifted to a wrong track. The general public perceives it as a struggle of divergent private interests rather than as a public search for the principles of a good polity. The pursuit of the common good is not part of the political process and it does not motivate the participants of politics. The concept of civic virtue that urges individuals to place the interests of the community ahead of their own private interests is unheard of. Little wonder, then, that laws lack the necessary authority. If free riding can go unpunished, there are no moral restraints to replace the legal enforcement mechanisms in motivating obedience. The authority of the state is in ruins. What is worse, Hungarian liberalism is not able so much as to identify the trouble, let alone fight it, because its own image of democratic politics is no other than that of a conflict of self-interests and bargaining.

The above analysis refines this diagnosis and the accompanying political proposals in one essential point and, I believe, radically modifies it in another. It refines what the Hungarian republicans have to say about the absence of common good as a political aspiration. But how to conceive of political community informed by such an aspiration? One possibility could be that the community agrees on what the common good consists in and what is to be done in order to achieve it. It is unclear whether the Hungarian republicans have such an agreement in mind. In any event, this would be an implausibly strong requirement. It is more realistic and more attractive to understand the presence of a shared aspiration to the common good as a mutual recognition of the members of the community as partners in an ongoing public debate. Once this mutual recognition is there, we have a true community informed by the common good as a shared aspiration. [36]

According to one of the possible views, we should strive for general and unanimous consensus in questions pertaining to the common good. My study presented a number of objections against such an answer. If I am right, the state of affairs to be desired is rather one in which representatives of the dominant trends of thought regard one another as partners in an incessant public discussion.

I believe there is a more serious disagreement on the explanation of the absence of law-abiding conduct, and about what should be done for the state to reestablish its ruined authority. It appears from what Hungarian republicans say on this subject that they blame deficiencies of civic virtue for the high frequency of violations of law, and that they hope the law will regain its authority through citizens' becoming more virtuous—more committed to the common good.[37] I believe, by contrast, that the praise of virtue may easily degenerate into empty moral preaching. What is mainly needed is to address the institutional disorders of democracy by looking for such written and unwritten rules whose success does not depend on the moral improvement of the citizens but on rule-following conduct's becoming more favorable for the individuals and on a closing of the gap between the individual and the common good.

Our reflections issue in a very simple claim—one that is, for that matter, among the dominant ideas of classical liberalism. It is the claim that the harmony of individual motivations with the common good depends on institutions. Institutions matter. The next study starts from this point.

NOTES

1 Cf. J. G. A. Pocock, *The Machiavellian Moment* (Princeton: Princeton University Press, 1975); Q. Skinner, "Machiavelli on the Maintenance of Liberty". In: *Politics* 81, 1983, pp. 3–15; Q. Skinner, "The Idea of Negative Liberty". In: Rorty–Schneewind–Skinner (eds.), *Philosophy in History* (Cambridge: Cambridge University Press, 1984).

2 The idea of ethical individualism had a decisive role in modern political and moral philosophy since Hobbes. On Hobbes' individualism see J. Hampton, *Hobbes and the Social Contract Tradition* (Cambridge: Cambridge University Press, 1986); and G. Kavka, *Hobbesian Moral and Political Theory* (Princeton: Princeton University Press, 1986).

3 The classical formulations of the principle that each individual may claim that maximum of liberty—protected by rights—that is consistent with the similar liberty of others are to be found in Kant. See, e.g., I. Kant, "On the Common Saying: 'This May be True in Theory, but it does not Apply in Practice'". Hans Reiss (ed.), *Kant's Political Writings* (Cambridge: Cambridge University Press, 1988), pp. 61–92.

4 This thesis was first propounded and supported with detailed arguments by Benjamin Constant. See his famed essay "De la liberté des anciens comparée par celle des modernes". In: *De la liberté chez les modernes* (Paris: Hachette, 1980), pp. 409–507.

5 The most famous formulation of the thesis of the economy of virtue is found in Adam Smith's economic treatise *The Wealth of Nations*; I will soon return to this. A. O. Hirschmann provides an excellent overview of the inception and development of the thought: *The Passions and Interests* (Princeton: Princeton University Press, 1977). The nature of this principle is discussed in terms of the relation between economic and political theory by G. Brennan, "Economics". In: R. E. Goodin and P. Pettit (eds.), *A Companion to Contemporary Political Philosophy* (Cambridge: Blackwell, 1993), pp. 123–156.

6 See Q. Skinner, "The Paradoxes of Political Liberty". In: S. Darwall (ed.), *Equal Freedom* (Ann Arbor: The University of Michigan Press, 1995), p. 37.

7 The expression itself—"the republican correction of the liberal outlook"—owes its existence to Péter Kende. See Kende, "A liberális szemlélet republikánus kiigazítása", *Világosság* 1996/2. Later, Kende gave numerous details of his thoughts to this effect,

which are published in his volume *A Köztársaság törékeny rendje* (Budapest: Osiris, 2000). The conception itself, as it is noted by Kende, originates with Gáspár Miklós Tamás, who discussed it in a whole series of articles. See "Arról, hogy a közjó délibáb", *Magyar Narancs*, 21 June 1993; "A nemzetállam védelmében", *Népszabadság*, 10 July 1993; "A magyar ideológia", *Magyar Narancs*, 7 October 1993; "Az új establishment", *Magyar Narancs*, 29 September 1994; "A közjó, amelyben testvériesülnek az állampolgárok", *Amaro Drom* (special issue) 14 May 1995; "Köztársaság és nemzet", *Magyar Hírlap*, 20 1996 January; "Közhaza és republikánus hit", *Magyar Hírlap*, 27 January 1996. Further important writings by Kende in this respect are "'Liberalism' as an insult", *Beszélő*, 1996/1, and "Erős republikánus állam nélkul ki fogja egyben tartani a magyar társadalmat?" *Mozgó Világ*, 1997/7. It is difficult to judge whether these writings are the products of an isolated endeavor, or, to the contrary, they are harbingers and path-breakers of the emergence of a broader intellectual trend. In any case, in her interview with young conservatives, Eszter Babarczy reports her observation that "it seems as though in our generation, republican liberalism of the brand of Tocqueville is gaining ground at the expense of human rights liberalism, that is, a kind of liberalism that emphasizes political participation rather than the protection of human rights and the minimal state..." See "A harmadik generáció", *Beszélő*, 1997/2. The present study does not examine the precise scope of the ideological impact of the attempted "republican correction". It only seeks to reconstruct its main theoretical theses and to see whether they are tenable—regardless of their ideological efficacy.

8 Ross Harrison's *Democracy* (London: Routledge, 1994) offers a very useful discussion of both Rousseau's and Bentham's and the elder Mill's conception.

9 That Rousseau's modern interpretation may be divorced from the thesis of direct democracy was shown by J.-F. Spitz, *La liberté politique* (Paris: Presse Universitaire de France, 1995).

10 Modern proponents of the preference-additive model usually go even further. They cast doubt on the possibility of speaking about an unequivocally and consistently determinable common good in democratic systems of decision making. See the influential work of William Riker, *Liberalism Against Populism* (San Fransisco: Freeman, 1982). We need not rely on this stronger thesis, however. Likewise, we need not discuss the problem of whether it is possible to aggregate individual preferences without voting, thus furnishing criteria for deciding which among the various electoral systems approaches best what is called the common good. To bring out the contrast with the ethical model it is sufficient to state that if there is such a thing as the common good, it can be nothing other, under the assumptions of the preference-aggregating model, than the sum of individual preferences that express self-interest.

11 One of Bentham and Mill's chief goals with their theory was precisely to provide reasons for the then revolutionary idea of universal suffrage.

12 Derek Parfit drew attention to this fact in his *Reasons and Persons* (Oxford: Clarendon Press, 1984), p. 351 *passim*.

13 Even the most consistent utilitarians admit that no one is obliged to give her last piece of food to the starving

14 This claim contradicts the manner in which the ancestor of the model, Rousseau, thought about democratic decision making. Rousseau thought that the outcome of

the vote does indeed reveal which view represents the common good, but only if it was *not* preceded by public discussion among the citizens. His reason for holding this baffling belief was that in Rousseau's view, communicating about controversial issues makes it possible for a group of citizens to conspire against and deceive others. On the other hand, Rousseau thought it vital that citizens make an informed decision, yet he said nothing about how, in the absence of their "communicating with one another", they might obtain the necessary knowledge. See J.-J. Rousseau, "On Social Contract", in Rousseau, *Political Writings* (New York: Norton, 1988).

15 On the republican conception's giving pride of place to public debates, see P. Pettit, *Republicanism* (Oxford: Clarendon, 1997), pp. 187–190. On the theory of "deliberative democracy" that puts public debate in the center of the normative interpretation of democracy, see S. Macedo (ed.), *Deliberative Politics* (New York–Oxford: Oxford University Press, 1999).

16 On the causes of disagreement between people who are seeking agreement see J. Rawls, *Political Liberalism* (New York: Columbia University Press, 1993), pp. 54–58.

17 On the costs of seeking unanimous consent see James Buchanan and Gordon Tullock, *The Calculus of Consent* (Ann Arbor: The University of Michigan Press, 1962). Buchanan and Tullock work with the preference-aggregating model, yet there is no such difference between the two models that would exclude extending their observations to the ethical model.

18 Since the question of what counts as respectable reasons may be just as controversial as the question of what the common good is, the considerations regarding the resources of time and energy necessary for discussion return at this point. Often such questions, too, must be decided by authoritative decision.

19 See T. Nagel, *Equality and Partiality* (New York–Oxford: Oxford University Press, 1991), p. 55.

20 The contemporary authors who developed the "economic" theory of politics usually take individuals to be *Homo oeconomicus*. See A. Downs, *An Economic Theory of Democracy* (New York: Harper & Row, 1957); D. C. Mueller, *Public Choice II* (Cambridge: Cambridge University Press, 1989), p. 2.

21 See A. MacIntyre, *After Virtue* (London: Duckworth, 1981); J. Habermas, "Three Normative Models of Democracy", *Constellations* 1 (1994), pp. 1–10. MacIntyre criticizes liberalism for its putative anthropological assumptions from the Right, while Habermas does so from the Left.

22 See G. Brennan and L. Lomasky, *Democracy and Decision* (Cambridge: Cambridge University Press, 1996), p. 2, pp. 9–14.

23 A. Smith, *An Inquiry into the Nature and Causes of the Wealth of Nations.* (Oxford–New York–Toronto: Oxford University Press 1993), p. 22.

24 Kant and Wilhelm von Humboldt already straightforwardly rejected legal paternalism; the first thorough formulation of the anti-paternalistic thesis is to be found in J.S. Mill's "On Liberty". See Mill, *On Liberty* (New York: Norton, 1975).

25 See J. Raz, "Liberalism, Skepticism, and Democracy". Raz, *Ethics in the Public Domain* (Oxford: Clarendon, 1993), pp. 113–117.

26 This claim is most emphatically made by John Rawls among the exponents of contemporary liberalism. See *Political Liberalism* p. 219.

27 See Raz, *op. cit.*

28 They will be mentioned in "Liberal Democracy" and in more detail in Chapter 3 of "The Constitutional Court in Balance" ("Nullification").

29 It is a quite separate problem that the market often gives rise to the illusion that moral considerations do not count. The decision-maker is usually justified in thinking, among market conditions, that whatever his decision may be, it does not affect the state of affairs as a whole; thus, it may appear to him that he has no obligation to refrain from doing what is wrong. Those who pollute the air by using leaded fuel are usually right in thinking that by switching to unleaded fuel they will not discernibly reduce the total consumption of leaded fuel, and that if they decide to use leaded fuel, the overall pollution will not recognizably increase. And if their decisions have neither good nor bad consequences, they are not subject to moral requirements. I call this belief the illusion of moral neutrality. Here I need not discuss why this belief is illusory.

30 This prompted them, on the one hand, to dismiss altogether the possibility that institutions should rely on moral motivations as well. It made them very optimistic, on the other hand, about what well-designed institutions may be capable of solely by mobilizing self-interest. Compare Madison's famous remark in *Federalist 72*: "The best security for the fidelity of mankind is to make their interests coincide with their duty." *The Federalist Papers* (New York: Tudor Publishing Co., 1937), p. 475. Even Immanuel Kant believed that a well-ordered political regime may rely on nothing but enlightened self-interest; that is why he claimed (in "On Perpetual Peace") that a constitutional democracy—or the "republican form of government"—could operate well even with rational devils: "Now the *republican* constitution is the only one which does complete justice to the rights of man. But it is also the most difficult to establish, even more so to preserve, so that many maintain that it would only be possible within a state of *angels*, since men, with their self-seeking inclinations, would be incapable of adhering to a constitution of so sublime a nature. But in fact, nature comes to the aid of the universal and rational human will, so admirable in itself but so impotent in practice, and makes use of precisely those self-seeking inclinations in order to do so. It only remains for men to create a good organization for the state, a task which is well within their capability, and to arrange it in such a way that their self-seeking energies are opposed to one another, each thereby neutralizing or eliminating the destructive effects of the rest. And as far as reason is concerned, the result is the same as if man's selfish tendencies were non-existent, so that man, even if he is not morally good in himself, is nevertheless compelled to be a good citizen. As hard as it may sound, the problem of setting up a state can be solved even by a nation of devils (so long as they possess understanding) ... For such a task does not involve the moral improvement of man; it only means finding out how the mechanism of nature can be applied to men in such a manner that the antagonism of their hostile attitudes will make them compel one another to submit to coercive laws, thereby producing a condition of peace within which the laws can be enforced." "Perpetual Peace: A Philosophical Sketch", Hans Reiss (ed.), *Kant's Political Writings*, pp. 112–113 (translated by H. B. Nisbet).

31 See G. Brennan and A. Hamlin, "Economizing on Virtue", *Constitutional Political Economy* 6 (1995), pp. 35–36.

32 Some modern liberal authors express this ethical thought, to be traced back to Plato and Aristotle, with great emphasis. See J. Raz, *The Morality of Freedom* (Oxford: Clarendon, 1986), and R. Dworkin, *Foundations of Liberal Equality* (Tanner Lectures on Human Values XI. Salt Lake City: The University of Utah Press, 1990).

33 This is an application of Bernard Williams' argument against utilitarianism. See. J. J. Smart and B. Williams, *Utilitarianism, For and against* (Cambridge: Cambridge University Press, 1973); and B. Wiliams, "Person, Character and Morality", in Williams: *Moral Luck* (Cambridge: Cambridge University Press, 1981).

34 This is a point made by Joseph Raz, who raises the possibility of conflicts between the demands of morality and the aim of pursuing one's own conception of a good life. See J. Raz "The Central Conflict: Morality and Self-interest", in Raz, *Engaging Reason* (Oxford University Press, 1999).

35 This argument adapts Bernard Williams' famous critique of utilitarianism; see. J. J. Smart and B. Williams, *Utilitarianism, For and against* (Cambridge: Cambridge University Press, 1973), pp. 108–118.

36 It was first in 1991 that I raised the question of how significant discussions may be pursued about political issues that are deeply divisive: "Az abortusztörvény és a köztársaság morális egysége", *Magyar Hírlap*, 24 December 1991. Another article by me on the same issue is: "Liberális szemmel", *Magyar Narancs*, 23 October 1996. Both studies are to be found in the volume *Az állam semlegessége* (Budapest: Atlantisz, 1997).

37 A recent statement by Gáspár Miklós Tamás, "The government is not too strong but too weak, to such an extent that it is hardly capable of collecting the taxes... Unless the government reestablishes its authority, liberty is doomed, for the citizens have no power whatever over a government contracted out to subcontractors. Such an authority, on the other hand, cannot be established without some sense of confident patriotism". *Heti Világgazdaság*, 13 December 1997.

LIBERAL DEMOCRACY

AGAINST THE COMPROMISE THESIS

1. Introduction

According to a widespread belief, liberal democracy tries to reconcile mutually exclusive values. No political regime can be both perfectly liberal and perfectly democratic, or so the claim has it; liberalism and democracy cannot be made compatible unless society makes concessions either from what it holds to be valuable about liberalism, or from what it values in democracy—or from both. What makes democracy attractive is that it realizes the rule of the majority, and what makes liberalism attractive is that it protects individual liberty; however, the majority tends to sacrifice individual liberty each time it can enhance its own prospects in this way. Therefore, only by restricting majority rule can liberty be saved, and majority rule cannot obtain unless liberty is restrained. The ideal of liberal democracy is that of a balance between these two values. In what follows, I will refer to this claim as *the compromise thesis*.[1]

The usual reasoning behind the compromise thesis goes as follows: the values of liberalism and those of democracy are separate, equally ultimate values (or if they are derivative values, they are nevertheless derived from different ultimate values). Since they are independent from one another, neither of them takes into account the requirements of the other. There is no such thing about liberal values that would compel one to reject states of affairs that are condemned as bad by democratic values; conversely, nothing about democratic values makes us reject that which is condemned by liberal values. Thus, conflict appears overwhelmingly likely, compromise unavoidable.

This explanation consists of two parts. First, it holds that ultimate values are independent of one another; second, it assumes that the values of liberalism and those of democracy are either equally ultimate or are derived from different ultimate values. Neither of these claims is obviously true.

First one has to face the following difficulty. Values are not facts of nature but rather normative ideals whose content is subject to *interpretation*; interpretation must satisfy the requirement of coherence. In other words, interpretations are expected to give a comprehensive view of the simultaneously approved values such that in it the latter cohere with and mutually reinforce and elucidate one another. Mutual inconsistency of ultimate values is a residual outcome of attempts of interpretation rather than an obvious starting point for them; it cannot be held unless even the best available interpretation must concede to a lack of coherence.

Mutual irreducibility of liberalism and democracy is also in need of justification. It is not evident that the two series of values do not belong to the same lineage with one of them being more basic and the other derivative. For instance, it may be claimed that the values of democracy originate in the more fundamental values of liberalism, by way of the latter being applied to the special problem of collective deliberation and decision making. Or the other way round, one may hold democratic values to be more basic and liberal values to be derivative.[2]

For my part, I am inclined to accept the coherence hypothesis; furthermore, I think liberalism is expressing basic political values, while democratic values are derivative. In this study, however, I do not argue for either of these claims but take it as my starting point that democratic values are derived from liberal values. Shortly it will be seen why this is justified in the context of the present study.

If the thesis claiming that liberal values are fundamental and democratic values are derivative is correct, then the usual justification of the compromise thesis is untenable. It is impossible that the values of democracy should require something that is rejected by liberal values.

Yet the analysis may not come to a rest at this point. Liberalism and democracy are not merely sets of values. Political values are realized through the medium of institutions. They cannot obtain unless such institutional rules and procedures are in place that combine the multitude of individual decisions in a way that makes the overall outcome approximate that which is required by these values. Liberalism is not exhausted by the fundamental ideas of liberty, equality and fraternity, but rather it also entails a specific institutional order, first and foremost the institutions of constitutionalism. Neither is democracy exhausted by the abstract ideas of collective deliberation and self-government and political participation but it also involves rules and techniques of collective decision making. A critique of the compromise thesis has to give an account of the way political institutions mediate between the guiding values and the multitude of individual decisions.

The next section locates the conflict predicted by the compromise thesis in the sphere of institutional procedures. Section 3 discusses the nature of the conflict, identifying the two pillars of the compromise thesis, that is the identification of democratic decision making with majority rule, and the identification of collective self-government with the principle that binding directives must be issued either by the participation of all community members or by representatives elected from among their own ranks. *Majority rule* is allegedly violated by the incorporation of liberal principles into the constitution, while collective self-government, also referred to as the principle of *popular sovereignty*, is supposed to be violated by constitutional review. Section 4 shows that the identification of democratic decisions with decisions by the majority presupposes a specific interpretation of political equality, one, for that matter, which we have no reason to endorse—this is the claim of Section 5. Section 6 reformulates the arguments of Section 4 in the contractarian language of constitution making. I have two objectives with this digression. On the one hand, I expect the reformulation to make the objections against the first pillar of the compromise thesis more complete and exact; on the other hand, I hope it will prepare the ground for undermining the second pillar of the compromise thesis, for in Sections 7 to 10 I will show that the contractarian theory is inevitably deficient. Before the contractarian arguments may come into play, the questions of who are the legitimate participants of the constitutive contract and what are the legitimate interests of the participants must already be settled in a substantive moral debate. The identification of the fundamental principles of liberalism must be carried out in this pre-contractual stage of reasoning. Section 11 first shows how the insights gained from the analysis of contractarian theories argue for the justification of liberal constraints, and applies these insights to the problem of constitutional review. It tries to show that, for the same reasons that make the original contract already presuppose the prior (non-contractual) identification of liberal principles, the intention of the framers of the constitution must entail that future judges apply the *correct* application of the liberal principles incorporated in the constitution, regardless of whether or not it coincides with *the framers' own* interpretation.

The compromise thesis represents a widely held dogma; its criticism is by no means superfluous. From a theoretical point of view, however, the refutation is interesting not so much in itself but rather for what it tells us about the nature of liberal democracy. Section 12 will briefly sum up these lessons.

2. The conflict

A collective decision does not raise any difficulty if it is made completely unanimously. Assume that a multitude of people has to decide about two alternatives, *a* and *b*. Assume, furthermore, that each person intends to vote for *a;* moreover, they intend to do so regardless of the voting intentions of the others. In this case the decisions are made in consensus, and no one would be justified in making objections against them. The main question of political theory—how can a binding collective decision and the duty to obey it be justified to disagreeing individuals—does not even arise.

Yet full consensus is a limiting case. Normally, decisions are divisive; there is no such outcome as to be equally favorable or approvable for everyone. Therefore, the question of political obligation is not something that could be avoided.

The liberal thesis requires that political decisions treat all human beings within their jurisdiction as *autonomous persons,* furthermore, that they treat them as *equals*. These theses imply that collective decisions should be made only within the constraints of rights and that individuals possess the same basic rights. The democratic thesis requires that the community should govern itself through its own decisions and that all members of the community should have an equal opportunity to participate in self-government. The minimal requirement of self-government is that the legislators who make rules for the community be themselves members of the same community; this is what is called popular sovereignty.[3] In direct democracy, popular sovereignty means that (almost) all adult members of the community are legislators, while in representative democracy it means that legislators are elected by the community of the subjects to the laws, and that they are elected from among the ranks of the electors themselves; that is, (almost) all members of the community have the right to vote and to run for elected office.[4] In fact, the requirement of democratic equality is implied by the principle of popular sovereignty; as members of the community, all have equal political rights, and as voters all have one and only one vote.

If liberal principles articulate basic values, while the values of democracy are derivative, then liberal principles set the boundaries for democratic principles. First, they mark out the domain in which the latter may be legitimately applied; second, they stipulate certain requirements for the way they should be applied. Democracy specifies the legitimate procedures of collective binding decisions, while liberalism claims, among other things, that there are certain issues that belong to the exclusive authority of individuals and of their voluntary associations.

Consider the issue of marriage. Imagine a practice whereby marital choices are made by the community. Even so if everybody would choose that specific spouse for everyone else that the person in question would prefer, democracy would be compatible with letting everyone decide for themselves, as a cheap substitute for collective decision making. If there were no such agreement, on the other hand, the democratic principle would require that there should be a vote, and that the choice made by the majority should be carried out. However, the liberal principle precludes the possibility of marital choice being settled by vote. Marriage is under any circumstances the private affair of two persons—and the community must accept their personal decisions, whether it coincides with its collective preferences or not. Should the principles of liberalism and those of democracy be mutually independent, the enforcement of the liberal principle would appear as a concession from the requirements of democracy. If, on the other hand, the democratic principle relies on the liberal, there is no question of moral concession. Democratic decision making is valuable only in the realm of public affairs. Its extension to private affairs is morally inappropriate.

One condition for democratic decisions to be legitimate is that political institutions clearly demarcate the realm of private affairs from the public realm, and restrict collective decisions strictly to the latter. Such a restriction does not implement a compromise between democratic and liberal principles. It does not give up anything of the things we value in democratic decision making; it only bans democratic decisions from a domain they ought not to invade. It seems as though the requirements of the democratic and liberal orders need not be reconciled.[5]

However, this argument cuts short the controversy instead of resolving it. For the problem of liberal democracy raises two separate issues. One concerns the *moral reasons* why the range of questions to be legitimately decided by democratic decision is limited, those justifying the limits being drawn in a particular way. The second problem concerns the *institutional procedures* a political community may adopt to decide between the competing answers that are given to the first issue. Suppose that members of a democratic community unanimously agree on the moral principles governing their co-existence; then the second question is pre-empted. No matter what kind of procedure they choose, the principles to be agreed upon would be the same. Modern societies, however, are divided by deep disagreements on a number of moral and ideological questions. The disagreements involve all domains of life; not only questions concerning how one should live, but also questions of what people owe to one another while pursuing their conception of a good life.

Thus, both questions must be examined separately. It is not sufficient to show that the authority of political decisions is in principle limited (say, by the boundaries of the private domain); it is also necessary to examine how this claim may become part of political decision making, provided that there is no agreement within a community about where exactly the limits of political authority lie.[6]

If it is true that certain decisions must be made—in accordance with the rules of democracy—by the community, while others must be left to be decided—in accordance with liberal rules—by the persons concerned, then further rules are needed to decide what should be decided in accordance with the rules of democracy and what should be left for the free decision of individuals, in accordance with the requirements of liberalism. Let us call the latter the *secondary rules* of a political regime. Primary rules concern the conduct of the participants of the regime; secondary rules concern the primary rules of the regime. They stipulate how primary rules can be made, amended, repealed, recognized and interpreted.[7]

Now, my claim is that secondary rules are subject to liberal and democratic requirements at the same time. First, they have to outline a decision making procedure that draws the line between individual sovereignty and the authority of collective decisions correctly—thus they belong to the jurisdiction of liberal principles. Second, they have to establish procedures for the community, and it is the community that has to endorse them as the procedures of its own rule making and rule application—thus they are inevitably within the jurisdiction of democratic principles. It is obvious that they can satisfy these two series of requirements simultaneously. It is not trivially true that there is no conflict here.

Democracy is a set of *procedural* requirements. It states the way the rules of the polity should be made, amended and repealed so that no one could reasonably object to their enforcement. It says nothing about the content of the rules. All rules made in accordance with the proper procedure are valid, no matter what their content may be. On the other hand, liberalism provides *substantive* criteria for the outcome of rule making. It excludes from the range of legitimate decisions any decision whose content does not possess the required properties. Hence the possibility of conflict between liberalism and democracy.[8]

All things considered, there is no guarantee that the majority required for drawing the proper line between the realm of private and public domains will be obtained in each case, as an outcome of an ideally regulated political discussion. There are issues that belong incontestably to the domain of private affairs (as the case of marriage just discussed); there are issues that belong uncontroversially to the public domain (as for instance the internal order and external security of a state). But the community is deeply divided on a number of issues, and competing political theories propose different boundary lines (consider the contemporary controversies surrounding sexual harassment in the United States).[9]

If it is uncertain whether the majority will adopt the correct conception of individual rights, the community may do one of two things. It may insist that the majority decision on the liberal constraints must have binding force. In this case, the institutions will satisfy the democratic requirements, but the liberal restrictions on collective decisions may suffer. Or it may want to establish safeguards for the enforcement of liberal principles. In other words, it may look for a procedure to reduce the danger of abandoning liberal principles. These provisions, however, depart from the democratic decision making procedure as it is traditionally conceived.

3. Constitutional constraints, constitutional review

The provisions protecting liberal principles are commonly said to depart from democratic decision making in two important ways. First, in constitutional democracies majority rule has no universal application to collective decisions. The rule of the majority means that support by the smallest possible majority is sufficient for an option to be declared the winner. In cases of binary choices, majority rule holds that the choice that receives at least one vote more than the half of all votes is to be the choice of the community. The constitution exempts the liberal principles from the scope of this rule. It makes fundamental individual rights and the requirements of equal treatment part of the *status quo*; and it requires some super majority to alter the *status quo*.[10] In what follows, I will refer to such procedural requirements as the liberal constraints of the constitution (or simply as liberal constraints). I will talk about constitutionalism whenever majority rule is subjected to liberal constraints.[11]

Second, it appears as though constitutional democracies violate the principle of popular sovereignty as much as that of majority rule. For the constitutional *status quo* does not have legal force unless such laws that are adopted by simple majority and are claimed to conflict with the provisions of the constitution lose their force for this reason. However, a law does not become null and void unless it is declared such by a body with authority to strike down. If the legislature itself is this body then there are two possible alternatives. Either it is the case that the same super majority may settle constitutional disagreements only as is required for amending the constitution. In this case, only such controversies can be settled that the legislature could handle through amending the existing constitution; therefore, the constitutional controversy could not be settled in precisely those cases where the constitution is supposed to constrain the legislature. Or constitutional controversies are settled by simple majority vote. In this case, the importance of the fact that constitutions are made by qualified majority is completely lost. Half of the representatives (plus one) may declare the contested piece of legislation to be constitutional, and the outcome is the same as though the constitution were amended by a simple majority. Thus, in order for constitutionalism to work, the protection of the constitutional *status quo* must be removed from the authority of the legislature.

But why not authorize another elected body? Because this body would not be identical with the legislature, neither would it be bound by the requirement of qualified majority—it is not its *own* two-thirds majority decisions that would be overturned by it. There are, however, further considerations that advise us against a second-chamber type solution. Constitutional review is supposed to establish whether contested provisions of law are or are not coherent with the rules and principles incorporated in the constitution. This and only this must be its outcome and motivating force. However, upholding or annulling a legal provision typically have different effects on different groups in society. In other words, constitutional decisions usually have significant distributional consequences, and from the voters' point of view the consequences of such decisions for their own situation are no less important than the consequences of the correct interpretation of the constitution for the contested piece of legislation. Therefore, it is reasonable to put the authority of constitutionally revising laws into the hands of such a body that is as much insulated from daily politics as possible. A necessary condition for this is that the members of the body entrusted with constitutional review must not be directly elected.[12]

Such a state of affairs would not raise the suspicion of violating the principle of popular sovereignty, had it been the case that the constitutional controversies were all due to the legislative majority transgressing self-evident constitutional constraints in transparently bad faith. In such cases, no one could claim that the guardians of the constitution make law despite their not being elected officials. They would only enforce such constitutional constraints against the current legislators that were erected by an earlier lawmaking or constitution-making assembly. In many cases, however, different good-faith interpretations of the constitution collide with one another; in other words, the narrow linguistic and logical reading of the relevant constitutional provision may allow for more than one—mutually exclusive—legal rule. It comes naturally to assume that in such cases the principle of popular sovereignty requires that the court choose that interpretation that corresponds to the intention of the framers of the constitution. Once it is allowed that the guardians of the constitution are not elected representatives, it follows that they must not change the laws by following their own convictions rather than what the constitution made by the representatives of the people entails. It is alone the representatives of the people who are authorized to decide about the laws they intend to give to the community.

But suppose that the intention of the framers is unclear, or the contested question is of such a nature that the framers could not possibly have foreseen it—thus no intention could be meaningfully attributed to them in that regard. It comes naturally to reply that in such cases the principle of popular sovereignty implies that the issue is beyond the competence of the guardians of the constitution, and so they have to refer it back to the legislature as the bearer of democratic legitimacy. Or suppose that even though the framers' own interpretation is discernible, it is informed by such false beliefs that are now commonly seen as having been refuted. Again, it appears as though the principle of popular sovereignty demands that, so long as the constitution is not amended, the guardians must enforce the false, obsolete interpretation of the contested provision.

Call the practice of the guardians *passive* if it adheres to these requirements. In case they adopt a passive stance, they are incapable of enforcing the liberal principles in exactly those contested cases where their decision is most needed. For what liberalism demands of constitutional democracies is not that they restrict the authority of collective decisions to those cases which the framers once *thought it to be right* for such decisions to be restricted to, but to those cases which it *is right* for them to be restricted to. Call a judicial practice *active* if it applies the principles of the constitution in that interpretation which, after carefully considering all the arguments available to the guardians, they judge to be the right one even though the framers had no stance whatsoever on the contested issue, or though they had a stance but it later proved to be wrong. Should the guardians adopt an active stance, they appear to amend the law by simply following their own convictions. And this is exactly what the principle of popular sovereignty prohibits—or so it seems. Either the liberal principles or the democratic principle of self-government are being infringed.

These are the claims that underlie the compromise thesis. In what follows, I will examine the two pillars of the thesis. First I examine the claim that the liberal constraints violate the requirement of majority rule, and then the other claim that they violate the principle of popular sovereignty. I will try to show that it is only in a special class of cases that democracy requires majority rule; therefore, even though the liberal constraints do indeed violate the majoritarian principle, the values of democracy itself are not infringed on that account. With regard to the principle of popular sovereignty, I will try to show that it may be satisfied even if the constitution may be actively interpreted by officials other than the elected representatives of the people; the makers of the constitution may endow the future guardians of the constitution with the authority to identify the authoritative interpretation of constitutional principles.

4. Political equality and rule by the majority

In the previous section I have been characterizing the putative conflict between democratic and liberal principles, in accordance with the traditional picture, as a conflict between majority rule and individual liberty. However, majority rule was not mentioned in my earlier characterization of democracy; I called those regimes democratic that satisfy the requirements of popular sovereignty and political equality. No doubt, this characterization departs from the usual view. Ever since the inception of modern democracy, the belief that democracy is identical with majority rule has been prevalent. John Locke claimed, in his *Second Treatise on Civil Government*, that the original contract, adopted by unanimity, privileges majority rule with regard to future decisions: "Every man, by consenting with others to make one body politic under one government, puts himself under the obligation to every one of that society, to submit to the determinations of the majority, and to be concluded by it."[13] Jean-Jacques Rousseau concluded to the same effect in *On Social Contract*: "There is but one law that by its nature requires unanimous consent. This is the social pact... Apart from this original contract, the vote of the majority is always binding on all the others; this is the consequence of the contract itself."[14]

As it will shortly turn out, this claim is false. From where does it derive, then, its force of persuasion?

There are two fundamental forms that theories of democracy take, and each gives a different interpretation about majority rule. One of them might be referred to as *collectivist*. The collectivist reading equates democratic self-government with the self-determination of the "people" understood as a person over and above the persons who constitute it. The self-government of the "people" then is the same at the level of the collective subject as what personal self-determination or the leading of an autonomous life is at the level of individual subjects. In this conception, the authority of laws in a democracy is derived from their being an expression of the will of the "people".

Just as the "people" stands above its members, so does "popular will" supersede individual wills and even the mere aggregation of individual wills. The majoritarian principle owes its special status to the fact that it realizes the self-government of the "people". Majority decisions are, as it were, the expression of "popular will"; the minority learns through the outcome of the vote that it had come to oppose the higher will of the "people".[15]

We need not discuss whether there are sufficient reasons within the collectivist reading for substituting majority decisions for the "popular will". If democracy were to derive its value from giving authoritative expression to the will of such a supraindividual "people", we would have no reason left as liberals to endorse democracy; thus we would have no reason left to see the constraints imposed on democratic principles as a loss, as a sacrifice of some genuine value. Liberalism adopts the position of methodological individualism; it attributes intentions, desires, wishes, volitions and acts only to flesh-and-bone individuals.[16] Furthermore, liberals are individualists in the ethical sense as well; they take it that nothing can be good or bad unless it is good or bad for at least one flesh-and-bone individual.[17] Liberalism is thus committed to an *individualist* reading of democracy. For the same reasons it does not admit that majority decisions, just because they represent the majority, are in principle of a higher dignity than the choices of the minority. But then what is it that gives such a privileged position to the majoritarian principle?

According to the interpretation acceptable for liberals, the majoritarian principle owes its special status to the fact that it, and it alone, satisfies the principle of *political equality*. In the individualist reading, the principle of self-government has a meaning different from the one it has in the collectivist one. Here, the principle claiming that in a democracy the totality of the subjects of the law must form a self-governing community is meant to exclude the possibility of the legislators becoming a group separate from the law subjects. This is just the egalitarian requirement; the legislators are not of a distinct species of people; they must not belong to a higher caste, order or elite separated from the addressees of the law. Democracy is valuable for liberals because under it (almost) all members of the community that is subject to the laws have the opportunity to participate in the process of electing the representatives authorized to make laws and to run for elected office. All adults have a vote and all have one vote only.

The principle of "one person one vote" is of symbolic significance. It recognizes that all people have equal status as members of the political community; no one's vote counts less just because it is cast by a person belonging to a particular class of voters, or because it expresses atypical views. It comes naturally to assume that the principle of the equal status of citizens involves a further criterion. It is not sufficient that (almost) all members of the community have one and only one vote. The way the electoral system weighs the votes when aggregating them is no less important. It would seem that if every vote counts as equal at the input, then no vote should count less (or more) at the output either, just because the person of the voter or her opinion is less (or more) valuable than that of the others. Let us call this the *principle of the equality of votes*. The principle of the equality of votes is more comprehensive than the "one person one vote" principle. It includes the former and something else—to wit, the requirement of equal weighing.

I wrote that once one accepts the principle of "one person one vote" it seems obvious to approve the more comprehensive principle of the equality of votes as well. Yet in what follows I will try to show that even though the extension seems obvious, it is wrong nevertheless. It is only under very special circumstances that the equality of votes makes people, as participants of collective decisions, equal. Before this may be shown, however, the content of the principle of the equality of votes must be further elucidated. A way to do this could be to look for rules that we would agree do violate the principle.

Such rules distinguish between people either according to their personal characteristics, or according to the characteristics of their views.

Imagine a voting system that involves the following rule. When aggregating the votes, every vote must be counted once, except for the votes of voters called Smith, which must be counted twice. Such rules are not anonymous, because the persons doing the counting cannot recognize the votes to be counted twice unless the privileged votes possess a name. The violation of *anonymity* clearly violates the principle of the equality of votes, and it is also clear that the violation is morally unacceptable; such rules select a group of voters by an arbitrary, irrelevant property (i.e. by their names), and accordingly give them special advantages as compared to the rest.

The requirement of anonymity may be easily generalized. Assume that a community must decide between two alternatives (*a* and *b*), and the majority prefers *a* over *b*. Let us distinguish two groups, *A* and *B*, within the two opposing camps in such a manner that *A* and *B* consist of an equal number of people. Now let us reverse the voting preferences of the people belonging to *A* and *B*: the members of *A* will now prefer *b*, while the members of *B* will prefer *a*. Provided that the voting system respects the requirement of anonymity, that is, it is indifferent to who are the supporters of the winning and of the losing alternative, no such reversal can possibly alter the outcome of the vote. If, on the other hand, the reversal makes the hitherto winning alternative into the losing one and vice versa, then the electoral rules violate the anonymity requirement. Such a system that counts the votes of Smiths twice obviously violates anonymity. But this is true for systems that weigh not according to personal names but according to some other personal criterion. If the system privileges certain groups of people by their social status, ethnic group or some other common property, then it may occur that the outcome of the vote is reversed when exchanging *A* for *B*. The main point is the same in all of these cases; the voting procedure must somehow be able to identify the members of the subclasses of the class of voters, so that it is able to properly weigh the votes of the participants.[18]

It is possible, however, for an electoral rule to privilege *standpoints* rather than *persons* or their groups. Let us imagine that there is a law in place that protects the overall *status quo*. Existing laws may be amended only by some super majority, which implies that it is sufficient for upholding an existing law that the motion to amend it fall short of receiving the requisite super majority. This rule is not neutral as far as the standpoints for or against the *status quo* are concerned, since the outcome of the procedure is sensitive to the content of the votes. Like the violation of anonymity, the violation of neutrality, too, infringes the principle of the equality of votes, since advocates of the *status quo* have a greater chance for victory than those who want to change it.[19]

The requirement of neutrality, too, may be immediately generalized. Assuming that a community decides between two alternatives (*a* and *b*), and that alternative *a* gets a certain amount of the vote that makes it the winner in the given voting system, the system is neutral if *b*, too, were to win if it were to get the same amount of votes as did *a*. If *b* loses, the system violates the requirement of neutrality.

The same requirement may be formulated with respect to two separate issues. Assuming that among the totality of voters the same number of people prefer option *x* over option *y* as the number of people preferring *v* over *z*, the decision making procedure is neutral as far as the two alternatives—*x* or *y*, and *v* or *z*—are concerned, provided that the outcome will be the same, no matter which issue is voted on. *X* will always be the winner if and only if *v* wins too, and *v* must always lose whenever *x* loses. The procedure violates the requirement of neutrality if the same distribution of votes makes *x* the winner of the first decision and it makes *z* the winner of the second.[20]

To sum up, in case of binary choices the principle of the equality of votes is satisfied by those and only those decision making rules that satisfy anonymity and neutrality. From this follows, however, that only majority rule meets the principle of the equality of votes. It was Kenneth O. May who demonstrated that in the case of binary choices there is only one minimally efficient rule—majority rule—that simultaneously satisfies the requirements of anonymity and neutrality.[21] Then it seems that equality of votes is indeed identical with majority rule. If votes are weighed equally at the aggregation, then collective decisions are made by simple majority, and if collective decisions are made by simple majority, then the votes are equally weighed. It follows that if we have reasons to accept that democratic equality means equality of votes, we also have to accept that democracy necessarily involves majority rule. In this view, genuine democracies are the ones in which representatives are elected by a simple majority and laws are made by simple majority decisions.

5. Equality of votes and equality of voters

But is it really the case that for a voting system to treat participants of the voting process as equals it must always grant one and only one vote to all of them and weigh the votes equally when it comes to aggregation? In what follows I will argue that this is not the case. It is only under special circumstances that equality of votes satisfies the requirement of equal treatment.

Let me begin with the requirement of anonymity. Assume that the community is divided into two distinct and well-recognizable groups, the Blue and the Pink ('Blue' and 'Pink' may refer to color, gender, age, religion, language, ethnicity, social class or whatever). Let us randomly select one person from each group and track down the way they vote in successive elections. If we find that the choice of both Blue and Pink tend to coincide with the preferences of the majority with approximately the same frequency, then it is the case that in the long run the two groups have a roughly equal share of the advantages and the disadvantages of collective decisions.[22] A rule violating the requirement of anonymity would make the outcome biased. It would give a disproportionately large share of the advantages of collective decisions to one group, and it would make the other group bear a disproportionately large part of the disadvantages. This would indeed amount to an unjustifiable, arbitrary distinction. But what makes it unjustifiable is not the fact in itself that the voting procedure deploys disparate weighing, but that disparate weighing arbitrarily advantages one of the groups while at the same time arbitrarily disadvantaging the other.

The situation is different, however, if Blue tend always to vote like other Blues do and Pink vote like other Pinks do, and one of the groups has a permanent numerical majority. Under such circumstances, the chances of Blues and Pinks voting with as the winners are radically unequal. The permanent minority becomes a permanent bearer of burdens, while the permanent majority becomes a permanent beneficiary of advantages. Adherence to the requirement of anonymity here is not necessarily fair, while departing from it is not necessarily arbitrary and biased. It is arbitrary and biased if it further increases the initial inequality and it is not so if it serves to diminish it.

Collective decisions allocate advantages and disadvantages among members of society. The voting procedure treats participants as equals only if in a series of decisions everybody has a roughly equal share in the advantages and disadvantages. The principle of anonymity does not always serve this more basic ideal of equality, but only if the distribution of preferences is such that in the long run everybody tends to vote with the majority with roughly the same frequency. If this condition fails to obtain, then all that can be said for anonymity is that it does not further aggravate inequality. However, this is not sufficient for us to judge an anonymous system to be more egalitarian than, or at the least as egalitarian as, a non-anonymous one that tends to offset the disadvantages of the minority. Insofar as the latter tends to equalize the chances of voting with the majority, it is morally superior to a strictly anonymous voting system. If our reason for being democrats is, among other things, that democracy applies the liberal principle of equal treatment to the case of collective decisions, then indeed we have no reason for finding such cases of departing from the requirement of anonymity objectionable. To the contrary, we have good reasons for objecting to voting systems that sustain the asymmetry between permanent majorities and permanent minorities.

What liberal equality requires is not that every rule treat every individual indiscriminately, but that disparate treatment should not put on anyone such burdens that are either arbitrary, unnecessary, disproportionate or based on prejudice and contempt towards her or her group. Unbiased positive discrimination is not prohibited by liberalism, thus neither is it prohibited by the liberal interpretation of democratic equality.

Such versions of positive discrimination that would give more votes to some members of the community than to others, thus directly violating the principle of "one person one vote", are certainly unacceptable. But the liberal interpretation of democratic equality forbids such discrimination not because it fails to satisfy anonymity, but because, as we have seen, the principle of "one person one vote" has a symbolic function in recognizing that all members of the political community are of an equal status. Yet one may depart from equality of votes while at the same time retaining the narrower condition of "one person one vote", because the weighing applied to the aggregation of votes has no such symbolic function.

Disparate weighing of votes may be carried out in a number of different ways. One of them consists in a direct violation of anonymity, taken by some federal systems. Suppose a certain community consists of two distinct ethnic groups. The constitution provides for a bicameral legislation. Members of the Lower House are elected indiscriminately by majority rule; the Upper House consists of two separate chambers, one for each ethnic group. Some of the bills are voted only in the Lower House, yet bills that meet a certain description must be passed by the Upper House, too. There is a simple majority decision both in the Lower House and in the two chambers of the Upper House, yet the bills that are read in the Upper House are turned into law only if they receive a majority in all of the three bodies. This system is not anonymous; it clearly privileges minority votes.

Another possibility is to depart from the requirement of neutrality rather than anonymity. Pieces of legislation that are vital from the point of view of the minority are set apart and made subject to a super majority rule such that they may not be passed without the approval of at least some members of the minority.

Furthermore, one may have reasons to depart from the requirement of neutrality other than making the vote of permanent minorities decisive. Neutrality of voting rules may prove to be undesirable directly from the point of view of equality. At first glance neutrality, not unlike anonymity, strikes one as an inherently egalitarian requirement. If the decision making system weighs two options differently (say, the one constructing a new subway line, as against the one of not engaging in the construction work), then it gives advantages to the proponents of one of the alternative options (if the opponents of construction possess one vote more than a third of all votes, for example, they can block the will of a majority of nearly two-thirds); on the other hand, if votes cast for all the alternatives are weighed equally, no one is given advantage. At a closer look, however, one will find that the neutrality of rules is no unmixed blessing, and it may be objectionable precisely from the perspective of equal treatment. For equality of weighing implies that a person's vote counts the same, regardless of whether the issue that is being voted on is vital for her or of marginal significance. Neutral rules are insensitive to the varying importance different issues may have for different persons. If one more person favors weakly that which is opposed violently by one less person, the weak endorsement will carry the day against strong disapproval. Let us imagine that this is the only occasion when the community decides by vote. In this case, the voting system does not treat the voters equally.

This complication draws our attention to the fact that equal treatment is not a self-evident idea. People may be treated equally or unequally in a variety of different dimensions. Voting systems, for instance, may make either the vote of every person equal, regardless of the strength of electoral preferences with respect to different decisions, or they may equalize votes that are weighed in accordance with preference intensity. Yet voters may be treated equally in both dimensions at the same time only if everybody has preferences of the same strength with regard to all issues that are voted on. If this is not the case, equality along one of these dimensions will exclude equality along the other. Before one could determine whether a voting system treats voters equally, it must be made clear which are the dimensions in which disparate weighing is prohibited by the requirement of equal treatment; to put it differently, it must be determined which is the dimension in which equality must obtain for the principle of equal treatment to be satisfied.

My claim is that the principle of equal treatment requires, with respect to voting systems, that votes are weighed in accordance with the importance of the issue rather than independently of it. Therefore, neutral rules do not satisfy the requirement of equal treatment unless some fairly specific conditions obtain. First, everybody should attribute roughly equal importance to the advantages brought about by victory and to the disadvantages brought about by defeat. Further, the importance attached to successive issues by different groups of voters should not differ significantly. Finally, it must be the case that everybody has a fair chance of not being on the losing side with disproportionate frequency and on the victorious side with disproportionate infrequency. Should it be the case that these conditions simultaneously hold, neutral rules will approximate well the performance of such more complex rules that are sensitive to the relative importance different groups attach to different issues and outcomes. If either one of these conditions are not satisfied, neutral rules will produce outcomes that diverge from those required by equal treatment.[23]

6. Contractarian theory:
the selection of voting rules

The insights of the previous section are close to the results the theory of collective decisions reached by way of studying constitutional choices. In what follows, I will briefly summarize the arguments of James Buchanan and Gordon Tullock, who outlined the theory in its classical form.[24] My hope is that such a summary will make the above claims about equal treatment of voters more exact and at the same time prepare the ground for discussing our second problem, the one that concerns the relation between constitutional review and popular sovereignty.

Suppose, goes the argument Buchanan and Tullock suggest, that the inhabitants of a country take it as their task to agree upon the constitution of their future state. The process of constitution making may be described as some sort of a hypothetical contract. Each party considers the available alternatives and approves of that which it takes to be more favorable than the rest (and more favorable than a state without constitution). The set of rules that is approved of by everyone will become the constitution of the state.

As part of the constitution, a voting system must be adopted. A voting system is the set of voting rules applied to the multitude of different collective decisions. In principle it is conceivable that the system will consist of one single rule (say, that all cases must be decided by simple majority), but it is equally possible that different rules will be adopted for different types of issues.

Suppose, so the argument proceeds, that every inhabitant of the country knows her own preferences and is able to consistently rank them. Thus, they are aware of the decisions they would make regarding the various issues put forward for vote after the constitution has come into force. Everybody strives to maximize their personal utility when making decisions. Therefore, everyone prefers that voting system which promises him or her the greatest personal utility in a long-term series of votes.

Provided that at the moment of constitution making the inhabitants of the country are conscious of the social distribution of preferences no less than they are conscious of their own preferences, they will be able to predict, for each future decision, the size of majority and minority as well as whether they themselves will belong to the majority or to the minority. That is, they will be able to tell, from case to case, the kind of voting rule that would be most favorable for them. Under such conditions it could occur only exceptionally that all would prefer the same voting system.

Suppose nevertheless that the exception indeed occurs; everyone votes for the same voting system. In this case, the voting system included in the constitution will depend exclusively on the (unanimous) preferences of the inhabitants. The outcome will not be affected by the kind of decision making rule that is being applied for the approval of the voting system itself. No matter whether unanimity, qualified majority or simple majority is required, or whether the decision depends on the will of only a few persons (or of a single one), the collective decision will always produce one and the same voting system. If there is no perfect consensus among the inhabitants, on the other hand, then the outcome of the decision about the voting system will depend on the voting rule that is applied for the constitution making itself as much as on the preferences of the inhabitants. Thus, prior to approving the voting system a rule must be approved which is to be applied to decide about the voting system itself. However, in the absence of unanimity, there must be a decision about *this* rule, too, and so on *ad infinitum*.

In order to stop this regress, Buchanan and Tullock suggest that we assume that even though the hypothetical inhabitants know how they will vote in the succession of future issues, they do not know how the others will vote, so they do not know whether they will belong to the winners or to the losers in any individual case, once the voting system is in place. Under such conditions, their decision about the voting system will not be influenced by their special interests, because no one will be able to guess which voting system would be more favorable for her (and her group) than for the others. Each of the partially ignorant inhabitants will make their decision as though they were contingently selected representatives of the totality of the population.[25] This assumption secures the unanimous agreement of all, and thus averts the danger of infinite regress.

The assumption of partial ignorance has a further consequence. None of the hypothetical constitution makers will be in such a position as to vote for a system that is exceptionally favorable for her or for her group.[26] Since the parties do not know whether they will belong to the majority or to the minority in any individual case, they are incapable of being biased either for or against the majority or the minority. Ignorance dooms them to impartiality. Everyone will be voting as though they were voting for everyone else.[27]

In other words, the hypothesis of partial ignorance is not some morally indifferent auxiliary hypothesis; it is not just one of many possible technical moves devised to arrest a looming infinite regress. It is privileged against other such moves by the fact that it compels hypothetical constitution makers to impartiality. It seems that a voting system that is approved of by individuals who are ignorant as to which rules are favorable or unfavorable personally for them necessarily satisfies the requirement of equal treatment.

Now, Buchanan and Tullock have shown that it is not always the rule of simple majority (i.e., the rule that satisfies the requirements of anonymity and neutrality simultaneously[28]) that is preferred by decision makers who are ignorant about their future position. Their argument proceeds as follows.

Whether the outcome of collective decisions is favorable or unfavorable for someone depends on whether she belongs to the winning or the losing coalition. The difference between advantages and disadvantages makes up the cost of the vote for the losers. This is what the authors call the *external costs* of decision making. The larger the external costs are the more important it becomes for a voter to avoid belonging to the losing side. And the larger the majority required by the voting rule for valid decisions is, the slighter the chances are that they will be on the losing side. If valid decisions require unanimity, then other people's decisions, can never incur external costs on an individual, for no majority, no matter how large it may be, may make valid decisions without her assent. Thus, assuming that decision making itself is a costless procedure, it is reasonable for constitution makers to adopt one single rule, that of unanimity.

However, decision making has its own costs, and the larger the community the higher the costs of reaching consensus will be. This is what Buchanan and Tullock call the *internal costs* of decision making. For any given size of the community, internal costs will increase in proportion to the size of the majority required for valid decisions. In case of a simple majority vote, it does not pose significant difficulties for a voting coalition if a voter makes her assent dependent on certain conditions. It may not appear necessary to bargain with her, since it may be easy to find someone else to take her place. As the required majority increases, however, the chances of replacement diminish and the bargaining position of would-be joiners improves. Keeping this correlation in mind, it may not be reasonable for constitution makers to agree on the requirement of unanimity in every single case. It will be reasonable for them to minimize the *sum* of external and internal costs of the decision, which will vary in each type of case, rather than minimizing external costs alone.

The rule of simple majority minimizes the bargaining costs of decision making. Yet the chances of ending up on the losing side are larger than with rules requiring a qualified majority or unanimity. It is reasonable to take this risk only if the constitution makers rely on the special assumptions mentioned in the previous section. First, all participants should attribute roughly the same importance to the advantages of a possible victory and the disadvantages of a possible defeat. Furthermore, the importance attached to successive issues may not differ from one case to another radically. Finally, all may reasonably expect not to end up on the losing side too frequently, or to belong to the winners with disproportionate infrequency. Should these requirements obtain, the framers of the constitution may hope that by adopting a simple majority rule, their gains will in the long run be in balance with their losses; thus, there is no point in adopting a more demanding—and therefore more costly—voting rule.

If, on the other hand, any of these conditions is not satisfied, commitment to a simple majority will be unreasonable. Suppose that though the constitution makers know the society is divided into permanent majorities and minorities, they do not know whether they themselves will belong to the majority or to the minority. Should they adopt the rule of simple majority, their decision would be unreasonable, for they would risk living in a regime where they bear all the burdens of collective decisions while others enjoy all the fruits thereof. Under such conditions, the adoption of some more demanding voting rule will be reasonable.[29]

Suppose now that the importance of different decisions is not the same, but rather varies from case to case. If so, then it is possible that even though everyone belongs to the winners and to the losers with approximately the same frequency, the balance of gains and losses will still be uneven. The higher the costs for someone of belonging to the losing side in a specific case, the more reasonable it will become for her to apply a rule to that specific case that is more demanding than the rule of simple majority. In extreme cases, it may even be worthwhile to insist on unanimity. However, this may prove unattainable in the real world; the time available for making a decision is usually less than what would be needed for reaching complete consensus. According to Buchanan and Tullock, it is reasonable to exempt such issues from the authority of collective decisions and to allow individuals to make sovereign decisions about them for themselves. These are the interests that the hypothetical framers would protect by individual rights.

To sum up, a variety of decision making rules are adopted in the course of constitution making. In certain cases, simple majority will be the reasonable thing to adopt; in other cases, it will be reasonable to insist on qualified majority; finally, it is reasonable for the most pressing individual interests to be removed from the domain of collective decisions and ranked in the domain protected by individual rights. Each time the rule of simple majority is abandoned, either the requirement of anonymity or of neutrality is violated, or both.

This is what rationality, the consideration of anticipated advantages and disadvantages, requires. And this is also what morality demands. We have seen that partial ignorance deprives the hypothetical constitution makers of the possibility of making biased decisions. A voting system that is unanimously approved under the conditions of partial ignorance would satisfy, beyond the requirements of rational prudence, those of equal treatment.

Thus, the majoritarian rule does not always conform to the moral requirements of equality. There are situations in which equal treatment demands of the voting system to abandon majority rule—even though this entails abandoning anonymity and/or neutrality. But this is only to assert that the choices generated by a voting system subject to the constraints of anonymity and neutrality do not always coincide with those required by equality; it may occur that an anonymous and/or neutral system is not egalitarian, or that a system providing for equal treatment is not anonymous and/or neutral.

7. A weakness of
contractarian theory

Thus, one of the two pillars of the compromise thesis has been removed. Since rules that are more demanding than simple majority do not in principle violate democratic equality, the latter does not prohibit the application of liberal constraints. Yet the second pillar is yet to be considered. If it is true that the liberal principles of equal treatment may be enforced against encroachments by the legislature only through judicial activism, and if it is true that an activist conception of constitutional review is incompatible with the principle of popular sovereignty, then it will still be the case that liberal constraints imposed on political decision making violate fundamental democratic principles. Hence the thesis that liberalism and democracy may be reconciled only through a compromise regarding their fundamental principles will remain true.

The model that conceives of constitution making as a hypothetical contract does not refute this belief. It provides no reasons for the judges who interpret the constitution in such a way that would justify their departure from "original intention", that is, from what the framers of the constitution themselves took to be the correct interpretation of their provisions. This is so, however, only because the model, as it will be seen shortly, fails to satisfactorily accommodate the liberal constraints themselves. If we can grasp the reasons for this failure, we will by the same token arrive at an understanding of why the belief supporting the second pillar of the compromise thesis is wrong.

The following sections will be devoted to examining the weaknesses of the contractarian model. I will focus on the so-called fundamental rights as instances of the liberal constraints, and I will examine whether an agreement reached by the hypothetical constitution makers posited by Buchanan and Tullock would cover the same rights as the ones required by liberalism.

Buchanan and Tullock merely make the claim that the hypothetical constitution makers would approve of basic liberal rights, but they do not attempt to prove this contention. True, they need not demonstrate it, since their aims do not include an establishing of the rights characteristic of liberal democracies. What they try to show is the general correlation between the properties of just and rational elections and those of individual preferences and of their distribution. Yet the theoretical value of their model partly depends on whether the properties and distribution of individual preferences are at least in principle capable of explaining the liberal constraints imposed on the majoritarian principle. This is what I will discuss now.

The hypothetical constitution makers of Buchanan and Tullock not only establish a rank ordering of the possible alternatives, say a and b. They also take into account the gains and losses that would be involved by a and b respectively. In other words, they are aware not only of the fact that realizing a is more (or less) advantageous for them than realizing b but also of how much it is more advantageous. Consider an imagined constitution maker, X. Suppose the issues to be decided by vote may be divided into two categories from the point of view of X. One of the categories comprises such issues where the value of a and b does not differ significantly for X (call these the "normal" cases). The other category comprises issues where the difference of values is significant (call them "special" cases). Let X expect the advantages and disadvantages incurred on him in 'normal' cases to be fairly balanced in the long run; it is reasonable for him to vote for retaining such issues within the authority of the majority rule. On the other hand, being on the losing side in "special" cases would represent unbearable disadvantages for X; he would be reasonable to want to refer these issues to the domain protected by rights—to the domain that is at the sovereign disposal of the individual. Suppose all constitution makers make the same distinction between "normal" and "special" issues. Yet would they agree in the list of individual rights? And would this list coincide with the set of liberal rights?

For this to be the case, the following conditions must be satisfied. First, it must be the case that for every liberal right there is at least one hypothetical constitution maker who regards the domain protected by that right as "special". Furthermore, everyone else must be at worst indifferent towards the protection of these interests. This assumption does not entail that each hypothetical constitution maker must hold exactly the same issues to be "special". But it still entails enough for it to be reasonable for us to ask: What is the ground for making it?

The ground could be that this assumption gives a good approximation of the distribution of preferences to be empirically found in the world. It is conceivable, for instance, for human nature to involve certain strong desires that are identical in (almost) every person. Hobbes made such an empirical assumption with regard to the desire to avoid violent death as a dominant desire of all. Yet even if there could be such anthropologically determined desires, it is certain that they do not account for the majority of basic rights recognized by contemporary constitutional democracies. For instance, what sort of anthropological interests do the rights concerning the protection of personal data or freedom of information express? Such rights are not even intelligible to people who do not live within the institutional framework and technical conditions characteristic of modern societies.

Another possibility would be that strong desires are not constitutive of human nature in general but of the nature of (the vast majority of) the people living in modern societies. Yet this, too, falls short of our empirical reality. Some of the liberal principles are for the most part approved of by citizens of democratic states; others deeply divide them, while there are yet others that are enduringly rejected by their majority. For instance, the so-called right to life is generally endorsed. On the other hand, unpopular minorities of descent, ethnicity, religion or life-style are to be found everywhere, and nowhere is there a clear agreement as to how they should be treated. And in most democratic countries the majority claims that under the liberal rule of law, "criminals" have more rights, unfortunately, than law enforcement agencies or the victims of crime, and that this situation should be reversed.

For there to be a strict correlation between strong preferences and individual rights, one must, thus, attribute *idealized* preferences to the hypothetical constitution makers. What I mean by the idealization of preferences is not that as a result of idealization better preferences are produced, such that are closer to our ideals. Idealized preferences are either better than ordinary ones or not. The main point is that many of the ordinary preferences are eliminated in the process.

Buchanan and Tullock do not furnish us with guidelines as to which of our preferences should be eliminated and on what grounds. They use a brute, uninterpreted conception of preference, such as was prevalent in the literature of economics at the time of the writing of their book. Below I outline a somewhat more refined yet still deliberately rudimentary typology of preferences, and take a look at a possible route of idealization by tracing the distinctions of this typology. I will show that filtering the preferences of the constitution makers does not help us out of the difficulty.

8. The typology of preferences

Call preferences such rankings of possible states of affairs where the ranking shows what, other things being equal, the person who made the ranking is disposed to choose. Call the person who makes the ranking the *subject* of preferences. Suppose that for this person, A, there are two possible states of affairs; he obtains either an apple or a pear. Then, A may prefer either obtaining the apple to obtaining the pear or obtaining the pear to obtaining the apple, or he may be indifferent to the two outcomes. Yet, such statements do not provide us with exhaustive descriptions of the preferences of A. They do not reveal whether A makes the ranking from his own point of view or from that of another person, B. They do not reveal whether what A desires is that he himself or B obtains an apple rather than a pear (or vice versa). Let us call the person from whose point of view the ranking is made the *addressee* of preferences. The first important distinction is between preferences where the subject and addressee coincide and between the ones where they do not coincide. In the first case, one may talk about self-regarding preferences of the subject, while in the latter case the preferences can be said to be other regarding.[30]

Preferences give priority to certain states of affairs over other states of affairs, but this need not mean that the person making the ranking believes the preferred state of affairs to be the best. Consider first the case of other-regarding preferences. Their ordering coincides with the order of evaluation only if the subject wishes well for the addressee of the preferences. It is conceivable, however, that the subject's preference ordering is governed by his hostility towards the addressee.[31] Thus one may distinguish between benevolent and hostile preferences. One may call this a distinction in accordance with (positive or negative) sign, for benevolent preferences preserve, while hostile preferences reverse, the order of evaluation of states of affairs. People are benevolent or hostile with respect to other people; they may be philanthropic or misanthropic; depending on such facts, they may either rejoice in other people's happiness and feel sorry for their sorrow, or, to the contrary, they may rejoice in their misery and experience their happiness as a personal loss. It is less obvious, yet it is true that the distinction according to (positive or negative) sign is neither meaningless nor vacuous with respect to self-regarding preferences, either. Think of self-hating people who wish bad for themselves.

A further distinction is as follows. When people in the real world identify their preferences, they do not always possess sufficient information about either the world or themselves so as to be able to precisely identify the true object of their desire. Should they acquire the necessary information, they may realize that what they in fact desire is not that which they believed they desired. Let us call such preferences as they are formed in ordinary life, in the absence of the requisite information, our *raw* preferences, and preferences that are established in the light of sufficient information and retained after careful review our *considered* preferences.[32]

For the most part, preferences rank such states of affairs that do not themselves include preferences. There are, however, such preferences that set up a ranking among states of affairs that involve preferences. The former may be called *first-order* preferences, the latter *second-order* preferences. Secondary preferences may be directed at what the first-order preferences should be like, or whether they be fulfilled or not. *B* prefers getting an apple to getting a pear; this is a first-order preference. *B* prefers preferring a pear to preferring an apple; this is a secondary preference. *B* prefers not getting the apple that he prefers to a pear to getting the apple; this, too, is a secondary preference. More specifically, these are such second-order preferences that are directed at *B*'s self-regarding first-order preferences. Yet second-order preferences may rank other-regarding first-order preferences as well. Such is the case when *B* prefers preferring an apple for *C* to preferring a pear for *C* (or *B* prefers *C* not getting the apple that he [*B*] prefers for her [*C*]). Furthermore, not unlike first-order preferences, second-order preferences, too, may be directed at others as well as at ourselves. *B* prefers *C* preferring an apple to a pear to *C* preferring a pear to an apple (or *B* prefers *C* not getting the pear that she [*C*] prefers for herself). These are other-regarding second-order preferences. More specifically, these are second-order preferences directed at another person's self-regarding first-order preferences. Finally, *B* may form preferences regarding the preferences that *C* should form with regard to a third person (or regarding the fulfillment of *C*'s preferences with regard to the third person).[33]

But what is the ground for forming particular second-order preferences that either approve of or reject first-order preferences? This is a further important question. Suppose *A* plays the piano in a bar every night. Before starting his work he spends his dinner with a friend, who is a great expert on wines. Each night, the friend proposes to share a bottle of excellent red wine. Should *A* drink his share, he will not be able to play the piano as well as he wishes. During the afternoon he still prefers good piano-play to the pleasure of the wine but by the time his friend makes his proposal, he prefers the wine. By morning, however, he regrets his decision. Now he regrets playing less satisfactorily than he would have desired. Now he desires not to have preferred the wine at dinner. The next night he will play the piano again and he will have dinner with his friend again. And now he desires that this time his preference does not change. This is his second-order preference.[34]

The moment of proposal is approaching, and *A*'s first-order preference is about to yield. Should he yield to the pressure or is it reasonable for him to subordinate his first-order preference to his second-order preference? It seems that there are two possible answers to this question. It is either the case that preferences of different order are allowed to compete with one another; if the first-order preference (that by this time favors the wine) is stronger than the second-order one, then it is reasonable to yield to it. Or it may be the case that second-order preferences are not competing with first-order ones that are in conflict with them, but simply exclude them from the range of motives that are allowed to influence when making the decision—but then there must be third order preferences requiring that the second-order preference be given priority, and so on *ad infinitum*.[35]

Yet there is no danger of infinite regress here. It should be noticed that second-order preferences are of a specific nature. On the primary level, it may be sufficient to prefer *a* to *b* to choose *a* rather than *b*. But for preferring that we do not prefer *a* to *b* it is not sufficient to prefer just this. It may appear that the problem of second-order preferences may lead to infinite regress only because one is implicitly assuming that second-order preferences are just the reflections of second-order desires. Yet our second-order desires are no mere desires or wishes. We desire that we do not desire something because we *disapprove* of that desire. *A* prefers preferring excellent piano-play as opposed to the pleasure of drinking wine in the decisive moment because he thinks playing excellently to be more valuable than the pleasure produced by drinking wine. His second-order stance is in fact nothing other than this value judgment; this judgment may be true or false, but it is not a tertiary standpoint that makes it true or false.

The fact that people take their stances with respect to their own preferences and those of other people on the basis of judgments opens up a very important dimension. First, when someone formulates his preference, he expresses what he favors over other possibilities. His statement is about his own attitude; thus, such statements depend on the person who makes them and the sort of things that characterize him or her. In this sense, preferences are susceptible to criticism only to a limited extent. People may very rarely be victims of desires that are irrational all by themselves. Such is the case with an unmotivated death wish, for instance (when one is healthy and has everything that is necessary for a successful life and yet wants to commit suicide). In other cases, one might locate one's immediate preferences mistakenly (when one desires to ease one's thirst rather than the taste of wine or to get drunk, yet one makes for the pub). In yet other cases one may be right about one's immediate preferences yet one may fail to take account of the longer-term consequences of satisfying them and thus may disregard one's own preferences with respect to such long-term consequences (when one desires the taste of wine and pays no heed to the ensuing hangover). It may also occur that one's preferences are inconsistent (when one prefers x to y and y to z and z to x). In such cases, and in a few similar ones, one may be justified in telling such a person that he identifies his preferences wrongly and ranks them unreasonably. Yet if this person's preferences are neither extremely irrational, inconsistent, nor grounded in ignorance or neglect of more distant consequences, then we have no reason to tell him that he is wrong, solely on the basis of what we know about him and his situation and attitudes.

On the other hand, if we desire that a person should prefer something else rather than what he actually prefers, or if we desire that he does not adjust his decisions to his preferences because we find that which he prefers (either that he prefers it or that he adjusts his actions to this preference) inappropriate and condemnable, then our desire has independent grounds. We desire that he desire something else not because we know that in fact he desires something else or because we would prefer something else in his place, but because it is *right* to do so, because he *should* form such preferences or he *should* decide *as though* he had such preferences. One may be wrong about this even if one is right about his actual preferences.

Furthermore, claims grounded in judgments are universalizable. They relate to whole groups of people (potentially to everyone) rather than to just those who have the appropriate propensities. If it were right for A to decide in favor of good piano-play over good wine, then, *ceteris paribus*, it would be right for everyone else as well to do so. It is conceivable for someone to be right about his personal preferences in the business of choosing between piano-play and drinking wine, and yet for the same person to be wrong about the sort of preference he ought to have.

This is a distinction of the utmost importance. Our sympathies and antipathies, wishes and desires are traits that characterize our personalities. They do not entail the claim that everyone else should share them. Our judgments, on the other hand, are true or false independent of the traits that characterize us, and if they are true, the claim they involve extends to everyone within their scope of application. And we have reasons to say that it is not right to stick to such preferences that are condemned by them.

9. Filtering the preferences of the contracting parties

The above typology is rather rudimentary, and it does not account for a number of factors that are relevant for human preferences.[36] Yet it is sufficient to give an overview of what the idealization of preferences of the hypothetical constitution makers may and may not involve.

First of all, it may involve excluding raw preferences. It is always better to make a decision on the basis of considered preferences than making decisions while we are not entirely clear about what we in fact prefer. The longer the time-span of a decision the more important it is that the preferences taken into account be as carefully considered as possible. The constitution establishes the principles and rules of the functioning of the state for an especially long term; thus it is especially important for constitution makers not to be influenced by brute, ill-considered preferences.

It can be seen that the elimination of raw preferences may bring us closer to accepting the liberal constraints. Consider the celebrated example of the death penalty. Even in some constitutional democracies with well-established traditions (such as the United States) a majority of the citizens opposes the abolition of capital punishment or, if it has been already abolished, they want to reintroduce it. Suppose the only reason proponents of capital punishment (or its reintroduction) have for favoring it is their belief that it is only through threatening possible perpetrators with death that the frequency of particularly grave crimes may be significantly reduced. Suppose now that one succeeds in persuading such people that there is no significant statistical correlation between introducing or abolishing the death penalty and the frequency of capital crimes. Suppose, furthermore, that they get acquainted with all the cases when the execution of a death sentence rendered a judicial error irremediable. These people will no longer favor the death penalty once they possess this information—at least if their preferences are grounded in careful assessment.

But suppose, on the contrary, that the expectation regarding a decline in crime is not the only reason for most of them to favor the death penalty. They think this is the *right* punishment to apply to certain crimes. What kind of a justice system is one, they may ask, that lets live a monster that serially raped and murdered helpless children? It is not sufficient against this reasoning to point out that capital punishment has no deterrent potential, for the argument takes it that its goal is not deterrence but retribution. So evidence of a different kind is needed, one that allows to choose between the retribution account and the deterrence account of punishment. Yet it might be the case that there is no decisive evidence at hand that would compel everyone to adopt the deterrence account rather than its retributivist rival (or vice versa). To put it differently, after carefully weighing all the available evidence, both the adepts of the deterrence account and those of the retribution account might in good faith persist in their initial position. If so, however, then the transformation of preferences demanded by a liberal theory of rights cannot be completed by narrowing the scope to considered preferences. Further screening is required.

But what else should be eliminated besides raw preferences? Approving retribution is a moral judgment—thus, certain moral judgments and such preferences that are dependent on them must go so as to reach an agreement on liberal constraints. It comes naturally to assume that approving the "eye for an eye" principle presumes dislike and hostility with regard to other people, and that this is the reason why it causes such complications. Should it be the case, one may try to eliminate judgments that presume disdain and hostility. But then, what should we think of Hegel's thesis that punishment is an expression of respect for the criminal—a recognition of the fact that he is a rational creature capable of grasping that his act is a crime and that he commits it knowingly, intentionally.[37] No matter what one may hold about this thesis, it certainly would not be justified to claim that Hegel only gave free rein to his disdain of criminals when he argued for a retributive conception of punishment.

To put it briefly, the range of moral judgments to be eliminated can hardly be restricted. We must assume that the hypothetical constitution makers do not subject their preferences to moral criticism at all.

Even so, it is still conceivable that some of their other-regarding preferences are undesirable. People full of hatred and having sadistic inclinations may feel a strong desire to retain capital punishment even though their desires are not being supported by moral reasons. Moreover, the elimination of moral judgments entails the elimination of the possibility of people being capable of disapproving of their own hostile preferences on moral grounds and thus of not allowing such preferences to guide their actions to them. Thus, the hypothetical constitution makers must be deprived of their other-regarding hostile preferences as well.[38]

However, not all violation of rights is based on hostile preferences. Suppose that a man finds excessive pleasure in sexual life with women but finds the thought of men having sex with other men utterly repulsive. Suppose, furthermore, that this man feels strong benevolence towards gay people. All he desires is that gay people, too, live a good life, and he cannot get rid of the thought that homosexual sex is perverted and disgusting. Since his decisions are not influenced by moral convictions (these having been eliminated in an earlier move), he is not going to accept sexual orientation's being relegated to the secure domain of private affairs—to the domain, that is, into which the collective decisions made within the limits of the constitution are not able to penetrate.

If it is true, then all other-regarding preferences, too, must be eliminated without remainder. It must be assumed that the participants of the contract are entirely indifferent towards one another.[39]

The idealization of preferences leaves us with a rather impoverished picture of the hypothetical constitution makers. One must imagine them as such people who feel neither sympathy nor antipathy for fellow human beings, and who are not governed by moral ideals in relation to their own lives or to that of others. Their first-order preferences are all self-regarding, and these preferences are examined at the secondary level only from the point of view of being properly considered. Should they have any second-order preferences beyond the former, they would be restricted to the wish that their (considered) first-order preferences be satisfied to the greatest extent possible.

This is a rather disquieting consequence. Liberal constitutions establish moral principles for the state and the society, and it is hard to approve these as well as accept that those who agree on these principles may be—or indeed should be—indifferent towards the requirements of morality and may not even feel psychological sympathy for the people to whom they give a constitution. Yet these consequences may be vastly compensated for by the advantages of simplification—that is, if it turns out to be the case that the drastic elimination of preferences enables the contractarian model to carry out its task successfully. For in that case one would have shown not only that, when put in the appropriate circumstances, the contracting parties would agree in the constitutional principles of *liberal* democracies (i.e. that the liberal constraints form part of the democratic order properly understood, rather than limiting democracy from without, as it were). One would have shown, in addition, that approving of liberal democracy does not depend on any of the different stances one may take in moral debates that tend to divide people. If this kind of contractarian justification for liberal democracy does indeed work, then what justifies liberal democracy is not controversial moral principles but the fact that people who are motivated by nothing else than the aim of self-regarding preferences and who do not form moral judgments at all find it favorable to accept it when put in the appropriate circumstances. And the circumstances of the hypothetical contract do indeed satisfy the requirements of morality because the radical filtering of available information creates symmetrical and egalitarian relations between the hypothetical decision makers. No one can make a biased decision while unaware of the distribution of preferences as well as much of his own preferences (such as his other-regarding preferences or the ones based on moral judgments). In this way, no one may be able to tell whether, when privileging one of the alternatives, he is giving advantages to himself, his own group, or to others, as the case may be.

The problem is that preference screening does not lead to the desired outcome. If it does not go far enough, leftover preferences may steer participants away from deciding in favor of the liberal constraints—we have seen that already. If it does go far enough, on the other hand, the absence of the preferences that were eliminated may be an obstacle to approving liberal constraints. This will be seen shortly.[40]

Is it really the case that constitution makers who are indifferent towards other people's interests and towards moral principles would agree that the state might not resort to capital punishment? One obstacle to agreement, the passionate insistence on the death penalty as an appropriate answer to capital crime would indeed be removed in such a hypothetical situation. But the passionate rejection of the death penalty would no less be removed. Neither moral disapproval of the death penalty, nor sympathy for the suffering person subjected to the procedure of execution would be present to motivate a choice of the abolition of death penalty. Nothing would make insistence on abolishing the death penalty reasonable. The passionate opponents of the death penalty are rarely moved by the desire to avoid the death sentence themselves, but rather by moral judgments and human feelings. If there is nothing left beyond self-interest, there is no reason left for insisting on abolition, either. The constitution makers who have undergone the elimination of preferences would most likely agree in leaving the issue of the death penalty for the ordinary legislation so that it may decide on the issue, depending on whatever it may think necessary for deterrence and what the majority of citizens could tolerate.

Yet it may seem that the issue of the death penalty is too extreme; it deeply divides the public and many who do not agree with abolitionism nevertheless approve of retaining more widely accepted liberal rights. I propose, therefore, to take a look at the case of a less-contested liberal right, such as freedom of speech.[41] The citizens of well-established liberal democracies tend to be highly sensitive about the state respecting freedom of speech. Does it mean that (almost) everybody would see it as a grave personal loss if the opportunity of speaking in public were restricted? Quite interestingly, this is not at all the case. There are but a few people who hold it personally important that they be not prevented from speaking publicly. The majority attributes much more significance to freedom of speech than to the personal preferences that are protected by it.[42] Freedom of speech is looked upon as a pillar of constitutional democracy and it is seen as a sign of moral decline if that pillar is being threatened. If the majority's moral approval of liberties were eliminated and there were nothing left but their personal interests to make their voice heard publicly without interference, they would not so passionately insist on freedom of speech. We have no reason to assume, therefore, that the right to public speech would be ranked among the fundamental rights by the hypothetical constitution makers. But if not even this, then what?

These are ad hoc illustrations, to be sure. Not all liberal constraints are treated so badly by the contractarian model. It may be easily seen that people maximizing their own personal utility, unless they are extremely irrational, would all attribute privileged importance to the protection of life and limb. They would presumably agree on the constitutional protection of property as well. The rights to *life, limb and property* would surely be approved by the hypothetical constitution makers. Even some of the more modern rights could be approved consensually, such as the protection of personal data. Or even, as we will see shortly, the hotly contested right of abortion.

Nevertheless, the lesson of the above examples may be easily generalized.

10. Moral discussion
before the contract

Let us assume that in ordinary life people are divided by enduring disagreements in questions of a moral nature, such as the right of religious people to be protected against public speech that hurts their sensibility or the right of pregnant women to have an abortion on demand. Contractarianism proposes to the disagreeing parties to settle their controversies by examining whether—among idealized conditions, and considering nothing but their own long-term utility—they would favor granting such rights or not. Suppose the hypothetical constitution makers would unanimously approve of the right to be protected against statements that hurt religious sensibilities or the right to an abortion, then it is reasonable to endorse them in ordinary life as well. I claim that this justificatory procedure is deficient. The contractarian reasoning will not compel Voltaire (in the first case) or Wojtyła (in the second case) to yield to the rivaling view. Nor would it compel their opponents.

Suppose our hypothetical constitution makers are about to reach an agreement concerning the limits of freedom of speech. They are aware of the fact that their society comprises faithful Muslims who would be deeply shocked by works mocking their religion. Yet they do not know whether they will be among the potentially hurt or not. They are ignorant about their convictions concerning religion; they do not attach emotions either to religion or to statements that are critical *vis-à-vis* religion. How would they cast their votes? Voltaire would suggest them to examine their preferences. Is there any one among these that would make criticism unbearable? No. Then he would urge them to concede that all preferences may be subjected to consideration, and it is reasonable to retain only those preferences that have passed the test of careful consideration. Those who want to suppress criticism are the fanatics. Should it be the case, then, that they would turn out to be fanatics in real life, it is still reasonable for them to be exposed to such statements that would hurt their feelings. They must concede that fanaticism is wrong, and their only chance of not falling prey to it is their being exposed to the freedom of criticism.

By contrast, Wojtyła would reply as follows. Mr. Voltaire's claim might appear urgent only because everything that people may hold to be sacred is purged from the perspective of the constitution makers. Thus they may easily concede that religious faith may be subjected to criticism as well as anything else. Yet this is exactly what is excluded by the nature of the sacred. Thus, purging preferences regarding the sacred is unfair with respect to believers. Purging the information available to the constitution makers does not result in a fair bargaining situation unless the convictions and emotions regarding questions of religion survive the screening process.

Voltaire, on the other hand, would respond that this is precisely what would not be fair. For if we allow fanatics to participate in the hypothetical constitution making, it is certain that the agreement reached would take their all-exclusive sensibilities into account. This, however, is unreasonable, because fanaticism does not justify any legitimate interest. The true interest of fanatics consists precisely in living in a world that gives them a chance to get rid of their fanaticism.

I believe Voltaire to be right; however, this is not a claim that would rescue the contractarian argument. For the controversy is not about which interests are legitimate and which preferences it is reasonable to take into account. Such questions are not answered in the process of making the contract; to the contrary, the hypothetical contract assumes that controversies of such a nature have already been settled antecedently. And now we have seen that they cannot be settled even by purging constitution makers of all preferences that might spoil the agreement. This procedure appeared to be acceptable because we assumed that the constitution makers are in a fair position with regard to one another behind the veil of ignorance, because they are incapable of making biased decisions. Yet later we have found that impartiality due to the veil does not necessarily grant the fairness of decisions. It is not fair to disregard true considerations when deciding which interests should serve as criteria for the possible alternatives. It is not fair to give ground to illegitimate interests and to exclude legitimate interests from the bargaining. Yet the contractarian model is incapable of accommodating this difficulty, for it takes the interests of the participants as given.

The abortion controversy yields the same insights. Hypothetical constitution makers who are deprived of all religious or metaphysical commitments as well as of other-regarding preferences and moral principles and thus have no views concerning the status of the fetus will have reason to have no difficulties endorsing the right to early abortion. Yet if someone opposes abortion because he is convinced that the moral status of the fetus in regard of *life, limb and property* is the same as that of the already born, then he will not have reason to accept such a decision as right. So he will reply to his partner that the contractarian test leads to false results because it is ill-conceived. The hypothetical constitution makers are already born women and men who do not entertain either moral convictions or sympathies and antipathies in relation to other people. It is only natural that some of them will strongly desire to have the last word about their own pregnancy. Since the rest will be indifferent in this issue, there will be some who strongly favor abortion rights while there will be none to oppose it. Yet the decision will be unjust because the interests of those hurt, i.e. of the fetuses, will not be represented by any of the parties. Just decisions should be constructed in such a manner, the pro-lifer would claim, that the as yet unborn be somehow represented among the hypothetical constitution makers. But then his opponent would promptly reply that providing a place for the as yet unborn among the hypothetical constitution makers is to already decide that the status of the fetus is the same as that of a human being after birth, and this is unacceptable.

This controversy shows once again that there are certain questions that must be settled antecedently for the contractarian model to be applicable. It is not sufficient that due to their partial ignorance the hypothetical constitution makers are incapable of making biased decisions *with respect to each other*. Before the hypothetical constitution makers are allowed to make their choice, it must first be decided *with respect to whom* they must be unbiased, and who has a legitimate claim to impartial decisions. Put it otherwise, who has the moral status that entitles him to have his interests considered in the course of the constitution making? The question concerning the moral status of the fetus may not be answered by the hypothetical contract, because the contract assumes that it has already been settled.[43]

In a word, the contractarian model may be applied only if the question of the legitimate participants of the contract and that of their legitimate interests has already been answered. But this must be done in substantive moral debate; the confrontation of the different positions may not be avoided by excluding all contested beliefs, feelings and desires from the range of information available for the hypothetical contracting parties.

Section 5 has shown that equality of votes does not necessarily coincide with equality of voters. The claims made there might be now reformulated in a wider context. There are collective decisions that concern merely the issue of whose preferences are to be realized. In other collective decisions the question is whose standpoint is to become the collective standpoint. Equality of votes does not coincide with equality of voters even in such cases that demand nothing but the aggregation of preferences. In such cases the voting system treats the participants as equals only if it gives an equal prior chance to all that collective decisions will coincide with their own choice, and if it gives an equal—and strong—guarantee to all that collective decisions will not violate their specifically important interests. This typically requires abandoning the requirements of anonymity and/or neutrality.

By contrast, when the controversy is not about the distribution of goods but about whose view is to become the collective view, the conditions of equality will be different. The principle of "one person one vote" must not be abandoned even in such cases. Yet it is no longer important that each person have such a chance for winning that is proportionate with the subjective importance she attaches to the issue that is voted on. Views are right or wrong regardless of what each voter may think or prefer. Suppose that the controversy is about whether the state should extend the institution of marriage to gay couples. The case is either that equal treatment requires such an extension, or that it does not. Let X think exclusion to be discriminatory and let Y hold that it is not. Suppose, furthermore, that the community decides in favor of extension, in the following procedure. The constitution makers state that exclusion is discriminatory, making gay marriage part of the constitutional status quo. Then, the opponents of gay marriage make a motion for amending the constitution. Even though they receive a simple majority of the votes, they do not command the two-thirds majority that is necessary for changing the constitutional status quo. Is Y justified in claiming that the voting system did not treat him equally because, even though the issue of gay marriage is no less important for him than it is for X, his view had smaller chances to prevail? I do not believe he is. We expect collective decisions to approximate that which is the right solution rather than that which we *believe* to be the right solution. Should the decision be right, the party that lost has no such interest as to give a more nearly proportionate expression of that which it *holds* to be right. Should the decision be wrong, the party that lost may object to it not because of its putative interest in having its belief weighed properly, but because of its interest in the community's approving that rule which it is right for it to approve. By the same token, it does not matter how intensely Y desires his view to prevail. Disappointment in his desire does not constitute such a psychological interest that should be taken into account. Y may not claim that even though he may be wrong, the voting system should consider that he is a fanatical opponent of gay marriage.

Put it briefly, whenever the community has to choose between views rather than between preferences, all decision making procedures that satisfy the minimal criterion of "one person one vote" satisfy the requirement of equality of voters as well. What matters beyond this is only that the procedure in force be at least as likely to yield right answers as any of its rivals.

Let us assume that liberal constraints increase the likelihood that the political community will reach the right answers with respect to the problem of treating its members as equal and autonomous persons. I need not discuss here what supports this assumption.[44] What is important for our present concern is that, provided that they do indeed promote our approximating the equality of citizens properly understood, introducing liberal constraints does not violate the requirements of equal treatment. The requirements of anonymity and neutrality of voting systems might be overruled in the interest of equal treatment.

Now one may proceed to discuss the second pillar of the compromise thesis.

11. The mandate of the guardians of the constitution

The fact that the only acceptable answer is the right answer does not imply either that the right answer coincides with one of the positions actually represented during the debate, nor that the available evidence would necessarily settle the question concerning the right answer compellingly. The thesis that questions concerning the liberal constraints require pursuing the right answer is compatible with the claim that at a given moment none of the participants are aware of the right answer or that none of them possess conclusive arguments that would make adopting their position compelling for others. Thus, even though it may be rightly claimed about liberal constraints that they have one and only one correct interpretation, the content of that correct interpretation may nevertheless be contested.

This is what gives the problem of constitutional review its urgency. The problem concerns the extent to which the guardians of the constitution may go in the course of interpreting a constitutional provision, given that the question of which interpretation among the ones compatible with the text is the right one is itself often being contested.[45] According to the "originalist thesis", they may go no further than reconstructing the original intention of the framers, because only the framers possessed the authority to make into a constitutional provision that (and just that) which they wanted to make into a constitutional provision. The intention of the guardians of the constitution does not possess legislative authority, because they are not elected by the citizens. Thus goes the originalist thesis.

But the originalist thesis is incompatible with the claim that liberal constraints articulate moral principles that may be interpreted correctly or falsely.

Suppose there is controversy on whether or not the prohibition of such statements that may hurt the feelings of religious people satisfies the requirements expressed by the principle of freedom of speech. Suppose, furthermore, that the available sources do not provide us with a sufficient clue to establish the original intention of the framers with respect to this question. It is conceivable that they had no opinion whatever about it because this question had not yet surfaced at the time. Or each of them might have had his personal view on this, yet their views did not coincide and it is impossible to establish which view to attribute to the body as a whole. In such cases there is simply no original intention with respect to the question. According to the originalists, in cases like that the judges must refrain from giving an interpretation to the principle of freedom of speech with respect to the contested question. Yet does this conclusion really follow from the originalist thesis? Does it really follow from it that future judges must refrain from pursuing the right answer just because the framers did not address the problem or because their individual answers do not unequivocally yield a collective answer?

In liberal democracies the guardians of the constitution derive their mandate from an authorization originating with the constitution makers. Their mandate is to examine the constitutionality of contested legislations and to annul all such provisions that they find unconstitutional. Yet what is the scope of this derivative mandate? Is it really the case that the mandate given by the constitution makers to the guardians of the constitution is restricted to enforcing their antecedently articulated intention in such cases that were foreseen by them? Or is it rather the case that the mandate extends to enforcing constitutional provisions that require interpretation with regard to unforeseen cases as well? Does the original intention of introducing the institution of constitutional review involve that the guardians of the constitution, when they are in the business of settling contested issues, must apply that specific interpretation of the moral principles incorporated into the constitution that they accept as correct in the light of all the arguments available for them? Or rather they must come to a halt where the foresight of the framers reached its limits?

These question may be understood in two different ways. In the first reading, the question is an empirical one concerning what the framers *thought* about the mandate of the future guardians. In the second reading, it is an analytical question of what the framers *should have thought* given the correct interpretation of their act of authorizing the guardians. The empirical reading allows that the authority of the guardians of the constitution may be different from country to country, depending on the whims of the intention of the framers. In that reading, it is possible that the order of one of the constitutional democracies demands strict self-restraint on the part of the guardians, while that of another gives them ample ground for active judicial practice. The normative reading goes against such variation. All depends on which reading is the correct one.

In my view the empirical reading is untenable. The demand that the guardians should come to a stop where the foresight of the framers had come to its limits is irreconcilable with the assumption that the framers were aware of what they were doing when they were incorporating the principle of freedom of speech—or any other principle of the same status—into the constitution.

Such provisions as "No one may be deprived of freedom of speech in the Republic" are not conventional rules (such as another constitutional provision stipulating that "Regular legislative elections must be held on the first Sunday in March of every fourth year") but moral principles. Moral principles have correct and false readings. What makes a principle itself true is not that the legislators made it part of the constitution; its incorporation into the constitution only makes it possible for it to function as a legal provision (as well). Thus, it is not the case either that the legitimate range of its application (or its correct interpretation in any given case) depends upon the choice of the framers. In other words, the moral principles incorporated in the constitution are consequential not only for the cases that were foreseen at the time when the framers approved them but for any number of future cases as well. From the point of view of interpretation, the status of cases that have occurred only after adopting the constitution does not differ from that of such cases that had already been known at the time of its adoption. Interpretations applied to new cases may be correct or mistaken no less than the interpretations formulated in connection with old cases.

Thus, the "meta-intention" of the constitution makers could not have possibly been to restrict the application of such principles to treating such cases that had already been known to them. It could only have been to extend the range of application to all cases to which its scope of validity does in fact extend. If it can be shown that the framers understood the competence of the guardians in the former rather than in the latter way, all it means is that one of the intentions of the framers (regarding the competence of the guardians) contradicts another of their intentions (regarding the point of the guardianship). One of the two must be altered for the sake of consistency. The intention regarding the point of the guardianship is more fundamental and in this way it is up to it to delimit the range of considerations regarding competence, rather than the other way around. Therefore, the intentions regarding competence must be altered rather than the definition of the point of the institution. On the other hand, the same conclusion is reached in a shorter way if it is not the case that the framers demanded self-restraint from the guardians; the mandate given by the constitution makers to future judges may not be restricted to the application of moral principles incorporated into the constitution, in the reading the framers themselves thought to be the correct one, to cases that were already seen by the framers themselves.

Let us now assume that an unequivocal intention may be attributed to the framers with regard to a contested issue. Suppose that it can be established beyond doubt that the constitution making body shared Wojtyła's view, that is, its members unmistakably held that incorporation of the principle of freedom of speech into the constitution does not prohibit future legislators from banning from the public sphere, on pain of punishment, such statements that hurt religious feelings. Thus, such limitations on of freedom of speech are not unconstitutional according to the original intention. Now assume that a hundred years later the guardians of the constitution find that, carefully considering all the arguments that in the meantime have become available, Voltaire was after all right. In other words, they contest the framers' interpretation of freedom of speech, and the available evidence shows that their position is correct while the framers were wrong. What makes it reasonable to claim that they should disregard the correct reading and adjust their decision to the clearly wrong interpretation?

The question may be answered by resorting to a strategy not unlike the one deployed above. One must start from the fact that it is the constitutive assembly that authorizes future guardians, and then one may proceed to examine what such an authorization involves. Put it differently, the question is, whether the nature of liberal constraints allows attributing an intention to the framers to the effect that future judges apply the reading originally believed to be the correct one—even though later it proved to be false. Such a "meta-intention" is no less incoherent than the "meta-intention" just examined above that excluded from the range of application of the correct reading of constitutional provisions cases that had not been foreseen by the framers.

Of course the constitution makers believe their own reading to be the correct one. By implication, they expect future judges to apply that very reading, being the correct one, to contested constitutional issues. Yet they may not preclude the possibility that new evidence will be discovered that was not available to them (or it was available yet they failed to take it into account) and which may alter the way the issue should be judged. They may not preclude that the reading they believed to be correct later proves to be false. If they are aware that they incorporate a moral principle into the constitution, then they cannot but demand, on pain of inconsistency, that the correct reading should be applied, whether it coincides with their own reading or not. In other words, they must demand of future guardians of the constitution to apply the original reading only up to the point it proves right and not any longer.

To sum up, the correct interpretation of the original "meta-intention" may be expressed through the following alternatives; if the original reading of a constitutional principle may be reconstructed and there is no urgent reason to abandon it, the court must enforce the original reading. On the other hand, if there is no way to reconstruct the original reading or there are pressing reasons to revise it, then the intention of the framers must be only that the court should apply its own reading if it proved to be more nearly right than the original one.

This implies, however, that there is no conflict between the principle of popular sovereignty and active constitutional review. The second pillar of the compromise thesis is shown to be wrong.

12. Summary and restrictions

.

In the introduction I have written that the refutation of the compromise thesis is interesting not in its own right but in what it shows us about liberal democracy. In the conclusion I would like to sum up this lesson.

First of all, we have gained criteria for the proper understanding of democratic equality. Democracy is usually described as a decision making procedure, where the outcome is legitimated by the procedure within the rules of which it was produced. Therefore, it comes naturally to think that the standards for selecting the appropriate procedure from the many available alternatives are such that set requirements for the different features of the appropriate procedure itself. One might call such standards, following Rawls, *pure procedural criteria*.[46] The anonymity and neutrality of decision making rules, as the two concepts were introduced by Kenneth O. May, are such pure procedural criteria.

There are in fact such institutions for which it is reasonable to apply only purely procedural criteria for their evaluation. Thus, the outcome of competitive games is fair (no matter what it may be), provided that the rules of the game satisfy the requirements of fair procedure. We tend to think that the same holds for democratic decisions as well; no matter what the content of the decision may be, it is fair if and only if the decision making procedure itself was fair. But this is wrong. Democracy is not such an institution whose operation could be judged to be fair merely in virtue of the fact that its procedures satisfy the requirements of the pure procedural criteria of fairness. First, we have found that retaining anonymity does not serve equality if the electorate is divided into a permanent majority and minority. In this case, the correctly selected procedural criteria are *input dependent*. Furthermore, we have seen that there are certain questions such that the decision is fair only if its outcome is fair, too. In such cases the fairness of the procedure has such criteria that are independent from the formal characteristics of the procedure itself; the procedure is fair only if it provides good chances for its outcome to satisfy the independent criteria of a fair resolution. This is the subclass of *output-dependent procedural criteria*. In such cases where it is reasonable to apply output-dependent procedural criteria, democratic equality will inevitably diverge from what democracy understood as a set of pure procedural criteria would require. Finally, we have found that even when it is reasonable to insist on the pure procedural criteria of democratic equality, it is not obvious that they coincide with what neutrality demands of the rules of decision making.

From all of the above it follows that it is only under special circumstances that the ideal of democracy coincides with majority rule. The rule of democratic decision making is identical with the majoritarian rule in those and only those cases where criteria of fair procedure are indeed merely pure procedural criteria and at the same time coincide with the requirements of anonymity and neutrality. By contrast, when these conditions are not met, the political morality of democracy does not privilege majority rule.

Second, our investigations put the institutional entrenchment of liberal constraints in a somewhat unusual light. Those critics of judicial review who appeal to the absence of democratic mandate when claiming that independent judicial interpretation of constitutional provisions is inadmissible usually draw the line between admissible and inadmissible interpretation with reference to the original intention of the framers. They claim that admissible interpretations may supplement the strict reading of the text of the constitution with no more than such information that refers to the original intention of the framers; inadmissible interpretations, by contrast, appeal (among other things) to the judges' own convictions. We have found, on the other hand, that the notion of original intention is more complex than it is usually thought to be. Intentions that are attributable to the constitution makers do not involve merely the reading in which particular constitutional provisions should be applied. Beyond these, one may attribute such second-order intentions to the framers that circumscribe the way future guardians of the constitution should proceed when confronted with cases in which there is either no discernible original intention if there is one, or it later proves to be grounded in a false interpretation. We have found that it amounts to attributing inconsistent intentions to the framers to claim that, on the one hand, they meant to incorporate moral principles into the constitution and, on the other hand, they demanded of the future guardians that they should not rely on the correct interpretation of these principles if it was not part of the original intention, or if it contradicts the latter.[47]

However, this claim is in need of being restricted; finally, I would like to add two restrictions. If it is the case that constitutions include moral principles, as much as conventional rules, then the reverse is also true; in other words, constitutions involve conventional rules no less than moral principles. And what is true of the latter does not necessarily hold for the former. There is no reason to attribute such a general intention to the framers that future judges should apply the "correct" reading of merely conventional rules of the constitution, regardless of whether there is an original intention in the contested issue and whether it coincides with the "correct" reading. In the case of merely conventional rules, it is not possible to make a distinction between "correct" and "false" readings. There is no room left for judicial activism in this domain.

The second and more important reservation is the following. When critics of judicial activism object that activist judges make law in the absence of democratic authorization, it is not only the absence of authority that they criticize. They usually add that since judges are not elected officials, they are not responsible to the voters; in other words, the community of citizens cannot hold them responsible for their decisions (in a way that representatives are held responsible for their deeds and failures at the time of elections). In the course of our investigations we have found that this is not necessarily a shortcoming. The reasons behind removing constitutional review from elected representatives and trusting it to such bodies that are insulated from partisan politics is exactly that dependence on electoral will is not favorable for the unbiased enforcement of constitutional principles. On the other hand, it must be admitted that the insulation of the judges goes at a price. It creates the possibility of what was described by László Csontos as the running amok of constitutional courts.[48]

Therefore, unless judicial practice is subjected to proper restraints and controls, the difficulties the constitutional courts were meant to remedy may be reproduced within the practice of judicial review itself. Yet this is a prudential remark rather than an objection based on principle. It does not express a belief that constitutional review is irreconcilable with the principles of democracy but that without proper checks and balances the advantages of judicial activism come at an all too high price. Put this way, the objection urges us to seek such procedures that retain the freedom of constitutional courts to actively interpret the constitution but at the same time considerably diminish the dangers of their running amok.

I would like to add that it is extremely unlikely that this pursuit would lead to the introduction of simple rules. What is needed is rather such prudential guidelines that may be adjusted to the various and varying nature of these dangers. This is, however, beyond the scope of the present study; my goal here was to consider such arguments against constitutionalism that are based on principle—such objections that are based on the principle of democratic equality and the principle of democratic self-government or popular sovereignty.

NOTES

1 On the compromise thesis, see the influential works of R. A. Dahl. *A Preface to Democratic Theory* (Chicago: The University of Chicago Press, 1956), pp. 14–33; *Democracy and Its Critics* (New Haven: Yale University Press, 1989), pp. 135–152. One of the earliest formulations of the thesis is to be found, as pointed out by Dahl himself, in James Madison. Yet it owes its notoriety to Alexis de Tocqueville and John Stuart Mill. Its most important modern proponent is perhaps Isaiah Berlin. See his *Two Concepts of Liberty;* an inaugural lecture delivered before the University of Oxford on 31 October 1958 (Oxford: Clarendon Press, 1958).

2 A further complication is presented by the fact that derivative values may be valuable in themselves or as means of realizing some of the more fundamental values (the former are called inherent values, the latter instrumental ones). However, we need not address this distinction here.

3 For more details on the principle of popular sovereignty, see Sections 2 and 3 of the study "Judical Review" in this volume.

4 In the strong interpretation, self-government or popular sovereignty means direct democracy, as articulated by Rousseau. See Rousseau, "On Social Contract", in Rousseau, *Political Writings* (New York: Norton, 1988). However, we have no reasons for accepting the strong interpretation. Be that as it may, liberal democracies are never direct, so it is convenient to rely on the weaker interpretation when discussing the compromise thesis.

5 Ferenc Huoranszki seems to argue against the compromise thesis along the same lines. See Ferenc Huoranszki, "Liberális demokrácia", in *Filozófia és utópia* (Budapest: Osiris, 1999).

6 On the distinction between philosophical principles and rules of political procedure see J. Waldron, "Rights and Majorities: Rousseau Revisited", in J. W. Chapman and A. Wertheimer (eds.), *Majorities and Minorities* (New York–London: The University Press, 1990), p. 44.

7 The distinction is from H. L. A. Hart's seminal work. See Hart, *The Concept of Law* (Oxford: Clarendon Press, 1961).

8 Moreover, the majority may even make such decisions that are contrary to the principles of democracy itself. It may suspend its own rule and authorize a dictator with the right to make decisions. This well-known paradox is of a piece with the one discussed here, but I need not address it in this study.

9 The private is the political—or so claims one of the fundamental tenets of feminist theory, rejecting the liberal distinction between the private and the public altogether. G. A. Cohen endorses the feminist thesis. See his "Where the Action Is: On the Site of Distributive Justice", in *Philosophy and Public Affairs* 26 (1997), pp. 3–30. On the

difficulties in drawing the line see Claus Offe "Legitimation durch Mehrheitsent-scheidung", in Guggenberger–Offe (eds.), *An den Grenzen der Mehrheitsdemok-ratie*. 2nd Ed. (Opladen: Westdeutscher Verlag, 1984).

10 This is the case where the fundamental rights and the principle of equal treatment are included in the constitution, and the amendment of the constitution requires a two-thirds (or even larger) majority.

11 Constitutional regimes contain constraints of other nature as well, such as the fundamental rules of government. But I need not address these problems here.

12 It is common to deploy further guarantees when appointing constitutional judges. The members of the United States Supreme Court, for instance, are appointed by the president, but the Senate may veto their appointments. Members of the Hungarian Constitutional Court are elected by the Parliament by a two-thirds majority, following the consensually made nominations of a parliamentary committee.

13 John Locke, *Second Treatise of Government* (Oxford: Basil Blackwell, 1966), pp. 49–50.

14 J.-J. Rousseau, *op. cit.*, p. 151 (translated by J. C. Bondanella).

15 It is one of the aspects of Rousseau's well-known thesis that in a well-ordered political regime, collective decisions express the general will rather than the sum of individual wills. *See ibid.*, p. 151.

16 This does not imply that there is no difference between individuals who merely take into account other people's intentions when making their decisions, and between individuals who intend to carry out something together with others. In the first case, the subjects of the action are the many individuals separately, while in the latter it is the group of cooperating individuals. Yet the group itself does not possess independent, supraindividual intentions.

17 Moral individualism does not imply the belief that individuals should exclusively attend to their own concerns. To the contrary, it is precisely moral individualism that entails that the interests of other people lay moral claims on us when pursuing our goals. See Nagel, *The View From Nowhere* (New York–Oxford: Oxford University Press, 1986), p. 164. Neither does moral individualism imply that the existence and flourishing of communities is not something valuable; moral individualists may admit that individuals may not have rich and good lives unless as members of communities. See Ch. Taylor, "Atomism", in *Philosophy and the Human Sciences*. 2nd vol. (Cambridge–New York: Cambridge University Press, 1985).

18 D. Rae–E. Schickler, "Majority Rule", in D. C. Mueller (ed.), *Perspectives on Public Choice* (Cambridge–New York: Cambridge University Press, 1997).

19 Since I have earlier written quite a bit about a certain requirement of political morality that is usually referred to as political neutrality, it seems necessary to note that the concept of neutrality used there differs from the concept of neutrality in collective decisions; it concerns acts of a different kind and specifies requirements of a different nature. See my "Az állam semlegessége" ("The Political Neutrality") in *Az állam semlegessége* (Budapest: Atlantisz, 1997).

20 See Rae–Schickler, *op. cit.*

21 K. O. May, "A Set of Independent, Necessary and Sufficient Conditions for Simple Majority Decisions". In: *Econometrica* 20 (1952), pp. 680–684. By minimal efficiency May means the satisfaction of two requirements—those of decisiveness and posi-

tive vote sensitivity. A voting system is decisive if it can produce an unequivocal decision for any possible distribution of votes. A system is characterized by positive sensitivity in the following case. Assume that every voter has formed his or her voting preference, and one single voter changes her mind. If she were to vote for x, now she is about to vote for y or to abstain. Provided that before her changing her mind x and y had equal votes or y had more than x, the system is positively sensitive if x cannot win the vote after her changing her mind. May's thesis is that in the case of binary votes there is one and only one voting rule—that of majority rule—that satisfies the requirements of decisiveness, positive sensitivity, anonymity and neutrality. As I referred to it earlier, the May thesis holds for such cases when there are only two alternatives. Three or more alternatives may produce complications even for majority rule, but we need not address this difficulty, because in what follows I will argue that democratic equality does not demand the satisfaction of the requirements of anonymity and neutrality (and thus the equality of votes) even for all cases of binary decisions. Therefore, it does not demand the rule of the majority for all cases, either. For a different establishment of the May thesis, see D. C. Mueller, *Public Choice II* (Cambridge–New York: Cambridge University Press, 1989).

22 It will be the case, that is, provided that consecutive decisions are of approximately equal weight. I will address this problem in the next step.

23 See C. Beitz, *Political Equality* (Princeton: Princeton University Press, 1989).

24 See J. Buchanan–G. Tullock, *The Calculus of Consent* (Ann Arbor: The University of Michigan Press, 1962).

25 Buchanan–Tullock, *op. cit.*, p. 96.

26 For Buchanan and Tullock, this feature of the hypothetical constitutional contract is not specifically important. What they want to show is that insisting on the rule of simple majority is reasonable only under special circumstances—in the sense of economic rationality. All the other modern representatives of contractualism, on the other hand, emphasize the fact that the "veil of ignorance" leads to impartial decisions. See for instance J. Harsanyi, "Morality and the Theory of Rational Behavior", in A. Sen–B. Williams (eds.), *Utilitarianism and Beyond* (Cambridge–New York: Cambridge University Press, 1982); and J. Rawls, *A Theory of Justice* (Cambridge, Mass.: Belknap Press of Harvard University Press, 1971).

27 Buchanan–Tullock, *op. cit.*, p. 96.

28 And the requirements of minimal efficiency: decisiveness and positive vote sensitivity.

29 According to Buchanan and Tullock, if the inhabitants of a country are divided to permanent majorities and minorities, they are unable to give a constitution to themselves; they may not constitute a political community. See Buchanan–Tullock, *op. cit.* p. 80. This is, however, not necessarily the case. Agreement is possible if the majority cannot exclude the minority from the cooperation or unilaterally subject it to itself, and if there is no intensive hatred between the two groups. The latter condition is mentioned by Buchanan and Tullock as well.

30 One may distinguish, prior to this, between personal and impersonal preferences. Personal preferences are the ones whose addressee itself is capable of forming preferences, and which rank possible states of the world from the point of view of such addressees. The addressees of impersonal preferences are not necessarily beings who

are themselves capable of forming preferences, and the possible states of the world are not set up from their points of view. See D. Parfit, *Reasons and Persons* (Oxford: Clarendon Press, 1984). Yet we need not consider this distinction here, and in what follows I will proceed as though all preferences were personal.

31 There may be preferences that are grounded on indifference towards the addressee, yet these must themselves consist in indifference relations. That *A* is indifferent towards *B* entails that it does not make a difference for him whether *B* is dead or alive. Conversely, if there is at least one such preference ordering that stipulates a preference relation other than indifference with respect to *B*'s possible states of affairs, then *A* cannot be indifferent to *B*.

32 The terminological distinction originates with D. Gauthier, *Morals by Agreement* (Oxford: Clarendon Press, 1986).

33 There may be such (third-order) preferences that are directed at secondary preferences, and so forth; yet we need not go into that difficulty here. Below I will call secondary preferences all preferences other than the primary ones.

34 See M. Bratman, "Planning and Temptation", in Bratman, *Faces of Intention*. (Cambridge: Cambridge University Press, 1999) p. 37.

35 See H. Frankfurt, "Freedom of the Will and Concept of a Person", in Frankfurt, *The Importance of What We Care About*. (Cambridge: Cambridge University Press, 1988).

36 For instance, it is but cursorily mentioned that preferences may be elusive or enduring, that there are prima facie preferences and concrete, all-things-considered determinate preferences.

37 See G. W. Hegel, *The Philosophy of Right*, §100.

38 Harsanyi calls them antisocial preferences. See Harsanyi, *op. cit.*, p. 56. It must be noted that antisocial preferences would prevent the incorporation into the constitution of not only such highly contested principles as this one. They would hinder the introduction of much more widely accepted rights as well, such as the right to property, for instance. If some of the constitution makers are motivated by a strong sense of envy, they may find it more important that their rivals not be able to rise above them than that the results of their own efforts have their proper protection.

39 This hypothesis is to be found, in addition to the already cited works of Rawls and Gauthier, in R. Dworkin's "What is Equality?", in *Philosophy and Public Affairs* 10 (1981).

40 In *A Theory of Justice* Rawls even goes radically beyond the moves described here. He proposes that when imagining the original contract one should assume that the parties are ignorant about their self-regarding preferences as well. All they know is that there are certain goods—Rawls calls them primary goods—that may serve whatever goals and are therefore reasonable for everyone to be desired, no matter what the structure of their specific preferences may be. In Rawls' view, fundamental rights and liberty belong to the primary goods. His treatise makes the claim of showing that parties to the original position, who are completely ignorant about their own preferences, would all choose to possess the greatest possible amount of primary goods, and that within the set of primary goods they would always give strict priority to rights and liberty; in other words, they would never sacrifice the latter for any other goods. If this demonstration were to be successful, the claim I made above would be

wrong; then, it would not be the case that after a certain point the elimination of preferences does not bring us closer to liberal rights. I have shown elsewhere that Rawls does not succeed in establishing his thesis. See "Az igazságosság elmélete (John Rawls magyarul)", in *Világosság*, 1998/8–9, p. 45.

41 Controversies about freedom of speech concern rather what the precise limits of freedom of speech should be. Yet there is hardly anyone who would want to draw these limits very narrowly. Everybody tends to agree that political criticism, academic discussion and artistic expression are under the full protection of freedom of speech.

42 One may reply that the majority merely wants to defend its interests in getting acquainted with the greatest possible variety of viewpoints as the receiver of public statements. However, this is not a reasonable assumption. Freedom of speech protects such expressions that do not involve valuable information as well.

43 Thus, the famous claim of the Hungarian Constitutional Court (in 64/1991 of XII.17) that the status of the fetus is a fore-question of any constitutional ruling is correct with respect to hypothetical constitution making. (ABH 1991, pp. 258, 266.) On the other hand, the claim is not tenable with respect to the constitutional interpretation to which the judges related it.

44 Section 3 of the next study will address such a justification in detail.

45 I address this problem in detail in Sections 2 and 3 of the study "Constitutional Review" in the present volume.

46 See Rawls, *op. cit.* p. 114.

47 Jeremy Waldron questions this conclusion. His objection relies on the claim that the decisions of an authorized body— in this case the court—may be regarded as the execution of the will of the authorizer if the authorized body possesses no freedom to consideration. See Waldron, "Precommitment and Disagreement", in Alexander (ed.), *Constitutionalism, Philosophical Foundations* (Cambridge–New York: Cambridge University Press, 1998). This argument is correct as far as first-order preferences are concerned, but it does not affect the above reasoning because it fails to consider the second-order (or meta-) preferences of the constitution makers.

48 The prime subject of Csontos' analysis are the problems issuing from the independence of central banks, yet his article points out that the solution of institutional insulation may give rise to the same sort of problems with respect to constitutional courts as well. See Csontos, "Mire szolgál és mit jelent a jegybank függetlensége?" In *Beszélő*, 5 /1996.

CONSTITUTIONAL REVIEW

1. Introduction

The Hungarian Constitutional Court is the offspring of the 1989 transition. Its creation and the fundamental principles of its operation were agreed upon at the national round table.[1] Its objectives, competences and procedural rules were specified by the constitution amended on October 18, 1989 and by the law on the Constitutional Court adopted on the following day.[2] The first five justices were elected in the course of the following month, while six justices were delegated by the new Parliament in June 1990. The mandate of the first members of the Court expired by the end of November 1998.[3] In June 1999 the other six had also reached the end of their term.[4] An era has come to its conclusion. With it, the time of summary assessment has also arrived.

The political institutions of the republic are familiar to the Hungarian society. The Parliament is a body with great tradition. The idea of a government responsible to the legislature originates with the revolution of 1848. The institution of the presidency as placed outside the executive and having strongly limited powers with respect to the legislature was first established in 1946, as a republican extension of the April laws of 1848 on constitutional monarchy. The autonomy of local governments is an inheritance from time immemorial.

By contrast, constitutional review has no precedents.

Hungary did not have a written constitution prior to 1949 and the institution of constitutional guardianship was unknown to it. The socialist constitution adopted in 1949 was a parody of constitutionalism; it was intended by its framers as an ornament that could be at any time dispensed with rather than as a source of individual rights and obligations for the state.[5] Political agents had to learn after 1989 what it is for them to live in a constitutional democracy, where all public institutions must act within the constraints of the constitution, and where a court oversees their adherence to the constitution.

1.1. TWO CONCEPTIONS

The general public as well as the legal community had, in 1989, such ideas about constitutional review that were for the most part reminiscent of the era that preceded that of constitutional democracies. These ideas were dominated by the traditional notion of *the rule of law* combined with parliamentary omnipotence.

Parliamentary omnipotence. This means that popular representatives are authorized to make laws to bind the state and its citizens, and all other government agencies must act within the constraints of the rules made by the Parliament. The Parliament, on the other hand, is bound by nothing else but the rules that were made for itself by itself and which it may amend at any time by the required majority, at its own will.

But the traditional conception combined the idea of parliamentary omnipotence with that of the rule of law, understood as the formal requirements comprised by the notion of *Rechtstaat,* which had been crystallized by the end of the nineteenth century. On the one hand, a *Rechtstaat* is a state whose authorities may not act against its citizens or against each other at their arbitrary will. They can enforce only such obligations against private persons that are specified by legal provisions and only if the addressees of such provisions had the chance to learn about these rules. And they may exercise only such powers that were granted to them by universally known provisions of law. On the other hand, the constraints of a *Rechtstaat* specify only formal procedural requirements; they are silent about the content of rules made and enforced. Any law enacted by the Parliament may be a valid rule if made in conformity to the legislative procedures. A state may oblige its citizens to follow some established religion and still be a *Rechtstaat.* Should there be no such rule that prohibits this, we may disapprove of the absence of the freedom of religion and of conscience, but our disapproval will be of a purely *moral* character, and it will not affect our *legal* assessment of the government's religious policy.[6]

Neither the idea of parliamentary omnipotence nor that of a *Rechtstaat* rule out the possibility of constitutional review as a matter of principle. The omnipotent Parliament has also the power to restrain itself by constitutional procedural rules. It has the power to stipulate, for example, that the amendment of constitutional rules requires some special majority. It has the power to declare that whenever there is a conflict between rules made in the ordinary legislative procedure and between constitutional rules, the ordinary rule that is in conflict with the constitution is automatically overruled.

finally, it has the power to bestow the authority of establishing such conflicts and of nullifying unconstitutional laws on a special body acting as the guardian of the constitution. Constitutional provisions may be understood as overriding legal norms within the rule of law.[7]

Yet in this way of thinking the role of constitutional review is reduced to a very narrow terrain. Conflict with the constitution may be established only if a rule in the constitution was violated in the course of lawmaking—either a procedural rule that was disregarded during the legislative process or some particular substantive rule that explicitly prohibits making laws with some specific content. For instance, if the constitution rules that the approval of laws requires the "yes" vote of the simple majority of all representatives present, yet an amendment of the Criminal Code reintroducing the death penalty was approved by a simple majority of the representatives who participated in the vote rather than by the majority of all the representatives present, then the court may establish formal, procedural unconstitutionality. If the contested articles were approved in flawless procedure yet the constitution contains a special provision stating that "the State shall not administer the death penalty", then the court may declare that the Criminal Code must not assign the death penalty to any crime. By contrast, provided that the constitution contains neither such procedural constraints nor such substantive requirements that were violated by the contested law, the conception of parliamentary *Rechtstaat* dooms the court to silence.[8]

The constitution of the third Hungarian republic contains no provision to the effect that "the State shall not administer the death penalty". True, it contains other provisions that might be read to apply to the issue of the death penalty. For instance, it declares that "everyone has a right to life and human dignity", or that "no one should be subjected to cruel, inhuman or humiliating punishment". Yet the conception of parliamentary *Rechtstaat* does not allow the court to establish the unconstitutionality of the death penalty by referring to such provisions. No legal rule could be struck down on the basis of *such* provisions. The statement that "no one should be subjected to cruel, inhuman or humiliating punishment" does not specify what counts as cruel, inhuman or humiliating punishment; therefore, it does not make explicit which forms of punishment are prohibited. At most, it confronts the lawmakers with the task of creating such rules of prohibition, that is, to specify the modes of punishment they judge to be cruel, inhuman or contrary to human dignity.

Thus, the conception of *Rechtstaat* divides constitutional provisions into two groups. On the one hand, there are precise, well-applicable rules; these make up the legitimate arsenal of constitutional review. And there are declarative principles, on the other hand, that at best provide legislators with a legislative agenda—but the court has nothing to do about them. The majority of the legal profession as well as large parts of the general public viewed the institution of the Constitutional Court with such notions in mind.

This was not the case with the Court itself. The first Constitutional Court did not rest content with applying constitutional rules to contested laws. It also vindicated the authority to articulate through interpretation what the abstract principles of the constitution—the fundamental rights, the requirement of equal treatment, as well as the very ideas of parliamentarism, of the rule of law or of popular sovereignty—demand with respect to various controversial issues. It started with great élan to formulate the auxiliary concepts and supplementary theorems that give substance to the loosely articulated principles.

Almost no component of the institutional arrangement of the republic was left unaffected by this activity. The Court had the final decision in conflicts of competence between the head of state and the prime minister on more than one occasion. It told the Parliament which provisions of so-called two-thirds laws must be adopted by qualified majority, and which provisions can pass by simple majority. It blocked referendum initiatives. It restricted the scope of provisions intended to deal with the communist past—such as the laws on restitution, on historical justice, on property and on lustration. It annulled important budgetary decisions. It prohibited the criminal persecution of extremist political speech. It declared the universal use of personal identity numbers unconstitutional and formulated the background conception for the law on the protection of personal data. It made its impact on the relation between the church and state. It abolished the death penalty. It declared that the army must not interfere with the marriages of its members and articulated in general the limits beyond which employers must not make rules of conduct with respect to the private lives of their employees. It stated that the Civil Code must not exclude same sex couples from the benefits of the institution of companionship.

Little wonder that the acts of the first Constitutional Court were accompanied by passionate controversies from the very beginning until its end. It was even proposed during the first legislative cycle that the whole institution should be abolished.[9] Today, no one goes this far, yet apart from the extreme idea of abolition, the whole range of possible questions is still being widely contested. There are controversies concerning the institutional place of constitutional review (whether it should remain an independent branch of power of its own, or rather it should be incorporated into the hierarchy of the ordinary judiciary), concerning its scope (whether the review should directly address legal provisions or be tied to the remedy of specific grievances), and concerning its procedure (whether or not the universal right to motion should be retained and whether or not the order of hearing the motions should be regulated).

The active judicial practice of the Court compelled legal theorists, politicians, public officials as well as ordinary citizens to reflect on the most fundamental theoretical and practical questions raised by the new republic: on that which differentiates the world of modern constitutional democracies from the more traditional world of parliamentary *Rechtstaat*. Only by thinking through this question is it possible to decide whether what the justices did was permissible or not, whether they were right to do something that is disallowed by the idea of *Rechtstaat*—as many of their critics were right to point out emphatically.

The answer depends on what precisely we take the constitution makers to do when they include abstract principles in the constitution. I suggest focusing our attention, for the sake of convenience, on the moral rights incorporated into the constitution. One may take it that the incorporation of such principles declares that the state provides its citizens with certain privileges—privileges that happen to coincide with the principles called moral rights by political philosophers. Or one may take it to declare that the state recognizes and respects the moral rights of individuals. The first suggestion leaves the notion of *Rechtstaat* unaltered. The second, by contrast, makes essential revisions to it. It develops it into a new doctrine of constitutionalism.

What distinguishes constitutionalism from the traditional conception of a parliamentary *Rechtstaat*? And which conception is the correct one? This is the root of the fundamental question with which the judicial practice of the first Constitutional Court confronted the legal profession and the general public.[10]

One should not be misled to believe that this question is of secondary importance for the participants of the debate. True, it is frequently the case that opponents of constitutionalism do not merely understand the procedural principles of democratic politics differently then the proponents of constitutionalism. It often occurs that objections against active constitutional review are motivated, among other things, by substantive considerations. Active review tends to involve a powerful practice of fundamental rights, and its opponents frequently oppose the extension of rights and the constitutional protection of unpopular minorities as well.[11] Yet the opponents of active judicial review may be ardent exponents of human rights who completely agree with the right-expanding rulings of the court in substantive terms.[12] And even opponents of the extension of human rights have independent, serious arguments against active judicial review.

Thus, it is no exaggeration to claim that the first years of the Constitutional Courts brought to light a fundamental question of principle about the order of the democratic republic.

1.2. QUESTIONS OF PRINCIPLE AND QUESTIONS OF REGULATION

The compromise about the Constitutional Court was made at the national round table at the last moment. Initially, the MSZMP was against conferring the power of striking down legislation on the Court[13]; while the opposition was against establishing new governmental institutions of the republic before the first free elections. At the last moment the opposition conceded; it agreed to approving the law on the Constitutional Court and to establishing the Court itself before the legislative elections with only five members. In exchange, the MSZMP also made consessions; step by step, it agreed to give the largest possible powers to the Court to oversee the legislature (power of striking down laws, the right scrutiny prior to, as well as after, the adoption of laws, and even the right of interpreting the constitution independently of any inquiry into the constitutionality of specific laws), and to define the right to motion so as to expand the powers of the Court (citizens having the right to initiate the constitutional review of legal provisions).

While the final agreement was reached on these issues in a fierce struggle, there was no time left for particular details. The hastily made law barely mentions the procedural rules of constitutional review, and it was left to the Court itself to establish its standing orders (with the assumption that the Parliament would make the proposal into law).[14]

Therefore, those who thought the Constitutional Court's powers to be too large could easily conclude that all their worries may be accounted for by the flaws of the political agreement made at the round table. It may have appeared to them that the extensive powers given to the Court reflect the concerns of the 1989 opposition in regard to the transition process rather than the demands of a consolidated democratic republican order. Indeed the opposition insisted on a powerful Constitutional Court as a counterbalance to the legislature because it believed that there was a good chance for the

MSZMP (or its successor) to win the elections and, relying on its parliamentary predominance, entrench its one-party rule within a parliamentary framework. The Court was thought to constitute a balance against such a danger. But, the objectors asked, what need is there for such a counterweight against the multiparty, democratic parliament, the supreme depository of popular representation?

Furthermore, the unsettled issues of procedure and standing order made it possible, or rather inevitable, for the Court to shape its competences by itself. Thus, the charge that it transgressed its legal competence and usurped those of other branches of power was brought against it from the beginning. Objections of this character tended to overshadow the more fundamental questions about the nature of constitutional democracy and constitutional review. I mean such objections that are made under the summary label of "activism".

The expression "judicial activism"—borrowed from American constitutional controversies—refers to a number of well-distinguishable yet related objections.[15] It may help to start by distinguishing between the different ways Hungarian authors use the expression "activism".

There is a point shared by all charges of "activism". Even though the republican constitution does not explicitly mention the separation of the different branches of the government, the reasoning has it, the institutional arrangement articulated in it belongs to the family of political regimes that is characterized by a trend towards the separation of competences and "checks and balances". The Court is one among the branches of the government that mutually restrain each other within the republican regime. Thus, it is a fundamental requirement that it must not exercise powers that belong to other branches.

Now, the expression "activism" in one of its uses implies that the Court, from time to time, transgresses its legal competence and embarks on such procedures or makes such decisions that it is not authorized to do either by the constitution or by the law regulating its own functions. It is frequently charged that the Court performed an *explicit transgression of competence* when it annulled the ruling of an ordinary court in 1991, even though it has no such powers according to common juridical understanding.[16]

However, it is not only through an explicit transgression of its legal jurisdiction that the Court[17] may extend its powers. It would be an explicit transgression of power for the Court to start a procedure ex *officio* where procedure is bound to motion. No such thing was ever done by the justices. On the other hand, it occurred quite frequently that they extended the constitutional review to such legal provisions that were not objected to by the party making the motion. This may be seen as an *implicit extension of powers,* for even though there is a motion, it does not contain some of the issues that served as the basis of the ruling, thus the review of such issues is not based on motions.[18]

Something different is meant by judicial activism when it is claimed that many of the rulings were motivated by *political bias,* by exploiting the uncertainties of procedural rules. To be sure, the suspicion of bias is difficult to establish. The fact that a court ruling is favorable or unfavorable for some one social group—or parliamentary party purporting to represent it—is no proof that the Court was motivated by sympathies or antipathies against that group when choosing that particular ruling from a number of alternatives. All Court rulings are almost always favorable for some and unfavorable for others; the Court cannot make such resolutions that do not have political *consequences* in this sense. Yet that which is to be proved is the involvement of political motives. If one were to infer to the involvement of political motives merely from the fact of political consequences, almost all Court rulings would prove to be biased. The involvement of politically biased *motives* needs further evidence for being established. Thus, the suspicion of bias may be given some reinforcement if, in a particular case, the Court conspicuously disregards important aspects that were taken into consideration by it in similar cases and which would have obviously changed the ruling.[19] Or if, even though the content of the resolution and its reasoning is immaculate, the decision making procedure conspicuously changes; for instance, if there are extraordinary differences in the timing of resolutions about motions of otherwise comparable weight.[20] Anyway, if the distribution of decisions is explained by politically biased motives, then again the Court has exceeded its constitutional powers and made such decisions that only other branches of the government are entitled to do.[21]

It is easy to see that the charge of "activism" raises issues of principle as well. Let us assume that it did in fact occur at a number of times that the Court explicitly transgressed its legal jurisdiction. This is surely inadmissible. But there may be different ways of correcting such an unlawful practice. One may want to restrict the Court within its official competence by making the rules more stringent. Or one may want to extend its official competence to the point where the Court itself has already progressed. Or one may even want to reduce the Court's legal powers to a domain narrower than its present official competence. But prior to selecting the preferred alternative one should clarify which variant is desirable and what sort of powers and room for consideration correspond to a defensible ideal of constitutional review. To do so, one needs a clear conception of the nature of constitutional democracy, of its value, and of the role constitutional review plays among its practices.

The derogatory label "activism" begs the question; it already prejudges that the criticized practice is beyond acceptability. From that point on, attention is focused on the ways one should amend the rules to impose discipline on judicial practice.

There is, however, a further version of the charge of "activism", one that does not—and cannot—lead to regulatory issues but directly raises issues of principle.

1.3. THE MEANS
OF JUDICIAL INTERPRETATION
OF THE CONSTITUTION

This fourth kind of objection, too, implies that the Court exceeds its competence; but the transgression is predicated not on the basis that the justices either explicitly or implicitly violate the provisions of the law, or that their rulings display bad-faith inconsistencies. It claims such a transgression that may be realized even though the law on the Constitutional Court regulates the body's function with all the desirable exactness and the justices confine themselves to the requirements of the law and make alike decisions in alike cases.

The objection again has two different versions. The simpler version may be formulated as follows: the Court's mandate is to *apply* the constitution rather than to *amend* it. Therefore, it must not deviate from the written constitution in the course of its practice. It must not lay down such rules that are not included in the text of the constitution and that may be arrived at only through recourse to extra-textual auxiliary concepts and theorems. The more the reasoning behind a resolution relies on such auxiliary concepts and theorems, the more the Court becomes the *maker* rather than the guardian of the constitution that was approved by the elected representatives of the people.

The second version of the objection may stand even if one finds that active interpretation does not necessarily amend the constitution. This variant focuses on the *grounds* on which the court strikes down a law when it relies on an active interpretation of the constitution. In this view, the Court's mandate includes only to examine the relation between two resolutions made by elected representatives of the people—one higher-order (constitution-making) and one lower-order (lawmaking) resolution. The lower-order resolution is invalidated on account of its being incompatible with the higher-order resolution; the Court's ruling merely establishes the fact of the conflict and declares its practical consequences.

For the lower-order resolution to become invalid, it must be in conflict with the higher-order parliamentary resolution and *only with* that; it is a violation of the principle of popular sovereignty if the higher-order resolution rules out the lower-order one only by being *supplemented with further premises*, that is, together with such premises that the Court itself adds to the resolutions of the people's representatives rather than borrowing them from the latter. And this is exactly what the Court does when it interprets the constitution in an active manner.

Either by amending the constitution or by striking down laws by relying on such theorems and concepts that were not provided by the people's representatives, the Court transgresses its competence when it grounds its rulings on active interpretation. This is the view expressed by the fourth version of the charge of "activism". Let us call it the charge of *interpretive activism*.

The ones who object to the Court's "interpretive activism" do not mean to imply that either the constitution or the law regulating the Court enumerates the interpretive moves the justices are permitted to rely on, and that the contested method is not among the ones enumerated. Neither the constitution nor the law on the Court contains any such enumeration, nor could they contain such a thing. This is an issue of competence in a more indirect and complex sense; the legitimate range of constitutional interpretations to be performed by the justices is determined by the mission of the Court and its role among the other branches of a democratic government. The charge is that "interpretive activism" exceeds the frameworks of constitutional review which might be legitimate within a democratic political regime. The boundaries of legitimate interpretive procedures are not specifiable by rules.

Where the boundary between legitimate and illegitimate interpretive procedures is to be drawn depends on the kind of theoretical assumptions it is reasonable to accept. First of all, one must formulate a defensible conception of constitutional interpretation. This theory, in turn, presupposes a comprehensive theory of constitutional democracy. The interpretation of a philosophical treatise adheres (in part) to different canons than that of a poetic or dramatic work, which again are different from the interpretive canons of a religious text; and all of the above differs from the way a constitutional document is to be interpreted—for the simple reason that these texts are embedded in different social practices, have different designations and institutional contexts.[22] After all, the way the authoritative interpreters of the constitution may proceed is an institutional rather than a hermeneutical question; the answer depends on what constitutional democracies are and why they are desirable, what the role of the written constitution is in a democratic arrangement and what the function of the guardians of the constitution is, and finally why it is reasonable for the latter to be persons insulated from the electoral system rather than elected representatives. Thus, the charge of "interpretive activism" inevitably raises the fundamental questions of principle. It will be seen that these questions are all related to the ultimate problem of how popular sovereignty is to be understood, why it is justifiable to accept its principle, and what kind of requirements this principle establishes with respect to political institutions.

The present study is devoted to this question.

1.4. A BRIEF OVERVIEW OF WHAT FOLLOWS

We have seen that the key to the understanding of the charge of interpretive activism is the thesis that the Court has no competence to amend the constitution or to strike down laws on the basis of active interpretation. In what follows, this thesis will be examined.

First of all we must think about what it is that may make the belief reasonable that in democratic republics the Court should not have such powers. In other words, the theoretical assumptions of parliamentary *Rechtstaat* must be made explicit. We will find that the idea of parliamentary omnipotence is an interpretation of the idea of popular sovereignty; therefore, it will be reasonable for us to start from the idea of popular sovereignty. Next, we will try to conceptualize what the justices are doing when they are, so to speak, caught constitution making.

Quite clearly, they do not add something to the text of the constitution, nor do they remove anything from it. The document called the "Constitution of the Republic of Hungary" is not being reprinted each time following a Court ruling. Therefore, if the justices can be said to be amending the constitution, they must be doing something that is *equivalent* to amending the text by the legislature, even though it is *not* a revision of the text itself. But there are no absolute criteria for what is equivalent to textual amendment approved by the parliament. Two prisms may be of the same height while their area is different, their areas may be the same while their height is different, and it may even be the case that their volume is the same even though they have no two sides of the same length. Or it may be that all of the above properties are different while their color is the same. Whether one judges the two bodies to be equal depends on what is relevant for us; their area, height, volume—or color. The same holds for the relation between constitutional amendment by parliament and constitutional interpretation by the Court. Whether one judges judicial interpretation of the constitution equivalent to constitution making depends on the criteria of comparison.

One may claim that the Court amends the constitution merely by stating such a rule to constitutional rank that is not included in the strict reading of the constitution.

Or one may claim that the Court amends the constitution only if it states such rules that are not included in the strict reading of the constitution and/or if it does so on such grounds that divide the public (that is, if it establishes constitutional rules by relying on the judges, own contested convictions).

Finally, one may claim that the Court amends the constitution if and only if it raises such a rule to the rank of the constitution that is in conflict with the strict reading of the constitutional text in force (in other words, if the constitutional rule established by the judges is tenable only on the condition of reading the constitution as though its text were different from what it actually is).

All three positions are to be discerned in the Hungarian controversies about constitutional review. Chapter 2 of this study will first try to clearly demarcate these positions and then to suggest some criteria for deciding which of the three conceptions of judicial constitution making establishes genuine equivalency between (activist) constitutional interpretation and amendment of the constitution. We will find that that the implicit revision of the text of the constitution is always equivalent to constitution making, and therefore it is to be rejected in all of its variants. The assessment of the two other variants, on the other hand, is a more complex matter.

If the Court indeed transgresses its competence by providing an interpretation that leaves the constitutional text unaltered, then the transgression is based—as it will be seen—on grounds that are different from amending the constitution through interpretation or, more accurately, through a ruling based on such an interpretation. It is at this point that the fourth conception of judicial activism, which holds that the justices usurp the authority of the legislature when they annul laws by relying on such concepts and theorems that they themselves add to the text of the constitution, comes to the fore. The discussion of this view requires that we articulate—and defend against the traditional conception of parliamentary *Rechtstaat*—a theory of constitutional democracy that was referred to here as constitutionalism.[23] This is going to be the subject of Chapter 3.

Our investigations will lead to the conclusion that judicial interpretations that do not amend the text of the constitution even implicitly are permissible, even though it is indispensable for them to state the principles that are only implicit in the constitution. At the same time, it will be argued that there are pressing reasons to proceed with this kind of interpretation with great caution—though these reasons have nothing to do with the charge that creative interpretation transgresses the competence of the Court. This conclusion will already be anticipated by certain sections of Chapter 2 (primarily Sections 2.7 and 2.9).

Chapter 3 will then go on to examine the objection that striking down legislation must not be based on active, substantive interpretations of the constitution even if such an interpretation is not equivalent with constitution making. First I will try to examine what it is that gives this argument its apparent plausibility. In other words, I will discuss the reasons that make it appear as though this argument is closely related to the principle of popular sovereignty. Then I will try to show that popular sovereignty is violated neither by the constitutional self-restraint of the Parliament nor by granting the guardianship over constitutional constraints to a judicial body. Finally, I will try to show that popular sovereignty is not infringed by the fact that politically not accountable judges annul such laws through active, substantive interpretation of the constitution that were made by politically accountable, elected representatives in a flawless legal procedure.

I hope that by the end of Chapter 3 it will be clear what sort of requirements it is justifiable to confront the practice of the Constitutional Court with. Thus, some of the objections occurring in our debates will be found groundless—provided that the theory presented here is tenable. Such objections should be answered not by showing that the Court in fact met the requirements made by the objector but by making it clear that it need not meet them. The actual practice of the Constitutional Court, then, should be subjected to the test of the remaining objections. That is what I attempt to do in the next study in this volume, dedicated to the assessment of the performance of the first Constitutional Court of the Hungarian Republic.

2. Interpreting
the constitution

2.1. POPULAR SOVEREIGNTY

In the introductory chapter I have characterized the ideal of parliamentarism as the thesis that holds that only popular representatives are authorized to make such rules that bind the state and its citizens; all other government agencies must act within the constraints of the laws made by the parliament, and no one might make rules that bind the representatives themselves. This is a very influential thought, because it appears to be the direct heir of one of democracy's basic normative ideas, the principle of *popular sovereignty*. In the next two chapters I try to show that the ideal of parliamentary *Rechtstaat* is not the only possible interpretation of what we understand as popular sovereignty; furthermore, it is not even its best interpretation.

The doctrine of popular sovereignty seeks to answer the question of the ultimate source of political authority within a given territorial state. Consider some government agency, for instance the bureau of river affairs. Suppose there is a controversy as to this bureau's right to issue binding provisions for the participants of river transportation. The controversy is about the authorization on which the bureau acts. Suppose that the parties to the controversy find that the bureau for river affairs was founded by the government and it was given proper competence to issue such provisions. Now one may ask, does the government have a right to establish such a bureau? This question leads to the further problem of who is the source of the government's authority and what is the scope of that authority. Suppose that the source is the Parliament and it includes the power to establish a bureau for river affairs. Then the next question may probe into the source of authority of the Parliament...

Let us say that a government agency's authority is *formally legitimate* if it was given to it in due process by the proper instance. It immediately meets the eye that the search for formal legitimacy leads to an infinite regress; if all authority's legitimacy depends on the existence of a further authority that is the source of the first authority, then one will never arrive at some such authority that does not depend on some yet further authority; therefore, no authority could be formally legitimate. For a state to have formally legitimate authorities, there must be some such ultimate authority whose legitimacy is not of a formal character, that is, which does not originate in some further authority. This ultimate authority is the *sovereign*. The sovereign is an instance of that which gives instructions or rules to others yet does not receive instructions or rules from others; it is that which authorizes others yet whose power does not originate in authorization by others. For the sovereign's authority to be legitimate it must display some such characteristic that may justify why the series of authorizations may come to an end at it. Thus, the sovereign's legitimacy must be *substantive* rather than formal.

Such a substantive feature may consist in a capacity to enforce obedience from everyone within the territory of the state. Sovereignty exists there and only there where everyone obeys the same ultimate authority. In order to find out whose instructions I must follow, I must learn whose instructions are followed by the other people within the territory of this state. The existence of an instance that is obeyed by almost all inhabitants almost all the time is a *necessary* condition of legitimate authority. Yet the capacity to enforce obedience is not a *sufficient* condition. Suppose that a group of organized criminals gain control over a certain territory. They issue rules, they enforce rule-following behavior on the inhabitants and they successfully marginalize all of their rivals. Yet their sovereignty over the territory under their control would still not be legitimate.

States make the claim that they are not merely organized gangs of criminals with extraordinary powers; they exercise legitimate sovereignty. Thus, they must possess some further characteristic that may give grounds for this claim. In pre-modern societies, rulers usually made appeal to descent, personal charisma or divine status. The doctrine of popular sovereignty summarizes and justifies the insight that all such grounds of legitimacy are untenable. The distinctive feature attributable to the ultimate source of political power is not to be sought in some fact that radically distinguishes it from the ordinary subjects; to the contrary, it is to be sought in the fact that it does not differ from them at all. The series of authorizations may legitimately come to an end only if the subject of sovereign power is identical with that over whom the power is exercised—that is, the "people". The source of all state power must be ultimately the "people"; the government is justified in issuing rules and instructions that impose constraints on its subjects only if it can be truly claimed about it that its authorization comes from the subjects themselves, that through it the "people" itself governs itself. But who is designated by the concept of the "people"? And what should we mean by authorization by the people?

It comes naturally to assume that the "people" is identical with the totality of inhabitants in a given country and that the inhabitants give political authority to the persons selected for that purpose through elections. Yet the problem is not that simple.

When one says that the bureau of river affairs is authorized by the government, which in turn is authorized by the Parliament, government and Parliament are thought of as legally defined agencies; their competence as well as who may exercise them and in what procedure are all specified by legal rules. Now, the "people" is either such a legally defined existent or it is not.

Suppose that it is. Say, it is identical with the totality of individuals that have the right to vote. Yet the existence of a "people" in this sense presupposes the existence of a constitution that determines who of all the inhabitants of the country is to have the right to vote and what that right is to include. Should the "people" be the totality of voters, it cannot be the ultimate source of all public power. The same constitution that defines suffrage also provides for the branches of power, their authority and the way they should be filled. But the constitution cannot originate in the "people"—to the contrary, the "people" originate in the constitution.

On the other hand, if the "people" is to be understood as some pre-constitutional entity, then it has no legal reality. Let us now suppose that this is the case. There are no such rules that would determine who the "people" would consist in, or the procedure through which its members authorize government officials. This renders it impossible to determine the occasions when one may rightly claim that the one who spoke was really the "people" or what counts as a declaration of the "people". Or at least this is the case where the revealed preference of the inhabitants of the relevant territory is not unanimous—which, we might assume, is the typical case.

In the first case, the "people" possess the legal definition necessary to perform the acts of authorization, yet it cannot precede that constitutional order that was supposed to originate in it. In the second case the "people" does precede the constitutional order, yet it lacks the legal definition necessary to perform the acts of authorization. It would seem that both interpretations make popular sovereignty unintelligible.

The "people" cannot make a constitution unless it is defined legally, that is, if its constitutive acts are preceded by a prior constitutive act determining the "people", its competences, and the procedures in which these competences may be exercised. Yet the subject of this prior constitutive act must be, due to the demands of popular sovereignty, the "people" itself; therefore, a further constitutive act is needed, and so on *ad infinitum*. The identification of the sovereign "people" with the collective agent of the first legal act leads us back to the very infinite regress the idea of popular sovereignty was supposed to arrest. This is the most serious difficulty with the classical doctrine of popular sovereignty.[24]

If, on the other hand, the "people" as the ultimate source of political authority is to remain without legal definition, the will of the sovereign is rendered indeterminate. First of all, it is impossible to determine the range of individuals whose will is to be taken into account when aggregating "popular will". Second, individual wills may be aggregated in so many different ways (it may be possible to reduce all decisions to binary options, or it may be possible to present three or more options for decision; binary options may be decided by simple majority or by some qualified majority; in case of three or more options, the options may be ranked in pairs or it is possible to attach cardinal numbers to each option and aggregate these numbers etc.), and the collective decision may be different depending on the procedure of aggregation, even though individual choices remain the same. It is impossible to unambiguously determine what the "people" wants (except in the limiting case where everybody chooses the same option).

It is easy to recognize in these two conceptions of the "people" the distinction made by the radicals of the French Revolution between *pouvoir constituant* and *pouvoir constitué*. *Pouvoir constitué* is the legally defined power, the one that originates in the constitution adopted. This power is not only the subject of well-defined competences but is also limited. It may do whatever it is authorized to do by the constitution, and nothing beyond that. Furthermore, it is not the ultimate power, because it cannot constitute itself; there must be a more fundamental power behind it, which creates the constitution and with it all the constituted powers. This more fundamental power is the *pouvoir constituant*. Unlike the *pouvoir constitué*, the *pouvoir constituant* is unlimited and unlimitable. It is for this same reason that it has no legal reality, for there is nothing that could constrain it. Furthermore, it is not something that would run its course and cease to exist after the completion of the first constitution. The *pouvoir constituant* persists as the ultimate source of all powers behind the constitutional order as well. It may abolish all regimes and give itself whatever regime it wishes.[25]

This is a dangerous consequence all by itself. The predicament is made worse by the fact that since the "people" is a totally undefinable reality, totalitarian leaders and organizations may claim themselves, by pointing to the unarticulated mass support that manifests itself on the streets, to be the mouthpiece of "popular will" and thus abolish democratic institutions and the collective decisions regulated by them.[26]

Therefore, liberal democrats often propose in good faith to abandon the doctrine of popular sovereignty altogether. I take this to be an all too hasty conclusion. The question of the ultimate source of state power does not wither away just because the idea of popular sovereignty is given up. Modern, democratic-egalitarian societies can give no satisfactory answer to this question other than suggested by the doctrine of popular sovereignty: the state is legitimate if its ultimate authority originates in those over whom this authority is exercised. The idea of popular sovereignty should be reconceived rather than abandoned. It should be given such an interpretation that, on the one hand, arrests the regress, and on the other, may not be mobilized for the purposes of totalitarian politics.

In order to transcend the dilemma, one must first examine its source. The conception of popular sovereignty claims that the ultimate source of all political authority is the "people"; put it differently, all political authorization comes from the "people". This thesis has led to the question of how the right of the "people" to political authorization should be understood. And it was this question that has produced the dilemma; either there are such rules and procedures that determine the subject of this right and the forms of its exercise, or there are no such rules and procedures. If there are, then the "people" cannot be the ultimate source of all political authority, for these rules and procedures must precede it. But, if there are no such rules and procedures in place then, again, the "people" cannot be the ultimate source of all powers because in the absence of such rules and procedures both the "people" and the will of the "people" are indeterminable.

Let us assume that there are no such rules and procedures. This is a reasonable assumption. After all, the right of the "people" to be the source of all political authorizations does not originate in a further authorization. This is an ultimate moral attribute of the totality of subjects of a state in the same manner as the human rights are the ultimate moral attributes of individuals. Thus, the right of authorization cannot originate in the people being enfranchised by someone—by the constitution makers. Human rights are recognized rather than created by the constitution makers; by the same token, the "people" is not made to be the ultimate source of political authority by the constitution makers but is only recognized by them as such. And here comes the decisive move. Earlier, it was simply taken for granted without further analysis that the legally undefined "people" exercises its sovereign power as though it were legally defined; that is, as though it were the *pouvoir constituant*, the subject that constitutes itself. This was found to be impossible. But this impossibility indicates merely that we were wrong about the nature of the sovereign "people". The "people" cannot be the ultimate legislator, the creator of the constitution. But this is not to say that on that account it cannot be sovereign. The pre-legislated existence of human rights confronts the makers of the constitution, no matter who they might be, with the task of establishing such a regime that respects these rights; by the same token, the pre-legislated popular sovereignty confronts them with the task of establishing such a regime that is consistent with the principle that all power originates in the "people".

According to the doctrine of popular sovereignty, state authorities are legitimate only if they govern in the name of the "people" rather than that of God, some aristocracy that was born to rule, or some other higher authority. The question then is this: On what grounds may someone claim to act in the name of the people?

Even though the grounds for such a claim might be conceptually distinguished from the source of authorization, the two obviously cannot be completely independent from one another. It might not be claimed that the governor delegated from the faraway imperial capital does his business in the name of those governed by him. Therefore, the question concerning the grounds of a claim of acting in the name of the people might be rephrased as follows: What sort of requirements must the actual practice of authorization meet so that the authorized may rightly derive their authority in the "people"? The doctrine of popular sovereignty sums up these requirements. Let us take a brief overview of them.

The first requirement is that the authorization must go from the bottom up, as it were, from the governed themselves; it may not originate in some higher instance over and above them. Those who give binding rules and instructions to the governed must receive their mandate from the governed themselves—either directly or indirectly. They must be elected by the ultimate addressees of the rules and instructions (the "subjects"), or by the officials elected by the latter.

The second requirement is that none of the subjects might be arbitrarily deprived of the right to participate in the act of authorization. There must be specifically strong reasons to justify the exclusion of some group of inhabitants from suffrage. Poverty or lack of education does not constitute such a reason. Neither does family status. It is reasonable to set an age limit, yet it should be specified at the youngest age allowed by the maturation of the capacity to make judgments in political matters. These claims command very wide acceptance in the community of democratic states today. There is no such agreement about giving citizenship within a reasonable period of time to those who permanently live within the territory of a state and are able to communicate with its officials, but the communities based on the ideal of political equality can hardly avoid accommodating this principle in the long run.

A third requirement concerns the way rights related to the act of authorization should be distributed among the subjects. Suppose an electoral system in which decisions are made by simple majority and almost everyone has one vote, except for a small group of individuals (say, people with an exceptionally high education), who have one vote more than everybody else. Even though it may still be true in this case that the totality of voters approximates the totality of inhabitants, and that public officials receive their authorization through elections, it might not be rightly claimed about this regime that political authority originates in the "people". Popular sovereignty demands that every voter without exception possess one and only one vote.[27]

All these requirements apply the fundamental idea of political equality to the problem of public authority; one may justifiably claim to act in the name of the "people" only if those who govern do not stand above the governed (i.e. they are either directly elected by the latter from among their own ranks, or they receive their mandate from officials elected by the governed), if no group of voters stands above the other voters (i.e. everyone has one and only one vote), and if voters do not stand above the rest of inhabitants (i.e. the scope of voters is as close to the scope of all inhabitants as possible).

In other words, the "people" as a subject before legal definition is not a collective agent authorizing to government instances and their incumbents. Rather, the collective agent is the totality of legally defined subjects—citizens and voters. The "people" is a regulative idea, an egalitarian principle that furnishes us with a criterion to judge whether the totality of citizens and voters is a legitimate source of public authority. The more the actual order of authorization of officials in a given state satisfies the requirements of political equality summarized above, the more that state can be said to be based on popular sovereignty.

Sometimes it is claimed that popular sovereignty and democracy are two distinct principles. Popular sovereignty demands that each people should decide for itself the kind of constitutional arrangement it wants to give itself. It does not demand that this arrangement should be democratic. The "people" might as well choose to favor dictatorship. As one of the consequences of the analysis above, this claim is shown to be wrong. Outside political regimes there are no political decision makers either; the "people" is not a source of decisions of public authority prior to the political organization of the state. Popular sovereignty is a *feature* of political regimes rather than something actually exercised *prior* to the establishment of political regimes. The question is not whether it was the people that created the state for itself by some original act but what the practice of authorization is like in the state, once it has been established. Provided that this practice is egalitarian, the regime satisfies the requirements of popular sovereignty. Popular sovereignty is a characteristic of democratic regimes.

If the concept of the "people" and the idea of popular sovereignty are understood this way, the danger of infinite regress is preempted. Furthermore, the fear that this idea may provide conceptual tools for totalitarian ideologies may also be dispelled; our interpretation is not in need of the (untenable) belief that the "people" as a legally undefined subject may make binding collective decisions that could override the decisions produced within the democratic institutions. Binding collective decisions are made only by voters, and the authorizations produced by them meet the demands of popular sovereignty only if the totality of voters is as close to the totality of inhabitants as possible, and if all voters may run for office as well, and if all who may run for office are also voters, and if public officials are either elected directly by the voters or are appointed by elected officials.

At this point, we have arrived to our proper problem. Popular sovereignty implies democracy, and if democracy cannot be direct, then it also implies the principle of parliamentary legislation. Laws might be said to be made in the name of the "people" only if the lawmakers are elected representatives. Yet popular sovereignty does not necessarily imply parliamentary governance; the head of the executive (in this case the chief of state) may be elected directly, and the government may be his or her cabinet, just as innumerable cases in between these two extremes are compatible with the principle of popular sovereignty. It is reconcilable with the demands of popular sovereignty even if the Parliament makes only relatively few, high-rank provisions, while authorizing some of its agents—the government, the ministries and other lower-level administrative authorities—with issuing all the remaining binding rules, provided that they act within the constraints of the laws made by the Parliament.

In parliamentary regimes, the executive itself functions on the basis of an authorization that it receives from the legislature; the prime minister is elected by the Parliament, and the Parliament authorizes the government, and the right of the members of the government to authorize other public officials, too, originates in the Parliament. But even where the head of the executive is elected directly it is still the case that the authorization given by the Parliament does not extend to all cases; it is explicitly forbidden to regulate questions of extraordinary significance by government decrees or administrative instructions (in Hungary, for instance, the exercise of constitutional rights may be regulated only by laws).[28] Furthermore, in case of a conflict between a statute or decree and a law, the conflict may not be resolved through bargaining or compromise; there is a strict hierarchy of legal provisions, and the arrow always points in the same direction. No decree may overrule any law, while laws may overrule all statutes and decrees; in cases of conflict, it is always the latter that are annulled and never the former. Thus, the persons who exercise public authority not as members of the legislature must act within the constraints of the laws made by the elected representatives. These legal constraints are simply external parameters for them; they may not revise or amend them. In complex, populous societies, where governance through elected representatives is as unattainable as the community's direct self-governance, popular sovereignty is preserved by the fact that public power may be exercised only by persons authorized by elected representatives and only within the constraints of the rules made by the latter.

It is this consideration that gives rise to the suspicion that constitutional review, if exercised beyond a very narrow range, gets in conflict with the fundamental principle of popular sovereignty. If the conception of popular sovereignty provided here is tenable, then the text of the constitution can be approved only by the body of representatives (or the totality of citizens) that was authorized to make a constitution. Written constitutions are at the apex of the hierarchy of legal provisions. The ultimate principles and rules articulating who, and in what sort of procedures and within what kind of constraints, may make lower-level provisions, are to be found here.[29] Popular sovereignty is surely violated if the text of the constitution is amended by some such body whose members are not elected representatives.

The justices of the Constitutional Court are not officials elected by the people, they are appointed by elected officials, and it will be seen (Section 3.5) that there are good reasons for this to be so.[30] It may appear, then, that the case is not simply that the existing Hungarian constitution and the law on the Constitutional Court *actually* do not give the Court the power to make a constitution. Rather, the case is that if they were to give the Court this power, this would contradict the principle of popular sovereignty and compromise that which makes democracy politically valuable. In democracies, constitutional courts *should not* have the power to make the constitution.

What is more, the Court's power of striking down legislation is necessarily restricted. The justices may declare some resolution of popular representatives null and void only if that is in conflict with some higher-order resolution of popular representatives. The resolution of popular representatives as lawmakers should be measured against the resolution of popular representatives as constitution makers. Once again, the question is not the powers the republican constitution *actually* gives to the judges. The question is rather this: What sort of powers may it give to the judges without violating the principle of popular sovereignty?

These are the theoretical considerations behind the conception of parliamentary *Rechtstaat*. But is it really the case that only a parliamentary *Rechtstaat* can satisfy the demands of popular sovereignty? Does it really follow from the principle of popular sovereignty that the Court may resort to that and only that constitutional text that it receives from the representatives of the people? Is it clear at all what this thesis really means?

In the present chapter I will examine the meaning of the charge that the Court is caught *constitution making* whenever it interprets the constitution beyond the narrowest confines of the text. The next chapter will address the problem of *striking down legislation*.

2.2. ONLY THAT WHICH IS "IN THE TEXT"

Let us begin with the narrowest conception of identifying constitutional interpretation with constitution making. In this conception, the Court is already amending the constitution merely by elevating such rules to constitutional status that are not included in the strict reading of the Basic Law. This conception surfaces with the greatest clarity in the Hungarian Court's statements about its own interpretive practice; its outlines are to be found both in dissenting opinions and in arguments supporting some of the majority decisions.

For instance, in one of the dissenting opinions against the first resolution on the president's competences one reads the following: "Assuming (but not conceding) that Section (1) of Article 29...is to be understood as a rule that regulates [the president's] authority, it is not only the constraint of authority cited [in the majority decision] that is compatible with it. It stands in the exact same correspondence with Section (1) of Article 29 to say that a rejection of an appointment by the president of the republic is constitutional only if;

- in his best judgment, making the appointment would be inconsistent with the democratic functioning of the state administration, or
- he reaches the conclusion that making the appointment would threaten the democratic functioning of the state administration, or
- he establishes beyond any doubt that making the appointment would block the democratic functioning of the state administration or would incur other such serious breakdowns in it that cannot be otherwise averted.

The cited textual variants stand in the same relation with Section (1) of Article 29 of the constitution. There are political arguments for and against each of them. But it is the task of the Parliament, vested with the right of constitution making, to choose—on the basis of political considerations—among the constitutionally equivalent variants that nevertheless have significantly different consequences for the authority of the president."[31]

In other words, there is a text, Section (1) of Article 29 of the constitution. There are variants of reading that are all equally compatible with the text and none of which is privileged by the text against any of the other variants. The text contains no indication as to which of the variants is to be chosen. As a consequence, the choice is a political act, rather than one of interpreting the constitution. The interpretation of the constitution might identify no more than that which is in the text.

But what does it mean to say that constitutional interpretation may identify only that which is "in the text"? In the strictest sense, this would mean that the judge who proceeds appropriately would do no more than read out the corresponding passages of the constitution on the contested pieces of legislation. This understanding is clearly untenable, yet it may be worthwhile to take a closer look at it.

What is wrong with the thesis that in interpreting the text, judges must not make appeal to anything beyond its content? First of all, this is simply impossible. Without mobilizing extra-textual information, the judges would not be able even to do so much as determine which are the relevant constitutional passages—not to mention deciding what follows from the relevant passages to the contested issue.

Consider the issue of who might be elected to become the president of the Hungarian Republic. It may come naturally to turn to the passage that lays out the requirements of eligibility for the presidency. This is Section (2) of Article 29/A of the constitution, which has it that "Every citizen who has the right to vote and who has reached thirty-five years of age by the date of the election may be elected for president." For the rules of citizenship, it may come naturally to turn to Article 69, and then to Article 70 for the electoral rules. But is it really the text that tells us where to turn? This is how it appears to be—yet this is an illusion.

Imagine a person who has a good command of the Hungarian language yet who is totally ignorant about the existing Hungarian constitution in particular and about modern constitutions in general—he had so far to do only with hereditary monarchies. He does not know the concept of the president of the republic; he has no idea that this office is filled through elections, furthermore, he does not know what an election is, or what it means for someone to be elected to an office. Our man may want to ask: Which office corresponds to the designation "king", and how is this office filled? Assume that the one who is being asked, instead of an explanation simply puts the text of the constitution before this man for him to browse it and search for the answer. Will he spot Section (2) of Article 29/A? Only in the case that he has at least so much general information about different political regimes as to realize that his initial question was wrong: the head of state of the Republic of Hungary is not a king. Furthermore, he will have to know when looking for the head of state who stands in for the king at least so much as to realize that the office-holder who "expresses the unity of the nation and is the guardian of the democratic functioning of the state" is likely to be identical with the person sought after, and he must know about the filling of public offices at least so much as to be able to recognize that the expression "may be elected for president" has something to do with becoming the head of state. All of this is of course trivial for us. But this is so only because we possess all the required information even before so much as touching the constitution.

The question thus is not whether the authoritative interpreter of the constitution may or may not take the liberty to rely on such information when choosing the relevant passages that is not included in the text of the constitution. In the absence of such supplementary information, even the very first move of the interpretation would be rendered impossible. The relevant passages do not point at themselves, they do not speak out of the constitution. More specifically, they speak only to those who already possess the background information required for recognition (for hearing the message). The right question is thus rather this: *What kind of* information is it permissible for the authoritative interpreter of the constitution to rely on?

Consider now a more complex problem. Section (1) of Article 54 of the constitution declares, "Every person in the Hungarian Republic has an innate right to life and human dignity, of which no one may be arbitrarily deprived." Suppose that we want to decide whether questions of the *quality* of life belong under this provision or not. The answer will clearly depend on what we mean by the right to life and human dignity. Those who understand this as the prohibition of being *deprived of* one's life and dignity will deny that this passage has any bearing on the issue. Those who think, on the other hand, that the right to life and human dignity obliges the state, beyond refraining from certain acts, to perform certain things—within the scope of its possibilities—that provide for the minimal material conditions of a life that satisfies the requirements of the right to human dignity will naturally extend the force of Article (1) of Paragraph 54 to questions about the quality of life.[32] Therefore, deciding about the relevance of this passage of the constitution for the issue in question already presumes the acceptance of some (contested) background conceptions. Once again, we have found that the text in itself, without external assistance, does not tell us which of its parts are relevant for some specific contested issue (or whether it has any relevant passages).[33]

To be sure, the real difficulties begin only when the selection of the relevant passages of the constitution has already been accomplished, and the interpreters begin their analysis. Let us return to Section (2) of Article 29/A, which appeared to be so straightforward and clear. What could be easier than to decide whether a presidential candidate has or has not reached thirty-five years of age by the day of the election? How much more difficult would it be to reach an agreement if the requirement were that the candidate "must possess the *experience, insight and judgment* of an average citizen of the age of 35"! And yet even the apparently perfectly unequivocal requirement to be found in Section (2) of Article 29/A is not really so.

Suppose that the election was called for May 1. A candidate who was born thirty-five years before the election at 00:01 on May 2 is surely not eligible for president. A candidate who was born thirty-five years before the election by midnight April 30 is surely eligible. Now suppose that one of the candidates was born between midnight April 30 and midnight May 1 (thirty-five years before the event). Is she eligible? This depends on what is to be understood by the expression "by the day of the election"; "00:00 of the day of the election" or "24:00 of the day of the election". The grammatical analysis of the phrase is of no help here, because it permits both alternatives. There may be such candidates (the ones born thirty-five years before the election, between midnight April 30 and midnight May 1) in the case of whom the provision permits both approval and rejection of their candidacy.

But is it not possible that such boundary cases are the products of mere lapses on the part of the people's representatives? Is it not conceivable that ideally informed and prescient constitution makers can eliminate all such interpretive uncertainties in advance?

In Chapter 3 I will show that striving for the utmost precision is not always an ideal that is worth pursuing. There are such regulatory issues in which the greatest possible precision is a reasonable objective, while there are others in which it is better for the legislator to refrain from drawing the limits all too precisely. For the moment, it may suffice to say that even if the utmost precision of rules would an ideal generally worth pursuing, this ideal would still be unattainable in some of the cases. Law is not a mathematical system of axioms; its language is not technical but draws on ordinary language. And it is an ineliminable feature of ordinary language that its concepts have vague boundaries. In the case of every single word there are cases to which it is certainly applicable, and others to which it is certainly not applicable. But the two domains are demarcated by a twilight zone rather than by a sharp boundary; there is a host of such cases where it is not at first glance determinable whether the contested expression has application for them or not.

Thus, constitutional provisions are never interpretable through the interpreter letting the constitution itself select, as it were, the relevant passages, and then letting these texts themselves decide—without external information—the contested issues. Interpreting the constitution—as well as interpreting any other text, for that matter—is an *active* operation, where the interpreter draws on extra-textual concepts, theorems and conceptions in his procedure, and mobilizes his own judgment.[34]

Therefore, the question to be answered is not whether the justices are allowed to involve extra-textual information in their practice of interpreting the constitution, but what kind of supplementary information they may take recourse to.

2.3. STRICT READING

No one would object to some of the additional information. No one would object to relying on the dictionary, paradigms and syntactic rules of the vernacular language. Nothing stands in the way of the grammatical analysis of the constitution. For instance, Section (3) of Article 22 of the constitution says "the Parliament must be summoned at the written request of one-fifth of the representatives, the president of the republic or the government." One may ask: Is the speaker of the Parliament obliged to summon the Parliament at the request of the enumerated persons, or does he have room for consideration here? The semantic analysis of the expression "must" gives an unequi-vocal answer to this question: yes, the speaker is obliged to summon the Parliament, and he has no room for consideration.

But why may reliance on grammatical rules be unobjectionable? Because these are identical for all competent users of the language; it is not the case that he who digresses from them holds a belief about the Hungarian language that is *different* from those of the other users but that he uses the language *inaccurately*. Therefore, it does not even occur to anyone that the judges would elevate their own personal views to the level of the constitution when they embark on a grammatical analysis of the constitution.

Yet grammatical analysis does not provide us with answers for all of our questions. Let us return for a moment to Section (2) of Article 29/A on the election of the president and let us ask the question whether someone under guardianship is eligible for president? The syntactic or semantic analysis of the cited passage leaves this question open. But Section (3) of Article 70 on voting rights says: "People under guardianship do not have the right to vote." This provision offers an answer to our question by inference, if we read it together with the previous one:

1. Every person with the right to vote is eligible for president [29/A (2)]; *therefore, because of 1,*
2. It is a necessary condition for a candidate to be eligible for president that it is the case that he/she has the right to vote; *and, because of Section (3) of Article 70,*
3. No person under guardianship has the right to vote; *therefore, because of 2 and 3,*
4. No one under guardianship possesses the necessary conditions to be eli-gible for president of the republic.

This reasoning infers such a proposition with the help of the formal rules of logic, by joining various passages of the constitution, which is not expressed by the constitution yet which is—as it is shown by the deduction—included in it.

Like the rules of grammar, the rules of logic, too, are applicable without further concerns. The rules of inference of logic are identical for every ratio-nal being; someone who might want to deviate from them uses logic *wrong-ly* rather than having a view of formal inferences different from that of the others. For this reason, it does not occur to anyone that the judges impute their own personal views to the constitution when applying the formal rules of logic, any more than in the case of grammatical analysis.

Yet not even the joint application of grammatical and logical rules would settle all the questions of constitutional interpretation. We have seen that according to Section (3) of Article 22 the Parliament must be summoned for an extraordinary session at the written request of the president of the republic, the government or one-fifth of the representatives. Let someone ask: Must an extraordinary session of the Parliament be summoned at the request of the chairman of the Constitutional Court?

One of us would promptly say the answer is no, since the cited passage of the constitution clearly indicates whose request has binding force, and the chairman of the Constitutional Court is not among those enumerated. Yet is this really the case? Only if the enumeration is meant to be exhaustive. Suppose the enumeration is not meant to be exhaustive. Then, the answer to the question is not an obvious one. In other words, before reaching the negative conclusion one must approve a further auxiliary hypothesis to the effect that "The subjects of constitutional entitlements are those and only those public officials who are specifically mentioned by the constitution as the subjects of such entitlements." Provided that we approve of this tenet, it does indeed follow from this and Section (3) of Article 22 *together* that the written request of the chairman of the Constitutional Court does not make summoning an extraordinary session of the Parliament mandatory. By contrast, the text of the constitution does not contain this tenet. It does not stipulate whether its enumerations are exhaustive or merely exemplary.

However, if linguistic and logical rules are safely applicable because they are identical for everyone, then why worry about applying this rule of legal interpretation, since this, too, is uncontested (this is why it appears superfluous to articulate it separately)? This observation might be generalized as follows: every information about which consent is (nearly) unanimous may be made use of.

Let us call *strict reading* such an interpretive procedure that draws in the interpretation, beyond the text of the constitution itself, only such information that enjoys (nearly) unanimous approval. Even strict reading inevitably goes beyond the bare text of the constitution, yet this gives rise to no difficulty; as I have said above, the addition is so trivial that it often goes unnoticed.

The difficulties begin where the interpretive issue cannot be settled through strict reading, that is, where there are two or more such answers for a contested question that are equally compatible with the strict reading of the relevant passages of the constitution. In such cases the range of possible readings might be further limited only if the interpreter resorts to such auxiliary theorems that divide the legal as well as the political community.

Shortly I will have to say more about this. For the time being, it may suffice to note that contested claims do not necessarily lead to such interpretations that contradict the strict reading. The interpretation might still be *textual* in a weaker sense of textualism, i.e. in the sense that the selected reading is one of those *allowed by*—or compatible with—the strict reading.

Naturally, not every interpretation that is compatible with a particular text may be regarded as one of its textual interpretations. The articles of a constitution do not exclude, taken either individually or collectively, the claim that the sun revolves around the earth. Nevertheless, the geocentric worldview might not be taken as a possible interpretation of the constitution. Nor does the heliocentric worldview (or any other rival of geocentrism, for that matter) belong to the domain of possible constitutional interpretations. The definition of textualism provided here assumes that the selected reading is a reading of the text in question, that it is meant to settle an interpretive controversy in regard of this very text. This is not the case with the theorems of the geocentric worldview and its rivals. One might say that the readings allowed by the strict interpretation may be regarded as textual only if they are relevant for settling an open question with regard to the meaning of the text. This is not the case with the theorems of the geocentric worldview and its rivals. One might say that the readings allowed by the strict interpretation may be regarded as textual only if they are relevant for settling an open question with regard to the meaning of the text.

By contrast, those who think resorting to contested auxiliary hypotheses is objectionable apply (either explicitly or implicitly) a stronger criterion of textualism. It is not sufficient for them for a reading to be compatible with the strict reading of the constitution; they want it to be identical with it. I shall call the *strict conception of textualism* the position which holds that the Constitutional Court must declare itself to be incompetent in all such issues that cannot be settled through the strict reading of the constitution—i.e. it must declare that the issue in question might not be settled through a judicial interpretation of the constitution.

According to this position, only those issues belong to the range of constitutional interpretation that may be decided by a strict reading of the constitution; everything beyond these are political questions and are deferred to the competence of such bodies that are authorized to make political decisions. The exponents of this position mean by interpretive activism—that is, interpretation that turns into constitution making—primarily such cases where the Court ventures to arbitrate issues left open by strict reading.

Which understanding of textualism should we settle on?

2.4. HISTORICAL READINGS

Suppose that the strict reading of a constitutional provision allows for a number of mutually exclusive interpretations, and that different interpreters endorse different interpretations. Yet it might occur that there is one such interpreter whose reading is endowed with a special constitutional status. This person (or group or body) may be the constitution maker itself or the totality of public officials who applied the contested passage over a long period of time in universal agreement.

Here is an example. According to Section (3) of Article 33 of the Hungarian constitution, "the prime minister is elected by the Parliament...at the proposal of the president of the republic". Is the president obliged to propose the candidate of the party with the largest number of seats to form the government, or might he authorize any candidate according to his best judgment? This question may not be settled by way of a strict reading. In the light of grammatical and logical rules as well as of consensual background information, the text of the constitution allows for both possibilities. Yet it does not follow from this that one should stop at this point. Let us assume that it might be established beyond doubt that when the framers of the constitution discussed and approved Section (3) of Article 33, they were driven by the *intention* that future enforcers should understand this passage as follows: "The prime minister is elected by the Parliament...at the proposal of the president of the republic. The president is obliged to first authorize the candidate of the party with the largest number of seats to form the government."

There may be some who question the reasonableness of the position of the constitution makers. For instance, they may envisage a situation in which the government resigns due to a grave economic crisis, the Parliament dissolves itself and new elections are held. The nation has no time for prolonged attempts to form a government; the leader of the largest party stands no chance of forming a government, what is more, neither does the leader of the second-largest party; by contrast, it is to be expected that the Parliament would approve a nonpartisan expert government. In countries with frequent economic crises, this may be a strong argument for giving more room for the president to select the prime minister. This consideration, however, does not overrule the intention of the framers, even though it may be supported by stronger arguments in the controversy. The original intention of the constitution makers is attributed this special significance not because the makers of the provision have the best knowledge of what the correct interpretation of these provisions is, but simply because this interpretation is *theirs*.

The constitution has binding force only because it was made by such a body that was authorized to make constitution for the community. It was the framers' intention to make the constitutional provisions binding with the meaning that they themselves attributed to them. Therefore, when one has to decide between two or more readings that are allowed by the strict reading, it is of special significance which one of them was intended by the framers. Provided that the available historical sources make it possible to answer this question, this is a way, other things being equal, to settle the interpretive controversy. Let us call this the position of *originalism*, and the reading that corresponds to it the *reading based on the original intention*.[35]

Yet it is not necessarily the makers of the constitution alone who can play such a privileged role. It may be the case that official agencies enforced Section (3) of Article 33 for a considerable period of time consistently in accordance with one of the possible interpretations. Initially, there might have been disagreements and tensions, but with the passage of time these were ironed out. Subsequent presidents consistently authorized the candidate of the largest party to form the government, and it did not even occur to them to deviate from this practice. In this case, it is the received constitutional custom which may settle the controversy. The justices who are petitioned to arbitrate in this issue may claim that the received practice prefers the reading according to which the president of the republic has no room for consideration: he must authorize the candidate with the largest number of seats. If they refer to this fact, they privilege the consensual constitutional interpretation of those who enforced the provisions of the constitution over a considerable length of time. Let us call the position which sees this as permissible the customary position, and the corresponding reading the *reading based on constitutional customs*.[36]

Should a judge rely on either the original intention or on constitutional customs, what he gives primacy to is not his own personal beliefs as against competing beliefs of his contemporaries, but to the understanding of such bodies that are generally acknowledged as authoritative sources of information regarding constitutional interpretation. Even though the reasonableness or usefulness of such interpretations may be called into question, it is usually recognized that such an interpretation is not just one among many; it has special authority. Since both the original intention and constitutional customs refer us to juridical history, I will refer to these two types of reading together as *historical readings*.

According to the historical position, the Constitutional Court must declare itself to be incompetent to arbitrate an issue only if the strict reading, when supplemented with information regarding the original intention and the constitutional customs, is still incapable of singling out one among the many possible interpretations. In this conception, only those questions that might not be settled through strict reading as supplemented with interpretation from historical sources are qualified as political questions—that is, such questions that must be left to elected representatives of the people.

If there is one such interpreter whose reading is recognized by everyone as having binding force, in virtue of being his or her reading, then it should not cause any major difficulty that the reading of this person or body is not shared by everyone. For in this case validity of the interpretation does not depend on whether the source is right or wrong; his or her reading must be accepted simply because it is his or her reading. On the other hand, if there is no such source to whose reading the Court could simply refer as binding, then the selection of the authoritative reading will depend on whose reading is correct. And if there is no compelling evidence in favor of the correctness of either of the readings, then the Court should refrain from making a decision.[37]

I will call this position *moderately strict textualism*. According to moderately strict textualism the Court is caught on judicial activism—that is, on interpretation that turns into constitution making—when it selects one among a number of readings allowed by the strict reading by resorting to substantive arguments—provided that these arguments are not compelling, that is, they may be contested in good faith even by those who share the judges' assessment of the circumstances of the contested question and about passages that are relevant for the case. In Károly Törő's expression, this is a case where the Court enforces its own conception.[38]

All such readings will be referred to here as *substantive readings*. These readings may differ radically, depending on the nature of the question and of the relevant arguments. Below, I will distinguish between two fundamental types of substantive readings, without any claim to comprehensiveness. One of these is the *moral reading*, which stirs most of the controversies. The other will be illustrated by the *structural reading*.

2.5. SUBSTANTIVE READINGS: STRUCTURAL INTERPRETATIONS

Section (2) of Article 2 of the constitution runs as follows: "In the Republic of Hungary, all power belongs to the people, who exercise popular sovereignty through its elected representatives as well as directly." That all power belongs to the people might not be understood as stating that all power is exercised by the people, because the second half of the sentence explicitly rejects this reading. What this passage is really about is what was attributed in Section 2.1 above to the principle of popular sovereignty; in the Republic of Hungary all power originates in the "people", that is, no public authority might be legitimate unless it is the case that it is exercised in the name of the "people", on the basis of the authorization by those governed.

Section (2) of Article 2 right away stipulates the most important institutional condition to be met so that the claim "all power belongs to the people" be true; no state meets the requirement of popular sovereignty unless legislators are elected by the totality of voters from among their own ranks (and are not, say, hereditary aristocrats), and unless every government agency is authorized by the elected representatives and acts within the framework of the laws made by these same elected representatives.

There is a straightforward relation between popular sovereignty and a legislature based on the principle of representation. If a considerable portion of adult inhabitants are excluded from the legislative elections or if the executive branch of the government is not subordinated to the legislature, then the principle of popular sovereignty fails to obtain. On the other hand, we have already seen (in Section 2.1) that the totality of voters is not identical with the "people". The "people" is a legally undefined multitude of individuals, while the community of voters comprises those who are recognized by the law as the bearers of the right to vote. The "people" never elects public officials; it is only the voters or their representatives who may elect officials. Therefore, the above claim decides only whether one may speak of popular sovereignty in *non-democratic states*. By contrast, it does not privilege any of the possible democratic alternatives—any rule of electing representatives, any legislative procedure, any formula of distributing competences between the legislature and the other branches of power. There are many conceivable institutional arrangements that might be equally compatible with the constitutional principle of popular sovereignty.

Let us now suppose, for the sake of argument, that the constitution does not provide for the procedure in which the president of the republic is to be elected. We have already seen (in Section 2.1) that popular sovereignty obtains both if the president is elected directly by the voters or if he is elected by the Parliament. One could say, on the other hand, that even though none of these solutions is excluded by popular sovereignty, the direct election of the president is nevertheless in a closer relation with this principle than an indirect election. Even though in general, the "people" exercises its power through elected representatives rather than directly, the principle of popular sovereignty is more fully realized in the direct exercise of power. Therefore, if the constitution does not provide for the procedure of presidential elections (as it was assumed here), then the institution of direct election should be preferred on the basis of Section (2) of Article 2.

But, first of all, it is not the case that the direct election of the president is in a closer relation with the principle of popular sovereignty than an indirect procedure. The appearance of such a correlation is due to the fact that we tend to identify popular sovereignty with the exercise of power by the "people". The better one approximates the ideal of direct democracy, the closer is the "people" to exercising its own sovereign authority by itself; the more the indirect forms of democracy predominate, the further removed is the "people" from being itself the sovereign, or so it is believed. On the other hand, it has already been shown that the "people" is not a legal agency; that is, it is not such an instance that could bear legal competences and make legally valid authorizations. An authority *originating* in the people is not identical with an authority *given by* the people; the realization or absence of popular sovereignty has nothing to do with the distinction between direct and indirect democracy.

The direct and indirect forms of exercising power are usually ranked with an eye on completely different perspectives, such as which of them guarantees more thorough civic participation in the political process, which of them produces more considered and informed collective decisions, and which of them is better compatible with the stability of the political regime, and so on. One may have good reasons to favor direct democracy against the indirect forms of democracy, at least if the former satisfies the other criteria of political decision making as well or nearly as well as the latter, for civic participation is in many respects desirable for itself. But these reasons are independent from the issue of the principle of popular sovereignty, for the latter is satisfied by any workable combination of direct and indirect democracy. Therefore, we are free to consider those reasons that speak against favoring direct democracy. One such argument is that the institutions of direct democracy, such as national referenda, rarely produce informed and considered collective decisions, or their all too frequent operation might endanger political stability. Should we find these reasons sufficiently serious, we may favor the institutions of indirect, representative democracy without doing any infringement upon the principle of popular sovereignty. Popular sovereignty does not decide whether one should favor direct or indirect presidential elections.

Second, the question of presidential elections is not an isolated one. Even though the constitution makers left this issue open (as it was assumed for the sake of the argument), they nevertheless settled a number of other issues unambiguously: the president is removed from the executive power, the executive branch—the cabinet—is subordinated to the legislature, not the head of state, and so on. The Republic of Hungary has a parliamentary regime. Considering all this, the following constitutional argument might be reconstructed in favor of electing the president by the Parliament, rather than directly by the people.

No matter what the options would be like prior to determining competences of public authority, once these are already stipulated in a certain way, the scope of possible alternatives with respect to the procedure of presidential elections is restricted, too. The direct or indirect election of the president is not equally well reconcilable with the existing structure of the distribution of power. The indirect election of the president would incur no difficulty for the smooth functioning of the governmental organization, while the direct election would very much do so. The head of state would be placed besides the Parliament and the government with respect to the source of its power. He or she would be endowed with a stronger legitimacy than the prime minister. This would inspire him to seek an extension of its competences. It would perpetuate controversies over the order of the distribution of powers. Therefore, once the constitution determined the structure of democratic institutions for the most part, with the Parliament and a government responsible to the Parliament in its core, there are strong constitutional reasons to settle the issue of presidential elections in a manner that avoids direct election by the people. Such reasons are referred to here as *structural reasons*, and an interpretation based on them is called a *structural reading*.

No doubt structural readings rarely decide constitutional controversies in a compelling manner. The controversy outlined here, too, divides the political community; the counter-arguments enumerated above are found by many to be inconclusive.[39] For the moment it may suffice to state this, and we may proceed to addressing another—more controversial and much more important—version of substantive readings.

2.6. SUBSTANTIVE INTERPRETATIONS:
THE MORAL READING

Consider Section (1) of Article 54 of the constitution: "Every person in the Republic of Hungary has an innate right to life and human dignity of which no one might be arbitrarily deprived." Now in Hungary, annually 400 to 450 people die of such kidney diseases that could be cured by transplantation.[40] Existing health regulations allow for living people to voluntarily donate one of their kidneys to a patient, but of course they do not allow for anyone being compelled to such a sacrifice. Suppose the lawmakers want to change this state of affairs; they argue that saving lives is more important than respecting self-determination over our own bodies. Does Section (1) of Article 54 prohibit the Parliament from making a law that compels Hungarian citizens to donate their organs?

The law would authorize the Surgeon General to register every citizen as a potential kidney donor and to produce a general registry of their medical data; when a patient's life could be saved only by instant transplantation, his or her data would be entered into the central registry that would produce the list of compatible donors. Then, the person to sacrifice a kidney to save the life of his or her fellow citizen would be selected by lot. Our question then is whether Section (1) of Article 54 permits this procedure.

It certainly does not contain such a clause that would spell out the prohibition of compulsory organ donation. It does not entail the ban on a legal regulation like the one outlined above even when coupled with other passages of the constitution. If it is still to be understood as prohibiting governmental disposition over human organs, then it does so only if further information is brought into the reasoning.

Suppose the problem of organ donation did not surface when the constitution was framed; no intention regarding compulsory transplantation can be attributed to the framers. Suppose, furthermore, that the question has not so far occurred to the law enforcers either; there are no constitutional customs available in this regard. In other words, the controversy might not be decided through resorting to historical sources. Substantive arguments are needed.[41] But what sort of arguments?

The provision cited above spells out a general moral principle: "Every person has an innate right to life and human dignity..." Nevertheless, this principle is immediately qualified by restricting its scope of validity to the jurisdiction of the Hungarian Republic. This duality allows for understanding the constitutional provision on life and dignity in two different ways.

According to the first conception, the textual coincidence of the moral principle and the constitutional provision has no *legal consequence*. What the whole of the sentence expresses is not that every person *possesses* the right to life and human dignity simply in virtue of being human—that is, independently of the legal stipulations by the state—but that the state of Hungary *provides* every person within its own jurisdiction with the privilege regarding life and dignity.

In the other conception, the cited passage *recognizes* a moral right rather than *creates* a privilege. It expresses a general moral principle and adds that the Republic of Hungary endorses this principle and incorporates it in its legal system.

A considerable part of constitutional provisions resemble Section (1) of Article 54; they contain such provisions that coincide with moral principles. The fundamental rights and the principles of equal treatment are of this nature and it can be shown that popular sovereignty and the rule of law as well exhibit strong similarities. The scope of further information one is permitted to bring into consideration when reading such passages will depend on which of the two conceptions mentioned above is the correct one.

Suppose we have reason to accept the first conception, that is, the one according to which the constitution creates legal privileges rather than recognizing rights rooted in morality. If so, then the right to human dignity cannot entail more than what the strict textual interpretation and the historical interpretation jointly reveal to be included in it. Therefore, a moral analysis of the relationship between dignity and control over one's body is not permitted to enter the constitutional controversy on compulsory organ transplantation. The decision of the issue will exclusively depend on the kind of rules with which the lawmakers gave substance to the privilege of human dignity and whether these rules allow for compulsory organ transplantation or not.

By contrast, let us suppose now that the constitution recognizes rights that have their origin in morality rather than distributes legal privileges. This assumption radically changes the interpretive problem. The question to be answered becomes not simply what the positive rules regarding dignity have to say about compulsory organ transplantation but rather what a defensible ethical conception of human dignity implies for this subject.

The primary task of the Court is to determine what the idea of human dignity that has been incorporated into the constitution consists in, on what grounds do we claim that people have a right to dignity, and what the correct conception of this right entails. Then, the institution of compulsory organ transplantation must be confronted with the thus developed conception. Now the moral issue of the right to dignity admits of right and wrong answers; conceptions of dignity claim truth to themselves, and the justices are expected to apply the true conception, with its practical consequences, whether or not these consequences are explicitly mentioned by the text of the constitution. Let us call this understanding of constitutional interpretation the *moral reading* of the constitution, and the position on which it rests the *position of moral reading*.[42]

Thus, the central issue is which understanding is the correct one. This is a hard question, even if the first position according to which there are constitutional provisions that happen to coincide with the statements expressing moral principles, but they are not expressions of moral principles nevertheless, seems to be highly implausible. But we need not enter into the intricacies of this debate here. It is a fact that the constitutions of the leading liberal democracies explicitly side with the second understanding. One way or another, they are all the heirs of the great human rights declarations of the eighteenth century.

And so is the constitution of the Republic of Hungary. We find in Chapter I, among the general provisions, the claim that "The Republic of Hungary recognizes the inviolable and inalienable rights of man; it is the primary obligation of the state to respect and protect these rights."[43] It is not only the verb "recognizes" that is important in this proposition but also the adjectives "inviolable" and "inalienable" associated with the fundamental rights. The expression "inviolable" expresses that the rights in question are such that it is forbidden for the state to infringe upon them. The expression "inalienable" refers to the fact that not even the subjects can resign from them. Finally, the cited provision claims about the state that it is its *obligation* to respect and protect these rights rather than merely having the *aim* to realize them. In other words, human rights are parametric data for the state; they impose inescapable normative constraints on its room of operation.[44]

Should this be the case, then we have good reasons to adopt the moral reading of the constitution. If individuals or their groups protest that the state's existing regulations violate the moral claims protected by the constitution, then, provided that the protest is not obviously ungrounded, the body entrusted with the safeguarding of the constitution is obliged to make an attempt to determine whether the complaint is justified. It is not allowed to avoid taking sides on the grounds that the controversy might not be decided by way of applying the strict reading of the text of the constitution. For if the relevant texts articulate moral principles, then these principles derive their sense from having a place within a wider moral conception, and the question of what this conception is admits of right and wrong answers, regardless of whether the strict reading of the constitutional text privileges any one of these. In other words, if we take the moral principles expressed by constitutional provisions for what they are—for moral principles—then the interpretation of the relevant provisions necessarily involves an appeal to the background principles that illuminate and justify those explicitly mentioned by the constitution's text. And the interpretation with regard to a particular legal problem, such as the one of compulsory organ transplantation, will make appeal to those principles and facts that jointly decide whether the constitutional provision (in this case, the constitutional right to human dignity) permits or prohibits the envisaged practice. If the moral reading of the constitution is an accurate one, then an appeal to the background principle stating one's right to control over one's own body is fully legitimate, even though such a principle is not explicitly mentioned by the text of the constitution.

2.7. SPECIAL OBJECTIONS: THE STRUCTURAL READING

At this point we already possess a rudimentary picture of the characteristics of substantive reading. In these lights, we may venture to examine whether there are good reasons to hold that when the Court rests its decision about constitutional controversies on such substantive arguments that divide the legal as well as the political community, it in fact impermissibly transgresses its competences.

These objections may be divided into two groups. Some of them claim substantive readings in general to be illegitimate, no matter which type they belong to. Some are directed against one or another type of substantive reading and leave the rest unaffected; they claim the objectionable type of reading to be illegitimate even though substantive reading in general is permissible. I will start with the latter ones; in this section, I will address the special objections directed against what I will call structural reading, while in the next section I will look at the ones directed at moral reading.

It appears that the more or less permanent "anti-activist" minority of the first Constitutional Court (Géza Kilényi, Péter Schmidt and Imre Vörös) objected primarily to the decisions based on structural reading. While they consistently protested when the Court made decisions based on such structural considerations that went beyond the strict reading in contested issues of competence (such as the signature rights of the president) that are left open by the strict reading, they never objected to deciding matters of fundamental rights on moral grounds.[45] There has not been a single dissenting opinion that rejected, on grounds of the charge of interpretive activism, either the famous clause of the Court's ruling 8/1990 (IV. 23) claiming that the Court "regards the right to human dignity as an expression of the so-called general personal right" and that "the general personal right is a "maternal right", that is, it is such a subsidiary fundamental right that might be cited by the Constitutional Court as well as the ordinary courts to defend individual autonomy, provided that none of the concrete, specified fundamental rights can be applied to a particular state of affairs,"[46] or any of the later decisions that were based on this clause. Therefore, it is reasonable to assume that the "anti-activist" minority was looking for special objections against structural readings rather than objections against substantive readings in general.

But why should the Court refrain from deciding controversies relating to governmental organization or competence in such cases where the strict and the historical readings do not privilege any of the opposing positions? What may be objected to the Court's resorting to structural arguments in such cases?

The statements of the "anti-activist" minority provide no clue in this regard. If they are really on the position that I have attributed to them, they do not forward specific arguments in favor of their position. I think, however, that the following reasoning recommends itself as plausibly theirs.

Structural reasons are about the sort of institutional arrangement that is reasonable for us to favor. The state's institutions, however, are not valued in themselves but are means that help society to realize various values and goals, and to make various principles respected. Therefore, no morally protected interest attaches in itself to any kind of electoral system, for instance, or to any specific distribution of competences between different state authorities.

Furthermore, as we have seen, promoting the same value, carrying out the same goal or securing respect for the same principle may be served by a number of different institutional arrangements. One such regime may be more efficient than another, but this is merely a question of convenience, and judging the efficiency of alternative institutional schemes does not belong to the domain of interpreting the constitution.

Provided that the constitution does not privilege any one institutional arrangement among a number of alternatives—for instance, among direct and indirect presidential elections—then we have further constitutional reasons to exclude one or another alternative only in the extreme case if it is straightforwardly contrary to the value it should promote, incompatible with the goal it should realize, or violates the principle it should protect (or any other constitutional principle). For instance, a regime in which the government may amend laws made by the legislature through statutes is certainly in conflict with the principle of popular sovereignty and the rule of law.

In such extreme cases the structural argument works well, but then it does not divide the community and is therefore in fact part of the strict reading. In less extreme conflicts, however, structural arguments have simply no justification, or so the objection goes.

What is more, this claim will be true in those cases as well where the structural arguments are based on the fact that a large part of the institutions have already been specified, thus the range of solutions for the as yet unspecified institutions is limited because of the need of coherence. Here, too, there will be cases where one or another solution is excluded by the already given institutional setting; here, structural arguments are legitimate, at the same time they are also compelling, thus are indeed part of the range of strict reading. In other cases, by contrast, specifying parts of the institutional setting does not eliminate the room for alternatives with regard to the rest of the institutions; in those cases, structural arguments are illegitimate.[47]

What should we think of this conclusion? On the one hand it is true that institutional structures are only means to reach other values rather than inherently valuable themselves. It is true that the promotion of the same constitutional goal, the serving of the same value or the protection of the same principle may be carried out by a number of different institutional arrangements, and that when the strict reading of the constitution does not privilege any one of these, then usually there are no reasons to look for further arguments in favor of constitutional restraint. It is also true that specifying some of the institutions—even though it may limit the range of available options—need not decide unambiguously about the selection of the as yet unspecified institutions. Therefore, it may be safely stated that structural arguments can settle constitutional controversies only in exceptional cases.

On the other hand, what the conclusion has to say about exceptional cases is not necessarily true. Exceptional cases are not necessarily so extreme as to rule out legitimate disagreement. For it can itself be a matter of controversy whether the contested structural solution in fact excludes the realization of the goal it is designed to promote, whether it conflicts with the accepted values or with a recognized principle, or it is merely relatively less efficient than some of its alternatives. The parties to the controversy frequently have different assessments of the dangers and the seriousness of the conflict. Then, differences of judgment often reflect differences of assessment of the political situation, which in turn may reflect differences of political position.

Someone who holds that a presidency undermining the institutions of parliamentarism and the rule of law has strong traditions in his country, and who opposes presidentialism, will think the risks of direct presidential elections to be greater than someone else who holds presidentialist traditions to be weak, or though strong but at the same time worthy of being resumed. Someone who cares first and foremost about the internal coherence of the decisions made at the peak of the executive power will think of the intrusion of the powers of a president elected by the Parliament into the executive branch of the government as more worrying than someone who rather fears the excess of power of a government left without proper checks and balances, and so on. What the parties disagree upon is not merely the coherence of one or another solution with the rest of the constitution but also the seriousness of the possible incoherence. That is, they disagree on whether the conflict is moderate or extreme, and thus could be resolved politically or it requires a decision by the Court. And such a controversy need not necessarily find a compelling resolution even if there is agreement to the effect that if the risks were really serious, then it would be necessary to abandon the contested institutional scheme.

To sum up, the methods of structural interpretation are indeed applicable only within a narrow range, but this range is not as narrow as to be part of the scope of strict reading. It cannot be meaningfully maintained that the application of structural arguments is inadmissible whenever they lack compelling force—because whether they are compelling or not is itself a matter of political conviction and judgment. The limits of structural argumentation cannot be determined by uncontroversial, technical means.

2.8. SPECIAL OBJECTIONS: THE MORAL READING

The critics of the first Court protested for the most part against the moral rather than against the structural reading. Károly Törő, too, in his already cited study, addresses the problem of moral reading. He complains that the judges ground their rulings "in many cases—and often in the most important cases—not on clear and detailed legal provisions but on declarative, so-called general fundamental rights that reflect mere moral principles that do not contain positive rules and can be interpreted in many different ways".[48] Let us consider now such arguments directed specifically against the moral reading.

One of the objections was formulated in the sharpest form by Béla Pokol. In his writings at the beginning of the 1990s, Pokol argued as follows. Apart from a few exceptions, fundamental constitutional rights are not formulated sharply enough to admit of legal applicability. This fact need not represent any difficulty, should it be the case that the judges suspend their use of jurisprudence until after the academic profession develops the conceptual tools of jurisprudence necessary to guide their application. Problems surface, however, when adjudication of fundamental rights goes ahead of this development. It can even occur that "such open principles and postulates become the center of constitutional review that withstand legal dogmatic precision".[49] In other words, if the requirements inherent in fundamental constitutional rights are sought to be determined through moral reading, then these rights will eventually overpower positive law's own life.

This concern is not entirely ungrounded. No doubt the moral reading tends to mobilize principles with no sharply defined boundaries. The domain of applicability of moral principles is not clearly demarcated. Since the boundaries are fuzzy, it is not clear whether the requirements of two separate principles may or may not be met simultaneously. In case of conflict, principles must be ranked; yet moral principles are undefined in the further sense that they do not have a clearly determined order of priority. The institution of law is necessary, among other things, exactly in order to mitigate the uncertainty of ordinary moral deliberation. This requires, among other things, the introduction of rules of great exactitude and refinement. The ideal after which law strives is a system of simultaneously enforceable rules with as clear ordering for the cases of conflict as possible. Should the Court interpret the constitution by resorting to moral principles, it may in principle subvert the aims of law.

Furthermore, this danger certainly will not materialize if the judges pay heed to Pokol's advice and "seek to avoid relying on those fundamental rights that...are not equipped with the requisite conceptual tools of jurisprudence". Judges who do not venture to morally interpret "bare" fundamental rights certainly cannot do any harm to the edifice of law. Thus, it may appear that they do well to claim, instead of providing an answer when confronted with such questions that cannot be answered without resorting to moral reading, that "The text of the constitution does not permit in the present case to make a decision by way of interpreting the constitution; therefore, we abstain from the decision."[50] However, such abstinence has its own perils.

First of all, "freezing" the fundamental rights provisions of the constitution is an all too high price for avoiding the dangers envisaged by Pokol. As I have shown in Section 2.5, if the Court takes this route it relinquishes the protection of constitutional principles of the utmost significance. If there is such a thing as individual rights vested in the constitution, then the rights bearers have a legitimate claim that the Court does not deny adjudicating their grievances. Therefore, before deciding whether the judges do well to abstain from decisions grounded in the moral reading it is necessary to examine whether there are better alternatives to abstinence.

We have all the more reason to look for alternatives because Pokol's conception entails much more than it explicitly states. He says that adjudication with respect to fundamental rights should be avoided only in cases where the fundamental rights in question are not yet equipped with the requisite conceptual tools of jurisprudence. However, this suspension has the curious consequence that developing the tools necessary for the application of fundamental rights will be delegated to the academics—to such a community, that is, that has no lawmaking authority whatsoever! If the Court is not allowed to develop jurisprudence, why would the corporation of academics be any more competent?

What is more, legal theorists do not discuss questions of jurisprudence in the ivory tower of academia. Their arguments are rooted in cases that occur in legal practice and in the analogies and distinctions that are tested there. Should the judges abstain from further developing the as yet "bare" constitutional principles in case law, the academic profession would be left with the results of legislation to see what specific rules make these principles applicable to particular cases. And this would lead to curious consequences.

As Albert Takács has pointed out in one of his early studies, if the moral reading is not admissible, then the relationship between provisions of the constitutional principles and specific laws becomes reversed. The scope and content of fundamental rights will not be determined by the constitutional provisions themselves that express them, Takács writes here, but by the laws in which "the legislators determine the specific rules related to fundamental rights". And if this is the case, then the Court might not substantively review precisely those laws that give shape to fundamental rights—for it is the laws that provide the criterion for determining the scope and content of fundamental rights. Such laws, then, could be ruled unconstitutional only on technical grounds, by claiming, that is, that some procedural rules were violated in the process of their making.[51]

But this implies that it is not the constitutional determination of fundamental rights that imposes constraints upon the laws subordinated to them but, to the contrary, the laws delimit the content of constitutional rights. The order of subordination between the constitution and the ordinary laws is reversed. The constitutional recognition of fundamental rights could not have legal consequences.

Fortunately, the difficulty can be avoided in ways other than abstinence with respect to fundamental rights. For the moral reading does not give freedom to the judges to apply their moral intuitions uncritically; it compels them to offer reasons, and constitutional interpretations deploying moral arguments have their technical procedures, measures and precautionary guidelines no less than any other interpretive method. I will specifically address this issue in Section 3.7. For the time being, let me only mention a number of examples.

Such a precautionary rule is that if there are a number of different arguments that yield the same decision in a certain question, and if one of these arguments is less controversial than the others, then this one should be adopted. Thus, if a law that violates fundamental rights may be struck down on the ground that it was made in an unconstitutional procedure, then it is preferable to give priority to this argument over a substantive examination of the conflict with some fundamental rights, because procedural unconstitutionality can usually be determined with greater chance to consensus than substantive unconstitutionality.

Furthermore, if the less controversial reasoning does the work in itself, then one should refrain from presenting the more contested reasons as redundant from the point of view of the decision. Such reasons should be deployed only in those cases where the decision cannot be sustained by less controversial reasons. The nature of the contested issue itself does matter, too. The more the reasoning divides the community, the stricter the requirements it must be subjected to. It is not advisable to ground constitutional interpretation on contested moral conceptions where the Court is asked to interpret a constitutional provision in itself, independently of any claim that a particular law is in conflict with that provision; moral reading is in place only where a particular law's constitutionality is at stake.

What is more, the considerations that guide the choice between moral and non-moral arguments are valid within the moral reading as well; when examining the constitutionality of a legal provision, one should bring only such background concepts and auxiliary hypotheses in the interpretation that are strictly necessary for the decision, and one should give preference to the less controversial views as opposed to the more controversial ones.

A further rule of thumb is that in cases that could be decided by a number of different interpretive conceptions, it is reasonable to choose the most economical conception, the one that has the least consequences for the as yet unexamined cases.

Finally, the moral reading is bound by the requirement of coherence. On the one hand, later rulings must be reconcilable with the earlier ones; possible deviations must be accounted for. One has to show either that the earlier ruling was based on error, or that even though the older ruling was right, there are essential differences between the cases and this may account for their differential treatment. On the other hand, from among the alternatives that are equally permitted by the earlier decisions, one should choose the one that better fits the existing legal material, which shows it in better light, and which is better illuminated by it.

Such a practice will yield ever more refined distinctions, more exact and detailed interpretive criteria, which gradually give substance to the abstract provisions of the constitution and restrict the scope of the judicial interpretation of the constitution.

Should the Court proceed this way, it will make piecemeal progress, the same way the ordinary courts circumscribe some specific legal domain with a multitude of precedents. It develops the operative interpretation of particular constitutional rights through a multitude of minor decisions rather than by one single major decision. In the meantime, other branches of power are allowed to do their business, too; the Parliament makes laws, the government issues orders, the ordinary courts make decisions while taking into account the rulings of the Constitutional Court; and legal scholars, philosophers and political scientists provide interpretive and critical commentaries to the growing corpus of constitutional decisions. In turn, the Court itself may take into account the body of such acts when it returns to old questions in new decisions. If it proceeds this way, it will be capable of applying the rights provisions of the constitution to such laws that belong within the scope of these rights, and it will not have to resort to these same laws to obtain standards for ruling about the laws—and yet, it will not make decisions with unpredictable scope and uncontrollable consequences.[52]

Later on, in Chapter 3, I will suggest ideas about what may justify the procedural restraint of the practice of moral reading. For the time being it may suffice to say that the absence of a finished jurisprudence offering detailed rules does not in itself represent sufficient reasons for refraining from the moral reading.

2.9. SUBSTANTIVE READINGS:
CRITICAL INTERPRETATION

A further special objection was also articulated in connection with the moral reading, one that is represented most vehemently by Károly Törő. The Court, Törő maintains, makes its decisions "on the basis of the 'invisible constitution' that stands above the written constitution and purports to represent its theoretical bases". And this "invisible constitution" is not given to it by the Parliament but is developed by itself. How should we understand the claim that an "invisible constitution" provides the theoretical bases for the "written constitution"? Even though Törő does not strive to precisely formulate his claim, he need not inevitably do so, because the metaphor of the "invisible constitution" was coined by the chief justice of the first Court, who in a frequently cited concurring opinion clearly expressed that the "invisible constitution" "serves as a safe measure of constitutionalism...above the constitution which is still being amended in the service of fleeting daily political purposes".[53]

Suppose that it follows from the constitution, which is being amended in the service of fleeting daily purposes, that p (for instance, that the death penalty is permissible), while from the "invisible constitution" it follows that not p (the death penalty is not permissible). Since it is the latter that serves as the safe measure of constitutionalism as against the former, one should adopt not p, even though this is excluded by the text of the constitution.

Let us translate this claim into the language of the apparatus developed in this paper. The correct moral reading of a constitutional passage is shown to be in conflict with the strict reading of the constitution. The question then is, which reading should prevail. Is it the moral reading that overrules the strict reading, or, to the contrary, the strict reading that overrules the moral reading? Should one amend the strict reading to the effect that the meaning of the given provision becomes morally acceptable, or should the moral reading be transformed so that it becomes compatible with the strict reading? Törő's article complains that the Constitutional Court gives preference to the moral reading as opposed to the strict one.

Whether this charge is well grounded as it is leveled against the first Hungarian Court will be discussed in the last study in this volume.[54] Here I would like to examine whether it is a necessary feature of the moral reading that it revises the strict reading. For a better elucidation of the question, I would like to return for a moment to the interpretation of the right to human dignity. Let us compare the following two cases.

In the first case, the relevant constitutional provision literally coincides with the cited passage of the constitution. Furthermore, it might be determined from other sources (for instance, from the records of the Parliament), that in the constitution makers' intention this provision was not meant to prohibit compulsory organ transplantation. Finally, the constitutional custom has corresponded for many years to the position of non-prohibition. But after many years a motion is filed with the Court to rule out this practice as unconstitutional. The Court decides that the right to human dignity contains, in its correct analysis, the more specific right of the people to dispose over the use of their own bodily organs. No doubt the makers of the constitution as well as its enforcers thought about it differently in the past. But what the constitution contains is the moral principle that "every person has a right...to human dignity" not their erroneous belief to the effect that the right to dignity allows for compulsory organ transplantation. The adequate interpretation of the constitution is identical with the correct reading of this principle, not with the mistaken readings attached to it in the past; and it does not matter that these readings were the readings of the makers and official enforcers of the constitution. Their beliefs do not have authority over the correct reading of the constitution. The moral reading overrules the historical reading.[55]

In the second case, it was not merely the intention of the framers when formulating the provision about the right to life and human dignity not to prohibit compulsory organ transplantation, but they included this intention in the written text of the constitution. "In the Republic of Hungary, every person has the right to life and human dignity...This right is not meant to rule out compulsory organ transplantation".

Suppose the belief that the right to dignity does not rule out compulsory organ transplantation was false before it was made into an explicit constitutional provision; then, it will be still false after having been included in the text of the constitution. One might infer from this that the moral reading can overrule the historical reading, then it can overrule the strict reading as well. In other words, it may occur that, rather than restricting the range of alternatives allowed by the strict reading, the moral reading commits the constitution to such an alternative that falls outside the range determined by the strict reading.

This response recalls the classical position of natural law. If the moral reading entails this position, then the doctrine of the moral reading of the constitution is indistinguishable from the natural law doctrine. It cannot be divorced from the thesis that immoral laws are null and void.

Such an interpretive practice would violate even the widest, most permissive criteria of textualism; it is in fact a critique rather than an interpretation of the constitution. Of course, no constitutional review could critically revise every single constitutional passage, case by case; and there is no such view that it should do so. But it is possible to conceive such a position that permits the interpreter to revise, occasionally, in the face of pressing reasons, the strict reading of the contested constitutional passages. Let us call such an interpretation a critical reading. If the critical reading regards moral reasons as such pressing reasons, we may call it a natural law reading.

The claims that revise the text of the constitution have two important characteristics. On the one hand, they are incompatible with at least one passage of the constitution, thus they violate the requirement that no interpretation is permitted to contradict the text that is being interpreted. On the other hand, provided that the constitution itself is non-contradictory, there are no such constitutional passages that they could be taken as the interpretation of; in other words, they fail to meet the requirement of textual relevance (on this requirement, see Section 2.3). If the simultaneous transgression of these two requirements were permitted, then of course a reading that transgresses only one of them would be permitted, too. Therefore, even though the concurring opinion of the president of the Court does not mention it specifically, the "doctrine of safe measure" involves the possibility of a weaker variant of critical reading, in which contested cases are decided by invoking theses that are allowed by strict reading but are textually irrelevant.

Suppose that the constitution does not include the article that "In the Republic of Hungary, every person has an innate right to life and human dignity." Furthermore, it has no chapter on the fundamental rights nor does it provide for such rights in an abstract manner. Nevertheless, the Court rules compulsory organ transplantation to be unconstitutional. It formulates the thesis of the right to life and human dignity all by itself, and it declares the unconstitutionality of compulsory transplantation by interpreting this thesis. The theorem on which the ruling is grounded does not contradict any one provision of the constitution, but neither is there a single constitutional provision which it could be taken as the interpretation of. With its introduction, the judges improve the constitution, as it were; they add to it something that was completely absent from it beforehand. It can easily be the case that when Törő protested that the Court grounds its decisions on the "invisible constitution" rather than on the written one, he had such a possibility in mind.

Of course, the critical reading does not require the interpreter to rely on textually irrelevant or contradicting theorems. Rather, it is characteristic of this conception that it regards textualism as a desirable ideal rather than a mandatory rule. It endorses the conception of desirable textualism. By contrast, all the other hitherto enumerated interpretive positions concur in that they endorse the conception of mandatory textualism. We may include among these positions that version of moral reading that rejects textual criticism based on natural law.

But is such a version conceivable? This depends on whether it is true that the answer to the question above is that there in no difference between the constitution makers' merely misinterpreting some of the consequences of the provision they have approved, and explicitly including the falsely interpreted consequence into the written text of the constitution.

In my view this is not true, for the allegedly only possible answer is false. Where there is a written constitution, the written text of the constitution possesses privileged authority. The written text is not merely one among a number of different sources of information which, taken together, may determine the valid constitutional rule with respect to a given question. The written text is the document itself the interpretation of which determines the constitutional rule. And a reading which is not compatible with the text but only with its amended version cannot be taken as one of its interpretations (because otherwise a conflict would be created between the written text, read with a view to the rules of grammar and logic and other consensual information, and this reading). In short, the strict reading of the text to be interpreted imposes constraints on all other legal rules or interpretations.

A moral reading that adheres to textualism presupposes, as it were, the outcomes of the strict reading. It takes the text of the constitution as given and in the first step it always subjects it to the procedure of strict reading— all that is settled by strict reading is taken for granted for the aims of further steps. All further moves are aimed at restricting the scope of interpretive alternatives allowed by strict reading. Therefore, if the text of the constitution contains both the provision that "every person has a right to life and human dignity" and the stipulation that "this right cannot be taken to mean the prohibiting of the introduction of compulsory organ transplantation", then in the interpretation of constitutional right to human dignity the range of possible readings must first be restricted to the variants that do not contradict the stipulation. The moral reading may enter only after this point, to select the morally most defensible variant within the thus outlined range.

A variant that has been excluded by strict reading may not be brought back by moral reading. If the two provisions have such a joint reading that is grammatically tenable and non-contradictory, then this reading must be accepted;

the interpreter has no right to presume that, even though there is such a (strict) reading, the constitution is nevertheless grammatically confusing (the second provision means something other than it states), or is logically contradictory (the two provisions simultaneously claim that the right to human dignity prohibits, and that it does not prohibit, compulsory organ transplantation). Further, it may not add such theorems to the text of the constitution whose deployment may not be justified on the ground that it helps to decide the interpretation of any one constitutional passage.

I hasten to add, for the sake of clarity, that my claim is not that the text is made inaccessible for all criticism. It may happen to be agrammatical and therefore in need of correction. In other cases, even though the text is grammatically correct, it beyond doubt deviates from what the lawmakers wanted to express; in such cases the American constitutional law speaks of the scrivener's error. For instance, there is a legal provision stating that "Certificates about the acquisition of real estate have to be submitted to the land registry office before December 31 of the given calendar year by the latest; otherwise the real estate is handed over to the state". It is beyond doubt that the lawmakers wanted to indicate the end of the calendar year as the critical deadline, thus in fact it meant: "by December 31". Thus, the expression "before December 31" is to be treated as an error. Finally, if the constitution has a long history, the lexical meaning of the expressions in it may shift; in such cases it may be reasonable to correct the original reading in the light of the modern one. Thus, grammatical mistakes, obvious errors and historical changes of meaning might constitute grounds for critically correcting the text. These reservations, however, leave our original principle unaffected, because none of the enumerated reasons is of a substantive nature; none of them demands us to revise the clear, unequivocal and semantically unchanged text on grounds of substantive—primarily moral, but also structural or other—arguments. And this is what is forbidden by the principle of the primacy of the strict reading.

A moral reading that adheres to textualism will represent in certain cases (as in the one in our fictitious example) not the morally best standpoint but only such a position that, given the constraints of the constitutional text, is morally the least bad. From this it also follows that the official interpreters of the constitution have good reasons to point out that the morally acceptable conception of the right to dignity would demand such lawmaking that prohibits compulsory organ transplantation.

To be sure, within the framework of mandatory textualism this is not a tenet of constitutional interpretation but an extra-constitutional claim, addressed by the interpreters to the bodies authorized to lawmaking and amending the constitution, as recommendations. The critique of the constitution may not be made part of interpreting the text of the constitution.

While the strict conception permits only the strict readings, and the moderately strict conception allows, beyond the strict readings only the historical readings, this third conception of textualism—let us call it the broad conception—accepts any reading as textual, provided that it is compatible with the strict reading. From this standpoint, the interpreters' procedure should be rejected as activism—as constitutional interpretation that turns into constitution making—only if they proceed as though it were a matter of judicial discretion to overrule the outcome of strict reading on the basis of some substantive reading.[56]

To sum up, the upshot is not that moral reading is inadmissible; we found only such interpretations that involve a critical reading to be objectionable. We have drawn a line, but this line runs between the substantive and the critical readings rather than between the historical and the substantive ones.

However, we have yet to examine the objections against substantive readings in general—the ones which, if tenable, rule out all substantive readings rather than only one or another of their versions.

2.10. GENERAL OBJECTIONS AGAINST SUBSTANTIVE READING

One of the objections is suggested by the argument just made against the natural law radicalism of the moral reading. I have said that the moral reading may not overrule the text of the constitution, because the text is not merely one among the many different kinds of of information one takes into account when deciding on constitutional matters, but embodies privileged information: every answer must be capable of being taken as an interpretation of it. But if this is the case, does it not follow that every answer must be confined to the strict interpretation of the text?

Is not this position a retreat to where we started from, i.e. to the thesis that the constitution is identical with the text of its articles, in the order they succeed one another? And if it is identical with them, are we not compelled to say that whatever goes beyond the strict reading of the text adds extra-constitutional claims to the constitution and thus amends it?

These claims, formulated as questions, are false; yet their close analysis—as that of the objections—may yield important insights.

Where there is a written constitution, the written text is no doubt the ulti-mate, definitive authority in identifying the constitutional order of this state. But when we reach for the tiny volume entitled The Constitution of the Republic of Hungary, what we want to find out is usually not the words and sentences that make up the text of the constitution. What we in fact want to find out is the legal norms contained in the constitution. These norms are to be found in part in the sentences of the written text, in part they may be inferred logically, from the joint reading of a number of sentences. That which is beyond these may not be claimed to be contained in the text, yet they, too, belong to the constitution—to the totality of constitutional norms.

And we have good reasons to take it as our starting point that the consti-tution contains more than that which is included in its written text. Constitutional norms regulate complex, multi-level practices: the legislature, the judiciary, the executive, the typical behavior of public and private organi-zations as well as of the multitude of individuals, and in the last analysis the content and identity of constitutional norms is decided in these practices. Such practices may restrict the meaning of the norms to be found in the text of the constitution, one or another norm may be altogether eliminated by them, or they may add further norms to the corpus of the constitution. This is what is acknowledged and made use of by the method of judicial interpre-tation of the constitution that was referred to above as the historical reading.

If the constitution were identical with its text, then the historical readings would be no more acceptable than the moral reading, because it, too, estab-lishes such norms that are not identified by the grammatical and logical anal-ysis of the text. If we restrict the range of the possible interpretations of the constitution on the grounds of the original intention and of the constitu-tional customs, then the constitution as a written text and the constitution as the totality of norms will not coincide. The historical interpretation pre-sumes that there is more to the existing constitution than the written text that represents its core.

Of course, it does not yet follow from this that substantive reading is acceptable. On the other hand, it does follow that in order to rule out sub-stantive reading, it is not sufficient to show that such readings go beyond the strict reading of the text. Some further reasons would be needed. One would need to explain why, once it is permitted that as a result of the refinement and adjustment of other public authorities, constitutional customs emerge which in turn further interpret the constitution, is it forbidden precisely for the Court to take part in shaping constitutional customs. For this is exactly what the Court in fact does.

Suppose that the Court refrains from adjudicating in the conflict of competences between the president of the republic and the prime minister. Suppose, furthermore, that none of the opposing sides has the required majority in the Parliament to amend the constitution. Then we are left with two solutions. Either the Parliament makes a law by a simple majority to fill in the gaps of constitutional provisions. Or the cooperation between the two public officials is allowed to shape the interpretation of the constitutional distribution of authorities. By assuming the burden of arbitration, the Court has taken precedence in shaping the constitutional customs over the Parliament on the one hand and over the president of the republic and the prime minister on the other. Let us for the moment disregard the possibility of the Parliament's shaping the constitutional customs by approving sub-constitutional rules, and let us instead face the question why, provided that it is allowed for the head of the state and the prime minister to shape the constitutional customs, is the same thing prohibited to the Court.

When the Court selects through its own interpretation one among the number of norms allowed by the text of the constitution, it in fact lets the other authorities of the state know that in the future they must adhere to this constitutional norm. If the Court in its future decisions adheres to its own provision—that is, if it treats the original decision as limiting its own freedom in its later decisions—and if it is capable of persuading the other government authorities to abide by its provisions, then it creates a new constitutional custom. Why is this a problem?

The ultima ratio of the critiques of the first Constitutional Court for rejecting all interpretive methods that go beyond the strict reading was that such an "activist" practice turns constitutional interpretation into constitution making. The demand of interpretive abstinence was grounded in the claim that the Court is not allowed to amend the constitution.

Either explicitly or implicitly, historical readings are usually exempted from this demand. When the Court restricts the range of interpretations left open by the strict reading through a reconstruction of the original intention or of some other constitutional custom, the reason for the exemption goes; it does not introduce a new rule by itself but rather makes explicit a rule that originates with such an authority that has the right to restrict the scope of possible interpretations left open by the text. We have to realize now that this distinction is inconsistent, at least with regard to constitutional customs.

If it is not allowed for the Court itself to change constitutional customs, because this amounts to constitution making, then we have no reason to suppose that other public authorities (with the exception of the Parliament) are allowed to do so—and then readings based on constitutional customs are no less unacceptable than, say, the moral reading. On the other hand, if we have good reasons to believe that other public authorities may develop constitutional practices, it is not clear why the Court is in need of the support of their authority to do the same.

We are now in possession of all the conceptual tools we need to answer the following question: Is it really true that any interpretation that goes beyond the strict reading amounts to amending the constitution?

Based on what we have learnt in the course of the earlier moves, we may safely declare this to be untrue: substantive readings that remain within the constraints of strict reading cannot be taken as constitution making.

2.11. CONSTITUTION MAKING

At the end of the first chapter of this study we distinguished between three possible conceptions of judicial constitution making:

1. the view according to which the Court amends the constitution by merely elevating a rule to constitutional status for such reasons that are not included in the strict reading of the constitution;
2. the view in which the Court amends the constitution by elevating to constitutional status a rule not contained by the strict reading of the constitution on such grounds that divide the legal as well as the political community; and finally,
3. the view in which the Court amends the constitution only if it elevates to constitutional status such a rule that is in conflict with the strict reading of the text of the constitution.

I would like to address these three positions in the light of our investigations so far, and to determine which of them is defensible.

Where there is a written constitution, it is the authority of the constitution makers (in the Hungarian Republic, the qualified majority of the Parliament) to amend the written text of the constitution. This is the last resort it may mobilize if constitutional customs evolve in an undesirable direction or if they fail to evolve in the desired direction. This is the resort that cannot be mobilized by any other public authority that does not possess the authority to make constitution.

The legislature itself may amend the constitution in three different ways. The first one is a wholesale change of the constitution: making a whole new constitution following the procedure of constitution making prescribed by the old constitution. The other two alternatives are confined to partial change. They may leave all of the old provisions unaltered and supplement them with a new one (supplementing the constitution), or they may repeal one or more old provisions and put new ones in their place (constitutional text-substitution).

It is conceivable in principle, although it is ruled out in practice, that a Court ruling would be equivalent to the wholesale change of the existing constitution. A Court that takes its mandate at least minimally seriously cannot display such a radically critical attitude as not to look for at least some fixed guidelines in the written text of the constitution. It must take at least certain constitutional provisions as given. Therefore, the charge of constitution making must protest either against an implicit supplementing of the constitution or against an implicit text-substitution on the part of the Court.

Both of these may occur; but if they in fact occur, we are within the domain of the critical reading.

The constitution of the republic declares, for instance, that "In the Republic of Hungary, every person is a legal subject."[57] The Court may not interpret this passage as saying that "In the Republic of Hungary, every being whose intelligence level reaches that of the person with the lowest level of intelligence is a legal subject." This reading could not be taken as an interpretation of the original rule but only as that of another one, substituted for the original. For the expression "every person" refers obviously not to just any being with the minimal intelligence of humans but to the individuals belonging to the human species—regardless of their level of intelligence. Reading the cited provision as extending legal capacity to any being in possession of the required intelligence amounts to altering the written text of the constitution. And the Court really does not have a mandate to do this.

Neither does it have a mandate to introduce, while leaving the text unaltered, such a theorem that, although allowed by the text, nevertheless indubitably falls outside its semantic scope. Suppose that the Court declares that "working on Sundays is prohibited in the Republic of Hungary", and it grounds the introduction of this norm in the passage that "in the Republic of Hungary, every person is a legal subject", which does not exclude the prohibition of Sunday work. The rules of labor do not interpret the principle of legal capacity, therefore it is little wonder that the latter is not in conflict with this or that regulation. The introduction of textually irrelevant provisions would really represent amending the constitution, and this is in fact not in the power of the Court.

Let us assume now, by contrast, that the Court commits itself to such a variant which is both textually relevant and is allowed by the strict reading. Suppose that the contested question is to whom the concept "person" refers in the use of the constitution; who are regarded, out of all individuals genetically qualified as human, as "persons" (persons with legal capacity, constitutional legal subjects). For the sake of convenience, let us assume that beings whose parents are humans have two natural states, the fetal (from conception to birth) and the post-natal (from birth to death). Let us disregard the possibility of a more refined periodization of ontogenesis or the possibility that individuals may possess rights that outlive them. The article on legal capacity confronts us with the following dilemma. The expression "every person" certainly comprises the totality of human persons already born (who would belong to this category if the people who live their own lives do not?). Yet it cannot be decided through strict reading whether the force of the expression extends to fetuses or not. Thus, the strict reading of the contested passage yields the following rule:

1. In the Republic of Hungary, all people who have already been born have a legal capacity; and
2. In the Republic of Hungary, human fetuses either possess legal capacity or not.

If the Court does not refrain from dispelling the uncertainty involved in 2, it will have to choose between the following two provisions:

2a. In the Republic of Hungary, human fetuses possess legal capacity.
2b. It is not true that in the Republic of Hungary human fetuses possess legal capacity.

No matter whether the Court endorses 1 and 2a or 1 and 2b as the reading of the constitutional provision, the rule contained by the reading will be different from the one contained by the strict reading of the text. The strict reading allows both 2a and 2b; thus, it does not provide us with further guidance for borderline cases, to decide whether a certain human being (of fetal state) possesses legal capacity or not. On the other hand, the reading selected by the Court allows either only 2a or only 2b. It gives us guidance in regard of the legal capacity of fetuses, but only at the price of putting another rule in the place of the one furnished by the strict reading. This suggests that there is an essential analogy between selecting a variant that falls outside the semantic scope of the strict reading altogether (critical reading) and between selecting a variant within the semantic scope of the strict reading (substantive reading). The latter no less than the former alters the original meaning of the provision.

But there is a crucial difference between the two procedures. In the former case, the Court carries out an implicit modification of the very text (substitution or supplementation). Even though it does not alter the written text of the constitution, it instructs us to read the given passage as though its wording had been altered. In the latter case, the interpretation leaves the text unaffected. It does not imply even an indirect modification of the text. In the former case, the Court has broken through the boundaries of the decision of the constitution makers—the boundaries of the text that was elevated to constitutional status. In the latter case, it has made its selection by respecting the constraints imposed by the decision of the constitution makers. The former case constitutes an obvious (covert) amendment of the constitution. On the other hand, it is not clear whether the latter case amounts to a (covert) amendment of the constitution as well.

A textually relevant substantive reading—like a decision about the status of the fetus—cannot even in principle amount to the wholesale change of the constitution, because it presupposes that at least one constitutional passage remains unaltered. It cannot amount to supplementing the constitution, either: that is ruled out by the requirement of textual relevance. We are left with constitutional text substitution, or replacing some old passages of the constitution with new ones.

But the decision cited in our example cannot be taken as a text substitution, either, because it falls short of critical reading. Text substitution entails the repealing of the text which is being substituted. And this is more than is performed—even covertly—by a choice between a number of variants that are equally allowed by the strict reading. Such a choice is compatible with the continued validity of the original constitution-making decision; what is more, it is grounded in it. One could say that the continued validity of the provision adopted by the constitution makers is a necessary but not sufficient condition of the validity of such an interpretation. To put it briefly, what the judicial interpretation of the constitution amounts to—provided that it remains confined to the scope specified by the strict reading—is not the making of a new constitution or a supplementation of the constitution, and neither is it a constitutional text substitution. It cannot qualify for constitution making.

This insight is consistent with the claim that the legal consequences of judicial interpretation must be weaker than those of constitution making. The Court may not strike down the text of the constitution as amended by the Parliament—unless there were some formal flaws in the procedure, for instance, if it was approved with a majority narrower than required. Parliamentary amendments are unalterable constraints for the Court. On the other hand, the Court may revise its own earlier interpretation. By contrast, the Parliament may revise its own earlier decisions as well as the constitutional rules that have their origin in judicial interpretation.[58]

Thus, there is an important analogy and also an important difference between parliamentary constitutional amendment and judicial interpretation. The analogy is that, not unlike the amendment, judicial interpretation, too, introduces a new rule. Just as the text as it was before the amendment does not fully determine the textual variant adopted by the constitution makers, the text to be interpreted does not fully determine the kind of constitutional rules to be set up by the interpreters who venture to arbitrate questions that have not been settled by the strict reading. The Court, if it resorts to means beyond the strict reading, alters some of the constitutional rules. This would make it appear reasonable to regard such practice as equivalent to constitution making and to declare that the judges have no power to do this.

On the other hand, the amending of the constitution by the Parliament and its judicial interpretation are also significantly different. The freedom of the constitution makers is not in the least restricted by that passage of the constitution that is being repealed, with regard to the kind of provision they want to introduce in its place. By contrast, the judges are restricted by the text to be interpreted with regard to the kind of rules they may establish. The new rule to be introduced must not fall outside the semantic range of the given constitutional passage, and must not take the place of annulled constitutional provisions. It presupposes that the text adopted by the constitution makers continues to be in force as it is. It rests on the validity of that text.

This duality should no longer cause any theoretical difficulties. The duality corresponds to the insight that the complete set of constitutional norms is larger than the set of norms included in the text of the constitution. It is consistent with the claim that the constitution can be developed by way of changing the constitutional customs no less than by the parliamentary amendment of its textual tenets. It allows for the Court to shape the constitution, as long as the change is confined to the domain of constitutional customs and falls short of even covertly amending the text of the constitution itself. It does not contradict the fundamental principle that the Court has no power of constitution making, that is, the explicit or implicit alteration of the text of the constitution.

Our insights are not affected by the fact that the substantive readings of the constitution are based on such contested views that divide the legal as well as the political community. The fact that there is no consensus about the right choice between a number of rules allowed by the strict reading of the text of the constitution does not turn such a decision into implicit constitution making. Whether a choice is contested or not has nothing to do with its leaving the text of the constitution unaffected or—covertly—changing it. Being controversial does not rule out its remaining within the domain specified by the strict reading of the text. The controversy then is about which alternative it is right to choose among the ones compatible with the text.

At this point the analysis given in this chapter reveals an important consequence that has so far remained concealed. We mentioned in Sections 2.3 and 2.9 the requirement that acceptable constitutional interpretations must be textually relevant. It is to be seen now that, provided that the interpretation satisfies the requirement of textual relevance, whether or not it divides the legal or the political community, it will be reasonable for everyone to accept it as a legitimate reading of the constitution.

This will be so because, even though there may be some who hold the interpretation to be mistaken, they cannot doubt that the reading that is unacceptable for them is a possible reading of a tenet that is included in the constitution. This would in itself secure only a weak consensus for judicial review. But the weak initial consensus is lent solid posture by the fact that the subsequent rulings of the Court presuppose one another and strive for coherence; the latter build on the results of the earlier, and the Court introduces, in the course of interpretation, such underlying principles that mutually reinforce one another and the concrete decisions justified by them, and that explain why, in a country where the constitution determines the ultimate rules of coexistence, it is right to rule this way rather than in any other way. This is important not only because this way the Court, provided that it functions according to the ideal of constitutional adjudication, makes the normative implications of the constitutional order better intelligible and more transparent, although this in itself is an achievement of great significance. However, it has a further consequence as well. It will be very likely that a great majority of the decisions will enjoy a fairly broad consensus, and it will be only a minority of cases in which the decision will be sharply divisive. Otherwise, the case would be either that the moral cleavage in the society is too strong for any constitutional political community to develop at all or it would be the case that, even though the citizens would approve of the same decision in most of the cases, the Court would systematically turn against this consensus. In the first case it would be the state that would be short-lived; in the second, the Constitutional Court. Where the state is solid and the Court enjoys broad acceptance, we may safely conclude that the majority of the Court's rulings do not deviate too far from the limits of tolerance of the consensus in the political community.

And if this is the case, then even the opponents of some one particular ruling must agree that the given decision, even though they think it to be erroneous, is nevertheless an application of a broadly consensual conception of the constitutional principles. All this takes is that they should be coherent with this wider conception and that the latter be transparently unified. No interpretation that ventures to arbitrate in issues that divide the public may strive to achieve more than this. A Court that, though it does not refrain from arbitrating questions that deeply divide the community, carefully avoids revising the strict reading of the text of the constitution, and at the same time seriously aspires to develop a coherent system out of its subsequent decisions, may enjoy broad authority even if some of its decisions are surrounded by passionate debates for decades.

To sum up, should interpretations resting on controversial views be impermissible, then the reason for their unacceptability cannot be that they turn into constitution making.

Most of the judicial rulings that divide the legal or the political community do not rest on the critical reading of the constitution, do not count as constitution making. Therefore, distinguishing between interpretation and amendment does not imply that the Constitutional Court should have no power of substantive reading. Should it have no such powers, it must be so because the Court strikes down laws on the basis of its own interpretations.

3. Striking down legislation

Constitutional justices are not elected representatives but are merely autho-rized by elected representatives; the mandate of this body is derived from the constitution makers, while the judges' own personal mandates derive from the lawmakers. Usually, ordinary judges, too, are not elected repre-sentatives; their authority is derivative as well. Yet there is a fundamental difference between constitutional justices and ordinary judges.

We have seen (in Section 2.1) that the principle of popular sovereignty demands that those authorized should act within the framework of rules set up by those who authorized them. The upshot of the previous chapter was that the judges who interpret the law may abundantly resort to supplemen-tary information when developing their reading, as long as they confine themselves to the domain specified by the strict reading. In the case of ordi-nary judicial legal interpretation, this is sufficient to prevent a conflict between the interpreters and the makers of the law. In Hungary, ordinary judges may not examine the constitutionality of laws at all; they must accept existing laws as given. But the situation is not fundamentally different where—as in the United States, Australia, Japan, Canada or India—at certain levels of the ordinary judiciary hierarchy judges have the power of constitu-tional review. For if an ordinary court finds some legal provision to be unconstitutional, it does not annul it but merely rejects applying it any longer. The legal provision continues to be in force even when it is "dor-mant", that is, when its execution cannot be enforced through the court. Therefore, it may be claimed that the ordinary court empowered to consti-tutional review does not take over the authority of the legislation; it neither makes nor repeals laws.

The case is different with Constitutional Courts. The mandate of the jus-tices concerns directly the control of legal norms, and it includes the power to strike down norms found to be unconstitutional. This once again con-fronts us with the question whether the institution of constitutional review is compatible with popular sovereignty. How could the Constitutional Court strike down laws, once it is true that it must function within the framework of laws?

The reply that first recommends itself runs as follows: the Court's mandate is to examine the existence or lack of coherence between some contested provisions and the constitution; the body annuls laws only if they violate the provisions of the constitution. Therefore, the judges examine in the cases brought before them the relation between two decisions both made by the elected representatives of the people—one lower-order (legislative) and one higher-order (constituent) decision. What overrules the lower-order parliamentary decision is not the judgment of the Court but the fact that it is incompatible with the higher-order parliamentary decision; the Court's ruling merely establishes the fact of the conflict and its practical consequences.

Therefore, striking down legislation by the Court does not violate the principle of popular sovereignty, as long as the Court does no more than establish the conflict between the lower-order and the higher-order parliamentary decisions.

It may appear obvious to add that constitutional review is consistent with popular sovereignty only if the law struck down by the Court is in conflict with the constitution and only with the constitution. The principle of popular sovereignty is violated if the higher-order legislative decision excludes the lower-order one only if supplemented by further premises, by such premises, that is, that are given to the Court not by the constitution makers (nor by the consensus in public opinion) but by itself. Only such a practice of constitutional review is consistent with the principle of popular sovereignty which merely applies the constitutional provisions issued by the Parliament and supplements the text of the constitution at most with generally accepted concepts and theorems. If the striking down of some law requires resorting to certain theorems that go beyond these and are also contested, then the conflict established by the Court is in fact not between a higher-order and a lower-order parliamentary decision but between a higher-order parliamentary decision supplemented by convictions not codified by the Parliament and a lower-order parliamentary decision. And this—the conclusion seems compelling—does indeed violate the principle of popular sovereignty.

In order that the Court does not transgress the authority which is compatible with democracy, it must confront laws and other legal provisions with that constitution that it received from the representatives of the people. It would seem·that this is not what the substantive reading does. No matter whether it rests on moral, structural or any other considerations, it chooses between a number of different, mutually exclusive beliefs, which are all equally compatible with the text to be interpreted. If this is really the case, and if the above reasoning is tenable, then the substantive reading is in conflict with the principle of popular sovereignty even if it does not amount to amending the constitution, at least when the Court strikes down laws on such grounds.

Thus, constitution making by the Court would be only one extreme case of rulings that violate popular sovereignty. Popular sovereignty is also violated if the Court—mandated by the constitution-making body—does no more than strike down some decision of the legislature by citing such controversial considerations that were not provided by the legislature. The objection thus reformulated is more general and therefore less easily tackled than the one addressed in the previous chapter, because it is valid even if the substantive reading leaves the written text of the constitution unaffected. We must now address this objection.

In so doing, we may pursue two different strategies. One may either accept without further argument that substantive readings violate the principle of popular sovereignty, and then proceed to show that constitutional review need not satisfy this principle. Or one may try to show that there is no necessary conflict between the principle of popular sovereignty and striking down legislation on the basis of substantive readings.

In the first case, the reasoning would run as follows: according to a generally accepted belief, in democracies every political decision must satisfy the requirements of popular sovereignty. There are certain issues, however, in which more important moral interests are at stake, which take precedence over the demands of popular sovereignty, i.e. the principles of such a treatment that is due to every individual simply in virtue of being a human person. If it is possible to show that the decisions made by elected representatives tend to violate these principles, then we can establish that the demands of popular sovereignty may be in conflict with such moral requirements that are prior to them. In such a conflict, popular sovereignty must yield. Therefore, if the Court is precisely in the business of protecting such a treatment that is due to every human person, then its practice need not satisfy the requirements of popular sovereignty.

The other strategy is the exact reverse of the former one; instead of trying to limit the range of the legitimate validity of the principle of popular sovereignty, it attempts to show that popular sovereignty is consistent with constitutional review even when the latter rests on a substantive reading of the constitution. To put it in a stronger form, popular sovereignty allows, while democracy demands, substantive constitutional review.

In what follows, I will examine both strategies. First I will discuss the thesis that constitutional review legitimately deviates from the demands of popular sovereignty. As it was already noted, this position rests on the well-known hypothesis that democratic decision making practices frequently come into conflict with the principles of a treatment due to human individuals. It would follow from this that the ultimate decision should be removed from the authority of elected representatives in all questions that concern liberty, human dignity, equality before the law, the prohibition of discrimination, and the like. Such explanations regard constitutional review as an extra-democratic institution, and constitutional democracy as a compromise between two colliding, though equally commendable values.[59]

Then I will proceed to examine the alternative strategy. This, too, regards the practice of striking down legislation based on substantive readings as a restraint on democratic decision making practice, but as such a restraint that is required by democracy itself and which therefore is in a complex relation with the principle of popular sovereignty, but not in one of conflict. The question it tries to answer is the following: What is it that democratic communities really try to achieve and yet are incapable of achieving, unless they tie their own hands, and what is the role of constitutional review in the democratic practice of self-binding?[60]

The constraints to be discussed are the provisions of the constitution. Therefore, it must be discussed first and foremost what difference it makes to democratic politics that constitutional constraints are imposed upon it. Then, we must proceed to examine why it is reasonable to make it the business of a judicial body to oversee that public authorities respect these constitutional constraints. Thus, I will assess the role performed by the constitution itself in the two strategies.

What is a constitution, then?

When the elected representatives adopt a constitution, they in fact restrain their own freedom of decision making. They impose such constraints on the republic that bind primarily the legislature itself rather than the authorities and persons subordinated to the legislature. From the point of view of the latter, it is indifferent whether their freedom of action is restrained by the constitution or by some other ordinary law; for them, the provisions of law are no less unalterable realities than the constitutional provisions. From the point of view of the legislators, on the other hand, the difference is indeed crucial. They are not bound by their own earlier legislation. When they pass a new law, they do not have to take into account the old laws; should there be a conflict between the new and the old piece of legislation, the new one automatically overrules the earlier one. By contrast, they may not make such laws that are in conflict with the constitution, nor pursue such a procedure that violates the provisions of the constitution. The provisions of the constitution are of a higher order than those of ordinary law. In case of a conflict, it is always the constitution that overrides the law that collides with it, and never the other way around.

One might want to say that the constitution stipulates an institutional status quo. It creates public authorities and offices (such as the Parliament, the government or the president of the republic, etc.). It distributes competences (the Parliament makes laws and approves the budget, etc.). It establishes procedures for the selection of the members of these bodies, for summoning their sessions and for their decision making processes (parliamentary representatives are elected by the voters every four years through universal, secret and direct ballot; the opening session of the newly elected Parliament is summoned by the president, otherwise it is the business of the speaker of the Parliament to summon ordinary legislative periods and individual sessions; a simple majority is required for the adoption of ordinary laws). It makes prohibitions (for instance, that no party may exercise public authority directly), and establishes the principles of treating human beings, which the state must respect and make respected (equality before the law, prohibition of discrimination, fundamental rights).

Yet the fact itself that the constitution creates an institutional status quo does not by itself mark it off from ordinary legal codes. The latter, too, stipulate a status quo, once they are adopted. The difference is that a status quo pinned down by an ordinary law is relatively easy to alter. All it takes to alter it is that one more than the half of all representatives supports the change. The proponents and opponents of the status quo are in an almost symmetrical position.[61] Disregarding the exceptional cases of minority governance, the government usually commands the parliamentary support necessary for changing the status quo, should it find it desirable to do so.

Of course, the constitution itself is not meant to last forever. It would contradict the principle of popular sovereignty if the constitutional provisions could never, under any circumstances, be amended.[62] There are procedures in place to change the constitution; in this respect, what distinguishes constitutions from the other rules of the system is that the constitution is the only set of rules that contains its own amendment rules.[63] But the constitutional status quo is given special weight by the fact that the rules of amendment upset the symmetry, in favor of the adherents of the status quo.

To amend the constitution, it is not sufficient that just one more than as many representatives votes for the amendment as would be necessary to reject the amendment. The change of the constitutional status quo requires a special majority—in the Republic of Hungary, two-thirds of all representatives. To sustain the status quo, by contrast, it is sufficient that a certain minority—in the Republic of Hungary, one-third of all representatives—does not support the change.[64] It is very rarely (even less likely than minority governance) that a government commands such a majority in the Parliament that it may amend the constitution without the consent of at least a part of the opposition.

In constitutional democracies, parliamentary omnipotence (discussed in Section 1.1) is an unattainable goal. It is the representatives authorized to constitution making who prevent the legislature from changing all the aspects of the status quo by simple majority.

This is the primary fact that we must understand. What is the point of a constitutional status quo? What purpose do the constitution makers serve by tying the hand of future legislators? Once we possess the answer to these questions, we may proceed to examinine the use of judicial review. Why is it good that the constitution makers granted to a judicial body the power to enforce the provisions of the constitution ?

3.2. "THE TYRANNY OF THE MAJORITY"

According to the conventional explanation, democratic decision making is the same as decision making by simple majority; and then, nothing prevents majority decisions from violating the fundamental moral interests of individuals. A person who is humiliated by the state, arbitrarily deprived of her liberty, forced to remain silent about her conscientious beliefs, or is discriminated against because of her origin, religion, ethnic group, gender or color, is subjected to no ordinary burdens. These are specifically grave damages that ruin her personality, self-esteem, dignity and capacity to lead her life autonomously. By contrast, these damages are treated by majority decisions as just any other damages; the voting system has no means for differential weighing. Every person has one and only one vote; when aggregating the votes, it is impossible to measure how important is the interest that moti-vates one or another vote. The weaker interests of many voters might pre-vail over the stronger interests of a lesser number of voters. It may even occur that the many sacrifice some of the most pressing, morally significant claims of the few for the sake of marginal advantages.

Furthermore, the burdens and benefits arising from acts that violate moral interests are typically distributed to different, well-distinguishable groups of people. Those who bear the costs do not enjoy the advantages and vice versa. Thus, the majority might easily disregard the losses from their decision.

Therefore, minorities might be secure in democratic regimes only if the majority is strongly motivated to avoid such collective decisions that, while being favorable for it, incur grave, morally relevant burdens to others. For the democratic decision to violate the fundamental moral interests of the minority it is sufficient that the majority be simply indifferent or neglectful with respect to the concerns of the minorities. Sometimes, however, the case is not that the majority is characterized by a mere disregard towards minor-ity interests. It might be rather positively hostile to minority customs, be-liefs and culture, and might strive to suppress or eliminate the hated "other-ness" from its environment. It was first and foremost such cases that James Madison, and in his wake Alexis de Tocqueville and John Stuart Mill, had in mind when they coined the expression "the tyranny of the majority".[65]

Their thesis might be immediately generalized: the voting procedures of democracy (one person one vote; the smallest majority carries the day) plus the plausible assumption that human individuals are no more altruistic in their role as voters than they are in other decision making situations,[66] and finally that there be such decisions that affect the fundamental moral inter-ests of a minority group distinct from those who enjoy the advantages from the decision.

In this manner, the constitutional entrenchment of treatment due to hu-man individuals could be justified by the shortcomings of principle of de-mocratic political regimes. Since the majority tends to sacrifice even the most fundamental moral interests of the minority, these interests must be removed from the scope of majority decisions. Popular sovereignty must yield where the domain of endangered moral interests begin. These are so important that they take precedence over the interest of popular sovereign-ty. They must therefore be protected by the constitution, and the ultimate authority in enforcing constitutional provisions must reside with such pub-lic officials who are neither elected by the majority nor accountable for their decisions to it.

In this conception, constitutional democracy brings about a compromise between mutually incompatible ultimate values. We have reason to approve of popular sovereignty as well as individual liberty and dignity. These two families of values might not be simultaneously and fully realized. One must concede either from the one or from the other, or from both. The desirable balance is established by the coupling of democracy with constitutionalism.

Majority decisions are incapable of assessing the kind of moral interests the state must respect and protect. These must be removed from the ordinary democratic decision making procedure (this is what happens when a special majority is required for the adoption or amendment of the constitution), and their protection must be made the business of some aristocratic body (in Hungary, this is said to be the Constitutional Court).

If this view is tenable, then the substantive interpretations of the constitution—including their most controversial version, the moral reading—are not excluded by the argument from popular sovereignty. The principle of popular sovereignty is valid but limitable; in assessing constitutional review, it is overruled by the requirement of protecting the moral rights of individuals.[67]

The theory of the "tyranny of the majority" carries some plausibility, because it articulates well-established facts (for constitutional review does indeed frequently protect unpopular causes), and arranges these facts in an intelligible relationship with well-established facts about democratic politics (for it does in fact frequently occur that a majority decision violates the fundamental interests of the minority) and with separation of powers characteristic of constitutional regimes (for judges do not bear political responsibility, and the voters cannot punish them for their rulings). Nevertheless, this theory is open to criticism from a number of aspects.

On the one hand, its consequences are more extensive than its proponents would like to allow. Such an unrecognized consequence is that compromising on popular sovereignty involves compromising on moral principles that govern the treatment of individuals. This is because the principle of popular sovereignty rests on the principle of moral equality. A person who was not elected by the members of the community from among their own ranks might not issue laws for the community because the lawmakers may not stand above the law subjects. Thus, if the violation of popular sovereignty is justified by invoking the fundamental moral interests of individuals, then one of the individuals' fundamental moral interests is allowed to overrule another such fundamental moral interest.

Furthermore, it may occur—or even appear desirable—that the constitution itself is adopted and amended in such a procedure that violates the principle of popular sovereignty. After all, what gives constitutional provisions their privileged significance in the "tyranny of the majority" theory is that these provisions protect the fundamental moral interests of individuals where the individuals whose moral interests are being threatened are in the minority. If it were permissible that the collective decisions affecting such interests are made in a way that deviates from the requirements of popular sovereignty, then it must also be permissible that the relevant provisions of the constitution be made and amended in a way that deviates from those requirements. If not the popular sovereignty, then what would block the move of giving constitution-making power to an aristocratic chamber, whose members are delegated, say, by the doctors of natural law from among their own ranks?

Someone could reply that if there is such an arrangement that secures the constitutional entrenchment of the moral rights of minorities as well as constitution making by doctors of natural law, and at the same time satisfies the requirements of popular sovereignty, then one should prefer this arrangement, because it combines the protection of the values of popular sovereignty and of individual rights better than aristocratic constitution making. And if the power to adopt and amend the constitution is trusted to elected representatives and at the same time bound to a qualified majority, then both families of values might be satisfied simultaneously. Popular sovereignty is sustained while the minority is given sufficient guarantees that its fundamental moral interests will be respected; the constitution could not so much as be adopted without the majority reaching an agreement with the minority, to begin with.

However, this answer is unsatisfactory. First of all, one or another minority could be left out of the constitutional agreements, for instance the very tiny ones, the politically unorganized ones, and the ones that are subject to prejudices even by members of other minorities.[68] The requirement of a qualified majority enhances the chances of creating a morally commendable constitution, but it does not guarantee it.

Second, what the fundamental moral interests of individuals consist in is not a matter of psychological dispositions but of moral judgment. The question is not what sort of treatment the individuals actually demand for themselves but rather what sort of treatment it is right for the state to grant to them, and what sort of treatment the individuals should demand. Representative politics, however, is guided by the former rather than by the latter. Candidates compete for votes, and the voters cast their votes for the candidate whose program and practical actions promise them the most, given their preferences. They cast their ballot in accordance with the sort of state of affairs they actually prefer rather than in accordance with the social state of affairs it would be right for them to prefer.[69] It may occur that the minority itself fails to stand up for the rights due to its own members as human individuals—and then, there is nothing left to guarantee that the constitution would be made in accordance with these rights.

We have good reasons to assume, therefore, that the composition and conduct of the constituent assembly would be more favorable if they were not elected by the citizenry but delegated by the chamber of the doctors of natural law from among their own ranks. But we would not accept this, and the "tyranny of the majority" account is not capable of saying why it is unacceptable; it would follow from this theory that it is unreasonable to stick to its democratic alternative.

The case of the Constitutional Court is similar. The justices are certainly not elected representatives. Nevertheless, they are not entirely insulated from the democratic process, for they are authorized by the elected representatives. This solution is far from being perfect; the selection of judges is often decided by inter-partisan deals that disregard the abilities and the background and constitutional views of the candidates. Possibly the makeup of our Constitutional Court would be much more favorable if its members were elected not by the Parliament but, once again, by the chamber of natural law doctors. But we would find this equally unacceptable. We insist on selection by the Parliament or some other democratic procedure, which makes the justices the delegates of elected representatives. And the "tyranny of the majority" account is incapable of giving an account of why this is preferable to the aristocratic arrangement even if it is less efficient than the latter.

There is a fourth disquieting consequence of the theory of the "tyranny of the majority". If democratic politics is in principle incapable of identifying the principle of the treatment due to every individual, and if therefore the protection of moral rights tolerates or even requires the introduction of such procedures that violate popular sovereignty, and furthermore, if these procedures are centered around constitutional review (as is the case in more and more constitutional democracies), while constitution making itself is the business of elected representatives, then there are two possibilities. The first possibility is to declare that, since constitution making itself is a political decision, and the rights of certain minorities might be violated even by decisions made by special majorities, therefore the text of the constitution might not determine the limits of possible judicial review. To the contrary, the judicial interpretation of the constitution furnishes the "safe measure" for assessing the text approved by the constitution makers. It is within the power of the Court to decide whether the adopted constitution is acceptable or not. In other words, one possible consequence of the theory of the "tyranny of the majority" is that we are brought to adopt the natural law position, which was rejected in the previous chapter.

Or, alternatively, we persist in rejecting the natural law position. But this may be made compatible with the "tyranny of the majority" account only if we accept that constitution making—although it belongs within the range of democratic political decisions—may be capable of identifying the principles of treatment due to human individuals. However, if it is possible to identify these principles through democratic decisions, then the theory of the "tyranny of the majority" is self-defeating, because it entails something the denial of which is presupposed by it.[70]

In sum, the consequences of the "tyranny of the majority" account are much more extensive than was foreseen by the proponents of the theory.

At the same time, this theory is incapable of accounting for every feature of constitutionalism. While on the one hand it is too general, on the other hand it is not general enough.

First of all, the constitution and the guardianship of the constitution comprise more than the principles of such a treatment that is due to human individuals—for instance, they include the basic scheme of government—but the "tyranny of the majority" account is applicable only for the protection of moral interests of individuals. What would make it reasonable that constitutional decisions requiring a special majority should be made about the most important institutions of the state, their competences and the way their offices are being filled, and entrusted with the power to review the acts that are meant to apply these decisions? The theory of the "tyranny of the majority" has no answer to these questions.

Second, the argument is not inclusive enough even with respect to the range of moral interests demanding constitutional protection. It is applicable only for those cases where the persons suffering the disadvantages of majority decisions are easily distinguishable from the ones enjoying their advantages. By contrast, it is not only such decisions that threaten the principles of treatment due to human individuals—as I will try to show in the next sections. The constitution protects the fundamental moral rights of individuals not only against discriminatory restraints but against illegitimate intrusions of all kinds, including the ones that concern those belonging to the majority no less than members of the minority. It secures the right to life, bodily integrity, freedom of speech, conscience, assembly and association, and to privacy for everyone, not only for the minority. Why is this necessary in representative democracies, where lawmaking is under the control of the majority? The "tyranny of the majority" account has no answer to this question.

To sum up, the justification of constitutional review might not rest on the thesis of the "tyranny of the majority" because this thesis has unacceptable consequences as well as consequences that are excluded by its own premises. We must look for another justificatory strategy.

3.3. THE POWER OF SELF-BINDING: ANALOGIES FROM INDIVIDUAL ACTION

The "tyranny of the majority" account of judicial review holds that when a Court strikes down legislation on the ground that the law conflicts with a substantive interpretation of a constitutional provision, the decision violates the principles of democracy, but there are circumstances under which democracy must yield to some other—weightier—moral interest. The defense of judicial review that I will outline in this section and Sections 3.5 and 3.6 will be based on a different sort of claim. My thesis will be that there is no conflict between judicial review based on substantive interpretation and democracy.

The no-conflict thesis has two different versions. The first version holds that judicial review is necessary to keep the political process democratic. Whether or not it meets the requirements of democratic procedure is immaterial; what matters is that the rest of the political process cannot meet those requirements unless coupled with the institution of judicial review. For example, elections fail to serve as vehicles of democratic decision making unless the voters are in a position to make free and informed choices; in the absence of freedom of expression, assembly and association, the conditions for free and informed electoral choice do not obtain; the majority, however, has a dangerous propensity to infringe upon individual freedoms and rights; constitutionalism and judicial review are necessary means to constrain such kind of invasions; therefore, constitutionalism and judicial review are necessary for upholding democracy.

In this version, the no-conflict thesis is not radically different from the thesis of the "tyranny of the majority". It holds that there is no conflict between protecting individual rights and protecting democracy, because individual rights are necessary conditions of the democratic character of politics. But it does not exclude the possibility of a conflict between the procedures required by the aim of securing individual rights and the procedures required by democratic principles. Or, more exactly, defenders of this version of the no-conflict thesis exclude the possibility of the conflict by way of definition: they claim that the issue of the democratic or non-democratic nature of a procedure depends on the outcomes of following the procedure rather than on its structural properties.[71] But this is question-begging. Suppose the only way to secure individual rights in a particular society is to allow another state to intervene in their defense. Regular interference from the outside may be a successful way to uphold the rights necessary for the rest of the political process to be democratic. But it is blatantly violating the principle of democratic self-government. So it looks more promising to explore the second version of the no-conflict thesis.

In this second version, the thesis holds that judicial review does indeed meet the requirements of democratic procedure. It is the community itself that ties its own hands by way of adopting a constitution that it is not possible to amend by simple majority, and it is the community that confers the power of enforcing the constitution on the judiciary. Call this the conception of *constitutional pre-commitment*.[72] This conception consists of two claims. It holds, first, that by adopting a constitution and by granting the judiciary the power to strike down unconstitutional legislation, the political community ties its own hands. Second, it maintains that constitutional self-binding is an enabling device: by constraining itself, the community makes itself capable of reaching important aims that would otherwise remain beyond its reach.

How can one enhance one's own powers by disabling oneself? When it comes to the discussion of constitutional self-binding, this question is clouded by a number of perplexing difficulties. The making and enforcing of a constitution are collective ventures. But the collective agency responsible for them is not a supra-personal person with attitudes, intentions or actions of its own: it has no existence beyond that of individual persons related to each other by mutual expectations, by attitudes and intentions directed to common activities, and by interlocking acts that they try to coordinate between themselves in such a way as to reach their aims together. Can it make sense at all to maintain that such an entity binds itself? This question has three aspects.

First, constitutions rarely if ever command unanimous consent. In general, they are adopted against the opposition of a more or less substantial minority. And when already in force, they are enforced against disagreement. How can one claim that those in disagreement with a constitution participate in a procedure of binding themselves? Is not it, rather, the case that they are bound by the decision of other people?

Second, constitutions are intended to govern the lives of many generations. The generations that come after the constitution is adopted do not take part in the constitution-making process. How can one claim that when a later generation is bound by the constitution, that is a case of self-binding? Should we not rather, say that one generation ties the hands of another?

Finally, ordinary members of a society do not take part either in constitution making or in legislation. Legislatures pass laws and Constituent Assemblies adopt constitutions. Members of one body (the Constituent Assembly) tie the hands of the members of another body (the legislature). How can one speak, nevertheless, about self-binding in this case and, particularly, about the ordinary members of society tying their own hands?

These are hard questions. But suppose the idea of enhancing one's powers by binding oneself does not make sense in the first place. If so, there is no reason to engage ourselves in an examination of these questions. So it is better to set aside the complexities of collective action for the time being, and to see whether or not self-binding is a meaningful enabling device in the domain of individual action. This is what I want to do in the present section. Restricting the focus on the one-person case will help us to reveal the conditions under which self-binding can be an enabling device rather than an act merely reducing one's options. These are the problems I want to explore in the present section. Sections 3.5 and 3.6 will extend the idea of self-binding from the case of individual action to the case of the collective action of adopting a constitution. Section 3.7 will show how constitutional self-binding involves the practice of judicial review.

Pre-commitment is an act aiming to determine in advance one's future acts. As Jon Elster has put it, "To bind oneself is to carry out a certain decision at time t_1 in order to increase the probability that one will carry out another decision at time t_2."[73] The action carried out at t_1 may consist in hardening one's resolve, as when Paul decides, while driving to a party, that under no circumstances will he accept more than two drinks. Such kind of resolution is not very likely to be effective. Paul's own intention is internal to his self; he can change it later on, and he knows in advance that once he has had two drinks he will be tempted to do so. He needs some safeguard that he will not be able to act according to his changed intention. And the safeguard must be beyond his control at the time of his stay at the party. Pre-commitment consists in setting up some obstacle at time t_1 that prevents one from acting in certain ways at time t_2, and that one has no power to remove at t_2. "The effect of carrying out the decision at t_1 must be to set up some causal process in the external world", Elster is saying.[74] Suppose what Paul really wants to avoid is not drinking too much but driving home in a state of drunkenness. In the house of his friend where the party is held there is a safe with a delaying device. Upon his arrival, Paul locks up the keys of his car in the safe. No matter how hard he will try in the night, he will not be able to have access to the keys.

Is it necessary for pre-commitment that the external obstacle consists in a causal process? In the absence of a safe with a timer, Paul could give the keys to Peter, his friend, taking his promise not to return them over the night. In this case, the act of pre-commitment operates through Peter's resolution at t_2 to honor the promise given at t_1. This is not a physical mechanism, the outcome will depend on Peter's judgment and decision.[75] In more complex cases, this might cast doubt on whether, by carrying out his mandate, the second person executes the intention of the first. I will return to this question later on. In this simple example Peter is just a substitute for a physical device. We can safely claim that by denying the request to return the keys, he executes his friend's intention. So it is not conceptually necessary that pre-commitments operate through mere causal mechanisms. An individual can pre-commit himself by engaging another individual to serve for external obstacle that prevents him from doing at t_2 what he wants at t_1 not to do at t_2.

But what makes it rational for an individual to pre-commit himself for future contingencies? Consider Paul again. Driving to the party, he is determined not to drive home in a state of drunkenness. But he knows from experience that once he has had more than two drinks he will not resist the temptation to drive home himself. Perhaps he will open his car, start it and yet think, even as he starts the car, that he should not. His beliefs and preferences remain constant from t_1 to t_2. Yet at t_2 he will not act upon them. He will act irrationally, against his best judgment. Such action displays weakness of will. The knowledge of his weakness provides Paul with a reason to pre-commit himself against having a third drink.[76]

The case is different when the agent's preference ranking changes over time. At t_1 Paul prefers not to have a third drink at t_2, but at t_2 he prefers having it. If he foresees such a change in his ordering of the options available to him at t_2, he has a reason to pre-commit himself at t_1. But there is an important difference between this case and the previous one. In that case, it is rational for Paul to expect himself to endorse, even at t_2, the decision he took at t_1 to eliminate the option of accepting a third drink at t_2. Whatever the time perspective from where he should look at his pre-commitment, it appears as the best choice he could take at t_1. In the case of the reversal in Paul's preference orderings, the same person ranks his options at t_2 differently depending on where he looks at them from. His pre-commitment has to be justified against the background of a natural question: Why should Paul-at-t_2 comply with the will of Paul-at-t_1 rather than doing what he currently wants most to do?

In our example, this question lends itself to an obvious answer. At t_1 Paul is sober, in full command of his decision making capacities. At t_2 Paul is drunk, and his capacity correctly to foresee the consequences of having yet another drink is significantly reduced. Thus, he has good reason at t_1 to consider his actual preference to represent his genuine will against his ordering at t_2. Elster suggests an interesting test for this distinction. We have to look at which self tries to bind the other one: "If we observe the sober self trying to bind the drunken self but never observe the drunken self trying to bind the sober self, we may reasonably identify the former self with the person's real interest."[77]

A further feature of this second case is worth mentioning. Although Paul's preference ranking changes from t_1 to t_2 the reversal is temporary. The day after the party Paul will wish that he had not had more than two drinks. So Paul-at-t_1 is reasonable to assume that Paul-at-t_3 will regret having accepted the third drink. The expectation of future regret justifies the decision to pre-commit oneself. In such cases, pre-commitment stabilizes action against a regrettable instability of preferences.

Sometimes, however, the preferences of the agent undergo a lasting shift. Suppose Jack likes vanilla ice cream, but soon after tasting it he always experiences some mild nausea. Although nausea is bad, Jack prefers licking the ice cream at the cost of enduring the after-effects to avoiding the after-effects at the cost of forsaking the pleasure of licking the ice cream. As the experience is repeated, however, the pleasure fades away, so that the rank ordering undergoes a permanent reversal. Does Jack have a reason to pre-commit himself against giving up vanilla ice cream? No, because the only reason for wanting the ice cream is that he wants it indeed. His life does not go worse if he stops wanting it. But not all preferences are of this nature. I have a less flourishing life if I fail to appreciate the value of friendship, for example, and therefore do not seek the company of friends. My life goes worse, in this case, because I fail to want what I should want. Ronald Dworkin calls what I should want my critical interests as opposed to my volitional interests the satisfaction of which is in my interest only because I want them.[78] Suppose now that one foresees a future change in one's preferences with regard to something that is in one's critical interest. One might abhor the change. If so, there might be a reason for one to pre-commit oneself against the effects of the future change.

Consider the celebrated story told by Derek Parfit: "[A] nineteenth century Russian…in several years, should inherit vast estates. Because he has socialist ideals, he intends, now, to give the land to the peasants. But he knows that in time his ideals may fade. To guard against this possibility, he does two things. He first signs a legal document which will automatically give away the land, and which can only be revoked with his wife's consent. He then says to his wife, 'If I ever change my mind, and ask you to revoke the document, promise me that you will not consent.'"[79]

Is the young nobleman rational to pre-commit himself against the (permanent) reversal of his attitudes towards the alternative of giving away or retaining his future estates? Certainly, he endorses his present desire and is ready to act upon it. But his approval of this desire goes beyond willingness to be moved by it. He is committed to this desire. He abhors the possibility that it may fade with time. And he wants what he now desires to come true in the future even if, at the time when this happens, he will not desire it any more.[80] And so the question is whether this commitment is rational to sustain against future preference changes.

Parfit's wording suggests that the changes do not respond to new reasons becoming accessible to the nobleman later in his life but to a fading away of his determination. If so, his pre-commitment is rational. There is nothing in the motivational set of his future self that could trump the reasons already available to him in his youth. But he cannot be sure that he will not encounter decisive reasons that would overrule his present determination. It would be incoherent to claim to know that there are no such reasons. So the young nobleman has to allow for the possibility that he will change his decision in good faith, reacting to a reason-based change in his convictions. Does this possibility rule out pre-commitment? I think it does in that version where a physical device could do the job as well as the intervention of a human person. It is not rational to ask his wife not to consent to the revoking of the document under any circumstances. But it makes sense to ask her to exercise her judgment. His socialist ideals are very important for the young nobleman; he cares about them, he is disposed "to be active in seeing to it that [they are] not abandoned or neglected".[81] Making it hard for himself to revise them or to give up their practical consequences fits naturally this commitment. The wife of the young nobleman is an intelligent person with a passionate love for justice and humanity. It is a reasonable safeguard against allowing the socialist ideals to be discarded too easily, that the legal document cannot be revoked without her consent, and that she promises not to consent unless he succeeds in convincig her that there is some fault either in the values that land distribution would promote or in land distribution as a policy to forward those values.

But, then, pre-commitment becomes less unproblematic as a case of self-binding. We are back with Jeremy Waldron's objection: the more the wife is allowed to deliberate and exercise her judgment, the more she is "capable of operating in ways that do not represent the intentions of the agent".[82]

But I think the objection, although persuasive, is mistaken. Suppose the husband asks his wife to employ her judgment when deciding about the fate of the legal document because he wants to make sure that the document will not be revoked. If this is his aim, then giving her a power of discretion is bad strategy. She may, after all, find that the newly accessible reasons do, in fact, overrule the original decision, and this outcome is contrary to the husband's intention. Her decision may be right, but it does not carry out his *will*.

However, if his intention is to reach a decision in the future that is as considered as possible, no matter what it should be, then so long as she applies her reason and judgment in a conscientious manner, the decision conforms to the original intention. It is the husband's will that is carried out by the wife's exercising the veto power obtained from him. This case, too, counts as one of self-binding. So the assessment of the wife's intervention will depend on which characterization of the husband's intention is accurate. I opt for the second. And, in any case, there are cases of delegating veto power with the intention of reaching considered decision, no matter what its outcome should be. In all such cases, it is legitimate to speak about self-binding.

In the stories discussed so far pre-commitment was made rational by the fact of a change of preferences through time. Sometimes, the preferences remain fixed, and a reversal of the standard temporal order between other variables causes the difficulty for planning and carrying out plans. For example, the normal temporal order of efforts and rewards is that the effort comes first and the reward is made available after it was duly expended. But the ordering may be the reverse one. Consider the famous toxin puzzle presented by Gregory Kavka. An eccentric billionaire approaches you with the following offer. If you intend, at midnight, to drink a disgusting but non-lethal toxin tomorrow afternoon, one million dollars will show up, tomorrow morning, on your bank account. You need not drink the toxin to receive the money; you have to intend to drink it. You are free to change your mind once you have the money. Clearly, it will be rational for you to change your mind. The toxin causes much pain, and at the time you are supposed to carry out your intention to drink it, there is no incentive to do so any more. Whatever you do now, the money is or is not on your bank account. Drinking the toxin cannot causally affect the transfer. The problem is that you foresee this at midnight. Because changing your mind at t_2 is rational, you indeed intend it at t_1. But, then, no matter how much you desire to receive the money, you cannot form the appropriate intention. You cannot intend at t_1 to drink the toxin at t_2 and, at the same time, intend at t_1 that you do not intend, at t_2, to carry out your original intention.[83]

Because Kavka's problem is a puzzle with intending, he makes the billionaire rule out self-binding as a means to get the agent off the hook. But he notes in passing that self-binding could be a way out of the puzzle. Suppose, he says, you sign a legal agreement that makes the one million transferable from your account to that of your least favorite political party, if you fail to drink the toxin. This will provide you with a sufficient incentive to carry out the intention tomorrow afternoon and, hence, to intend it at midnight.

In the toxin case, the normal ordering of efforts and rewards is undermined because the billionaire sets a prize directly on intention formation— a very unusual offer. But such reversals can be due to more ordinary circumstances. Buying and selling cars may be an example. The buyer is supposed to pay the price when he gets the car. But there might be many faults in the vehicle that cannot be immediately detected. Repairing these might be a very costly business. Perhaps the supplier is ready to take care of all repairs for free. But how would it be sufficient for the buyer to rely on such readiness? At the time the faults are detected, the price of the car will already have been fully paid. The supplier may have the intention now to undertake all the burdens related to repairing the car in the future, but his intention might change with time. This circumstance could prevent the deal from coming into effect. One way to overcome such obstacles is for the supplier to issue a legal document that guarantees free repair of all faults not due to an accident for a reasonably long period.

This example is special in an important respect. Self-binding by the supplier is part of an interpersonal action where the outcome depends on the moves of more than one agent. The supplier wants to sell cars and, in order to succeed in this, he has to give rise to secure expectations in the potential buyers. Pre-commitment is a means of favorably influencing the expectations of other people. Even so, this last example does still belong to the domain of individual rationality. One binds oneself in order to make it more likely to reach a personal aim that presupposes appropriate conduct by others.

The proper domain of our discussion is different. We will assume that a group of people jointly bind themselves in order to reach some common aim.

3.4. COMMUNAL AGENCY

In contemporary political theory the pre-commitment view is presented as an extension from the interpretation of individual action. Historically, however, the idea of self-binding originated with an interpretation of collective political agency. Rousseau was the first to maintain that under certain conditions the laws of a community are devices through which community members bind themselves in order to become free. It was this idea that Immanuel Kant translated into a conception of individual autonomy.

Rousseau's problem was how, if members of a community disagree on what laws to make, the law adopted by majority vote can be a means of communal self-binding rather than a means by which one part of the community binds the other. His answer boils down to the claim that if the majority decision is met under appropriate conditions, the result of the vote counting dissolves the disagreement prior to it.

The law of a community, Rousseau can be reconstructed as maintaining, purports to regulate action in such a way as to forward the common good. The questions regarding the common good admit of answers that are right or wrong. When casting their ballot, citizens are supposed to express their judgment on which of the alternative options represents the right answer. They have a decisive reason to vote for the option they believe to be the right choice, because they have a decisive reason to want the right answer to prevail. Note the difference between voting for what one believes to be the right answer and desiring that what is, indeed, the right answer, prevails. One has nothing else but one's warranted beliefs to act upon, yet at the same time, one is conscious of the fact that those beliefs are fallible. What a voter has a decisive reason to want to be law is not what he believes to be the right answer but what, in fact, is the right answer. Now, according to Rousseau, the majority is more likely to pass a correct judgment on the issues that admit right and wrong answers than the minority, or such is the case if the voters form their judgment independently of each other. Actually, Rousseau claims that if, indeed, the voters cast their ballot with the bona fide aim to promote the common good and undisturbed by the persuasive discourse of demagogues, then the majority vote will unmistakably represent the common good. Under such conditions, the majority decision expresses the General Will, because it is what all the voters have an overriding reason to will. The outcome of the vote is a test that reveals for all, including those who end up being in the minority, what their genuine will consists in.[84]

We can imagine in Rousseau's vein that after the result of the vote count is published, a second ballot is taken on the same issue. If he is right, then this time the proposal is most likely to pass by unanimous agreement.

Clearly, it does not make any difference for the outcome of the vote whether the voting procedure is applied to popular referenda or to legislation by a representative body. If in the first case the re-vote yields a decision by unanimity, then so it must in the second case, too. Nevertheless, Rousseau believes that only the first is a case of self-binding. Even if the community comes to endorse the law, the approval is not sufficient to make the law a means of communal self-binding. The subject restrained by the law must be part of the agency that makes it. Only direct democracy is a system where freedom prevails. Representative systems are not unlike those of slavery, Rousseau concludes.

So Rousseau develops a critical theory that purports to show two things. First, wherever the law is made by agents other than the law subjects themselves, liberty is absent. Second, the absence of liberty is not due to the fact that legislation is a collective venture where a particular individual's contribution may not make a difference at all, but to the fact that it is delegated to a special body. A directly self-governing community is free, and so are all its individual members, including those whose ex ante will proves to be different from that of the majority.

This is a problematic conception. First, modern societies are too large and too complex to allow for legislation by direct popular vote. If Rousseau is right, we are doomed to be subjected to political slavery. Furthermore, Rousseau failed to show how direct popular vote, even if it could become the usual way of lawmaking, would take us into the realm of freedom. The claim that vote counting can serve as a test for the rightness of the voters' ex ante position cannot be sustained as a general thesis. The belief that the majority is more likely to pass a correct judgment on the issues up for decision holds under very restrictive assumptions only.[85] More often than not, the vote decides issues about which there is genuine disagreement or conflict of interest. So Rousseau's intuition that a community can be self-governing even if its members disagree on how to govern themselves needs a better-elaborated support. A more promising account seems to be implicit in what Ronald Dworkin calls "the communal conception of collective action".[86]

Dworkin opposes the communal conception to what he calls the statistical conception. According to the statistical view, an individual's act is part of the collective action if it has significant antecedent chance to make a difference for the outcome. For example, where the choice is between accepting and rejecting a proposal, each voter has three options: either to vote for, or to vote against, or else to abstain from the ballot. Voter X has a part in the collective choice, in the statistical sense, if ex ante she has a reason to believe that her own choice will have an impact on the outcome of the vote. X has no part in the collective choice, in the statistical sense, if whatever she should do (abstain, cast her ballot for the proposal, cast her ballot against it), the outcome is expected to remain the same. Now Dworkin maintains that even in this second case, an individual might have a part in the collective action if collective action is understood in the communal sense.

In order to see how this is possible, we have first to consider the nature of collective political action. The government of a country amounts to much more than the acts of those who occupy the official positions. It entails, minimally, the fact that a sufficiently large majority of the governed go along with the laws and other binding directives. There is no government without the requisite degree of compliance on the part of the subjects. So the existence of a government and the carrying out of its plans involves the action of the many. The acts of the individual subjects are not independent of each other, though. It is not only the case that they are coordinated by the same official directives. Individuals engage in law-abiding action in the expectation that a sufficiently large number of others will do so. In other words, the subjects' intentions are conditional on each other. Each intends to carry out the required action on condition that enough others have the same intention. And the availability of the requisite interdependent intentions must be public knowledge.

Now individual intentions are interdependent in many various types of interaction. Participants of market transactions, for example, form intentions that mutually depend on each other. But market transactions do not constitute communities. In order for a group of interacting individuals to form a community, they must believe that they do so. It must be the case, first, that its members consider themselves as belonging to it and, second, that those who consider themselves to belong to it mutually recognize each other as belonging to it. Individuals interacting on the market are not united by such a shared belief and by mutual recognition. Individuals participating in collective political action may be united in this way. In this case, thus, we can speak about shared intentions and a joint agency. Members speak about their joint agency as "us".

But, Dworkin says, a de facto community is not necessarily a true community. A subject of a state might not have a genuine part in the processes of governing her country, whether or not she is recognized as "one of us" by the other subjects, if the government is not elected, or if she is deprived of the vote. She may be excluded from the class of those who can run for office, etc. Thus, the use of the first person plural does not entail that the subject is a member of a self-governing community. In order for the latter claim to be justified, a number of normative conditions must obtain (I will list these in a way slightly different from the enumeration by Dworkin).

Consider a society, S_1, where the following assumptions hold true. First, all the government offices are occupied by individuals who are either elected by the governed or appointed by elected officials. Second, all the non-elected officials are bound to act within the law made by elected officials. Third, the elected officials, although they enjoy a wide margin of discretion in choosing policies and means to carry these out, are accountable to the governed, who have the power to remove them from office, and have the freedom to express their views and to conduct public debates in order to make sure that they meet competent choices when it comes to the vote. Fourth, the office holders are selected from among the governed themselves; (virtually) all the governed have an equal right to run for office and to cast their vote in the elections, and the voting system treats all the voters in a fair manner. Finally, the rules of the regime constrain the government to treat all the governed with equal concern as bearers of interests, and to pay equal respect to them as autonomous persons.

In S_1 the government derives its mandate from the governed themselves, by way of a bottom-up authorization: the governed are able to make informed judgments on how they should be governed; they are able to constrain the government officials to act within the bounds of their judgments; and they are treated as equals as choosers of the office holders and as objects of the latters' actions. Compare now S_1 with S_2 where the government's authorization comes from outside the society of the governed, or the latter do not have the power to remove the rulers from office, or if they do, they are not able to make informed judgments on matters of governance, or where the equality conditions of S_1 fail to obtain. We would not say about S_2 that it is a self-governing society.

Now, even in S_1 the governmental decisions are met without direct participation of the governed. But here the political process as a whole lends itself to a characterization as that of self-government. And so in S_1 the governed are justified to consider themselves as participants in a complex process through which their society governs itself. Ordinary members of the society do not directly participate in the legislative process, but they do have the opportunity to participate in the wider political process that constrains legislation, and they are positioned as equals with regard to this process. Nobody has better ex ante chances to run for election and to cast a vote in the election, or to make her voice heard in other ways, or to have her interests treated with greater concern by the government, than anybody else.[87] Under these circumstances, the members of the society are justified to consider themselves as having their part in an ongoing process of collective self-government. They are justified to think and speak about the rules adopted by their officials as "our laws, the laws adopted by us". They are justified to think and speak in these terms even if their personal action did not make any difference for the outcome, and even if they disagree with some of the laws and voted for a candidate who promised to resist their adoption.

The view outlined here does not rely on the dubious assumption that the vote is a mechanism that automatically yields agreement. It is rather based on the idea of political community. As Dworkin has put it, "If I am a genuine member of a political community, its act is in some pertinent sense my act, even when I argued and voted against it, just as the victory or defeat of a team of which I am a member is my victory or defeat even if my own individual contribution made no difference either way."[88]

Thus, even if we drop Rousseau's unacceptable assumptions, the extension of the idea of self-binding from individual to collective action remains a workable project. But there are further steps to carry out for the analogy to be complete. In the case of the individual, the agency that is supposed to bind itself is given. The individual person's separateness and identity are matters of natural circumstance, not of social construction. Her spatio-temporal boundaries cannot be redrawn by social agreement or cultural convention: whatever their social and cultural environment, individuals think of their past or future states in the first person singular ("I had a headache yesterday evening", "I hope tomorrow I will not have headache"), and refrain from thinking about their selves in an expansive mood (they never say, for example, "I am lifting my hand" when someone else standing nearby is lifting his hand). Communities are different. Their temporal identity and spatial separation are social artifacts. Before asking the question as to whether a group of people is self-governing, we have to ask whether it is a unit about which the first question can be meaningfully asked.

Let a state be given together with its territorial domain. And let the conditions of political community obtain within that state. And suppose that, if so, then all the inhabitants of the state's territory are prepared to recognize any other inhabitant as "one of us". Under such circumstances the fact that the political community—unlike the individual person—is a social construct, does not raise any special difficulty. Although the mutual recognition that transforms a population into a community is a result of historical processes rather than being given as a natural circumstance, once the shared identity is there, it is no less real.

This view helps to put the problem of the intergenerational impact of constitutional constraints in perspective. Individual agents have their natural limits at birth and death. Those limits cannot be removed by a later person taking the place of the earlier one. Communal entities are not limited in this way. Their boundaries are social constructs not natural circumstances, whether in space or in time. The existence of a community can continue indefinitely so long as there are living human individuals who identify with them and who accept each other as sharing in this identity. When a father makes his will to take care of the future of his children, he does not believe (and is rational not to believe) that he is taking care of his own future. But the framers of a constitution can legitimately declare that they are securing justice and rights "for us" until the end of time, "us" meaning the community stretching over an indefinite number of generations to come. And the relationship works in the opposite direction as well. The generations living in the present can legitimately speak about the deeds of generations who were living in the past in the first person plural. "We Hungarians fought a war of independence against the Habsburgs in 1848/49": this sentence is legitimately uttered by people who did not live in the nineteenth century. It can be legitimately uttered even by people whose family ancestors were not Hungarians at the time of the war of independence. The Hungarian nation extends over those people in the present who are prepared to speak about the history of the Hungarians in the first person plural, together with those people in the past whose deeds the Hungarians now living remember as constituting that history (provided that they, too, were prepared to speak about that history in the first person plural).

An early, beautiful expression was given to this fact of historical continuity of communities in the famous statement of Edmund Burke, according to which society is "a partnership not only between those who are living, but between those who are living, those who are dead, and those who are to be born".[89] But if communities have such a historical dimension, then the fact that not all of those constrained by a constitution belong to the generation of the constitution makers is not more potentially damaging for the pre-commitment view than the fact that not all the members of the constitution-making generation take part in the sessions of the Constituent Assembly. "[I]t is more than likely", says Jeremy Waldron, "that the requisite sense of membership and community will extend across generations, so that in principle there is no difficulty about being bound by the decision of one's ancestors. So, if our forefathers deemed certain pre-commitments necessary, the mere fact that those pre-commitments are supposed to extend over time, and outlast those who enacted them, is not in itself a reason for not honoring them or for condemning them as incompatible with the idea of self-government."[90]

The upshot is that the transition from the domain of individual conduct to that of collective action does not make, in itself, the idea of self-binding inconsistent. But the collective acts of constitution making might have further properties that are damaging to the attempt to interpret the entrenchment of a constitution as an act of communal self-binding. In the next section I want to discuss some of these difficulties that seem to me decisive if valid.

3.5. CONSTITUTIONAL SELF-BINDING

The first is relatively easy to deal with. Here it is as raised by Jon Elster: "The individual who wants to bind himself can entrust his will to external institutions or forces, outside his control, that prevent him from changing his mind. But there is nothing external to society, barring the case of pre-commitment through international institutions with powers of enforcement."[91] This is a conceptual argument. Self-binding works through some external agency, physical or intentional. Constitutions are not entrusted to external (international) agencies for enforcement. Therefore, constitutions cannot serve as means of self-binding. Constitutional "pre-commitment" is no different from what an individual does when he hardens his resolve: it is not genuine pre-commitment because the agent who purports to bind itself is always in a position to undo the tie.

However, what matters for the individual to be able to bind herself is not that the agency she involves in her action is external to her but that it is outside her control. Externality is a requirement only because nothing internal to a person's intentional action is outside of her control. This is true in principle about societies as well. If a community is able to adopt a rule for its members, it is also able to repeal it. But it may not be able to repeal it easily. One way of constraining the community's power to amend its standing rules is to make the amendment conditional on the agreement of a very large majority, say four-fifths of the community members. The rule is even more firmly entrenched if the four-fifths must express their agreement on two or more occasions. Yet another way to constrain the amendment procedures consists in dividing the acts of amending between separate institutions and to provide these with incentives to check and counterbalance each other rather than to add up their forces easily. In the latter case, the constraints will be external to the relevant institutions, although not to society at large. In summary, because society is a complex collective agent, the means of its self-binding can be internal to it.

But here a new, although related, difficulty emerges. What looks like constitutional self-binding usually proceeds through a division and separation of powers. The legislature, the government and the judiciary do not tie their own hands: they tie each other's hands, according to rules set by a fourth power, the Constituent Assembly. So self-binding, at the level of society, may not be self-binding after all.[92]

The communal conception of collective agency is capable of dealing with this difficulty. For it, constitution making, judicial review and parliamentary control of the executive make part of a much wider web of activities that is communal self-government. The joint agency to which these activities are attributed is the community at large. It makes sense to claim that the political community ties its own hands by separating the branches of government and playing them out against each other to serve as mutual checks and balances. The Constituent Assembly does not bind itself but the other powers; the community, however, binds itself through the acts of the Constituent Assembly.

Let me address now a more serious objection, leveled against the conception of pre-commitment by Jeremy Waldron. Waldron's point is that there is a diversity of states of mind that might bring a person to entrust the enforcement of her intention to an external agency: sometimes she is firmly committed to the intention and wants to protect it against future deviation she knows she will regret later on at other times she acts under genuine uncertainty, or under the impact of changes of mind, etc. It is only in the first case that carrying out the request of the agent counts unmistakably as an act through which she binds herself, Waldron states. In the other cases, it rather seems like taking sides in an internal dispute. Therefore, Waldron maintains, in order to be able to speak about upholding another person's pre-commitment, we need to be able to draw "a clear line between the aberrant mental phenomena the pre-commitment was supposed to override, on the one hand, and genuine uncertainty, changes of mind, conversions, etc., on the other hand".[93]

This might be a relatively easy task where self-binding of an individual is at stake. But when it comes to the constitutional pre-commitment of an entire community, the dividing line becomes fuzzy. Any sufficiently large and complex society is pervaded by deep disagreements, and the controversies reach up to constitutional issues. Constitutional provisions are adopted against dissenting minorities; legislative proposals that arguably violate a constitutional provision are passed with the support of some who oppose the constitutional provision adopted earlier; the legislative enactment is found unconstitutional by a court against a minority of the judges holding that no morally acceptable reading of the constitutional provision would support that decision. "It is the same disagreement all the way through", Waldron says, "though the weight of opinion shifted back and forth."[94]

If so, then we might be unable to tell a case of preemptive rationality where an agent entrenches her decision taken at a "calm hour" against intertemporal inconsistencies from a case where opinions shift and majorities change. But, then, we are not justified to treat a constitutional constraint as a device that protects the genuine will of the community in face of decision making pathologies, Waldron maintains. We have rather to see it as "the artificially sustained ascendancy of one view in the polity over other views while the complex moral issues between them remain unresolved".[95]

This consideration lends special significance to the intergenerational dimension of constitutional pre-commitment. Suppose, Waldron says, the framers entrench a provision on free speech that reflects what they believe to be the correct view on the issue of expression. And suppose generations later the majority comes to see this view as utterly wrong given what they know about the media, electoral campaigns, and the like. It is possible for the members of the majority to "resist the pre-commitment characterization, not because they are overwhelmed by passion or anger, but because they disagree with the ideas about free speech that seemed plausible to their ancestors".[96]

To be sure, no community can be capable of constitutionally pre-committing itself unless it is divided by pervasive disagreements and conflicts of interest. If a conception of free speech is adopted by unanimity at t_1, and at

t_2 the people come to the unanimous view that the original conception was wrong, then it is impossible for the constitutional entrenchment of that conception to survive the judgment at t_2, because a community can repeal any constitutional provision by unanimity.[97] Disagreement and conflict of interest are necessary conditions for a society to be able to bind its future choices. So any interesting case of intertemporal inconsistency in communal intention and action is accompanied by disagreement over which of the conflicting intentions should be carried out. It does not follow, however, that in all such cases the intertemporal inconsistency boils down to a mere shift in the opinions, so that if we succeed in describing the disagreement correctly we have said all that can be said about the case.

In what follows I will try to show that, as a matter of fact, this is not so. There are independent reasons to believe that an important asymmetry holds between the moments of constitution making on the one hand and those of legislative action and of ordinary politics on the other, the first being more favorable for "calm", "lucid" reflection and deliberation than the latter. If, indeed, it is the case that the framers of the constitution are more likely to reach decisions that the community has reason to endorse in the long run than ordinary legislators are, then it is rational for the community to tie its own hands by way of making a constitution. And if it is the case that ordinary legislatures are unlikely to reach the agreement that is needed to undo the constitutional tie, then self-binding is indeed possible. Let us see, first, whether the constitutional moment is more likely to be a "calm moment" than the moments of legislative battles.

At times, democratic societies are carried away by panic or hysteria. Decisions taken in such pathological states of mind are regretted later on, and so the community is rational to preempt them. Nobody denies either that such phenomena do indeed occur or that it is rational for the community to pre-commit itself against them. But the possibility of collective panic or hysteria is too narrow a basis for a theory of constitutional pre-commitment to stand on, so in what follows I will not pursue this line of argument. Rather, I will start from the observation that for a collective decision to be irrational, it is not necessary that the participants of the decision making process are in an irrational state of mind, one by one. A choice can be collectively irrational even if it is rational from the point of view of all the participating individuals, given certain circumstances.

Suppose the circumstances that provide for collective irrationality are pervasive facts of ordinary legislation and politics. Suppose they can be remedied by subjecting ordinary legislation and politics to constitutional constraints. And suppose a constituent assembly is in a better position to look at the problem with a detached regard and to take the steps suggested by that regard than an ordinary legislature would be. If these assumptions can be shown to be true, then the pre-commitment view of constitutional constraints is vindicated against the objection from disagreement.

Constitutions divide into two main chapters: provisions on governmental organization and a bill of rights. In Section 3.2 I mentioned among the weaknesses of the "tyranny of the majority" account that it is unable to explain why constitutions should include a chapter on governmental organization. In the following paragraphs I will bring up examples from both domains to show that the "self-binding of the community" account is capable of covering the whole of constitutional regulation.

Consider a problem related to constitutional organization first. States consist of a number of organizations, any of these being defined by a set of roles and the competences, powers and obligations of the persons who occupy these roles, plus the rules of succession of the incumbents. In a democratic society these persons are supposed to act on behalf of the community, either as its agents or as trustees of its interests. It makes a great difference whether we adopt the idiom of agency or that of trusteeship, but for our present aims this difference does not matter. What matters is that the office holder is supposed to act—whether as an agent or as a trustee—in the interests of the community. At the same time he has his own interests, too, that motivate him to depart from the goals set by his function. This unavoidable tension creates the need for mechanisms that narrow the distance between the interests of the community and those of the public official.[98]

The system of periodic elections is commonly understood as such a mechanism. Democratic party politics is a competitive game where the parties are running for a fixed number of parliamentary seats and, ultimately, for the power to form the government. Although occasionally one-election parties may show up, they are a negligible phenomenon in democratic politics. A typical party plays the game repeatedly on an indefinite number of occasions. So it is interested in maximizing the number of its mandates over a series of elections, and to stay in power as long as possible. Whichever party should be in government, it is held by the practice of periodic elections under the constant threat of losing too much if it departs too far from forwarding the interests of the public.

Suppose now that the electoral regime is regulated by ordinary legislation (the Parliament is able to change the rules by simple majority), and consider the following scenario. In Year Zero, the Blue Party wins the elections under a system of nation-wide party lists, the parliamentary seats being distributed in proportion to the votes cast on each list. Towards the end of the parliamentary cycle, public opinion polls signal a shift in party allegiances. Under the proportional system, the Blues have no chance of winning the elections again. However, the distribution of allegiances makes it likely for them to be the winning party if the elections are held under a majoritarian system where individual candidates compete for seats on a winner-takes-all basis. If the Blues are, as we have good reason to assume, strongly interested in staying in power, they will find it rational to abandon the proportional system for a majoritarian one. And they will have the power to do so. Towards the end of the next parliamentary cycle polls may signal that the Blues are likely to lose the urban agglomerations while still having a chance to win the sparsely populated countryside. So they have a strong incentive to redraw the electoral districts to make sure that fewer voters elect a representative in the countryside than in the urban areas, and so on. If, by bending the electoral rules to their momentary interests, the incumbents can secure victory for themselves whatever the distribution of party allegiances in the electorate, then the elections fail to work as checks on the conduct of the government, and the power holders obtain a very wide discretion to pursue their own interests at the cost of those of the community.

But suppose the amendment of the electoral regime is tied to one of the following two conditions (or both): it cannot pass unless supported by some qualified majority of the representatives; or it cannot come into force before the next elections. The first condition makes the amendment dependent on the concurrence of the opposition or at least of a part of it, while the second makes it hard for the legislature as a whole to foresee, at the time when the amendment is made, what electoral system would best fit their particular interests at the time when the new rules come into force. If adopted, such devices (requirement of a super majority in the first case, delay between the vote on the bill and its coming into force) tie the hands of the Parliament and, in so doing, they protect the capacity of the community to punish the incumbents if they depart too far from pursuing the common good.

But of course making the electoral regime safe from easy amendment is a curse rather than a blessing for the community if the entrenched rules are biased in the first place. Imagine a constitutional electoral regime that systematically favors agrarian parties against their urban competitors or vice versa: clearly, it would do more damage to democratic accountability than the same regime not protected by the requirement of special majorities or by delaying devices, or by other methods. For constitutional entrenchment to be a means of democratic self-government, the framers of the constitution must be more likely to give priority to the common good over aims that conflict with it than the majority in an ordinary legislature. In other words, the community has a reason to subject the change of the electoral system to constitutional constraints if and only if it also has a reason to trust more the judgment and motivation of the majority of a Constituent Assembly than those of the legislative majority.

It obviously does if the delegates to the Assembly cannot be party members and are barred for their future life from occupying any public office. But even if the same parties that will compete for seats in the legislature are represented in the Constituent Assembly, the latter body can be shown to be a more reliable agent of the common good than the former. We can allow that the overwhelming majority of the legislators are loyal to the political community and are committed to the principles of democratic governance. This loyalty and this commitment may constrain to some degree the pursuit of the special interests even in the ordinary legislature. But the motivating force of the latter are predictably much weaker in a Constituent Assembly. When the majority of the Assembly adopts principles and rules for the future republic, they assess the effects of these from the long-run perspective. Their interests are not focused on the outcome of the next election but on the outcomes of an indefinite number of elections; not on what happens during the next parliamentary cycle but on what happens over an indefinite number of cycles. Suppose there are two parties in the Assembly, and suppose that their constituencies undergo oscillations from election to election. If so, then the advantages and disadvantages of bending the electoral rules to some special interests will cancel out each other, whether the bias is entrenched for many cycles or is allowed to shift every four or five years. An entrenched bias is likely to favor one party in roughly one half of the elections, and to be to its disadvantage in the other half, and so is the decision to allow the majority in power to amend the rules at its will. Therefore the majority in the Assembly is likely to be indifferent, in so far as their special party interests are concerned, between biased and fair electoral systems and between entrenched rules and the rules being up for grabs for any momentary majority. And this increases the probability that their commitment to democracy and their concern for the good of the community will carry the decision. The electoral rules chosen by a Constituent Assembly are thus likely to be worthy of being entrenched as a constitutional status quo that remains in force as a default position so long as the special majority required for change is not there.

The same logic applies to the issue of the freedom of information and criticism. Democratic parties are likely to value the transparency of the government and free deliberation on public matters. But while in power they have an interest in limiting the access to information concerning the government's activities and in restraining the criticism addressed to them. When in opposition, they are of course interested in more information and criticism. But if the provisions on freedom of expression can be amended by a simple majority of ordinary legislatures, it is always the party in power that decides about the range over which this freedom will be protected. And so, although in a two-party system and in the long run each party is likely to be interested as often in restricting the scope of freedom of expression as it is in widening it, and although the community has a constant interest in a very wide definition of this freedom, the political system will encourage a trend towards more and more restraint. Not so if freedom of expression is entrenched as a constitutional right. In the Constituent Assembly where decisions are taken with an eye on the long run, each party can be assumed to be indifferent, as far as its special interests are concerned, between a set of rules that ensure freedom of expression in a wide reading and a set of rules that narrow that reading to a significant degree. Therefore the commitment to the value of freedom of expression is more likely to carry the decision than in ordinary legislatures working under a simple majority rule.

To be sure, freedom of information and criticism is only a part of what we generally understand by freedom of expression. The argument outlined above does not show how a Constituent Assembly's platform is superior to that of an ordinary legislature with regard to regulating non-political speech, artistic expression or pornography, for example. To generalize: some of the basic rights are related to the political process while others are not. I hope I have succeeded in showing that the logic of democratic politics makes it rational for the community to trust better a body framing a constitution for the long run than an ordinary legislature to take care of the protection of politics-related rights. But it remains to be seen whether this is also true about those rights that are not (at least not directly) related to the political process. Because of a lack of direct relationship, the interests of a party in power and those of a party in opposition are not necessarily asymmetrical with regard to such rights. Some other mechanism is needed to explain why a Constituent Assembly is more likely to take the appropriate attitude towards non-political rights than the majority in an ordinary legislature.

I will continue to assume that the parties share some degree of commitment to the principles underlying a democratic system, including basic rights.

I will also assume that the community at large takes those rights seriously, although there is disagreement on the question of their scope and their requirements. Jeremy Waldron seems to believe that this shared commitment is either absent and, then, a constitutional protection of rights is no more feasible than their protection through ordinary legislative enactments, or it is there and, then, there is no reason why ordinary citizens and their legislators are not able to do justice to the rights in question as well as members of some special elite such as the judiciary.[99] In what follows I will try to show that even if we assume the community and its legislators to be committed to respect the basic rights of the individual, it is rational to allow the constitution makers to tie the hands of ordinary legislatures when it comes to drawing the boundaries and to define the requirements of these rights. As a first step I will discuss a case where the legal abridgement of a right is likely to harm any randomly selected member of the community. In conclusion I will extend the argument to the case where one part of the community (a permanent majority) harms another one (a permanent minority).

Imagine a country where organized crime is rising sharply. Suppose the government submits to the legislature a plan to curb mafia activities, and that plan includes measures such as making the personal data (bank accounts, tax returns, social security balances, medical files) of any private individual freely accessible to the law enforcement agencies. Suppose that the legislators' vote on the bill is guided by their expectation as to what the voters want them to do. Suppose, finally, that the average voter is moved by two concerns: on the one hand, he is seriously concerned about the deterioration of public security; on the other hand, he is clear about the dangers of the repeal of the protection of personal data. If he compares the bads he expects to suffer as a result of rising organized crime with the bads he expects to suffer on the assumption that his own personal data will certainly be disclosed to law enforcement agents, he finds the costs of combating criminality unbearably high. But if he compares the bads expected from crime with the bads he expects to suffer on the more realistic assumption that the probability of his own personal data being disclosed is vanishing, then the costs shrink to insignificance.

To be sure, the voter is casting his ballot not only for himself but also for the community as a whole. He has some view on the right everybody has to have control over the disclosure of his personal data to third persons. Whatever this view, he will agree that a free access of the law enforcement agencies to anyone's personal data would eliminate this right. And some members of the community would inevitably suffer damage as a consequence. Any voter would understand this cost to be unbearably high for those people. But before making a decision, the voter does not only discount his own prospective loss with the probability of its occurring. He does the same for the potential losses of all other people as well. So he finds that no matter whose point of view he should take, it is rational to accept the repeal of the data protection measures. The average voter will support the anti-mafia policy, and so will the legislature under the control of the electorate.

The constitution makers do not find themselves under this control. They frame the constitution in a "calm hour" when the public does not face a direct challenge from the rise in organized crime. They may foresee the possibility of such a challenge and ask themselves how to draw now the right concerning personal data given that at some future point in time the public may be prepared to compromise on this right to a very high degree. This deliberation is not under the control of the future electorates. We can assume that both the constitution makers and the members of later legislatures have some conception of the right of the individual to be sovereign over her personal data, but the constitution makers are more likely to decide the issue on the basis of their beliefs on what that right requires. It is not that we assume their beliefs to be more accurate than those of the legislators coming perhaps generations later. That may or may not be true. What we assume is that they are better placed to act on them.

In order to make the argument complete we have briefly to see what happens when it comes to attempts at bending the constitution to the momentary interests of the parliamentary majority. This cannot succeed unless the majority is able to win additional support to reach the requisite super majority. But if all the voters tend to discount the cost of being deprived of their right to control the disclosure of their personal data, then forming the requisite super majority coalition does not look that difficult, after all. Nevertheless it is very difficult. Ordinary legislatures work on the basis of a division between government and opposition. Presumably, the opposition votes against the government's proposals. This is the case, typically, even if the opposition agrees with the government on the merit of the issue. Those who vote for a bill take responsibility for the consequences of its adoption. But the consequences depend partly on the way the government proceeds to apply the law. As a rule, the opposition has no means to influence this. It is only under the pressure of exceptionally strong reasons that it is moved to vote with the government. So there is a presumption that the opposition votes against the motions of the governing side.

In all the cases discussed above this presumption is supported by further reasons based on the opposition's interests, on its structural position in the parliamentary system. Clearly, the opposition has a strong interest in preventing the majority from bending the electoral rules to its expectations. It has a strong interest in protecting freedom of information and criticism. Data protection seems to be different in that the assessment of the burdens of the relaxing of its safeguards is neutral between the constituencies of the government party and of the opposition party. But the perspective of the opposition politicians is special. Free governmental access to personal data is dangerous because it can be abused. And the acts of abuse do not necessarily target the citizenry in a stochastic manner. Some groups attract the interest of government officials much more strongly than others. Political adversaries of the party in government are among the privileged targets. Free access to personal data secures uncontrolled power for the governing party to try to destroy its opponents by way of collecting information on their bank accounts, medical files, sexual habits, and so on. So the opposition has a direct interest in blocking the proposed amendment, even if its electoral constituency has no objection to it.

In sum, once a constitutional status quo is pinned down, the division of the legislature into a governing majority and an opposition makes the amendment of it extremely difficult.

Let us briefly consider, in conclusion, the case where the benefits and the burdens of following a rule fall on two separate groups—the case the defenders of the "tyranny of the majority" thesis have in mind. It does not take complicated arguments to show that the "self-binding of the community" thesis can successfully deal with such cases. Basic rights are universal, they are rights all human beings are bearers of, morally speaking. "No one must be deprived of the right to life and dignity", "No one must be subjected to cruel and humiliating punishment", "No one's freedom of conscience must be infringed upon", and so on. The racial, ethnic, gender, religious etc. differences which may divide the population of a country into permanent majorities and minorities are irrelevant from this point of view. A majority that agrees to base the community on the rights of the individual, commits itself to treat any permanent minority as equals and to refrain from discriminating against, excluding, stigmatizing or humiliating their members. This is what is more likely to happen at the "calm hour" of constitution making than at the "heated hours" of legislative battles. The rest of the argument follows the logic presented above.[100]

Let me take stock. Individuals sometimes tie their hands in order to enable themselves to reach certain aims. The concept of self-binding can be extended to communities: constitution making lends itself to an interpretation as an act of communal pre-commitment. If so, there is no conflict in principle between the requirements of democratic decision making and the adoption of constitutional constraints. It is not only the case that democracy must be constitutionally constrained in order that its conditions exist at all. It is also true that the very act of constraining is a democratic act, an act of self-constraining by the community.

The finding that the community is divided by lasting disagreements on virtually all issues, including those of the conditions of democracy and the way these can be secured, does not invalidate this result. We have good reasons to assume that there is an important asymmetry between the position of the constitution makers and that of the later legislatures. A constitutional moment can indeed be characterized by the image of the "calm moment" or "lucid moment" as opposed to the moments of the "heat of the legislative battle", even if no panic, hysteria or other pathologies of the mind are assumed to accompany the latter. And this characterization holds whether or not the same disagreements continue to divide the public over time, although with shifting majorities. The framers' position is not beyond fallibility. It may be the case that they are wrong and posterity is right (or, more precisely, that the required majority in a Constituent Assembly is wrong and the majority of later legislatures is right). Nevertheless, the decisions taken in a Constituent Assembly are more likely to be carried by beliefs (correct or mistaken) concerning the common good than those made by ordinary legislatures. Therefore, the community has good reasons to make it hard for the latter to revise those decisions. And, in fact, the division of the legislatures into government and opposition usually takes care of this aim. Only exceptionally do governments command a majority that is sufficient to carry through a constitutional amendment without the opposition's concurrence.

But revision is only hard, not impossible. Remember the case of the Russian nobleman: as a young socialist he is appalled by the thought that in the future his egalitarian convictions may fade away, but—as we have found—he cannot exclude the possibility of new evidence, not available to him now, becoming accessible in the future, providing him with a conclusive reason against equality. We concluded that he is not rational to make it impossible for himself to undo in the future the decision taken now. But it is rational for him to make such unbinding very difficult. The pervasive facts of disagreement put the community in a similar position. Self-binding in the sense of imposing absolutely non-amendable constitutional constraints on itself would be unreasonable. But self-binding in the sense of making the amendment unusually difficult is a reasonable thing to do.

Furthermore, the possibility for new reasons to emerge makes it reasonable to constitutionally entrench principles that are as abstract as possible, and to leave it to posterity to specify the content of those principles in the light of information becoming available after the constitution is made. Or at least such is the case with the principles of the Bill of Rights. This point brings out a last question: Whom should the community entrust the task of interpreting the specific requirements that flow from the abstract principles for more concrete conditions? The following section will be dedicated to this problem.

3.6. JUDICIAL REVIEW, SUBSTANTIVE READING

The constitutional status quo does not have any regulatory function unless the ordinary laws that violate the provisions of the constitution are null and void. But their being null and void—i.e. unconstitutional—must also be declared by some instance. If this is to be the business of the legislature, then there are two possibilities. First, constitutional controversies might be settled by such a qualified majority as is required for adopting a constitution. In this case, only such constitutional controversies might be settled that could be resolved by the legislature through amending the existing constitution. In other words, the compatibility or incompatibility of the contested legal provision with the constitution would be impossible to establish in precisely those cases where the constitution is supposed to constrain the legislature. Or, second, constitutional controversies could be settled through simple majority. In this case, the significance of the fact that the constitution itself was adopted by a qualified majority is completely lost. The exact same majority that passed the legal provision of contested constitutionality could rule that there was in fact no violation of the constitution. The outcome is the same as though the constitution were amended by a simple majority. Therefore the power to safeguard the existing constitutional status quo must be removed from the authority of the legislature.

But why should not one confer this power to another elected body? Since this would not be identical with the legislature, it would not be subject to the requirement of a qualified majority either (it would not be its *own* two-thirds decisions that it would thus strike down by simple majority). But there is a further consideration that advises against an upper-chamber sort of constitutional guardianship. Constitutional review must determine whether some contested legal provision is consistent with the rules and principles specified by the constitution. The aim of the decision can be nothing else but establishing the existence or lack of such a compatibility. On the other hand, it is a matter of fact that the choice between upholding or annulling a legal provision has—apart from extreme borderline cases—unequal consequences for different groups of people. In other words, constitutional decisions have severe distributional consequences, and these consequences are no less important for the voters than what follows for the contested provisions from the correct reading of the constitution. By contrast, the advantages and disadvantages of the outcome are indifferent from the perspective of the constitutional controversy. Such collateral consequences might not influence the content of the decision. Therefore it is reasonable to confer the power of constitutional review on such a body that is insulated from daily politics—whose members are not elected representatives of the people.

The judiciary is such a body.[101] But if it were distinguished from the bodies of elected representatives merely by the fact that its members do not bear political responsibility, it would not be capable of doing the job. The absence of political responsibility has serious drawbacks as well as considerable advantages. The judges may not do just anything; they are bound by the rules of their functioning laid down by laws as well as by the obligation to adhere to the constitution. But they may be held accountable for the violation of these obligations only in extreme cases of impeachment. Furthermore, the Constitutional Court is the ultimate seat of judgment; there is no court to which one could appeal against its decisions. No doubt, the Parliament might alter the Court's decisions, but not by showing that they rest on a false interpretation of the existing constitution—the Parliament has no power to do this. The body of representatives may overrule the judgment of the Court only by amending the constitution on which the judgment rested. If it were easy to do this, the constitution could not do the job it was designed to do. On the other hand, if it is difficult to amend the constitution, then the decision of the guardians of the constitution is for all practical purposes immutable, apart from exceptional cases.

It is for this very reason, however, that it is so important for the Court to be subject to public control in a different sense; and it is in this respect that the fact that the Court is a *judicial* body becomes so significant. To be sure, Constitutional Courts are unlike ordinary courts in important respects. Ordinary courts adjudicate particular grievances of particular individuals; they never engage in a direct assessment of laws independently of the particular cases to which the laws are supposed to apply. What Constitutional Courts are mostly doing is to assess the constitutionality of laws, not to adjudicate personal complaints. Ordinary courts follow an adversarial procedure, while Constitutional Courts tend not to do so. In this and some other senses Constitutional Courts are not genuine courts. But they are similar to genuine courts in being obliged to offer reasons for their rulings.

To be sure, it is not only the courts that offer reasons, for the House of Representatives itself is a privileged scene of political disputes and thus of political arguments. But the arguments voiced in the debates of the Parliament are subject only to the most relaxed requirements. The reasons offered in favor of a new law need not be consistent with the reasons offered in favor of earlier ones; no rule is violated, furthermore, if a representative or group of representatives gives up its earlier position for no specific reasons, and supports causes that are incompatible with it. Political turns of this nature are to be expected in the Parliament. Neither the sponsors nor the critics of a bill are obliged to argue in such a manner that their positions remain consistent over time. It is not infrequent that the opposing parties borrow one another's arguments as they switch from government to opposition and from opposition to government.

By contrast, judicial rulings are subject to strict consistency requirements. Decisions must be reasoned and the reasons must show how later decisions might be ranked among the earlier ones without contradiction; they are supported by earlier decisions and they in turn reinforce them. If this is not so, they must show why one or another of the earlier decisions was wrong. The judges are not allowed to spare this work for themselves. The constitution cannot be consistently enforced unless the norms entrenched by it form a coherent order; otherwise, everything could be ruled constitutional and unconstitutional at the same time, according to the guardians' momentary preferences. This is why it is so important that the rulings protecting the constitution be as consistent as possible, and judicial decisions stand a better chance of achieving this than the representatives' decisions, if only because of the stricter formal requirements made against judicial decisions.

On the other hand, the reasoning of the judges might be subjected to public discussions. The judges must offer reasons for their decisions while being aware that their reasons must hold their ground before the seat of the legal, political scientific and philosophical professions as well as before the general public. If an argument proves untenable in the public discussion, it must sooner or later go. Conversely, nothing could be a more appropriate measure of the correctness of their decisions than that they survive public scrutiny. Sanctions without the sanction of public criticism are that which constitute the ultimate limit of the judges' freedom of decision, and criticism is that which redirects constitutional review to the democratic political process.

It is reasonable, therefore, for the guardians of the constitution to function as the courts do, even if they are not part of the ordinary judiciary hierarchy but are separated from it.[102]

It was shown that elected representatives might tie their own hands by adopting a constitution, no less than the individuals who might tie their hands to achieve their goals. We have seen that the principle of constitutional self-binding corresponds better to democracy than the principle of parliamentary omnipotence. We have seen that there are good reasons to confer the power of enforcing constitutional constraints on a separate, judicial body, not unlike when individuals entrust another person to be the means of their own self-binding. We have yet to show that, just as it might be reasonable for individuals to give the power of consideration and judgment to the person they make the means of their own self-binding, the constitution makers, too, act in accordance with their aims if they confer the power on the Constitutional Court not merely to enforce mechanically applicable rules, but also to apply such abstract principles that might be realized only through substantive interpretation, consideration and judgment. If this holds true, then the traditional *Rechtstaat*-conception of the rule of law (see Section 1.1.) is not tenable either, and we will have good reasons to think in terms of democratic constitutionalism rather than those of parliamentary *Rechtstaat*.

It was already mentioned in Chapter 2 (Section 2.2.) that legal provisions are not susceptible to perfect precision. This of course should not be taken to mean that the degree of exactness of legal provisions is immaterial. It is reasonable to demand that, to the degree possible, the lawmakers eliminate uncertainties and approximate the ideal of rules whose application is beyond controversy. I wrote "to the degree possible" because this demand is not equally attainable in all areas. There are certain domains where it is relatively easy to attain, whereas there are other, more difficult, domains where this is not so.

The constitution belongs among the difficult domains. Since it introduces such a status quo that is very difficult to change, its provisions are meant to last for a long period. By contrast, the longer a constitutional provision endures, the greater the possibility of changes in the world which it is meant to regulate. The number of situations that the framers did not foresee at all, or at least did not foresee in all their essential details, will increase. There will be an ever-larger number of cases for which it will be impossible to decide, through strict reading, which of the constitution's provisions are relevant for them, and what they have to say about them. What is more, it is not merely the situations in need of constitutional regulation that change but their assessment as well. The boundaries between commendable and condemnable, tolerable and intolerable conduct, between conducts judged to be good, indifferent or bad, will shift too. Changes in society's attitudes will suggest new considerations, insights, arguments and reasons, put old disputes in new lights, and may finally lead to the realization that what the framers thought to be the correct interpretation of the principles they adopted are in fact in many respects mistaken. As recently as in the last few decades, constitutional democracies witnessed dramatic shifts in thinking about the death penalty, abortion, euthanasia, extra-marital sexuality, marriage and family itself, and homosexuality. Convictions once thought to be indisputable have become subject to controversy. The interpretation of constitutional rights concerning privacy, individual self-determination, and the freedom of conscience has been transformed, too, while the text of the constitution remained unaltered.

Can we avoid such challenges through making constitutional provisions more exact? Detailed regulations may certainly diminish interpretive uncertainties, but only at the cost of inviting two other risks. First of all, if the definitions are too strictly adjusted to the current or currently predictable state of affairs, then a host of new relations may arise in the future, which by their nature will demand constitutional regulation and which, nevertheless, will simply fall outside the sharply demarcated domain of constitutional interpretation. What is and what is not protected by the constitution will depend on contingent facts. Imagine that Section (2) of Article 61 of the constitution, which declares that "The Republic of Hungary recognizes and protects the freedom of the press", had been supplemented in 1989 with an enumerated list of the forms of communication through the press, which was meant to be comprehensive. This list, however, as it was made in 1989, would not include the Internet. (Had it been compiled in the 1920s, it would not include the television; had it been compiled before the end of the nineteenth century it would not include the radio). In this manner, the governmental regulation of the Internet would not belong under the force of the constitutional principle of the freedom of the press.

The other danger is that the framers stipulate the entrenched principle in the interpretation that they *believe* to be correct, yet, later this *may prove* to be wrong, ruling out the possibility of correcting its reading, as long as the provision is in force. The Founding Fathers of the United States, for instance, declared that "The Congress shall make no law...abridging the freedom of...the press". We today consider this to be a robust prohibition, but the American framers were far from including in it everything that we, especially after the practice of the US Supreme Court in the last half a century, tend to understand by it. Under the abridgment of the press they meant primarily, in accordance with the prevailing conception of the period, prior censorship.[103] If they were explicitly to formulate this conception, the first Amendment would protect the press only against such challenges that no one is likely to undertake anymore.

Therefore the framers do well to aspire to detailed regulations only where the change of circumstances might not affect the rules determined by them. There is room for such detailed regulations in the domain of governmental organization, that is, in the domain where the constitution specifies public institutions, confers competences, creates offices and regulates the way they are filled, and makes rules of procedure and decision making. Such provisions are not likely to be threatened by the danger that the relations they are meant to regulate may be left outside the domain of regulation if they are defined too strictly, or that they enforce outmoded values on posterity. The organizations they regulate do not have an existence independent of them; they are created by the constitutional provisions themselves. The competences of the Parliament, the government, the president of the republic or the judiciary might not shift unless the constitution itself is amended. Therefore it is reasonable to aspire to sharp contours when drawing the constitutional boundaries of governmental organization.

If it were the case that the moral principles entrenched in the constitution created rather than merely recognized the values they protect, the ideal of sharp contours and mechanically applicable rules would be worthwhile to pursue in this domain as well. We have already seen, however, that the constitution does not create the moral principles incorporated in it but merely expresses that the state is obliged to respect and protect them. The moral principles expressed by the constitution are right or wrong, true or false independent of the framers' intentions, and which one is to be regarded as their correct interpretation has legal consequences. Thus, in this domain the strategy to be pursued is not the making of ever more exact rules but the highest possible level of abstraction that leaves ample room for later reinterpretations.[104]

3.7. THE LIMITS OF
CONSTITUTIONAL REVIEW

The theory of constitution and of constitutional review developed here supports the position according to which there is no difficulty, in principle, in the justices making decisions based on the substantive reading of the constitution, or rather, the nature of constitutional legal disputes explicitly demands such interpretations. It is only the critical reading of the constitution that is prohibited, which overrules or in any other ways amends the text of the constitution.

We have found, furthermore, that the conventional institutional peculiarities of the judiciary, which traditionally inspired the suspicion against decisions based on substantive readings, are in fact necessary conditions for the justices to be able to approximate the correct answer with a better chance in the issues brought before them than the legislature, which is responsible to the voters. The Court might perform the function conferred on it by the elected representatives effectively only if its members are free of political responsibility.

It is now necessary to qualify this insight. There are certain decisions that of their nature require the decision makers to be free of political responsibility. These are the questions that should belong under the competence of the Court. But there are also decisions that demand political responsibility. These are inevitably outside the competence of the Court. In the present section, I would like to expand on this claim a little further. I do not venture to develop a general theory of the questions that require political responsibility—that is, of political questions. I would like to illustrate through a single example that such questions do indeed exist.

This example concerns the extent and structure of the government's budget. It is very widely accepted that budget decisions are paradigmatic cases of decisions that do not belong under the competence of the Court. Budgets constitute a system of equations with a number of variables, with a complex correlation between the variables. It is not merely that the sum of expenditures may not exceed that of the revenues; furthermore, it is not merely whether the expenditures are covered in whole by taxes or by loans taken by the state as well. The designers of the budget must make assessments about such issues as the impact of loose fiscal policy on expectations concerning inflation, or the impact of a one percent increase in budget deficit on interest rates, or the impact of international financial markets on the ability of the government to take loans, etc. There is wide agreement to the effect that

Courts are not capable of making such estimates and calculating the putative correlations. On the other hand, there is no agreement as to why they are incapable of this. For my part, I find the usual arguments to be mistaken.

One of them is that the justices are not capable of grasping and considering such divergent empirical correlations as the makers of budgets must take into account.[105] But if the Court were given the power to make budget decisions, it would also have to be equipped with an expert economic apparatus, and it is hard to see why the economists working for the justices would be less prepared for the job than their colleagues in the Ministry of Finance.

According to another argument, adjudication consists in decision making based on hearing and considering the views of the different parties, and since different budget conceptions involve the different parties concerned, the scope of those involved is uncertain; therefore the making of budget decisions by the judges is simply not practicable.[106] This is no doubt an interesting point with regard to the ordinary judiciary, but it certainly does not concern the practice of constitutional adjudication as it has emerged in countries with a civil law tradition, like Hungary; the Constitutional Court does not hear cases in a direct adversarial procedure, thus the uncertainty of the parties concerned need not affect its rulings.

Finally, there is a third argument according to which a judicial review of the budget would protect such interests that demand of the government that it do something (provide some service to its citizens) rather than that it refrain from doing something (for instance, from interfering with the privacy of its citizens). By contrast, the Court was designed to protect the second rather than the first type of interests, to enforce negative rather than positive rights. In this conception the government's constitutional obligations are confined to protecting the negative rights of its citizens; the government has no obligation to positive assistance; therefore, the citizens have no positive rights either.[107] Thus, it would follow that, whether the courts are capable of deciding budget issues or not, they are simply not in the business of doing so.

But, first of all, the distinction between the so-called negative and positive rights is not identical with the distinction between doing something or refraining from doing something by the bearer of obligations with respect to the bearers of rights. The exact same act might be described as a positive assistance in one case and as protecting a negative right in another, depending on what one should accept as the baseline against which the various claims are to be assessed.

If the government takes a certain amount of money from A to hand it over to B, it certainly does something rather than refraining from doing something. This act, however, may cover a number of different things. It may be the case that the government levies some tax on the income of A, who has no children, and gives it to B who has a large family. In this case, the government serves a purpose that requires positive, assisting interference. But it might also be the case that A has beforehand unlawfully acquired B's money. In this case, the government merely protects B's right to property against A's illegal intervention; i.e., it protects B's claim to be free from intervention to that which is his own. Furthermore, it is also possible that even though the sum taken from A has never been in B's possession, yet B nevertheless rightly claims that it should not have become A's possession to begin with, because A acquired it by taking advantage of his grossly superior bargaining strength.

Furthermore, among the fundamental constitutional rights—the rights, that is, whose protection certainly belongs to the competence of the Court—are positive no less than negative rights. Equality before the law, for instance, includes everyone's right to legal counsel; the government must appoint a counsel to a defendant, provided that he cannot afford to hire a lawyer. The right of assembly includes that the police must be present with a substantial force in case the antecedently registered demonstration is threatened by the intervention of violent intruders, and so on.

In other words, the arguments habitually made against budget decisions made by judges are not tenable. I propose a fourth argument for consideration.

Budget decisions do indeed differ from typical court rulings, but not in that the number of relevant variables is larger, or the scope of those concerned is more uncertain, or that the demands budget expenditures must answer are of a positive nature. The relevant difference is this. Typical court rulings enforce such provisions whose addressees have two possibilities; they either adhere to the rule or violate it. Decisions related to the budget are different. The government must levy taxes to finance its planned expenditures. But the possibilities present to the addressees of tax rules are not confined to paying the proper amount of taxes due after a given amount of consumption, income or investment profit, or to pay less than legally required. If consumption taxes make their regular purchases too expensive for them, they might decide to reduce their consumption, or to switch to cheaper articles. If income taxes take too much of their salaries, they might choose to work less and compensate themselves with increased leisure. If they find profit taxes too high, they might decide to invest their money in real estate or other valuables instead. They do not on that account violate the law. They in fact exercise their rights. But if too many people act this way, the actual revenues of the budget will not cover the planned expenditures.[108]

The makers of budget decisions do not merely decide about how much tax to collect and how to spend it. Compare the planned revenues and expenditures for the next budget year with the accounts of the already closed budget year. The latter does not include anything beyond the figures for revenues and expenditures. The former, by contrast, must involve estimates as to how economic actors will react to the rules laid down by the budget; first of all, how they intend to adjust their consumption, savings and investment decisions to the alterations in tax rates. They must develop such a tax structure that predictably invites the actors to make favorable decisions, that makes it in their interest to consume and to earn income and profits at least as much as is necessary for delivering the amount of taxes required to cover the planned expenditures. This is the main task of the budget, and this is not one designed for judges.

Not because the judges would be intellectually unfit for tackling it. The sophistication of their budget decisions might as well equal those by the Ministry of Finance. It is a task not designed for judges because estimates concerning the expected behavior of economic actors is at best only very likely; therefore, the decisions that are based on them about the optimal rate of taxes, the amount of expected revenues, and with it the limits and structure of expenditures, inevitably involve risks. Budget choices will depend on the accuracy of estimates as well as the amount of risk the decision makers find tolerable. The advantages of accurate estimates and well-considered risk taking will be enjoyed by the citizens of the state, while the costs of false estimates and excessive risk taking (or extreme caution) will also be paid by them. If all the risks are taken by the citizens, while the job, income and status of the decision makers are insensitive with respect to the consequences of the decision, then it is overwhelmingly likely that they will make wrong decisions.

This is in and of itself an undesirable consequence. Institutions must be so designed as to make optimal decisions for the community. But beyond such unintended consequences, it is unacceptable in democracies, where the legitimacy of governance is derived from serving the interests of those governed, that the decision makers do not share any of the risks of the decisions. They must bear responsibility for their decisions, and this responsibility is eminently political. If they misconceive the possibilities (the environmental conditions, the reaction of taxpayers to the change of tax rates, or the sensitivity of the beneficiaries of budge expenditures), or inaccurately judge the amount of risk to be taken, they must pay the cost. Budget decisions must be made by people who can be dismissed by the voters, should they be dissatisfied by their performance.

We have seen, on the other hand, that it is reasonable to insulate the judges from the whims of public opinion, because they must decide questions that have answers that are either correct or false, and the correctness or falsehood of the answers is independent of the expectations and conduct of the citizens. The chances of making the right decision in such questions is enhanced by the existence of such an ultimate court of appeal whose members do not bear political responsibility. But this same fact makes this court ineligible for making budgets—or, more generally, for making such decisions that require political responsibility.

3.8. PRECAUTIONARY GUIDELINES

The claim just made cannot be generalized without further ado. It does not follow from our reasoning that the Court might not *for any reasons* interfere with the state budget.

First of all, almost every decision has budgetary implications. In countries with a heavily polarized political community, street demonstrations are frequent, and are frequently disturbed by violent intruders; the securing by the police of the right of assembly is costly. In countries with high number of abortions, and where the costs of such surgeries are covered by the social security, the recognition of women's right to self-determination incurs costs on the budget that guarantees the finances of the social security. Such budgetary effects are sometimes negligible, but sometimes they may be considerable. The protection of constitutional rights would be of little use if the government could take these rights off the agenda by merely pointing out the costs they involve.

Second, the provisions themselves that form part of the budget—the tax rules, for instance—may be objected to on the basis of such considerations that may be judged independent of any economic estimates. Imagine a tax system that imposes a heavier burden on the registered members of churches than on the rest of the taxpayers. This system would be discriminatory, and collecting the information necessary for its implementation would violate freedom of conscience as well as the right to protect personal data—regardless of whether the expected surplus is really indispensable for the budget or not.

Finally, the creation and amendment of the budget invites purely procedural questions as well, and the assessment of the latter does not require taking a stance on the economic hypotheses that serve as the basis of budget decisions. I would like to expand on this aspect a little bit.

The legal rules for tax-rates, pension indexation, and credit allowances have a similar role in the relation between the state and private persons as the conditions stipulated in contracts have in the relation between private persons. With the declaration of these rules, the government determines the conditions private persons must take into account when making their decisions about purchases, savings and investments. Just as it is important for the contracting parties that none of them might deviate from the agreement as long as it is in force, and that the agreement itself might not be unilaterally modified, it is equally important for the private persons who are subject to the rules that the state might not deviate from the declared conditions, and that it might not unilaterally modify them. If the government is allowed to disregard or arbitrarily change its own rules, it might occur either that they make such decisions, trusting the stability of the rules, the costs of which they are not able to cover, or that, in the absence of sufficient trust they fail to make the decisions the issued rules were intended to foster. In the first case, the legitimate interests of individuals are being violated; in the other case, legitimate collective goals fail to be realized. (The two harms may combine: the number of people who trust the government decreases, thus the intended effect fails to materialize, but the ones who unreasonably trusted the government pay for their credulity.)

In the case of two equal parties making a contract, there is always a higher instance that enforces the contract and prevents unilateral modification of its terms. By contrast, the government makes and changes its own rules all by itself. Should it be perfectly free to do whatever it wishes, the private persons subjected to it could not count on its trustworthiness. It must tie its hands so that its own laws may regulate the expectations of private persons to an extent comparable with the way contracts regulate the moves of equal parties. The classical norms of the rule of law had already a similar function, like the provision that the budget must be regulated by law or that the government must submit the accounts of the budget of the previous year to the Parliament, which must approve the accounts in a resolution.

Constitutional constraints do the same, only at a higher level. Such constraints may consist in the provision that separate laws must provide for pension indexation or for mandatory social security payments; or that such laws might be amended by simple majority only after the expiration of a certain delay period (say, five years), otherwise the amendment requires a qualified majority. Reviewing the adherence to such procedural requirements might be made the business of the Court, since the decision does not require the substantive examination of the budget.

The difficulties begin where the procedural rules of the constitutional rule of law are not violated, yet austerity measures are nevertheless objected to on grounds whose merits cannot always be detached from the economic assessment of the budget. The social commitments of the constitution—its promise to guarantee a minimum standard of living or health service for all—are such grounds, because we cannot always judge whether they were violated or not without assessing the financial position of the budget. Issues whose proper management requires the absence of political responsibility might be intertwined with ones that require the existence of political responsibility.

Such an intertwining might be avoided by resorting to either one of two diametrically opposed substantive standpoints. According to the first, the social obligations of the government are the expressions of social rights, which are no less categorically binding than, say, the right to life. Just as no scale of economic catastrophe might justify the government in reducing its financial burdens through the mass killing of those in need of public assistance, similarly, no degree of economic hardship might authorize the government to reduce the guaranteed minimum standard of living. If this is true, then the government's social obligations might be judged without assessing the financial position of the budget.

In the other view, the government has no constitutional obligations whatsoever to sustain any guaranteed social minimum. Its obligations are confined to protecting the individuals' right to life, limb and legally acquired property, and to enforce their appropriately established, voluntary contracts. Therefore, so the argument goes, the Court need not deal with budgetary issues, because under normal circumstances the protection of these rights does not necessitate such expenditures that would impose any perceptible burden on the budget.

The first view has not been proposed by any serious author since the crisis of welfare capitalism. The second view, which could be traced back to the nineteenth-century version of liberalism, has once again become popular since the crisis of the welfare state.[109] The author of the present paper is attached to the liberal tradition, but he does not share this conception referred to as neoliberal. He agrees with those modern liberals who take it that the principles that justify constitutional democracy involve that the government has constitutional obligations towards those of its citizens whose living conditions are incompatible with the status of "persons with equal dignity". And safeguarding the constitutional obligations of the government is the business of the Constitutional Court.

Therefore, I think we have here a genuine difficulty that must be dealt with in the practice of constitutional adjudication. In the previous chapter I have mentioned that even though the Court's authority includes the mandate to the substantive interpretation of the constitution, this power must be exercised with great care, and with the introduction of and, adherence to, certain precautionary guidelines. Now we are faced with an immense set of problems that the judges might embark on discussing only if they, simultaneously with making their decisions, or in fact as part of their decisions, develop the precautionary guidelines they adhere to.

Such guidelines may consist in the careful choice of stronger and weaker constitutional tests. A weak test of the constitutionality of restraining rights is, for instance, that the restraint has a "reasonable goal"; a strong test is that the restraint is "absolutely necessary", and that its goal should be "proportionate" to the inflicted harm. The test of "reasonable goal" requires no more than examining whether the official reasons behind the austerity measures are in themselves tenable or not: Is there a rational reason for austerity? Are the initial data credible? Are the calculations accurate? Is there any plausible connection between the goals and the chosen strategy? The Court need not possess its own budget conception to answer these questions. The test of "necessity/proportionality" demands much more than this; it is not satisfied merely by the reasonableness of some austerity policy. The budget adopted by the legislature must be confronted with other possible conceptions, and it must be shown, on the one hand, that there is no such solution that would realize the intended goals at lesser costs (necessity), and, on the other hand, that the failure to realize these goals would involve at least as heavy burdens as are caused to some by their realization (proportionality). It is the stronger test that confronts the Court with difficulties.

The difficulties become manageable if the justices resort to the test of "necessity/proportionality" only in those cases which do not require a revision of the budget: for instance, if the cancellation of a certain support does not have any discernible effect on the whole of the budget; or if the cancellation is justified by a change of policy by the government rather than by austerity. For instance, if it so far has supported the survival of disappearing small settlements, and now it decides to spend the same funds on the human development of urban agglomerations. And the judges confine themselves to applying the test of "reasonable goal" if the test of "necessity/proportionality" would be applicable only by producing an alternative budget—that is, by showing that the austerity is either unnecessary or might be realized without reducing social allowances (or by reducing them to a lesser extent than is approved by the legislature).

In sum, precautionary guidelines are necessary, on the one hand, because questions within the competence of the Court (ones that require that the decision maker has no political responsibility) are not always separable from questions outside the competence of the Court (ones that demand that the decision maker has political responsibility). But this is only one of the reasons. Another reason resides in the fact that the absence of political responsibility on the part of the judges implies the possibility, no less than any other institutional solution, that by eliminating certain anomalies, one creates new ones.

The judges might perform their function properly because they, unlike parliamentary representatives and members of the government, do not depend on the will of the electorate. Their mandate is non-renewable, and their salaries are independent of their performance on the bench.[110] While the representatives compete for votes, which urges them to adjust to the whims of public opinion during their time in office, the judges are not influenced by such incentives, nor are they subjected to the supervision of external authorities. This is a rare, though not completely unheard of solution; the relation between the one who authorizes and the authorized is usually regulated in such a way that the authorizer might control the activity of the authorized, and may even put in place certain incentives to encourage the latter to pursue the goals provided by the authorizer ever more closely. The justices, by contrast, are insulated from any dependence of this nature. Although appropriate, this situation is not without risks. It may give the power to a body of nine to eleven members to interfere with the business of legislature or government through the agreement of merely six of its members, and to serially make decisions of the utmost importance.[111]

This danger might be reasonably reduced through the control of the public as well as through introducing rules of competence and procedure. But there is no such amount of public control or such set of rules that could prevent the judges from what László Csontos referred to as "the running amok of the Constitutional Court", should the judges be inclined to do this.[112] It is impossible to recognize the right of the Court to substantive readings on the one hand and to impose rules without breaks on its interpretive practice on the other hand. One either accepts that safeguarding constitutional obligations demands the intellectual and moral courage of the judges to substantively interpret the constitutional principles—even if it is impossible for them to furnish a non-controversial interpretation—and then we must also accept that the Court might perform this task only in the possession of a freedom of deliberation and action. Or one constrains the judges' freedom, but at the cost of preventing them from performing their proper function. This dilemma can be overcome only by the Court itself developing certain precautionary guidelines to constrain its own practice, and applying them with sufficient consistency.[113]

3.9. SUMMARY

When the framers give a constitution to their state, they tie the hands of the legislature. Through this act, the community ties its own hands. The Constitutional Court is a means of communal self-binding; its mandate is to apply the higher-order (constituent) decisions of representatives to lower-order (legislative) decisions.[114] But this task might not be performed by the judges unless they are authorized to arbitrate controversial interpretive questions through substantive arguments. This is especially true about the application of the moral principles entrenched in the constitution, because the correct interpretation of moral principles might not be laid down by fixed rules. There are two types of objection habitually made against substantive constitutional interpretations; on the one hand, it is claimed that such interpretations amend the constitution; on the other hand, it is claimed that nullification based on such interpretations makes the trustee of the Parliament into a seat of judgment above it. I have shown in the previous chapter that substantive readings, as long as they remain within the bounds of the strict reading, are not equivalent to amending the constitution. In the present chapter, I have shown that nullification based on substantive arguments does not exceed the mandate given to the Court by the constitution makers simply on account of the fact that these arguments mobilize, among other things, controversial convictions.

There is no conflict between substantive reading by the Constitutional Court and the fundamental principles of democracy. What is more, if the constitution really establishes moral principles (among other things) for the republic, then the enforcement of these principles not only allows for substantive interpretation, but positively demands it. Substantive interpretation turns into objectionable activism only if it involves the covert revision of the text of the constitution.

Nevertheless, the mandate of the justices is exceptional and differs from that of the other trustees of the representative body. The special nature of their task requires that their authorizers give them ample freedom of deliberation and decision, and do not try to stir their rulings through incentives. This construction averts certain dangers while inviting others. The risks are tolerable only if the judges themselves develop and apply certain precautionary guidelines in their interpretive practice.

All of this requires a sense of proportion and wisdom, because the Court must carefully constrain its own freedom of action by not dodging the main task it is designed to perform: to protect the constitutional rights of individuals and to prevent the transgression of competences by the various different branches of power.

But self-restraint in itself is not sufficient to avoid all the dangers inherent in the absence of political responsibility. The fact that the Court is obliged to offer reasons and that its arguments are subject to the criticism of the political as well as the legal community is no less important in this regard.

The theory outlined here—a theory of democratic constitutionalism—suggests that part of the objections made against the first Hungarian Constitutional Court are unfounded. I have offered unconventional reasons for some of the other criticisms. But I hope it was made clear that in my view the Hungarian political writers and legal scholars did an invaluable service to the republic by subjecting the interpretive practice of the first Constitutional Court to harsh criticism.

The primary objective of my study is to provide a systematic perspective for continuing this dispute. But the merits of this perspective might be judged only if it is applied to the activity of the Constitutional Court itself no less than to the disputes about constitutional adjudication.

In the next study I will try to show that the judicial practice of the first Constitutional Court might be arranged into a meaningful picture with the help of the theory outlined here. I will not address the correctness or falsehood of the content and background hypotheses of the rulings, but only that which has been the subject matter of our investigations so far: What kind of interpretive canons has the Court adopted? How have these canons changed? Did they involve the substantive reading of the text of the constitution? Did they allow its critical reading? Did they include the inevitable precautionary guidelines of constitutional adjudication? And of course I examine the kind of attitude implied by the Court's interpretive conception towards the purpose of the Constitutional Court and its place among the institutions of the republic.

NOTES

1 Trying to hold on to the increasing pace of events, the Parliament had adopted a minor package to revise the constitution as early as 10 January, 1989 (1989:I). This package reformulated the constitutional tenets of freedom of association, freedom of assembly and freedom of speech (Articles 9 and 10), acknowledged the right to conscientious objection to military service (Article 11), and introduced a few changes in state organization. The establishment of the Constitutional Court was one of these (Article 6), but this Court was different from the one actually created by the end of the year. It did not have the right to strike down laws but only lower-level provisions [Section (2) of Article 6].

2 1989:XXXII on the Constitutional Court.

3 Only three of the first five justices have served their full mandates: Antal Ádám, Géza Kilényi and László Sólyom, who served also as the chief justice between 1990 and 1998. Pál Solt became the chairman of the Supreme Court in 1990, while János Zlinszky retired in 1997 when he reached 70.

4 Of them, only Tamás Lábady, Ödön Tersztyánszky and Imre Vörös have served their full mandates. Géza Herczegh left for the International Court in the Hague in 1993, while Péter Schmidt and András Szabó retired in 1997.

5 During the disintegration of the post-1956 regime a Constitutional Council was created (1984:I) with virtually no powers at all, which only made itself conspicuous by its absence during its five years of existence and played no role whatsoever in the preparation of the transition.

6 This conception of the rule of law is well reflected in Max Weber's sociology of law. See Weber, *Economy and Society*, vol. II, part 2 (Berkeley: The University of California Press, c1978).

7 Hans Kelsen, the father of European constitutional courts, endorsed both the formal understanding of the *Rechtstaat* and the necessity of judicial guardianship of the constitution. See Kelsen, *Introduction to the Problems of Legal Theory:* A Translation of the First Edition of the Reine Rechtslehre or the Pure Theory of Law (Oxford: Clarendon Press, 1992).

8 See Kelsen, *Wer Soll der Hüter der Verfassung sein?* Dr. Walter Rotschild (Berlin–Grünewald, 1931).

9 Traces of this position were discernible in the election programs of the MDF and KDNP in 1994.

10 For the distinction between the formal (legalist) and substantive (constitutionalist) conceptions of the rule of law see R. Dworkin, "Political Judges and the Rule of Law", in Dworkin, *A Matter of Principle* (Cambridge, Mass.: Harvard University Press, 1985), pp. 9–32; and R. Dreier, "Konstituionalismus und Legalismus", in *Archiv für Rechts- und Sozialphilosophie*, Supplement 40, pp. 85–97; and R. Alexy: "Rechtsystem un Praktische Vernunft", in Alexy, *Recht, Vernunft, Diskurs* (Frankfurt am Main: Suhrkamp, 1995), pp. 213–231.

11 A characteristic representative of this standpoint is Béla Pokol. See especially his article "Az emberjogi ideológia", *Napi Magyarország*, 10 October 1998.

12 This view was taken by Tamás Bauer in the early 1990s (see his article "A Bölcsek tanácsa", *Beszélő*, 4 May 1991) and Gáspár Miklós Tamás ("Bírói jogalkotás és parlamenti mindenhatóság", *Beszélő*, 25 May 1991).

13 See the proposal of the Ministry of Justice on the law on the Constitutional Court. In *Magyar Hírlap*, 6 May 1989 and the minutes of the constitutional subcommittee (No. I/1) of the national round table. In András Bozóki (ed.), *A rendszerváltás forgatókönyve*, vol. VI (Budapest: Új Mandátum, 2000).

14 Tamás Bán's study gives a good description of the establishment of the Constitutional Court: "Az Alkotmánybíróság létrejötte", *Világosság*, 1993/11. From the point of view of the Németh government, see Kálmán Kulcsár, "A kormányzat és az alkotmánybíráskodás", in László Lengyel (ed.), *Kormány a mérlegen*, (Budapest: Korridor, 1994). From the perspective of the Constitutional Court itself, see László Sólyom, "Az Alkotmánybíróság hatáskörének sajátossága", *Benedek-emlékkönyv* (Pécs, 1996).

15 Tamás Győrfi's excellent study is an exception in this regard. See his "Az Alkotmánybíróság politikai szerepe", *Politikatudományi Szemle*, 1996/4. In what follows, I will propose an analysis that is significantly different from his. Therefore, it is especially important to emphasize that his study influenced me greatly in thinking through this issue.

16 57/1991 (XI.8), ABH 1991, 236. See Péter Szigeti, "Hatalommegosztás – Alkotmánybíróság", *Világosság*, 1993/1, p. 54.

17 In what follows, I will use "Court" instead of "Constitutional Court" and "justices" instead of "constitutional justices", for the sake of convenience. I will make it clear when I am referring to ordinary courts and judges.

18 The Court resorted to implicit extension of its powers from the very beginning. In the first instance, a motion was made to annul a passage from the government statute on the alienation of state property and a passage from a related Budapest municipal statute. By contrast, the Court upheld the two passages but annulled another article of the municipal statute. See 14/1990 (VI.27), ABH 1990, 170. Another motion was made against a government statute from 1981 that restricted the range of administrative decisions subject to judicial review. The body found the motion well grounded, but it did not put up with annulling the statute: "It extended the review to the law [serving as the basis of the statute] as well and established unconstitutionality in that regard, too." See 32/1990 (XXII. 22), ABH 1990, 145, 147. This practice was characteristic of the first Court through and through. See 4/1997 (I.22), [ABH 1997, 4], that examined, going beyond the motion, whether the Court may annul already ratified international treaties or 29/1997 (IV.29), [ABH 1997, 122] that established, again independently of the content of the motion, that the parliamentary procedure might not hinder the prior norm control of the standing order of the Parliament.

19 In November 1995 the extra-parliamentary Workers' Party submitted nearly 180,000 signatures to the Parliament to initiate a referendum on the following issue: "Do you want Hungary to become a member of NATO?" Nearly 140,000 of the signatures proved to be authentic. The regulations in force at that time [1989:XVII, Section (1) of Article 10] required that in case of submitting more than 100,000 authentic signatures, the Parliament must call a referendum, without any room for discretion. Instead, the Parliament rejected the initiatives by citing reasons that are external to law.

The chairman of the party filed a motion with the Constitutional Court. The petition was rejected by the Court, claiming that the rejection to call a referendum by the Parliament is not a legal provision but a singular measure containing a concrete decision, whose review is beyond the competence of the Constitutional Court [3/1996 (II.23), ABH 1996, 361]. By contrast, in 1997 the Court agreed to review a parliamentary resolution about a referendum initiative. The Court reasoned that in the meantime the Parliament had amended the constitution and made participation in a referendum a fundamental right [52/1997 (XI.14), ABH 1997, 331]. However, the constitutional amendment made no change in matters of principle, for Section (2) of Article 2 of the constitution already defined a referendum as a form of exercising popular sovereignty, thus making it a fundamental constitutional right (though in the section of general provisions rather than in the section summarizing fundamental rights) that is exercised by the citizens collectively. Thus, it is difficult to avoid the bad feeling that the justices rejected the Workers' Party's motion in 1996 because they shared the worries of all parliamentary party leaders concerning the political consequences of an ill-timed referendum.

20 In 1992, a motion objected that the budget for 1993 included the budget plans of Hungarian Radio and Television within the budget line of the Prime Minister's Bureau. Even though this was repeated in 1993, at the approval of the budget for 1994, the Court made its resolution establishing the unconstitutionality of the procedure only in late 1994, i.e. after the change of government [47/1994 (X.21) ABH 1994, 281]. Cf. Andrew Arato, "Az Alkotmánybíróság a médiaháborúban", *Világosság*, 1994/2. By contrast, the decision about the partial unconstitutionality of the government statute ordering the reduction of the staff of higher education institutions was made in an especially hasty procedure, in three weeks from the submission of the motion [40/1995 (VI.10), ABH 1995, 170]. The question inevitably arises: What might have motivated the extremely different treating of the two issues, other than the fact that the nation had a different government after May 1994 than before it?

21 All hitherto mentioned forms of judicial activism are thoroughly dealt with by András Sajó's article discussing the first three years of the Constitutional Court. See "A 'láthatatlan alkotmány' apró betűi: a magyar Alkotmánybíróság első ezerkétszáz napja", *Állam- és Jogtudomány*, 1993/1. A more recent overview is provided by Gábor Halmai, "Az aktivizmus vége? A Sólyom-bíróság kilenc éve", *Fundamentum*, 1999/2.

22 See Richard Posner, *Law and Literature* (Cambridge, Mass.: Harvard University Press, 1988), p. 209.

23 Chapter 3 of the present study forms a unified whole with the piece titled "Liberal Democracy", also in this volume, which expands some of the questions in more detail than was possible here.

24 See E.-J. Sièyes, *Qu'est-ce que le tiers état?* and C. Schmitt, *Die Diktatur.* (Munich–Leipzig: Duncker & Humblot), 1928, pp. 137–143.

25 See J. L. Talmon, *The Origins of Totalitarian Democracy.* (London 1955.)

26 Carl Schmitt, *Die Diktatur,* Talmon, Origins.

27 On what is implied by the "one person one vote" principle and what is not implied by it, see "Liberal Democracy" in this volume.

28 Constitution, Section (1) of Article 8.

29 See András Bragyova, "Normák normák ellen", *Világosság*, 1993/2.

30 It was the legislature that approved the constitution they are designed to protect, as well as the law that determines their authority and procedure; finally, the judges themselves are elected by the legislature for nine years.

31 48/1991 (IX. 26) Constitutional Court Ruling, ABH 1991, 189, 208. Dissenting opinion by Géza Kilényi, Péter Schmidt and Imre Vörös.

32 It was by the end of the mandate of the first Constitutional Court that it made it explicit that its conception corresponds to this latter, positive interpretation. The instructing section of 32/1998 (VI. 25) Constitutional Court ruling took the following position: "The right to social safety as determined by Article 70/E of the constitution contains the guarantee by the state of such a minimum living standard, provided by the totality of social allowances, that is necessary for the realization of the right to human dignity". [ABH 1998, 251.]

33 This fact has a further consequence, to the effect that the application of constitutional provisions and the justification of decisions are not strict deduction. But I need not address this problem separately. See N. MacCormick, *Legal Reasoning and Legal Theory* (Oxford: Clarendon Press, Oxford, 1978), p. 19.

34 This claim evidently concerns the interpretation of ordinary legal provisions as well. Nevertheless, the interpretation of the constitution exhibits a number of distinctive features, addressed by the remaining sections of this chapter below. To use András Bragyova's summary formulation, the chain of inferences is especially long in constitutional interpretation. See András Bragyova, *Az alkotmánybíráskodás elmélete* (Budapest: Közgazdasági és Jogi Könyvkiadó–MTA Állam- és Jogtudományi Intézete, 1994).

35 That the authority of a legal provision presupposes the lawmaker whose *intention* it is to make the draft before its binding is argued by J. Raz, "On the Authority and Interpretation of Constitutions: Some Preliminaries", in L. Alexander (ed.), *Constitutionalism* (Cambridge: Cambridge University Press, 1998).

36 On constitutional customs see S. Perry, "What is the 'Constitution'?", in Alexander, *Constitutionalism*.

37 Of course it may occur that the reconstruction of the original intention or of the constitutional customs are just as ambiguous in some issues as the substantive positions themselves. If the proponents of the historical reading want to be consistent, they should reject decisions based on contested reconstructions as well as decisions based on contested substantive arguments. However, I need not go into this difficulty, because—as I will try to show— the last word is not that of historical reading in this issue.

38 Károly Törő, "Az alkotmánybíráskodás és a 'láthatatlan alkotmány'", *Magyar Jog* 1992/2, p. 86.

39 See Pál Vastagh, "Közvetlenül vagy közvetve?", *Népszabadság*, 25 March 1999, and Gábor Halmai, "Dönthet-e a nép?", *Magyar Narancs*, 22 April 1999. The question is directly related to the way one is to conceive of the constitutional status of the institution of referenda. See István Kukorelly, "A népszavazás nem antik nosztalgia", *Népszavazás*, 22 May 1997. The author of this study, too, expressed his views on the

role of referenda in the order of the third Hungarian Republic. See "A nép és alkot-mánya I–II", *Magyar Hírlap*, 10 and 11 May 1999.

40 "Kevés a transzplantálható szerv", *Népszabadság*, 30 March 2000.

41 For the time being, I do not consider the case when historical readings come into conflict with the moral reading. I will return to this question later on, in Section 2.7.

42 The expression was coined by Ronald Dworkin. See *Freedom's Law—"The Moral Reading of the American Constitution"* (Cambridge, Mass.: Harvard University Press, 1996).

43 Section (1) of Article 8.

44 The characterization discussed above, to the effect that everyone has an innate right to life and human dignity, has a similar function as the adjectives "inviolable" and "inalienable"; it expresses that we enjoy this right not due to our social status, thus not due to the legislature's decision to make it a rule, but simply in virtue of our having been born as human beings. Finally, the articulation of the constitutional prohibition of negative discrimination has a similar function as Section (1) of Article 8. The Republic of Hungary guarantees human and civic rights to every person on its territory, without any discrimination. See Section (1) of Article 70/A.

45 At least as far as the rulings did not go beyond deciding between alternatives left open by the strict reading of the text. It occurred on one single occasion that at least one of the three judges objected to a ruling on fundamental rights on the grounds of interpretive activism. It was Péter Schmidt who, in his dissenting opinion (ABH 1990, 88, 94) attached to the decision that ruled the death penalty to be unconstitutional (23/1990), alleged that the majority was transgressing its authority on account of its establishing a contradiction between two passages of the constitution and venturing itself to resolve the contradiction right away. This objection, however, was not directed against the moral interpretation of the given passages but against the revision of the given text on moral grounds. I will return to this question briefly in Section 2.8 and in more detail in the last study included in this volume.

46 ABH 1990, 42, 44.

47 Readers might have noticed that this argumentation is conspicuously close to what the reasoning of the Constitutional Court's majority opinion has to say on the relation between judicial independence and ministerial control, or between the independence of the media and the controlling authority of the government.

48 Béla Pokol, "Az alapjogi bíráskodás", *Társadalmi Szemle*, 1991/5, p. 85.

49 *Ibid.*, p. 61

50 Béla Pokol, "Aktivista alapjogász vagy parlamenti törvénybarát?", *Társadalmi Szemle*, 1991/5, p.70.

51 For instance, they could claim that some of the procedural requirements for adopting the law were not satisfied. See Albert Takács, "Az alkományosság dilemmái és az Alkotmánybíróság ítéletei", *Acta Humana*, 1990/1, p. 47. In his later writings, Takács has somewhat distanced himself from this position and has become more permissive with respect to fundamental rights adjudication. See Takács, "Az Alkotmánybíróság Magyarországon – tegnap és holnap között", in Antal Ádám (ed.) *Alkotmányfejlődés és jogállami gyakorlat.* (Budapest: Hans Seidel Alapítvány, 1994). Nevertheless, it is still important to discuss his original position, for it highlights an important argument.

52 Cass Sunstein refers to the strict adherence to such precautionary guidelines as judicial minimalism. See Sunstein, *One Case at a Time* (Cambridge, Mass.: Harvard University Press, 1999).

53 László Sólyom's parallel opinion attached to court ruling No. 23/1990 (X. 31), ABH 1990, 88, 98.

54 I examine there whether the Court's ruling that abolished the death penalty was in fact based on a type of argument outlined two paragraphs above, and whether this type of reasoning was a constant characteristic of the first Constitutional Court's rulings or a unique digression.

55 I develop in detail the bases of this claim and its connections with the two-level structure of the original intention in "Liberal Democracy".

56 That interpreting the constitution must not involve a critique of the constitution is maintained by R. Dworkin. See his "Natural Law Revisited", *Florida Law Review* 34, pp. 166–188.

57 Article 56.

58 So far, there has been one single instance of such revenge by amendment in Hungary: in March 1990, the Parliament included in the constitution that part of the electoral law that had been annulled by the Court, thus excluding from active suffrage all Hungarian citizens who are abroad on election day, even if they have a permanent address in Hungary.

59 "Liberal Democracy" in the present volume examines the compromise thesis in detail, as well as a number of other questions that will surface in the following sections.

60 Such a distinction between "antidemocratic explanation" and "democratic explanation" is similar to, but not identical with, what András Bragyova refers to as the "weak justifications" and the "strong justification" of constitutional courts, in analysing the relation between democracy and constitutional review. See Bragyova, "Demokrácia és alkotmánybíráskodás", *Szentpéteri-emlékkönyv* (Szeged, 1996).

61 Proponents of the status quo consist of two groups: first of all, there are those who strongly oppose the change (who vote against the proposed bill), and those who weakly oppose it (who abstain from the vote). This is so of course only in such voting systems that require for the approval of the bill that "yes" votes exceed the total number of "no" votes and abstentions taken together. In voting systems where it is sufficient for the bill to be approved that the number of "yes" votes exceeds that of the "no" votes, the requirement is even weaker. In extreme situations, it may even occur that only the sponsor of the bill votes for it while everyone else abstains, and yet the proposal enters into force. Here we need not discuss either this difference or the respective advantages and drawbacks of the two systems.

62 This would imply that the generations living today could not elect representatives who can amend the constitution made by representatives elected by generations of the distant past; the dead would rule over the living. It was Tom Paine who first recognized this difficulty. Paine took the position that to secure the self-determination of later generations, each generation must be given the power to revise the constitution it inherited without constraints. At the same time, he also thought that the old generations are incapable of preventing the new ones from exercising this right. Thomas Jefferson put forward similar views roughly at the same time. He thought

the way out of the difficulty would be to repeat the act of constitution making once in every twenty years, out of nothing, as it were. A new constitutional beginning every twenty years would of course have unacceptable consequences, and fortunately the difficulties may be avoided in other ways as well—nevertheless, it does follow from Paine's and Jefferson's observations that a constitution meant to last for ever, ruling out all amendments, is inconsistent with popular sovereignty. See S. Holmes, "Pre-commitment and the Paradox of Democracy", in: J. Elster–Slagstad (eds.), *Constitutionalism and Democracy* (Cambridge: Cambridge University Press, 1988), pp. 200–205.

63 See András Bragyova, "Módosítható-e népszavazással az alkotmány?", *Népszava* 6 May 1999.

64 This requirement is weaker than the requirement of a third plus one votes against the proposal. It is sufficient that a third plus one do not take part in the vote or abstain. The success of the proposal requires the approval by the required majority of the change as against the status quo, while all it takes for the proposal to fail is that the required minority be indifferent in regard of the change and the status quo.

65 See no. 10 of the *Federalist Papers* [Hamilton–Madison–Jay, *The Federalist*], and Alexis de Tocqueville's *Democracy in America*, or John Stuart Mill's essay "On Liberty". The thought that majoritarian democracy leads to the tyranny of the majority is already present in Edmund Burke's *Reflections on the Revolution in France* (1790) (Indianapolis–Cambridge: Hackett, 1987), p. 109.

66 Geoffrey Brennan and Loren Lomasky claim that this assumption is not true for such situations where the impact of individual voter decisions on the outcome of the vote is inconsequential. See Brennan–Lomasky, *Politics and Process* (Cambridge: Cambridge University Press, 1989), pp. 42–59.

67 This thesis may be made compatible with the acceptance of democracy. One might claim that no democratic decision making is possible where the fundamental moral rights of individuals are not respected; intimidated individuals deprived of the freedom of expression and assembly are incapable of making real communal decisions. See J. H. Ely, *Democracy and Distrust* (Cambridge, Mass.: Harvard University Press, 1980). But this supplementary argument is not necessary for the above justification of restricting popular sovereignty; furthermore, this argument does not affect the claim that—in the above reasoning—constitutional review resting on substantive reading violates the principle of the supremacy of the people. At most, it might now be claimed that the supremacy of the people might not be so much as partially realized unless it is restricted—but the Court is still looked upon as an institution that infringes upon popular sovereignty.

68 It may occur, for instance, that the members of some persecuted religious minority approve of the persecution of gays, or that members of a minority group that is discriminated against because of its origin are hostile against another group that is equally discriminated against because of its origin.

69 See R. Dworkin, *A Matter of Principle* (Cambridge, Mass.: Harvard University Press, 1985), p. 359.

70 See J. Waldron, "Majorities and Minorities, Rousseau Revisited", in J. Pennock—J.J. Chapman, (eds.), *Majorities and Minorities* (Nomos XXIII. New York: The University Press, 1991).

71 For the outcome-based view of democratic procedure, see R. Dworkin: „Political Equality", in Dworkin *Sovereign Virtue*. (Cambridge, Mass.–London, Harvard University Press, 2000).

72 The term is borrowed from Jeremy Waldron, a critic of this view. See Waldron, "Precommitment and Disagreement", in L. Alexander, (ed.), *Constitutionalism*. For important formulations of the pre-commitment view, see S. Holmes, "Precommitment and the Paradox of Democracy", in J. Elster and R. Slagstad, *Constitutionalism and Democracy*, (Cambridge: Cambridge University Press 1988). S. Freeman, "Constitutional Democracy and the Legitimacy of Judicial Review", *Law and Philosophy* 9 (1990), pp. 327–370.

73 See J. Elster, *Ulysses and the Sirens: Studies in Rationality and Irrationality*. (Cambridge: Cambridge University Press 1984), p. 39.

74 *Ibid.*, 42.

75 Waldron, *art. cit.*, p. 277.

76 See J. Elster, *Ulysses Unbound*, (Cambridge: Cambridge University Press 2000), p. 9f.

77 *Ibid.*, p. 22.

78 See R. Dworkin, "Equality and the Good Life", in Dworkin, *Sovereign Virtue*. (Cambridge, Mass.–London: Harvard University Press 2000), pp. 242–245.

79 D. Parfit, "Later Selves and Moral Principles", in A. Montefiore, (ed.) *Philosophy and Personal Relations*, (London: Routledge and Kegan Paul 1973), p. 145. The example is discussed by Elster in *Ulysses and the Sirens*, 109, and *Ulysses Unbound* p. 57.

80 On being committed to a desire, see H. G. Frankfurt, "Caring and Necessity", in Frankfurt, *Necessity, Volition, and Love*, (Cambridge: Cambridge University Press 1999), p. 162.

81 *Ibid.*

82 Waldron, *art. cit.*, p. 278.

83 See G. Kavka, "The Toxin Puzzle", *Analysis* 43 (1983) pp. 33–36.

84 See R. Harrison, *Democracy*, (New York: Routledge 1993), Ch. 4. See also "Common Good and Civic Virtue" in this volume.

85 The probability that a randomly selected voter will cast his ballot for the right answer must be greater than 0.5, for example.

86 See R. Dworkin, "The Moral Reading and the Majoritarian Premise", in Dworkin, *Freedom's Law*. (Cambridge, Mass.-Harvard University Press 1996), p. 22.

87 As Dworkin observes, this cannot be true unless the political system is isolated from the impact of economic inequalities. See his "Free Speech, Politics, and the Dimensions of Democracy", in Dworkin, *Sovereign Virtue*. (Cambridge, Mass.: Harvard University Press 2000).

88 *Ibid.* Cited also in Waldron, "Precommitment".

89 See E. Burke, *Reflections on the Revolution in France* (1790). (Indianapolis–Cambridge: Hackett 1987), p. 85.

90 Waldron, *art. cit.*, p. 288.

91 *Unbound*, 94f (italics in the original). Cf. J. Elster, *Solomonic Judgments: Studies in the Limits of Rationality*. (Cambridge: Cambridge University Press 1989), p. 196.

92 *Unbound*, p. 93.

93 J. Waldron, "Freeman's Defense of Judicial Review", *Law and Philosophy* 9 (1990), p. 38.

94 "Precommitment", p. 283.

95 *Ibid.*, p. 284.

96 *Ibid.*, p. 289.

97 Some constitutions make their most important provisions unamendable. But, then, the provision prohibiting amendment can be changed by unanimity.

98 On the principal–agent relationship, see J. Miller, *Managerial Dilemmas*, (Cambridge: Cambridge University Press 1992), p. 120.

99 See J. Waldron, "Rights and Majorities: Rousseau Revisited", in J. W. Chapman and A. Wertheimer, (eds.), *Majorities and Minorities*, (New York: The University Press, 1990), and J. Waldron, "A Rights-Based Critique of Constitutional Rights", *Oxford Journal of Legal Studies* 13 (1993) pp. 18–51.

100 See Pierre Rosanvallon's excellent book on the way the abstract principle of equality exerted an irresistible pressure in the direction of extending the right to vote to excluded minorities: *Le sacre du citoyen*, (Paris: Gallimard 1992).

101 In the case of appointing judges, it is common to resort to further guarantees. The members of the U.S. Supreme Court, for instance, are appointed by the president, but the Senate may veto the appointment. The members of the Hungarian Constitutional Court are elected by the Parliament by a two-thirds majority, following the selection of candidates by a parliamentary committee that functions on a consensual basis.

102 Two further reasons tend to surface. First, the judges decide in small bodies, where the personal position of one or another judge has a considerable impact on the decision; therefore, the personal responsibility of the judges is much greater than in bodies of representatives where decisions are made by dozens or hundreds of people. Second, if the guardians of the constitution are judges, then individuals who think they have suffered some harm because of an unconstitutional law may seek legal remedy with them. By contrast, the bodies of representatives are not accessible to individuals in this way; the latter might exert some influence on them only as voters, by casting their votes. These arguments do not appear compelling. Representative bodies, too, might confer the discussion of such cases on a smaller group of its members (true, in this case the uniformity of decisions must be taken care of), or may launch investigations at citizens' initiatives. The two features discussed above, by contrast, appear to be special.

103 Less than ten years after adopting the constitution, they did not think it unconstitutional to make such a rebellion law that threatened with jail or a fine all those who published "false, outrageous or intriguing" claims about the public authorities of the United States. See L. W. Levy, *Emergence of a Free Press* (Oxford–New York: Clarendon Press, 1985).

104 Therefore, the constitution makers would make a wrong decision to create such a provision as the one we have construed in Section 2.9, for the sake of argument: "In the Republic of Hungary, every person has the right to life and human dignity...This right is not meant to exclude the introduction of the compulsory donation of organs." Even if they believe the right to life and human dignity to be compatible with the compulsory donation of organs, they do not act reasonably if they try to tie the hands of future interpreters.

105 See Tamás Győrfi, *art. cit.*, p. 91.

106 See L Fuller, "The Forms and Limits of Adjudication", in *Harvard Law Review* 92, pp. 353–409.

107 On the distinction between negative and positive rights, see D. M. White, "Negative Liberty", in *Ethics* 80, pp. 185–204; and M. Levin, "Negative Liberty", in *Social Philosophy and Policy* 2, pp. 84–100.

108 See János Kis, "On Liberty–A Dispute with György Márkus", in Constellations 1999/9.

109 The most elaborate representative of this view in the current Hungarian legal literature is András Sajó. See Sajó, "Szociális jólét és rossz közérzet", *Beszélő*, 1996/3, and Sajó, "A jogosultságok lehetősége", *Beszélő*, 1997/1.

110 The existing Hungarian law on the Constitutional Court allows for reelecting the judges at one occasion, but the established consensus rules this out.

111 See Zoltán Szente, "Ki ellenőrzi az Alkotmánybíróságot?", *Népszabadság*, 16 October 1995.

112 See László Csontos, "Mire szolgál és mit jelent a jegybank függetlensége?", *Beszélő*, 1997/1.

113 I enumerated some such characteristic precautionary guidelines in Section 2.7 of the previous chapter.

114 And to the provisions issued by the authorities subordinated to the Parliament; but this represents no theoretical difficulty.

THE LEGACY OF
THE FIRST HUNGARIAN
CONSTITUTIONAL
COURT

1. The interpretive practice of the Constitutional Court

This study examines the interpretive practice of the first Hungarian Constitutional Court in the light of the general conception of constitutional review, developed in the previous study. I will show that the collective stance of the Constitutional Court included the claim to substantive constitutional interpretation; that the judges saw it justified to resort to substantive interpretation primarily in cases that require the moral reading—that is, in rights adjudication. It will be shown, furthermore, that initially they saw the critical—natural rights oriented—revision of the text as permissible. The fact that the judges soon retreated behind the confines of text-bound interpretation will be established, together with the vagaries of this retreat: first it swung to the extreme position of strict textualism, to settle around 1992 at the acceptance of text-bound substantive interpretations. We will see, furthermore, that after having accommodated the norm of textual relevance, the impetus of rights adjudication has gradually subsided. In accounting for this trend I will show that it may be attributed not so much to having given up the natural rights-based critical reading as to the substantive views of the Court. Finally, it will be shown that, while the judges ventured less and less to embark on an expansive interpretation of fundamental rights, their welfare-protective conception has been gradually radicalized to the point of breaking through the boundaries of their competence set by the lack of political responsibility.

Since these tendencies concern primarily the issues pertaining to moral interpretation, in what follows I will not address the questions of structural reading.[1]

1.1. THE SELF-UNDERSTANDING OF THE COURT:
SUBSTANTIVE READING

The Court is a body of many different actors, and it is most unlikely that all of its members share the same view about their joint mission. The disagreements and disputes dividing the first Constitutional Court have not yet been properly processed, yet they have well-documented monuments in the dissenting opinions that were attached to some of the decisions (furthermore, many of the concurring opinions contain more references to objections than to specific reasons for the collective decision).[2] Nevertheless, when we try to reconstruct their collective self-understanding that emerged as the vector of the numerous individual views, we may in the first analysis disregard the disagreements. It may suffice to discuss the conception that best covers the majority decisions of the Court.

This conception might be attributed primarily to László Sólyom, the chief justice between 1990 and 1998. Sólyom played a distinguished role in shaping the judicial practice of the first Court; his contribution went far beyond that which inevitably follows from the position of the chief justice. Therefore, it will be hardly misleading if in the following sections I will focus on the reasoning of the rulings prepared by him, on the concurring opinions written by him, and on his articles and other statements.

In a lecture given in November 1991, Sólyom said that the Court must undertake "the articulation of such resolutions whose *possibility* is contained by the constitution but which would be left enclosed in the rules by the current public opinion".[3] This claim concerns constitutional rights adjudication only. The lecture referred to makes a clear distinction between issues of governmental organization and issues of constitutional rights. Within the domain of governmental organization, the lecture sees the Court's task in stabilizing the rules laid down by the constitution: "The Constitutional Court...is extremely rigid and self-restrained where the *governmental organization* specified by the constitution is at stake, that is, with regard to the disputes concerning the 'calibrating' of the competences of the new governmental organization."[4] Within the sphere of constitutional rights, on the other hand, Sólyom saw the Court's task in expanding the domain of individual liberty guaranteed by the constitution: "The fundamental rights chapter of the constitution has *taken over the text of international conventions*, which means that it represents a *minimal common denominator* that was acceptable for every signer of the international convention. The task of the Constitutional Court is to *heighten* this level of requirements."[5]

This distinction is not identical with the one between substantive and strict readings, but is related to it. For the Court will much more likely be required to undertake substantive reading where the task is "to heighten the level of requirements" of the constitution than where its business is only to stabilize the already existing constitutional arrangement.

In other words, the chief justice of the first Court saw it not only permissible but unavoidable, due to the tasks before the Court, that some of its decisions should rest on the substantive reading of the constitution. He made this claim with reference to the mission undertaken by the Court, that is, that its activity "will shift more and more in the direction of constitutional rights adjudication."[6]

We read in the lecture cited above that "It is a compelling duty as well as an aspiration of the Court to take a decisive part in developing the constitutional rights doctrine."[7] Proceeding from case to case, the Court "formulates the theoretical basis of the constitution and the rights included in it, and forms a coherent system with its rulings".[8] This characterization, which is to be found in his parallel reasoning attached to the decision that abolished the death penalty and was reiterated a number of times later on, is very close to what is referred to after Ronald Dworkin as the moral reading of the constitution. In one of his relatively late interviews, Sólyom himself has admitted the influence of Dworkin, and has reinforced once again that the judges have undertaken the moral reading of constitutional rights on the one hand, and, on the other hand, they have been aiming to formulate a "coherent system" of the underlying principles they resorted to in the course of the interpretation.[9] This "coherent system"—that interprets the provisions of the written text, explicates its internal relations and highlights their coherence—is what was referred to by László Sólyom as the "invisible constitution".

It seems justified, therefore, to assume in the beginning that the Court's self-understanding is on the most important points very close to the theory developed in the previous study: through and through, the Court has claimed the power to substantively—i.e. primarily morally—interpret the constitution, and to strike down laws on the basis of such substantive interpretations.

Nevertheless, I will claim that there have been significant alterations over the years within this relatively solid framework, and the major part of this study will be devoted to reconstructing these shifts.

One of the changes came to its conclusion rather early, in 1992. While in the beginning—that is, in 1990 and 91—the "invisible constitution" was seen as such a set of principles that could serve as the basis for critically revising even the written text of the constitution (the "invisible constitution" "serves as the safe measure of constitutionalism...above the constitution that is still being amended out of fleeting daily political purposes", as László Sólyom has written in one of his famous concurring opinions),[10] this shade of its meaning had disappeared by 1992 at the latest. From then on, the judges carefully avoided appealing to principles which may not be related to at least one provision of the constitution as its interpretation, or even presupposed the revision of the text of one or another constitutional provision.

In the second section I will say a few things about why László Sólyom and the majority centered around him first thought that they might critically treat the text of the constitution; then I will try to show, by an analysis of the Court's ruling 23/1990 (X. 31), that this belief not only pervaded the Court's self-understanding but also had its impact on its judicial practice. In at least one instance, the decision made by the judges did indeed break through even the broadest boundaries of textualism, and went so far as implicitly amending the text of the constitution.

Then I will proceed to reconstruct the kind of insights that have helped to stir the Court back to an unconditional respect for the text of the constitution. First I will take a look at the dilemmas with which the Court was confronted by its own death penalty ruling in relation with the abortion case, and then I will survey the lessons arising from the analysis of the first transitional justice legislation.

Another shift began soon after this. As we have seen, the Court initially understood its primary task to be the protection of constitutional rights; accordingly, between 1990 and 1993 there was a series of consequential decisions that expanded the conception of rights included in the constitution. However, this current dissipated in 1993, and there have been only minor rights decisions ever since. At the same time, an opposite tendency has emerged in a domain outside the sphere of classical fundamental rights, that is, in the realm of the social allowances and benefits provided by the government. While initially the Court adhered to a minimalist conception of the constitutional protection of the claim to such allowances, in the period between 1992 and 1994 the apparatus of an expansive conception of social rights was being formed, and a breakthrough occurred in 1995; there was a large number of rulings that struck down budgetary austerity measures in the name of social safety. While the Court became less and less active in safeguarding the constitutional rights whose protection does not require taking political responsibility, it interpreted more and more expansively the constitutional status of such allowances that might be protected only by such agents who are politically responsible to the public.

In the last sections of this study, I will discuss the nature of this shift and the reasons behind it, and raise questions concerning its reasonableness.

1.2. CRITICAL READING: THE ABOLITION
OF THE DEATH PENALTY

Our starting point was that the "invisible constitution" is not another constitution, independent of the written constitutional text; it is bound by the written text adopted by the Parliament. But what does the requirement of textual relevance demand? Does it permit or prohibit the "coherent system" developed by the Court occasionally to revise the text of the constitution (or, more specifically, its strict reading)? I have claimed in the previous section that the original articulation of the conception of the "invisible constitution" involved this possibility.[11]

The chief justice of the first Court was no doubt guided by a respect for the constitution. However, a respect for the *constitution* does not necessarily imply a respect for the *text* of the constitution. The constitution is valuable on account of its embodying *constitutionalism*; its text may, however, deviate here and there from that ideal. If we find that there is indeed a tension between the written constitution and the ideal of constitutionalism, then the guardian of the constitution is faced with a dilemma: Should it adhere to the text or revise it? For its mandate is not simply to safeguard the text of the constitution but to guard constitutionalism itself. In the beginning László Sólyom did indeed think that there is a less than desirable fit between the text of the constitution and the ideal of constitutionalism. He had a number of reasons for thinking this.

One of them is referred to by the succinct phrase cited above; this was fleshed out by Sólyom as follows in a lecture delivered in 1992: "You may recall that the expression "invisible constitution" was coined two and a half years ago. At that time, this conveyed a very important message. It was the summer of 1990, when the constitution was continually amended out of fleeting daily political purposes; during the spring there occurred the modification of the election of the president of the republic, then the return to the original situation; then there was the "pact" and the profound constitutional amendments involved in it. Then the Constitutional Court contrasted with this text, amended week after week, the fact of the existence of another constitution, which is more enduring than the former and has a true foundation in principles, and which is here to stay even though the existing text changes."[12]

The reservations concerning the text of the constitution might have been motivated by the frequent amendments springing from various political agreements, as well as by the hurried phrasing of the original text and the "constitutional errors"[13] that may be attributed to it. Finally, there was the fact mentioned above that the 1989 constitution took over its provisions on fundamental rights from the European Convention on Human Rights, representing an international minimum, while the Court understood its task as consisting in, among other things, heightening this minimal level of requirements.[14]

I claim, therefore, that at the time of the establishment of the Constitutional Court, the chief justice saw the constitution as an unstable, less than sufficiently considered text, which was being frequently amended on the basis of ephemeral reasons, and which contained a minimal compromise on human rights, which therefore did not always meet the norms of constitutionalism. And this image might have suggested to him and the majority that took shape around him that the judges, while specifying the solid and carefully harmonized norms of constitutionalism by proceeding with the interpretation from case to case, might in limiting cases go as far as revising the text of the constitution itself.

The claim to correct the faults of the constitution makers certainly goes beyond that which the guardians of the constitution may do without usurping the competence of the Parliament; thus, in democratic states the Court is supposed to refrain from it. But is there really more to it than a mere assertion? Did the first Court really pursue the program of critically applying the "safe measure" against the constitutional text? In what follows I will try to show that the answer is, in at least one instance, affirmative. The ruling that abolished the death penalty did exactly what was described through the metaphor of the "invisible constitution" in Sólyom's concurring opinion: far from merely interpreting it, that ruling revised the existing text of the constitution.

Four passages of the republican constitution may be brought to bear directly on the problem of the death penalty. Section 1 of Article 54 states that: "In the Republic of Hungary, every person has an innate right to life and human dignity, of which no one must be arbitrarily deprived". Section 2 of Article 54 claims that "No one must be subjected to torture or cruel, inhuman or humiliating treatment or punishment". Section 2 of Article 8 has it that "In the Republic of Hungary, the rules concerning fundamental rights and duties must be determined by laws, but the essential content of fundamental rights must not be restrained even by laws". Finally, Section 4 of Article 8 stipulates that "During a state of war, state of emergency or state of crisis the exercise of fundamental rights…might be suspended or limited" except for a number of enumerated fundamental rights, among them the right to life. The ruling draws on the first and third of these four passages.

The strict reading of Section 1 of Article 54 implies the following. First, the deprivation of someone's life is either arbitrary or not arbitrary. Second, the right to life prohibits the arbitrary deprivation of someone's life. Third, the right to life does not exclude those cases of the deprivation of life that are not qualified as arbitrary.

The content of Section 2 of Article 8 might be articulated as follows. There is no general principle prohibiting the restriction of constitutional rights categorically. Nevertheless, any restriction must respect two crucial conditions. The first one is formal: constitutional rights might be restricted only by laws. The second condition is substantive: the essential content of fundamental rights might not be invaded even by laws. What this "essential content" consists in is left unexplored by Section 2 of Article 8; it seems obvious that this must be made explicit from case to case, by way of interpreting the particular right in question.

Clearly, if the two passages lend themselves to a joint reading such that under it they do not contradict one another, then this interpretation must be given priority to its alternatives that involve contradictions. This rule expresses a requirement of strict interpretation that was already referred to above, i.e. that the reading of the text must not violate the demands of logic.

What kind of interpretive possibilities are excluded by this requirement? Section 2 of Article 8 would in principle allow the following alternatives:

1. The essential content of the right to life involves certain *special conditions*, under which the intentional deprivation of someone's life is prohibited;
2. The essential content of the right to life involves *all cases* of the deprivation of someone's life, therefore, the intentional deprivation of someone's life is always prohibited.

By contrast, Section 1 of Article 54 makes a distinction between the arbitrary and non-arbitrary cases of depriving someone of her life, and declares a general prohibition only for the arbitrary cases. Read together with this passage, Section 2 of Article 8 might not be interpreted as claiming that the essential content of the right to life involves *all cases* of depriving someone of her life, because according to Section 1 of Article 54 the non-arbitrary deprivation of someone of her life is not prohibited *in itself* (by the right to life). In other words, Section 2 of Article 8 should be read in the first variant enumerated above.

But what are the special conditions that make the deprivation of someone's life prohibited? According to Section 1 of Article 54, we must certainly include here the *arbitrariness* of the deprivation. If the essential content of some fundamental right includes those special conditions under which the given right must not be abridged even by laws, then the prohibition of the arbitrary deprivation of life certainly belongs to the essential content of the right to life. However, Section 2 of Article 8 and Section 1 of Article 54 do not stipulate any further condition that belongs to the essential content of the right to life, and which could therefore be the basis of prohibiting the restriction of this right. Therefore, the joint reading of the two constitutional passages allows two, mutually exclusive, readings, such as:

1. The essential content of the right to life includes the prohibition of and *only of* the arbitrary deprivation of someone's life; and
2. The essential content of the right to life includes the prohibition of the arbitrary deprivation of someone's life *and further things as well.*

Therefore, the strict reading of Section 2 of Article 8 and of Section 1 of Article 54 does not tell us which variant is to be accepted as valid. It allows for both.

Thus far extends the strict, joint reading of the two constitutional passages. The interpretation offered here is consistent; in other words, the categorical protection of the essential content of fundamental rights is fully compatible with confining this categorical protection, in the case of the right to life, to the prohibition of the arbitrary deprivation of life. At the same time, this consistent (strict) reading leaves open the question whether the criminal code's provisions specifying the death penalty infringe upon the essential content of the right to life (in the case they are not arbitrary, i.e. if they satisfy the requirement of the rule of law). If in the correct constitutional interpretation the essential content of this right involves the prohibition of and only of the arbitrary deprivation of life, then they do not infringe on it. By contrast, if the essential content of the right to life implies more than the prohibition of arbitrary deprivation of someone's life, then it must be decided through further investigation whether such provisions infringe upon the essential content of the right to life. Here is an example.

I have already cited Section 2 of Article 54, according to which "No one must be subjected to torture or cruel, inhuman or humiliating treatment or punishment." The Court did not draw on this provision in its reasoning, though it could have done so. All it takes is to accept that" the death penalty is a cruel, inhuman and humiliating punishment". If this tenet is true, then one may substitute in Section 2 of Article 54 the death penalty for the phrase "cruel, inhuman and humiliating...punishment", and the outcome will be the constitutional prohibition that "No one might be...subjected to the death penalty".[15]

Of course, it cannot be deduced from the text of the constitution that the death penalty is a "cruel, inhuman and humiliating" kind of punishment (although that it is not such a punishment cannot be deduced from it either). The question whether Section 2 of Article 54 may be brought to bear on the death penalty might be decided only through developing the criteria of cruel, inhuman and humiliating punishments, and then discussing the case of the death penalty in their light. Of course, this entails the establishment and application of a moral conception that goes beyond the strict interpretation. But this conception need not contradict the strict reading of the two sections of Article 54.

Furthermore, the above outcome might be joined with Section 2 of Article 8, and thus may be further reinforced. We have already seen that even though the joint reading of Section 2 of Article 8 and Section 1 of Article 54 does not require, neither does it preclude that the essential content of the right to life implies more than merely prohibiting the arbitrary deprivation of life. And then one might claim, on the basis of Section 2 of Article 54, that the prohibition of the deprivation of life as a cruel, inhuman and humiliating punishment is a constitutive part of the essential content of the right to life (even if the procedure is not arbitrary). Therefore, considering the thus further interpreted essential content of the right to life, Section 1 of Article 54 does indeed prohibit the death penalty.

This interpretation allows that there are such cases of depriving someone of her life that are neither arbitrary nor cruel, inhuman and humiliating, and are therefore acceptable (such cases are those of justified euthanasia or legitimate self-defense, and maybe homicide in extreme necessity as well). This is so because the constitutional prohibition of the death penalty is related to such features that it is an exercise of the government's punitive power, and is at the same time cruel, inhuman and humiliating, which features do not apply for the cases of justified euthanasia, legitimate self-defense, or homicide under extreme necessity: that is, to such features.

The Court pursued a different strategy. It did not seek for a special reason for excluding the death penalty, but desired to constitutionally prohibit the intentional taking of human life in general, and then went on to apply this general prohibition to the death penalty as a special case of depriving a human person of her life. The features that distinguish the death penalty from other cases of taking life (such as that it is ordered as a punitive sanction by a court ruling and is executed in institutional procedure) do not play any part in the Court's reasoning. It draws on such a feature that is true of all versions of the intentional taking of life: that it is complete and irremediable: if someone's life is taken, then everything is taken from her and her life might not be given back to her.

The Court's ruling admitted that Section 1 of Article 54 "allows for the non-arbitrary taking of life and human dignity",[16] and thus it did not in principle exclude the death penalty. On the other hand, it established a contradiction between Section 2 of Article 8 and the criminal code provisions specifying the death penalty. The conflict is allegedly caused by the fact that these provisions "do not merely infringe upon the essential content of the right to life and human dignity, but allow for the full and irremediable annihilation of life and human dignity and the right that secures them".[17] Since the annihilation of the essential content is a more severe violation than mere infringement, if infringement is prohibited, then so must also be annihilation. Thus is the Court's argument.

However, the ruling draws a further conclusion. It claims that "Section 2 of Article 8 of the constitution and Section 1 of Article 54 are incompatible" with one another.[18] This laconic and never further detailed claim refers to the fact that, in the Court's interpretation, Section 2 of Article 8 says that "the deprivation of someone's life and human dignity is *always* prohibited", while Section 1 of Article 54 implies the claim that "the deprivation of someone's life is *not always* prohibited (but only if it is arbitrary)". In other words, there is a direct contradiction between Section 2 of Article 8 and Section 1 of Article 54.

True, the contradiction might be eliminated, as indicated by the concurring opinion of László Sólyom. It is sufficient to introduce an auxiliary theorem according to which depriving someone of her life and human dignity can *only* be arbitrary (it is "conceptually arbitrary").[19] If this is true, then the adjective "arbitrary" in Section 1 of Article 54 is redundant, because "arbitrary deprivation" (of life) is equivalent to "deprivation" pure and simple. And the redundant mentioning of arbitrariness does not entail the possibility of non-arbitrary deprivation, which is approved by the constitution. Section 1 of Article 54 is thus made compatible with Section 2 of Article 8.

But this solution comes at the price that now the suggested interpretation of Section 1 of Article 54 is in conflict with the strict reading of the same passage, for in the strict reading the adjective "arbitrary" is *not* redundant, and its addition entails the possibility of non-arbitrary—and therefore, under the given provision, not necessarily prohibited—forms of taking life and human dignity. In other words, the Court's interpretation creates a contradiction either between the two constitutional passages or between the substantive reading of one of the passages and the strict reading of the same passage. Either way, the interpretation violates the fundamental requirement of textualism already referred to, according to which if there is a consistent reading of the text under discussion, then that reading must be taken as valid, and the full reading might not contradict the strict reading of the text (provided that there is at least one consistent reading).

In other words, if there is at least one such grammatical-logical analysis of the two constitutional provisions in which they do not contradict one another, then such a reading—developed by relying on moral convictions—that creates a contradiction between them must not be taken as an interpretation of the constitution. Furthermore, if the grammatical and logical analysis of the constitutional formulation of some right excludes the possibility of taking this right as absolute, then a theorem that holds this right to be beyond any restrictions under any circumstances must not be taken as an interpretation of the constitution.

The ruling on the death penalty inevitably violates at least one of these two requirements. The procedure of the Court would be defensible only if the ruling could demonstrate that its interpretation of the right to life reflects a universally accepted moral judgment, and is part of society's moral consensus—that there is indeed no other, morally defensible interpretation than that of the Court. If there is in fact such a consensus, then this must be satisfied no less than the rules of grammar and logic.

However, nothing of this sort was so much as implied by the judges. Their thesis in fact expresses rather complex and by no means obvious beliefs; we have no reason to think that they form parts of the moral consensus.[20] All this excludes the Constitutional Court's reading from among the ranks of acceptable interpretations even under the broadest criteria of textualism.

But it may be the case that proponents of the majority decision did not knowingly venture to critically revise the text; maybe they simply failed to recognize that the alleged contradiction between Section 2 of Article 8 and Section 1 of Article 54 disappears once the strict readings of the two passages are combined. If it were the case, then their error would not demonstrate that the decision was based on the critical reading of the constitution. All this would show is that someone who holds critical reading to be unacceptable must also reject the reasoning of this decision. But there is something else here as well, which was for sure considered by the Court.

If it were true that the two passages might not be maintained simultaneously, then at least one of them must be altered. But such alterations belong to the authority of the Parliament. So long as the legislators did not decide which passage was to be amended so as to remove the contradiction construed by the Court, no Court ruling might rest on either of the passages. For if it were otherwise, Court itself would decide which of the passages should be retained and which should be removed, which is in fact a constituent decision. By contrast, the Court ruling 23/1990 (X. 31) did in fact make this decision. It takes as authoritative Section 2 of Article 8, thus implicitly establishing that the fallacy lies not here but in Section 1 of Article 54. And then, this feature of the ruling for sure was not lost on the Court, because this move was explicitly objected to in Péter Schmidt's dissenting opinion.[21]

1.3. STRICT TEXTUALISM: THE ISSUE OF THE LEGAL STATUS OF FETUSES

The reasoning against the death penalty that is based on its being cruel, inhuman and humiliating differs from the one based on the conceptually illimitable nature of the right to life and human dignity not merely in the fact that while the latter creates a contradiction between the relevant constitutional passages, the former does not. A further important difference is that one of the reasonings restricts the Court's scope for later decisions much less than the other one. If the decision rests on the unconstitutionality of cruel, inhuman and humiliating *punishments*, then its consequences are limited to the range of juridical acts. By contrast, if it rests on the universal prohibition of *taking human life*, then it may have an impact on the constitutional status of a number of acts outside the sphere of criminal justice. It has serious consequences for a series of such issues that currently still deeply divide public opinion (abortion, euthanasia, in vitro fertilization, embryo experiments, etc.).[22] Furthermore, it makes the treatment of a number of cases that do not divide the public this way very difficult as well (such as obliging soldiers not to take anyone's life on the battlefield, or drawing the boundaries of legitimate use of weapons by policemen).[23]

In the previous study I have mentioned that the Court does well to make an incrementalist stance towards answering specific questions; that is, it does well, provided that two different answers settle the issue in the same way, if it chooses the one that binds less the decisions to be made about future cases. In the present case, nothing about the ruling and the individual reasonings attached to it implies that the judges might have considered resting the abolition of the death penalty on a more incrementalist reasoning than the one offered by them. Be that as it may, they were shortly confronted with the wider implications of the reasoning they chose.

In the course of 1990 and 1991, a large number of motions were filed with the Court that demanded it strike down the government statute (and other related rules of law) that permitted abortion, and urged that the Court declare the fetus to be a human being and, by implication, abortion to be homicide, the violation of the right to life, and therefore strictly forbidden. These motions confronted the Court with a serious dilemma.

If they were to meet these demands and declare that, legally speaking, fetuses are human beings and therefore the constitution regarded fetuses to be legal subjects that have the constitutional rights of human beings—among them the right to life—then they had also to declare that "abortion...might be practiced exclusively in those cases in which the law tolerates the choice between human lives and therefore does not punish the taking of life. Such a case is, for instance, when saving the mother's life necessitates abortion".[24] If they wanted to refrain from drawing this conclusion, they had to declare that the fetus does not belong to that class of beings that are recognized by the constitution as human beings. In what follows I will examine what the judges did in the face of this dilemma.

"In the Republic of Hungary, every person is a legal subject", says Article 56 of the constitution. But who belongs to the category of "every person"? Nowadays, it is only at the margins of the general public that one may venture to deny that all born human beings belong here, without exception— but does the fetus belong here as well? And if so, from what point in time? The answer will depend on the kind of properties that form the basis of our *obligation* to treat all beings that are biologically regarded as humans—that are the offspring of humans—in a privileged manner. In the language adopted by the Court, it depends on the properties to which the *dignity* of humans is attached.

The term "dignity" in its primary use refers to the moral rank of humans, the special *status* which is the basis of the special treatment that is due to every human individual; that they are the bearers of rights and all others are bearers of duties with respect to them. In this primary sense, dignity is not an empirical property that could be observed and measured like the level of intelligence or the capacity to concentrate. When we speak about human dignity in this sense, we formulate the judgment that humans are worthy of special treatment. But this judgment must be grounded one way or another. We must be able to point out the properties characteristic of human beings, and only of them, that justify the claim for special treatment. Human dignity is a *supervenient property*; it is not in itself observable, and it may be attributed to someone only if she possesses certain other properties (for instance, she is capable of leading a rational life and of revising her desires and beliefs in a critical manner) in virtue of which it is justified to ascribe the feature of dignity to her as well.[25] This implies, on the other hand, that what gives substance to the concept of human dignity (in this primary use) is the kind of independently observable properties it is attached to, because its different conceptions offer different interpretations about it, and they differ from one another precisely in the kind of properties to which they attach the special moral status of humans.

The decision abolishing the death penalty commits itself to a very specific conception. It claims that "human life and human dignity constitute an inseparable unity". This claim might be read, in principle, in two different ways. It may be interpreted as entailing that human life is worthy of special protection only if the living human being possesses the prerequisites of dignity (which are not identical with the facts that the individual in question was born of humans and is alive). Or it may be interpreted as saying that human dignity invariably accompanies human life and is attributable to every living human individual, irrespective of any other properties. In the first reading, dignity is a precondition of the distinguished worth of life. In the second reading, life itself is the very precondition which, if satisfied, is the reason for treating every person as a being with special moral status. The decision that abolished the death penalty does not tell us unequivocally which interpretation it takes as the correct one, but László Sólyom's concurring opinion makes it plain that the Court intended the second reading. Moreover, the abortion ruling uses the same unambiguous language as the parallel opinion of the chief justice: "Dignity is such a quality that is in principle inseparable from human life", we read here.[27]

This claim may at first glance appear as surprising, for a few lines below we find the following: "The right to human dignity means that there is a center of individual autonomy and self-determination, free from the disposition of anyone else, due to which, in the classical formulation, human beings are subjects and must not be treated as means or objects."[28] The cited formulation relates dignity to autonomy or self-determination, and thus makes it dependent on the possession of such a property which is not invariably given with human life.

However, the contradiction might be eliminated. The confusion is caused by the fact that the concept of human dignity has, beyond its primary use which is the focus of our discussion here, a secondary use as well—that is, one related to and presupposing the primary use—and the ruling oscillates between the two uses. In its secondary use, the concept refers to the property of individuals of conducting their lives in a manner that is worthy of their moral status. It recognizes that the individual is aware of the moral status marked by dignity, and acts accordingly. The individual who conducts her life in a manner worthy of her being as a human acts, among other things, in an autonomous way, and the right to human dignity protects her autonomy. But all this does not exclude that dignity, in its primary and fundamental meaning, characterizes human beings in the entirety of their lives, that is, from their conception until the irreversible breakdown of brain functions. In other words, even if one contests the conception embodied in the ruling (as does the author of this paper), one might not contest it on the basis that it harbors blatant inconsistencies.

Let us proceed, then, and examine the reasons the decision offers for adopting this position. "Human dignity...is inviolable in the case of everyone who is a human being, regardless of her physical or intellectual capacities or state, and of how much she has realized of her human possibilities, and why only so much", the judges established.[29] Therefore, dignity is equal for all human beings[30], and is insensitive to the level any one individual reaches in regard of such qualities as, for instance, rationality, awareness, will, or the capacity to grasp, follow and criticize rules. From this the justices concluded that these morally important features might not influence the status of human beings, for if they could, then the status of different individuals would not be equal. Therefore, human dignity is independent not only from the degree any one individual might reach in these specifically human properties, but also, and for this very reason, from these properties themselves. "It is a characteristic of the fundamental legal status of humans that their legal capacity is independent of any one property. This is fundamentally true about the right to life and human dignity as well", is the conclusion drawn by the ruling.[31]

On the other hand, if this is really the case, "If the legal capacity expressing the human quality of the already born person is unaffected by either their individual properties or the properties typical of certain states (such as age), then the level of development and other properties of the fetus might also be indifferent from the point of view of legal capacity and the right to life and human dignity."[32] In fact, they must be indifferent.

Therefore, the interpretation of the constitutional idea of human dignity offered by the decision involves the thesis of the legal capacity of the fetus. The inference might be summarized as follows:

1. The observable properties of human beings are of a scalar nature, i.e. they have degrees and might be ordered according to the relationship of more and less;
2. Human dignity, on the other hand, is independent of the degree to which any one individual might display the properties characteristic of human beings (human dignity is a non-scalar property: it either obtains or does not obtain); *therefore,*
3. Human dignity is independent of whether a human person shares any of the specifically human characteristics at all or not; *therefore,*
4. Human dignity is independent of whether an individual possesses any of the properties of the already born human beings, or is still in the state of fetuses, or in the specific state of fetal development it may be in; *therefore,*
5. Fetuses must be treated in the same privileged manner as already born human persons (independent of the phase of development they happen to be in); *therefore,*
6. The constitutional principle that "every person is a legal subject" includes fetuses as well (independent of the phase of development they happen to be in).

The ruling does not merely imply but explicitly endorses this conclusion: "The nature and significance of such an extension of legal subjecthood is comparable only to the abolition of slavery, only that it would be even more significant", we read in the reasoning. "With this, the legal subjecthood of human beings would reach its logical limits and completeness..."[33]

In my view, this conception is mistaken, even though not wholly unmotivated. The root of the fallacy lies in the transition from step 2 to step 3 in the chain of inferences above. The fact that the moral status of persons is insensitive to the differences of degree in the scalar properties that underlie it does not entail that it must also be insensitive to the presence or absence of these properties themselves.[34] The decision does not tell us why we should adopt a conception of the unity of human life and human dignity in which dignity is supervenient on the mere life of genetically human beings rather than one in which dignity is tied to other properties (to rationality, to the capacity for autonomy, for example), and life is protected by dignity only if these properties obtain. And if it were to try to justify this choice, it would encounter momentous difficulties. Suppose that we know it to be true about every being with dignity (and only about them) that they are shorter than two meters and weigh less then two hundred kilos. Then, someone who claims that dignity is supervenient on being shorter than two meters and weighing less than two hundred kilos would identify that very class of beings of which it may be truly claimed that they are to be treated as beings with dignity. But he would refer not to those primary qualities that *justify* attributing dignity to them. The relation between body size and weight on the one hand and dignity on the other is contingent. There is nothing in the first that would explain why beings shorter than two meters and weighing less than two hundred kilos should be treated as beings with dignity. The fact of biological human life is in the same relation with dignity. If we disregard beings that share the capacities of humans but are only possible rather than real, then this property delimits the class of beings with dignity rather precisely. But it still does not justify our ascribing special moral status to the members of this class.

However, my aim here is not that of subjecting the position taken by the Court to substantive criticism. I ventured to reconstruct the chain of inference of the abortion decision only in order to show that the ruling entailed the conclusion that fetuses are legal subjects. (True, the inference was fallacious, but the fallacy was explicitly made by the decision.) And still, the judges refrained from endorsing this claim; we will shortly see why.

They escaped the difficulty by retreating from critical reading straight to the principle of strict textualism. They declared that "the question of the legal subjecthood of the fetus might not be decided through an interpretation of the constitution...The legal situation is fundamentally different if the fetus is a legal subject than if it is not so. The legal consequences of the two interpretations are mutually exclusive, but both of them are compatible with the constitution."[35]

Should the Court have adhered to this extremely austere interpretive conception from the beginning on, it could not have made its decision abolishing the death penalty, or the one prohibiting the criminal prosecution of defamatory speech, or the rulings on restitution, or the decision prohibiting the unrestricted use of a personal identification number, and many others...In other words, the abortion ruling is incompatible with the interpretive practice of the Court unless it can show that it had special reasons for saying that the question of the legal subjecthood of fetuses (and only this question), which was left open by the strict reading, might not be decided through substantive interpretation.

The reasoning enumerates a number of possible explanations. First of all it claims that the question of the legal subjecthood of the fetus "is not about determining which of the possible interpretations within a universally accepted and value-free concept are reconcilable with the constitution and which are not".[36] But neither was the ruling that abolished the death penalty about this! It is compatible with the strict reading of the text of the constitution that there are arbitrary and non-arbitrary cases of taking life, yet this possibility was ruled out by the Court without substantive discussion, and the consequences are momentous: if it is possible to take life in a non-arbitrary manner, and if, furthermore, the death penalty is a non-arbitrary measure, then the death penalty is not ruled out by the joint reading of Section 2 of Article 8 and Section 1 of Article 54; if it is impossible to take life in a non-arbitrary way, then Section 2 of Article 8 prohibits the death penalty. And this observation might be swiftly generalized.

Competing interpretations of constitutional rights might be the interpretations of the *same* rights because in a large number of cases they draw the boundaries in the same manner; for instance, all plausible interpretations of the right to life concur in that homicide for its own sake is forbidden, while killing in self-defense is not. On the other hand, competing interpretations may be *different* interpretations of the same right because there are certain cases for which they draw the boundaries differently; thus, some interpretations permit, while others strictly forbid, medical euthanasia for terminally ill and suffering patients. If there was not a single case for which two interpretations draw the boundary between permissible and impermissible acts differently, then we would really be dealing with different formulations of the same interpretation rather than with two different interpretations. On the other hand, if the received use of the concept were to draw a clear-cut boundary where the two interpretations do not coincide, then at least one of the competing interpretations could not count as an interpretation of *this* concept ("he who has the power to kill someone may do so" is not an interpretation of the right to life).

A further explanation for the special treatment of the question concerning the legal subjecthood of the fetus was that the issue involved in this question would amount to "a redefiniton of the legal status of human beings", and this is "a question logically prior to the interpretation of fundamental rights, which requires a decision which is...external and might not be deduced from the internal coherence of the constitution".[37] No doubt the list of rights that are due to human beings does not specify the range of beings who count as human. It must first be determined whether fetuses are human beings or not to be able to decide whether they are protected by the fundamental rights or not. No interpretation of the *fundamental rights* may yield a clarification of the legal status of fetuses. But this does not mean that no interpretation of the *constitution* may yield such a clarification, for the constitution consists of more than a list of fundamental rights. Above I have reconstructed a possible (though I believe false) constitutional interpretation which is to be found in the Court's abortion ruling itself. I may add that this interpretation was not a mere logical possibility for the Court. Since it was coherent with the reasoning of the decision that abolished the death penalty, the judges should have taken it into account in their decision, for they had to read the text of the constitution together with their earlier interpretations.[38]

Finally, the ruling claims that "The decision about the legal subjecthood of the fetus is...substantively a constitutional decision, which should be most appropriately regulated by laying it down in the constitution."[39] The Court has no authority to make constitution; therefore, if the status of the fetus is a question to be settled by the constitution makers, then it might not be decided by the Court. But this argument is not sufficient in itself. The question of the status of the fetus is in fact of constitutional significance; the answer to be given to it will determine the meaning of the phrase "every person" in Article 56 of the constitution. But the decision about this question belongs to the exclusive authority of the constitution makers only if it might not be carried out through an interpretation of the existing text of the constitution. If this were really so, the argument from constitution making would be superfluous: the impossibility of settling the issue through interpretation would in itself conclusively close the debate. By contrast, if this is not so (and we have seen that it is not), then the question of the legal status of fetuses need not be a constitution making one, for it would not require altering the text of the constitution.

In sum, there are no good reasons for the Court to treat the question concerning the status of fetuses with such distinct caution, that is, to retreat to the position of strict textualism from the substantive interpretation daringly deployed in earlier decisions. It would have corresponded to the practice of the Court to apply the principles it had introduced in the course of discussing the death penalty to the problem of the status of fetuses as well. And we can go even further.

The abortion ruling affects the problem of the status of fetuses in two different aspects. First, it must answer the question whether the status of fetuses entails the criteria of legal subjecthood. It is in this regard that the Court claimed the impossibility of determining the status of fetuses through constitutional interpretation. But it also brings up a further question, which is also related to the problem of the status of fetuses—that is, to the principles of the treatment that is due to fetuses. This question runs as follows: What are the consequences if the constitution makers were to rule that fetuses are not legal subjects? Does it follow that the pregnant woman is alone to decide (at least in the early stages of pregnancy) whether to bear or abort her fetus? According to the ruling, even if fetuses do not possess legal capacity, the right to self-determination of pregnant women might not prevail without qualifications. In this case, the life of fetuses is protected by the fact that human life is an objective value to be upheld in and of itself. How did the Court reach this insight?

The constitution does not stipulate that human life is an objective value, nor does it mention objective values in general. On the other hand, Article 54 declares that every person has a right to life, and Article 8 declares that the protection of the fundamental rights of people is a primary duty of the state. Since the right to life is enumerated among the fundamental rights, it follows from the joining of these two claims that protecting the right to life is a primary duty of the state. It is through interpreting this duty that the ruling concludes that protecting the objective value of life is a further duty of the state.

The right to life imposes the duty on the state, the abortion ruling claims, not only to refrain from violating this right but also to provide for satisfying the conditions necessary for the realization of this right. This is what is referred to by the reasoning as the state's duty to provide the institutional protection of life. And the idea of a duty to provide the institutional protection of life leads to the conception of an objective value of human life. This duty "protects human life and its conditions of existence in general as well as...human life in general"—that is, human life as a value is the object of this protection".[40]

But if life as an objective value can be the object of protection, then the scope of the institutional protection of life might be divorced from the scope of the subjects of the right to life. It may be extended to such living human beings who are not the subjects of the right to life—that is, to fetuses as well. From this the ruling draws the conclusion that abortion must be made dependent on official permission, and granting the permission must be made dependent on specific reasons that lend themselves to verification even if the legislature does not extend legal subjecthood to fetuses.[41] The reasoning proceeds as follows:

1. The state bears an institutional duty to protect life;
2. The institutional protection of life goes beyond the protection of the subjects of the right to life, and it protects human life as an objective value; *therefore,*
3. The scope of the institutional protection of life extends further than the class of beings who possess the right to life, it extends to every living human being;
4. Fetuses are living human beings; *therefore,*
5. The institutional protection of life extends to fetuses as well; *therefore,*
6. Abortion must not be the private affair of pregnant women (abortion without justifying reasons is unacceptable).

The critical move is to be found in steps 3 and 4 of the chain of inference. If we claim human life to be an objective value which is to be protected in itself, independent of the right to life of constitutional subjects, then it is indeed possible for the objective protection of life to extend to a domain which is larger than that of the protection of the subjects of the right to life. Nevertheless, we must be able to say where this domain begins and ends; in other words, how far human life, which is to be objectively protected, extends. When specifying this domain one makes a claim about the status of the beings within its boundaries: one claims that they, in contrast to the existents outside its boundaries, are under the objective, institutional protection of life.[42]

Thus, the reasoning reconstructed here involves a position about the status of fetuses, not with respect to legal subjecthood but with respect to the norms of the objective protection of life. The conclusion might be drawn only if it was antecedently established about the fetus that it stands under the objective, institutional protection of life.

Whether this is so is a question prior to the one about the prohibition of abortion without justifying reasons, in the same manner as the question of the legal subjecthood of fetuses logically precedes the problem of whether the right to life, provided that fetuses possess it, allows abortion, and if so, under what sort of circumstances. Still, the Court wanted to exclude the latter from the range of questions determinable through constitutional interpretation, while it answered the former without any scruples.

This is a serious logical error. If it is not determinable through constitutional interpretation whether the status of fetuses entails the predicate of legal subjecthood (because the question about the status of the fetus is logically prior to that concerning the right of constitutional subjects), then it might no more be determined through constitutional interpretation whether the status of fetuses entails the predicate of the objective value of fetal life (for the same reason). However, the ruling settles the second question. But if the second question might be settled through constitutional interpretation, then there is no reason why the first question should not be settled through interpretation as well. But the ruling wants to leave the first question open.

If we find an explanation for the differential treatment of the two questions, we might understand why the abortion ruling retreated in its most important issue, from the natural rights reasoning of the the death penalty ruling to strict textualism. Now, there is only one relevant difference to be found between the two issues. From the objective value of fetal life the decision inferred only that abortion must be bound to justifying reasons, but it did not specify any constitutional criteria as to the nature and weight of these. By contrast, it made it plain that if fetuses are to be regarded as legal subjects, then it is only the most serious reason (the endangerment of the pregnant woman's life) that might make abortion permissible. My assumption is that the ruling did not refrain from establishing the objective value of fetal life only because the judges could reach an agreement to the effect that such a need for justification that is based on this is acceptable.[43] On the other hand, the Court rejected to establish the legal subjecthood of fetuses because the majority was reluctant to accept its consequences—a strict prohibition of abortion.[44]

But why would strict prohibition follow from attributing legal capacity to fetuses? Because if they are legal subjects, there are no grounds for denying that they are the bearers of the right to life as well. And then, the ruling that abolished the death penalty offered such an interpretation of the right to life in which it has an absolute, non-limitable status. At the same time, the conception of the unity of life and human dignity entailed the extension of legal capacity to fetuses. This is how the dilemma of the abortion ruling has obtained. The ruling on the death penalty had such consequences which only a minority of the judges were willing to endorse.

Had the Court rested the abolition of the death penalty on the concept of "cruel, inhuman or humiliating punishment" rather than on the thesis of the non-limitability of the right to life, it could have avoided the dilemma outlined here. It could also have avoided the dilemma through an interpretation of the right to life as less than absolute even if it had established the legal subjecthood of fetuses. For instance, it could have followed the abortion ruling of the German Federal Constitutional Court in 1975, which recognized fetuses as persons and bearers of the right to life, yet established that pregnant women might not be obliged to bear their fetuses if that incurs a disproportionate burden on them.[45]

1.4. A SHIFT IN SELF-UNDERSTANDING:
TRANSITIONAL JUSTICE

The embarrassing difficulties that arose in relation with the abortion ruling warned the Court against such interpretations that predetermine later decisions. Of course, that a ruling has far-reaching consequences and that it rests on a critical revision of the text of the constitution are logically independent from one another. There might be momentous decisions that respect the results of strict reading, and there might be modest decisions that nevertheless revise the strict reading of the text. Still, it is very likely that the Court will venture to knowingly undertake an interpretation that covertly amends the text only if it intends to carry through some very consequential conception. This was certainly the case with the interpretation of the right to life. Therefore, the lessons must have had an impact on the way the Court treated the possibility of critical reading. These lessons called for greater caution. First, the pendulum swung right to the other extreme: the abortion ruling stipulated the limits of interpretation at the principles of strict textualism—at least with respect to the legal subjecthood of fetuses. In other cases, where the judges' hands were not directly tied by the theses of the the death penalty resolution, they did not exercise such a degree of self-restraint.[46]

To be sure, greater practical precaution need not in itself imply renouncing in principle the claim to critical reading. That takes more than this. It required the Court to revise its self-understanding and the way it understood its own mission. We have seen that in the beginning the Court—or at least the chief justice who decisively shaped its attitude—saw that the judges must uphold constitutionalism even against the haphazardly amended text of the constitution. However, the Court was soon to face such a task that compelled it to reformulate its self-understanding.

The 1989 constitution outlined the enduring institutional arrangement of the democratic republic, even though its preamble claimed that it was made with the temporary aim of promoting "the peaceful political transition" in view. It does not contain temporary rules and institutions at all. "For all practical purposes, with the constitutional amendment published on 23 October, 1989 a new constitution has come into force", the Court itself claimed.[47] But then the question inevitably arose: Should the constitution that was designed for the future be applied without remainder to the circumstances of the transition as well, or do the unique and extraordinary tasks of the transformation make a deviation from the constitution necessary and therefore permissible? This question was brought up first and foremost in relation to the legacy of the old regime—how the state might meet its obligation to compensate the victims of the injustices of the past, and what it might do with the perpetrators of past crimes that were comitted out of political motives and left unpunished for political reasons.[48]

The Parliament raised the issue of the closing of the past in 1991. Subsequently, in 1991/92 a number of questions were addressed to the Court with respect to the relation between the constitution and the transition that had realized the new constitutional order.

It was first in relation to the third restitution resolution that the Court declared that "the transition imposes unique, special historic requirements" on the government, which may demand extraordinary measures.[49] The Restitution Act approved by the Parliament on April 24, 1991 granted priority purchase rights to former landowners against agricultural cooperatives; former landowners were given so-called restitution vouchers to pay for the land. If the transition had left the property of the cooperatives unaffected, the constitutionality of creating purchase rights against it would have been questionable, since creating purchase rights by law is a severe interference with the right of the owners to dispose over their holdings, and the property of the cooperatives—just like any other form of property—is under the protection of the constitution. This was the position of the first restitution ruling of the Court.[50]

The property of the cooperatives, however, did not remain unaffected. At the time of drafting the Restitution Act, the amendment of the provisions on the cooperatives was already underway, making the transformation of cooperatives into shareholding companies possible. Therefore, the second and third rulings on the Restitution Act assumed that the Restitution Act had been approved at a special moment, at the moment of the transition, when the forms of ownership appropriate for a market economy were being born, and the government was confronted with the moral obligation to redeem the injustices done at the time of abolishing private property.

This was the moment, the Constitutional Court claimed, when creating purchase rights against the property of the cooperatives was permissible. But the reason was not that the extraordinary situation could make unconstitutional measures acceptable, but because in the extraordinary situation the imposition of purchase rights was not unconstitutional.

The law on cooperatives under preparation at the time made it a precondition of the transformation that the property of the cooperatives be distributed among members. Therefore, the members expected to get free property from the property of the cooperative that had formerly been treated as indivisible. Thus, the Court could claim that if the right to purchase was enforced against the cooperatives at the time when their property was being distributed, then the state in fact established the purchase right against the new property which was being born; thus, it restricted such properties for which the would-be owners had no prior claim—since the members of the cooperatives received the property not in virtue of such a claim but in virtue of a new legal disposition, and not in return for payment but freely, as beneficiaries of the transition to a market economy. Therefore, the new recipients of the property had no right against the state's imposing a part of the costs of the transformation on them—as a precondition of distributing the property, as it were.

Prior to the beginning of the transformation, the indivisible property of the cooperatives enjoyed constitutional protection against expropriation without compensation. *After* the completion of the transformation, the divided property of the cooperatives enjoys the same sort of protection. The time of the transformation, however, was a special moment, when the claim to the constitutional protection of property was mitigated, and the sharing of the costs of peaceful transformation became possible.

Therefore, the Court established, the Restitution Act did not violate such property rights that are under the protection of the constitution: "There is no constitutional barrier that should prevent the laws that effect the transformation of the system of property from distributing the burdens of the creation of societal property and the obligations introduced by the amendment of the constitution on 23 October, 1989 between those who acquire this societal property freely."[51]

Thus, the question was not whether the unique, extraordinary circumstances of the transition made the evasion of the constitutional protection of property acceptable. As the first ruling on transitional justice observed retrospectively: "It was never the case that the Constitutional Court considered the situation extraordinary from the point of view of constitutionalism; in other words, it never even occurred to suspend the demands of constitutionalism."[52]

This had to be emphasized with such force because the sponsors and supporters of the Transitional Justice Act approved in October 1991 tried to offer reasons precisely for a suspension of the requirements of constitutionalism, by referring to the extraordinary nature of the task. Zsolt Zétényi, who was (along with Péter Takács) the sponsor of the bill, said at the 8 October session of the Parliament: "The rule of law might not serve as a protective shield for the perpetrators of injustices. The re-establishment of the rule of law must mean that no deed deserving punishments remains without punishment...The statutes of limitation or the general principles of the rule of law are not in the business of perpetuating or preserving pre-legal or unlawful situations. To sum up, the application of the provisions of the rule of law is obligatory under the rule of law, but they must not be applied in a way that once and for all exempts unlawful situations from the jurisdiction of criminal law. I do not question the logical consistency of the argument that the requirements of formal law are violated by the above measures, but I do contest that in the given situation there is no other solution than doing nothing...In a state where the law was being violated day after day, it would be an affront to the rule of law itself if the formerly violated tenets of law were mobilized against the natural law..."[53]

The proponents of transitional justice legislation argued, thus, that there is a conflict between substantive justice demanded by the rule of law and the formal provisions of the rule of law, and that in this conflict justice should take priority. The government says to its citizens, by attempting to enforce political justice, that the unlawful practice of the old regime has gone, once and for all; by contrast, failing to enforce political justice would convey the message that the perpetrators who were left unpunished under the dictatorship are exempted from the legal consequences of their deeds. Revealing and punishing past crimes is a weightier interest than the strict enforcement of constitutional provisions, or so Zétényi and his comrades have argued.

For its part, the Constitutional Court struck down the law on the whole as well as in detail. What is more, it did not merely declare the provisions that would have restarted the statutes of limitation to be unconstitutional and therefore void. It saw it to be necessary to emphatically declare that "The given historical situation might be taken into consideration within the framework of the rule of law and for the sake of establishing the rule of law. On the other hand, one must not disregard the fundamental guarantees of the rule of law with reference to the historical situation and the justice demanded by the rule of law."[54]

The direct application of natural law might be justified when the legal system is being suspended—during revolutions or in such situations as emerged as a result of the collapse of the Nazi regime and the military occupation of Germany. The transition from communism to democracy and a capitalist market economy was not accompanied by such a legal rupture. True, the republican constitution and the fundamental laws that were adopted with it have introduced "such changes that, from a political point of view, amounted to a revolution".[55] However, these provisions "were established within the legislative procedure of the old regime, in a formally flawless manner, and they derive their binding force from this fact".[56] To sum up: "The transition was brought about on the basis of the old regime."[57]

This entails the important consequence that "the old law continues to be in force. With respect to validity, there is no difference between law 'before the constitution' and law 'after the constitution'."[58] There are no two different standards: "Irrespective of the time of its adoption, every existing provision of law must satisfy the demands of the new constitution."[59] If the statutes of limitation are in accordance with the present constitution—and this is in fact the case—then they might not be retroactively disregarded.

"A fundamental component of the rule of law is legal security. Among other things, legal security requires the protection of acquired rights and that the legal relations that have already been accomplished or otherwise definitively concluded be left unaffected."[60] Once the statutes of limitation have ran out for a crime, "the perpetrators have a right not to be punished", no matter what their deeds might have been, and no matter what the reasons for their avoiding the punishment had been.[61]

And here comes the decisive claim of the resolution: "The unjust outcome of the legal relations...is not in itself an argument against legal security...Legal security that rests on objective and formal principles always has priority over the ever partial and subjective justice."[62] The priority of legal security means that the fundamental principles enshrined in the constitution and the guarantees of their enforcement might not be evaded for considerations of natural law.

This claim was made by the Court with respect to legislation; however, it was not based on the special status of the legislature, but on a general conception of the relation between formal legal security and substantive justice. Arguing against the proponents of transitional justice, the judges offered such an interpretation of the conception of the rule of law that from then on binds their own hand as well.

The tenet contained in Section 1 of Article 2 of the constitution that "the Republic of Hungary is...under the rule of law" might in principle be interpreted in two different ways. The first alternative is to identify the rule of law, beyond its merely formal conditions, with the substantive requirements of justice, fairness and respect for the fundamental rights. In this case the rule of law would be equivalent with the rule of constitutional rights; the formal aspects of the rule of law would merely amount to being means for the realization of these broader, substantive requirements. Since the Court had been committed, right from the beginning, to the moral reading of the constitution and the active protection of fundamental rights, this so to speak broad interpretation would not have been alien to it.

The other alternative was to choose a narrow understanding for the rule of law, that is, to include in it only the formal conditions required by legal security. No doubt, the narrow understanding could have come into conflict with the fundamental rights commitments of the Court. But the possibility of such a conflict would not imperil the judicial protection of fundamental rights unless it were coupled with the further thesis that all constitutional requirements beyond the demands of the formal rule of law are mere ideals, declarative principles without regulatory force. But such a thesis is not entailed by the formal understanding of the rule of law. Thus, the possibility was left open for the Court to understand the principle of the rule of law narrowly and then articulate the moral principles latent in the constitution by making appeal to other constitutional passages.

In 1992 the judges opted for the latter option. But what were the stakes in this move? What is the difference between the two conceptions that are otherwise equally compatible with the Court's commitments? The difference lies in that by clearly separating the formal and the substantive constitutional requirements, the narrow understanding allows for establishing an order of priority between them. It was for the sake of this ranking that the Court opted for the narrow definition of the rule of law. It wanted to stipulate that under the rule of law, adherence to substantive values might not break through the barriers of formal procedural norms.

The thesis that the procedural norms of the rule of law were to have strict priority over the enforcement of substantive values was a new element in the doctrine of the Court, and it was bound to have significant consequences for the critical reading of the constitution. The formal understanding of the rule of law demands that no constitutional interpretation may come into conflict with the text of the constitution. The judges must have noticed that the objection they had made against the Transitional Justice Act might equally be made against their own position held in the ruling on the death penalty. If the priority of legal security applies to the legislature that is subordinated to the constitution, then it equally applies to the interpretation of the constitution. Judicial interpretation of the constitution might no more violate the formal requirements of the rule of law than a legislative decision. And then, a constitutional interpretation that implies a covert amendment of the text of the constitution frustrates the expectations attached to the stability of the text, and therefore violates legal security.

Thus, when the Court declared that the requirements of substantive justice might be realized exclusively within the framework of the guarantees that serve legal security, it introduced, once and for all, a binding principle of self-restraint for itself as well. That principle implied that the Court must carefully refrain from reading the constitution in ways that rest on a critique of the text.

It is by no means a coincidence that it was precisely in contemplating the 1992 resolution on political justice that the chief justice said that "The Constitutional Court...relies, instead of ideologies or ideological natural law principles, on a sort of (limited) constitutional positivism."[63] As far as I am aware, the term "constitutional positivism" has never been used by Sólyom either before or after this occasion in summarizing the creed of the Court.[64] And now, all of a sudden, when the conflict between legal security and extralegal claims confronted the Court with the problematic nature of natural rights oriented treatment of the constitution, he resorted to this term. "It is a historical experience", Sólyom added, "that after the fall of dictatorships it is often natural law that fills the ideological as well as the legal gap not merely in the period of transition but even after the consolidation of the new regime."[65] To illustrate this, he referred to the practice of the German Federal Constitutional Court during its first decade, when the court had not yet refrained from passing judgments that rested on the "value system of the constitution". The Hungarian Constitutional Court, by contrast, "works with legal concepts rather than with the 'value system of the constitution', and among these concepts are preeminent those of legal security and of (primarily procedural) guarantees".[66]

To sum up, at the time when the Court began its career, the emphasis in its self-understanding was put on the fact that it is authorized to confront the text of the constitution—bearing the marks of a host of improvisations and political bargains—with the "safe measure of constitutionalism". I might say that in the beginning the view of the majority was that the Court is the depository of the paradox of constitutionalism. By contrast, when the judges were faced with the basic questions of the transition, the emphasis of the Court's self-understanding shifted to the fact, and this is a real citation, that "the Constitutional Court is the depository of the legal revolution".[67] With this shift, the claim that was still raised in the beginning that the "invisible constitution", reconstructed through constitutional interpretation, might offer grounds for revising the text of the constitution itself has vanished without a trace. The period when the Court was prepared for natural law adjudication was over.

1.5. THE DECLINE OF RIGHTS
ADJUDICATION

This shift was soon to be followed by yet another one. Up until 1993, in each year at least one rights resolution of far-reaching political consequences was being met. In 1990, the Court abolished the death penalty. In 1991, it determined the principles of the protection of personal data and of freedom of information. In 1992, it provided for the constitutional understanding of the freedom of expression, and determined the conditions under which the punitive power of the government might be deployed. In 1993, it interpreted the freedom of religion, and the principle of the separation of church and state; furthermore, it made a resolution about the meaning of the independence of the judiciary and about its special institutional preconditions. The common feature of these rulings is that they have laid down comprehensive principles and theses, and that they—to use László Sólyom's expression—significantly raised the level of requirements of the protection of constitutional rights. Between 1990 and 1993, the practice of the Court was in line with its self-understanding according to which the primary aim of constitutional review is to protect the—expansively conceived—fundamental rights. After 1993, however, the current of formative rights decisions dissipated. What are the reasons behind this drop?

There is an apparently obvious answer to this question. "In the first four or five years, there was much more ground to lay down basic principles, because at that time we had to give substance to the fundamental rights out of nothing; for all practical purposes, we had to develop the constitution", László Sólyom claimed in his interview already cited above.[68] The view offers itself that after the making of the far-reaching rulings of principle, there was little more left but the developing of details and the refinement of distinctions. If this picture is correct, then the rupture in the series of formative resolutions only indicates that by 1993 the doctrine of the Court had reached completion.

However, the suggested explanation is not spelled out in sufficient detail. A number of further conditions must be met so that one could agree with it. First, it must be true that the Court already covered all major areas of constitutional rights, and developed both the principles that underlie the constitution and the tests of the application of these principles. The second condition is suggested by the absence of correlation between the scope of decisions and their significance; the fact that the later decisions dealt only with details does not imply that they were mostly of a trivial nature. Therefore, for

Sólyom's explanation to work, it must be true that even though the scope of the later decisions is typically narrower than that of the earlier ones, their implications is typically no less serious than those of the earlier ones. Third, it is not sufficient that the Court be prepared to make far-reaching resolutions; it is also necessary that the consecutive rulings point in the same direction, and that the growing corpus constitutes an unambiguous trend.

If we apply these tests to the changes in rights adjudication after 1993, our observations will not justify the belief that the shift was due to the maturation of the Court's doctrine.

First of all, a number of highly important areas were not so much as touched by the Court. There is no decision about the constitutional requirements of the use of force and restriction of freedom by the police, even though numerous motions were filed in this regard after 1995. A motion objecting to the immigration law has not been heard since 1995, either; the Court has simply no view on the principles of how the government should treat asylum-seekers and other foreigners taking the soil of this country. There is no decision about the phenomena of non-punitive use of force or restriction of freedom, such as, primarily, the mandatory hospitalization and treatment of psychiatric patients, even though a series of motions have been filed with the Court since 1994. The Court is yet to address the issue of patients' rights, and is yet to hear the motion made in 1993 about euthanasia. Even though it has developed detailed tests for the assessment of discrimination, these are simply not applicable to the most urgent and widespread cases of discrimination in Hungary—i.e. racial discrimination—and they are equally inapplicable to the characteristic cases of discrimination against women. However, the Court did not see it necessary to do anything about the proper development of further tests.[69] What occurred in 1993 was not a complete removal of the blind spots from rights adjudication but rather the abandonment of charting these blind spots.

Second, it was not merely the scope of rights resolutions that was narrowed—the Court usually gave priority to the less consequential issues over those that had serious political implications. This is well demonstrated in those two areas—that of freedom of expression, and of data protection and freedom of information—in which the Court made consequential, formative resolutions in 1991 and 1992.

Resolution 30/1992 (V. 26) no doubt laid down the doctrine of the freedom of expression, and set the guidelines for judging all later cases in this domain. But there was subsequently a large number of significant cases that all demanded resolution by the Court. In 1993, a motion was filed against the law about criminal prosecution of the use of totalitarian symbols; in 1994, a motion was filed against the criminal law provisions on derogating from the authority of public officials; in 1995, the criminal case of an offence against national symbols, in 1996, the new criminal case of hate speech, and the criminal case of spreading false rumors were objected to. Another motion was filed against passages about prior censorship of the 1986 law on the press. These are all issues of significant consequence, and yet until November 1998 (the retirement of László Sólyom) only two of them were heard by the Court—that of the derogating from public authority and of prior censorship. In the first case, the Court made an unobjectionable decision.[70] In the latter case, by contrast, a highly ambiguous decision was reached. On the one hand, the ruling declared that the prosecutors might not suspend the publication of press products with reference to the personality rights of others (independent of the will of those concerned), and that they might not ask for prohibition by the court; on the other hand, the Court upheld the authorization of the prosecutors in cases where the intervention is justified in the interests of public morality.[71] Beyond this, the Court made one single resolution in the area of freedom of expression; it found unconstitutional the rules providing that different economic and social organizations might purchase only such art objects that had previously been assessed by a panel of experts.[72] This is a correct but trivial decision; its significance is not comparable with those the judges failed to hear.[73]

The future career of the very consequential resolution on the protection of personal data and the freedom of information shows a similar tendency. In 1994, the Court declared, in relation to the first Lustration Act, that those under surveillance by the secret services of the old regime had a right to access their files, and that information about the spying activity of former secret agents was in the public interest and therefore might not be made secret.[74] On the other hand, it failed to hear the motion made in 1996 that initiated that all the files created at the different departments of the former secret services should be made accessible for those that were under surveillance.[75] It never discussed the passages of the Police Act that were suspect from the perspective of data protection, and it never addressed those provisions of that act regulating the treatment of medical data that were again objected to. And while in these highly significant issues the Court allowed, by inaction, the practice of data protection to deteriorate, it addressed and resolved a series of minor issues in the same area—in good spirit, but with trivial consequences. Thus, in 1995 it declared that the restriction on accessing real estate registries was unconstitutional[76]; it repeatedly prohibited compulsory property declarations[77]; it determined the requirements to be met at public criminal courts when presenting expert opinions on the mental state of the defendant[78]. And in 1998, it provided that defendants might not be denied the right to have access to such data that support the prosecution but which are qualified as official secrets.[79]

We find an even less favorable picture if, by taking a wider perspective, we examine all the resolutions made between 1994 and 1998 that in one way or another concerned constitutional rights. Such resolutions were made in large numbers: the restriction on the number of cabdriver's permissions violates the freedom of enterprise;[80] it is against the freedom of competition that chimney-cleaning might be delivered only through one specific company[81]; the statute of the local government of the capital violates the requirement of legal security when it fails to make it explicit whether it is compulsory or merely permissible to put clamps on cars parking without paying the appropriate fee;[82] it is unconstitutional that civil procedure does not provide for legal remedy against appellate court resolutions ordering fines and expert fees;[83] it is unconstitutional to make a distinction between the order of enforcement of such civil law claims that are regulated by the criminal procedure, provided that the distinction has the consequence that in one of the cases essential procedural guarantees are disregarded;[84] the higher education law is unconstitutional in excluding, without the possibility of differentiation, from all types of institutions, branches, levels of training, and forms of higher education, those persons who have been prohibited from participating in public affairs;[85] it is not acceptable that in some cases employers are wholly responsible for the harms incurred on third parties during the exercise of employment, while in other cases the responsibility is shared between the employer and the employee, the only difference being in the form of ownership of the employing company;[86] the legal prescription of temporary compulsory work constrains fundamental rights and therefore it is not permissible unless the law specifies the essential guarantees of the protection of this fundamental right;[87] if the president of the republic suspends on probation the execution of a punishment through pardon, then the conditions of the lapse of individual pardon and the procedure of the subsequent execution of the punishment must be specified in law;[88] the criminal case of the abuse of the freedom of association represents an unnecessary and disproportionate restriction (this case obtains if someone creates or leads an organization whose goal is to commit crimes...;[89] and so on. The series of such more or less well-meaning but inconsequential rights rulings is hardly interrupted by significant resolutions between 1994 and 1998.

There was only one single instance after 1993 when the Court made a truly consequential rights decision in a previously uncharted territory: this occurred in 1995, when the Court established that the exclusion of same sex couples from the civil law institution of partnership is discriminatory and therefore unconstitutional.[90] This resolution could have turned out to be such a landmark decision in the constitutional treatment of forms of life, sexual and cultural attitudes, as the 1992 resolution on the freedom of expression in fact has been in the sphere of speech. But this was not to be. Hardly a year later, when the Court had to decide whether it was permissible to set special requirements for the registration of a gay rights organization, the judges in full agreement ruled in a spirit diametrically opposed to the earlier decision.[91] At the same time, the Court failed to discuss up until the end of 1998 a motion filed in 1993, on the grounds of discrimination against sexual orientation, against the criminal case of unnatural sexual perversion, nor have they heard a 1996 petition against the discrimination inherent in the criminal cases of rape, offences against decency, seduction, incest, unnatural sexual perversion, and in the institution of private action.[92]

The ambiguity on gay rights is not the only indication of the disorientation of rights adjudication. The first abortion resolution has already deviated from the series of decisions that unambiguously "raised the level of protection"; in 1995, the Court all of a sudden threatened the public with tightening the rules,[93] and even though it did not realize this threat, in 1998 it compelled the legislature to restrict the existing regulations.[94] The 1993 resolution on the freedom of conscience and religion was followed by such a decision on the institution of army chaplains that would hardly survive the test either against the principle of the separation of church and state, or against that of the religious neutrality of the state and of the abolition of religious discrimination.[95]

Therefore, third, disorientation and hesitation is to be witnessed in the Court's practice after 1993 in relation with the great rights questions.

In a word, the full picture implies the loss of impetus of rights adjudication rather than its reaching completion, and this requires some explanation.

First of all I would like to rule out a possible explanation that would immediately recommend itself from what has been said so far. Then I go on to suggest another answer.

The ebbing away of the current of fundamental rights resolutions almost immediately followed the turn described above as the Court's retreat from the critical reading of the constitution. The assumption suggests itself that the rejection of natural rights adjudication warned for greater caution in the treatment of fundamental rights. To be sure, if an expansive interpretation of fundamental rights is necessarily divorced from the text of the constitution and might even revise it, then the caution would in fact have been justified. Yet, as I tried to show in the study on "Constitutional Review" there are strong reasons for rejecting the assimilation of the moral reading of the constitution to critical reading. Relinquishing natural law adjudication need not at all compel the judges to turn their backs on the active protection of constitutional rights.

But, one may argue, even though the rejection of natural law adjudication does not logically imply such a turn, it might nevertheless psychologically foster it. This is in fact conceivable, but the practice of the Court suggests otherwise. For even though after 1993 the judges became more and more cautious in the sphere of rights adjudication, they at the same time grew more and more courageous in the active defense of social allowances and benefits. If the rejection of natural rights adjudication warned them to caution in one domain, it should have sent the same warning in the other domain as well. Therefore, we must find such an explanation which simultaneously motivates the recoil in one of the domains and the growing momentum in the other one. Where should one look for this?

I suggest taking a look at the way the views of the judges were divided. That is, I propose to ask what sort of decisions could hope to acquire a majority in the Court? My hypothesis is the following: the issue of the freedom of religion was the last great rights issue where the expansive interpretation commanded a sufficient majority. In the issues that came after, there was no way to secure a majority for such interpretations. Thus, the Court could do little else but to put these cases aside, or if it ventured to make a decision, it either deviated from the series of resolutions that "raised the level of protection", as the first abortion resolution, or did not show a clear trend (but rather signs of disorientation) if taken together with other decisions on the same subject, as the rulings concerning gay rights, or the separation of church and state and religious discrimination. By contrast, the access to social allowances was initially understood by the majority as enjoying such weak protection that no individual claims can be based on it. Between 1992 and 1994, however, the prerequisites for reaching a new consensus were gradually formed, which led to dramatic decisions in 1995.

The two parts of this hypothesis are not equally easy to test. The analysis of the second part can be carried out relatively easily, through an examination of the resolutions accessible to the public; all it takes is to go through the shift in the doctrine of the Court, decision after decision. This is what I will do in the next section. The first part of the hypothesis, by contrast, could be tested only by mobilizing different types of information, because the decisions that were put aside do not leave traces behind, and it is very rarely that one could determine, without systematically interviewing the judges and their clerks, whether a decision was set aside because there was no chance of bringing the necessary majority together, or because of completely different reasons. Such investigations would exceed the confines of this study.

Nevertheless, the published resolutions do in fact provide certain evidence, and this material was surveyed in the present section. If the chances of reaching an agreement were no smaller in the case of coercive measures by the police and by the medical profession, of immigration rules, euthanasia, and the so-called offences against sexual morality, than in the case of, say, the death penalty, then what was the reason why no decision was met on these issues? If the consensus on important details of freedom of expression or data protection was no less determinate than in the broad outlines drawn by the first, formative resolutions, then why did the Court set most of the relevant, important motions aside? If the judges were not ambivalent with respect to gay rights, then why did they make conflicting resolutions? If the Court continued to adhere to its emphatically declared initial program, then why did it waste its precious time and energy on trivial issues rather then continuing to raise the level of protection of fundamental rights?

The tendencies between 1994 and 1998 of the Court's rulings cohere well with the hypothesis that the majority behind expansive rights adjudication vanished after 1993. If one compares the decided cases and the ones left undecided, one will find that the collective position of the Court concerning the general principles of political liberties (freedom of expression, data protection, freedom of conscience and religion) was close to the conception of liberalism, but in the domain of many of the applications of these same general principles, not to mention other families of issues like questions of life and the death, of the individual conduct of life, of racial and gender discrimination (such as abortion, euthanasia, artificial insemination, homosexuality, women, the Roma), it was much farther from it. This is, in my view, what explains the loss of the initial momentum of rights adjudication. At the moment that the formulation of principles in the areas where the consensus among the judges corresponded to the liberal position was completed, the program of raising the level of protection of fundamental rights could no longer be continued.[96]

Let us now consider the other aspect of the story: the emerging consensus behind strong judicial protection of social allowances.

1.6. THE UPSURGE
OF WELFARE PROTECTION

The chapter on fundamental rights of the constitution enumerates a few "social rights" as well. The most important one among these is the right to social safety laid down in Article 70/E, whose subjects—that is, the citizens—might claim, in case of necessity, "such allowances that are sufficient for their subsistence". This article consists of two sections: the first determines the content of the right, while the other stipulates the sort of measures the government must deploy in protecting the right in question. Section 1 entails that the government must not leave any one of its citizens without at least some minimum social provision; Section 2 entails that the government must deliver such institutions as are necessary for preserving social safety (for instance, it must establish and operate the organization of social security).

Right from the beginning, the Court understood these requirements in a very guarded manner. In interpreting the first section, it established that the mandatory minimum social allowance is not a predetermined quantity; it is impossible to specify such a level of allowances that the government could be compelled to deliver to the needy, regardless of the state of the budget. The violation of the right to social safety might be established only in the limiting case when the needy are altogether left without allowance; the executive and the legislature possess a wide margin of discretion in determining the level and quality of social provisions. With regard to Section 2, too, the Court has claimed that all the government is compelled to do is to establish some sort of a practicable institutional order; the executive and the legislature have a wide margin of discretion in choosing the relevant institutions. According to the Court, the content of the right to social safety is the following: the government must maintain practicable institutions to secure social provisions, and at least some of these institutions must be specifically designed to take care of the needy. Apart from the limiting cases of the total absence of institutions or the total failure of provisions, the usual constitutional standards do not apply to the right to social safety. The government has no obligation to maintain the once achieved level of provisions forever or to never alter the once established institutional order. Accordingly, up until 1995 the Court had consistently refused to intervene, to protect social rights, in the budgetary decisions of the executive or of the legislature.[97]

The judges have never explicitly abandoned the conception outlined here. But they departed from their well-guarded practice. In May 1995, the Parliament approved an Economic Stabilization Act. The joint application of the austerity measures would have reduced government deficits with a total of 132.4 billion HUF. The Court addressed the stability measures in 15 resolutions, and it annulled many of them. Taken together, its resolutions removed 31.4 billion HUF from the proposed savings, or 23.72 percent of the total.[98] This was an unprecedented intervention in the budgetary competence of the legislature; it did not merely deviate from the European practice of constitutional review, but it also effected a dramatic change compared to the domestic precedents. How could such a radical turn come about?

The most straightforward answer is that the resolutions that cut back the stability program brought unprepared, arbitrary changes in the practice of the Court, which could not have been predicted by the executive or by the legislature.[99] This view could be held in good faith in the summer of 1995; those who focused primarily on the dispositive parts of the earlier resolutions were justified to expect that the stabilization program would mostly pass the hurdle of constitutional review. Thus, the belief that the Court merely gave free rein to its political biases when it invalidated almost one-quarter of the budgetary cuts, were not altogether ungrounded.[100] But still it would be superficial and erroneous to explain the 1995 resolutions solely with the misgivings of the Court majority against the government. In the past, the resolutions that stirred political controversies had always divided the judges.[101] By contrast, this time the Court acted almost unanimously.[102]

This fact distinguished the resolutions examining the stabilization law and the supplementary estimates of 1995 not only from the other, politically sensitive decisions but from the earlier rulings on social safety as well. To be sure, prior to 1995 the Court had never struck down any budgetary legislation that negatively affected the well-being of a group of citizens, but the upholding of such legislation never enjoyed full consensus. It was first in 1991 that the judges had to decide on a case of revoking a government subsidy. At that time, the question was whether it is permissible to raise, by a legislative act, the interest rates on housing loans that were originally offered at below-the-market conditions. There were two dissenting opinions attached to the upholding resolution.[103] In 1993, when the issue was whether it is constitutional to raise pensions at a rate smaller than that of the increase of real wages, and to set a cap on pensions so as to change the income relations among pensioners, the number of dissenting opinions approximated the half of all the justices on the bench (four out of the ten objected to the resolution).[104] In 1994, in a related area, more specifically in a ruling on the "right to protect the environment", it already became the majority view that this right "means the government's obligation to maintain the natural basis of life", and the thus determined obligation was said to include that the government might retreat from the once achieved level of environmental protection only under special circumstances, that is, under such circumstances "when the restriction of the fundamental rights of the subjects would be admissible, too". Seven out of nine judges subscribed to this view.[105] When it came, finally, to the Stabilization Act, the majority had been already perceptibly transformed. One should explain at this point how the shift occurred.

For my part, I would suggest the following explanation. Between 1990 and 1995 an interpretive apparatus was formed that allowed the judges to declare many of the welfare austerity measures to be unconstitutional while at the same time retaining the minimalist discourse on the constitutional protection of social rights. Thus, a proper assessment of the 1995 decisions requires that we take a look at the apparatus that forms the grounds of the new consensus. We must go beyond the dispositive section of the rulings concerning the social commitments of the government, to see how the changes were gathering in the reasoning section, to the point of transforming the very disposition at a particular historical moment.

As early as the first mentioning of the question of social safety we find a curious reference. We read that even in cases where the reduction of guaranteed social provisions does not reach the critical limit, it might be constitutionally objectionable, but what is objected to in such cases is not the reduction of allowances and benefits in itself but rather something else, for instance that the supports were taken away in a discriminatory manner, disproportionately affecting certain groups, or by violating acquired rights.[106] We may for this time set aside the issue of discrimination, for this is not a constitutional reason to prohibit the state from reducing social allowances; discrimination might be remedied by depriving everyone of the support of the government to the same degree. The doctrine of *acquired rights* is the conceptual tool that will give a handle to the Court to form its new consensus.

Originally, the Court meant by acquired rights—or acquisition of rights— that someone purchases, at an earlier time, certain later services, and thus acquires a right to the later enjoyment of these. Thus, an employee who paid his pension contributions regularly acquired on this account the right to have a pension after retirement. The thus interpreted acquired right is not in itself a constitutional concept, but the principle of the rule of law, enshrined in Article 2 of the constitution, or more specifically one of its aspects, the principle of *legal security*, gives it constitutional protection. For one might purchase in advance future services on a reasonable calculation only if the purchaser might expect that in the intervening period of time the provider will not arbitrarily modify its commitment to perform the services in question. It was on this ground that the Court declared as early as the beginning of 1991 that "the revoking of acquired rights violates the principle of legal security, which is a constitutive element of the rule of law".[107]

In the cases discussed here, the principle of legal security meant the secure enjoyment of the right to property. The purchaser's right to future service for his payments is a property right, and later the Court made it explicit that the right to future services acquired through earlier payments is to be assessed in accordance with the criteria of the constitutional *protection of property*.[108] This is a compelling reading, though one might want to add that the intervening period between the payment and the service entails certain risks, and the proportion in which the parties should share these risks is a matter of further clarification.[109]

Of course, the person who pays the contribution acquires a right only if the two parties made a prior agreement that the contributions of the one will be returned by the later services of the other. Therefore, this case of acquired rights might be understood as an entitlement based on the contract between the parties, which binds the party that offers the service on the ground that 1. it made an agreement with the other party, who 2. for his part has performed the obligations incurred on him by the contract.

However, entitlements based on contracts are not necessarily of a property-like nature. Contracts may serve as a basis of obligations even without it being the case that the obliged party received any payment. In the next step, the Court examined the constitutional aspects of such a case. This was the case of subsidized housing loans.

Here, the story was that the National Savings Bank offered housing loans to married couples at a below-the-market interest rate, and the government took responsibility to cover the difference each year. If one dissects this complex case, one has two, partly different instances.

In one case, the bank offers loans to the purchasers at market interest rates, but the market rates significantly and enduringly increase. Then the question is whether the original contract may be adjusted to the changed market conditions. The recipients of the loan did not purchase the right to unchanged interest rates; if they have such a right it is certainly not one based on the acquisition of property. But the principle of legal security demands even without this that the original conditions of the contract should not be altered arbitrarily, by unilateral decision. When somebody takes a long-term loan, he must consider the burdens that the paying of the installments incur on him. He may make reliable estimates, and take a responsible decision on whether he will be able to perform his obligations to pay only if he has no reason to fear that the burdens will increase unpredictably in the future. No long-term contract might be made without some stability of expectations. Therefore, we might say that by making the contract, the recipient of the loan purchases a right to the stability of the terms of the contract. This, too, is an acquired right, though not one of property. The principle of legal security requires that the already signed contract be modified only by the voluntary consent of the recipient of the loan or, in the absence of this, through court action, and that a judicial amendment of the contract be effected only under very strict conditions—i.e. when the initiator of the modification can prove that due to an unpredictable deterioration of conditions that exceeds ordinary risks, maintaining the original terms of the contract would impose intolerable burdens on him. It is not a sufficient ground that the credit institution could have more favorable options to allocate its money, had it waited with the making of the contract until this time; it must also be true that the wholly unexpected change in the financial market conditions imposes such severe payment obligations on it that it would not survive the new situation without an increase of interest rates.

At this point, let us focus on the government, which took responsibility, in a legal provision, to regularly pay the difference between the fixed low interest rates and the market rate. If the original obligation did not stipulate a cap on the difference, then the legal provision obliges the government to take the whole burden of inflation upon itself. In this story, the role of the government differs from that of the bank in the previous story in a number of respects. First of all, the government is not one of the contracting parties; it takes on itself the burden of paying the loss of the bank by a unilateral act. Second, the government undertakes this obligation not in return for some service but in order to realize one of its policy aims—to promote housing construction. Third, it is not the government's own money with which it supports housing construction, but the contribution of taxpayers. The taxpaying capacity of the citizenry is limited, and so the goal of supporting housing construction inevitably competes with other policy aims, which are also expected by the taxpayers to be realized. This is a peculiar situation with peculiar consequences.

If it nevertheless remains true with respect to the government as well that the recipients of the loan have a right to the stability of the terms of the contract, then the scope of the application of the concept of acquired rights is extended to a new domain; even though the acquisition of right is still based on a contract, it is enforced against such a party who did not take part in the contract. And this is exactly how the Court saw the case to be. The resolution cited above claims that the government might modify through legal provision the obligation it took on itself under exactly the same conditions which would move a court to change the terms of a contract made between two parties.[110] This might sound an all too strict qualification, but it is intelligible why the Court saw a resemblance between the obligations of the contracting parties and those unilaterally undertaken by the government. For the government promised to pay the difference between the subsidized and the market rates precisely with the intention to promote contracts between housing constructors and the National Savings Bank; the promise concerned not merely the background conditions of the contract but its very content; therefore, its revoking affects the content of the contract itself. Even though the government is not one of the contracting parties, the claims made against it are based on a contract—on such contract, for that matter, which was fostered by it.

From this, it takes only one further move to declare that the principle of legal security restricts the government in revoking its unilateral promises even if these promises are not related directly to contracts made between private parties, and if, therefore, the claim to stability is not based on contractual obligations. The decisive move was made by the Court in 1994, when it examined whether the government might revoke tax benefits granted to foreign companies.[111] The structure of the argument is the same here as in the case of contractual obligations. If the legal provision grants certain benefits without a deadline, then the expected advantages are built into the calculations of the beneficiaries. They might adjust their long-term projects to the hoped-for allowances, and the revocation of the latter might make the actions already begun intolerably costly even if it was not a contract in which the government made its promise, and even if the beneficiaries did not pay a dime for it.

Thus, the Court was heading towards a conception according to which the stability of purchased rights or of rights acquired through other contracts are only a special class under the principle of legal security. Each time the government induces, by its conduct, individuals or their organizations to expect the enduring existence of some benefit or indemnity, the government has an obligation to secure these, provided that in the hope of the stability of the favorable situation, the agents concerned undertook such burdens that will be returned only in the long run. Therefore, even though the government might later on revoke unilateral advantages that were offered without any service in return, its discretion is not unlimited in such cases.

It is in this latest sense that the Court uses the concept of acquired rights in most of the resolutions that examined the Stabilization Act. "An accustomed, well-known and predictable system of provisions, which...has been maintained for decades" creates "recognized and acquired rights" simply in virtue of the fact that in the past the government made a unilateral promise, which it kept for a long period of time.[112] The beneficiaries of the past services of the government acquire a right to the future maintenance of these services, regardless of what the reasons behind the launching of the services had been (original entitlement or merely some policy aim by the government), and the basis of the acquisition of right is that the government made a promise in law to realize the service, and it kept its promise for a sufficiently long time.[113]

Let us summarize what has been said so far. The source of the acquisition of entitlements is in all cases some act, the consequences of which are protected by the principle of legal security. But the nature of the act that creates the entitlement may differ from case to case; accordingly, the principle of legal security contributes to the acquisition of entitlement in different ways. In some of the cases, it is the entitled person herself who acquires the right through her payments, and the principle of legal security protects her right to property. This is the case of rights acquired through purchase. In other cases, it is an agreement made between the contracting parties that determines certain entitlements (not to property), and the principle of legal security protects the good-faith expectations attached to the contract. In a third case, the contracting parties acquire certain entitlements against the government as an extra-contractual party, and the entitlement is based partly on the unilateral promise made by the government, and partly on the contract that was made on the basis of the government's promise and was subsequently kept by both parties; here, the principle of legal security protects the expectations with respect to the government as a third party that promoted the contract. This is the case of rights acquired through the legal guarantee of contracts. Finally, the unilateral promise of the government might in itself be a source of entitlements; in such cases, the principle of legal security protects the expectations based on the incentives provided by the government. This is the case of rights acquired through mere legal promise.[114]

The extension appears to be obvious. But the farther we leave the paradigm case of property rights, the weaker the binding force of acquired rights becomes, and the weaker the requirements of the norm of legal security will be. A claim based on a unilateral promise might not be as solid as an entitlement based on purchase. From step to step, we need less and less pressing reasons to make the acquired right yield to the interests that are opposed to it.

At the decisive point, the Court understood the issue in the same way. Even though it did not address the difference in force of acquired claims, and it established an explicit equivalence between the conditions for changing a contract and for changing unilateral of legal promises that form the ground of contracts, it nevertheless emphatically declared that the claims that were created by unilateral declaration might be revoked by the government by unilateral declaration. Such a revocation need not be justified by "compelling necessity". In revoking unilaterally offered benefits or allowances, all that is expected from the government is to provide "a reasonable period of preparation" for those concerned. The demonstration of compelling necessity is necessary only if the government wants to introduce the restrictions immediately, *without transition*.[115] In other words, compelling necessity and the sufficient preparatory period are not supplementary but alternative conditions in the case of the weakest version of acquired rights; if either one or the other obtains, the revocation of such allowances that were granted for an extended period of time does not violate the constitutional requirement of legal security. This conception, too, was fully preserved in the 1995 resolutions. The protection of acquired rights means, we read here, that "services and the expectations attached to them might not be radically changed without proper constitutional reasons or from one day to the next...Changes without a transitory period require special reasons."[116]

As for the concept of preparatory period, this was taken over from the Act on Legislation. Originally, it indicated the period of time that must pass between the publication and the entry into force of a law so that those subject to the law might be expected to be aware of it.[117] This period, of course, might not be negative; that is, the law must not prescribe obligations retroactively, for the period that preceded its publication.[118]

The first two rulings of the Court on this issue declared only retroactive force to be explicitly unconstitutional, and the third and fourth resolutions did not deviate from this practice.[119] Later on, however, the Court's position shifted. First it declared that the date of publication and of entry into force must not coincide, because this would violate the principle of legal security—for those obliged by the law have no time to get acquainted with their obligations. But the resolution that declared this still made the point that if the law enters into force later than the date of publication, then there is no ground for constitutional investigations as to the length of the period between the two events (the question of appropriate time "is a matter of consideration that requires taking into account economic, organizational and technical facts; that is, it is not a constitutional problem").[120]

In the next move, the Court modified this thesis and extended the range of constitutional assessment to the length of the period of time between publication and entry into force. It was in early 1994 that it first declared that an insufficient preparatory period might be unconstitutional.[121] From then on, it became a requirement of legal security that between publication and entry into force, at least so much time must pass that it might be claimed in good faith that the absence of knowledge of the law could not give indemnity from the consequences.

The same resolution that declared that the length of the period of time between publication and entry into force may be a matter of constitutional assessment brought about a further innovation: it mentioned among the criteria for determining the sufficient preparatory period the need for adjustment created by the revocation of the antecedently promised allowances or benefits—in this case of tax benefits.[122] It made it plain that when the government revokes such subsidies that are granted by law, the sufficient preparatory period must include the time that is necessary for adjustment to the changes for those who undertook long-term liabilities in the expectation of the allowance which is now being revoked.

By the time the constitutional assessment of the Stabilization Act was undertaken the next year, all the devices the Court needed were in place to be able to radically intervene, while maintaining its doctrine on the constitutional protection of social rights, in the legislative reduction of government allowances. The growth of the interventionist minority made it perceptible that the judges are attracted by the thought of the constitutional protection of welfare benefits, and should they acquire the necessary interpretive apparatus, they would not refrain from acting. By 1995, the apparatus was complete. All they needed was the right moment to mobilize the apparatus of legal security, acquired rights and sufficient preparatory period, so that they could strike down legislation even in such areas where the conceptual framework of social rights alone would not have done the trick.

What is more, since the apparatus developed between 1990 and 1994 is independent of the concepts of social rights and the theses associated with it, the new apparatus enabled the Court to extend constitutional welfare protection to such areas that are not covered by social rights at all. The rulings that cut back the 1995 Stabilization Act and the supplementary estimates addressed need-based entitlements only as an exception.[123] The welfare policies they undertook to protect were designed for the most part to promote specific demographic policies; they fostered childbearing either directly, as the child allowance, or indirectly, as the subsidized housing loan offered to couples with children. The remaining part was made up of striking down measures intended to extend social security contributions (the inclusion of copyright fees, the specification of the industrial accident insurance fee to be paid by individual entrepreneurs in part-time employement) or the provision that shifted the starting date of the payment of disability allowance to the 26th day of disability. This was not a need-based policy; it had nothing to do with the constitutional passages that protect social rights.

In the next section, I will take a look at the basic questions of the practice of welfare protection as it was tested in 1995. Before doing that, however, I would like to sum up the picture that was drawn by the tendency described in this section, if coupled by the one described in the previous one.

We have traced the shifts in the Court's practice in two dimensions. One of them was that of rights adjudication. At the two extremes one finds here expansive and conservative protection of liberty. Initially, the Court's resolutions were to be found close to the expansionist extreme, but as early as before the half time of the Court's mandate they had run of issues in which an expansive resolution could hope to win a majority. As we have seen in the previous section, a shift toward the conservative extreme (where the already achieved level of protection is not further raised but only at best maintained) could have been avoided only if the majority of the judges were close to the liberal standpoint not only in the area of political liberties, but also in the issues of life and the death, individual lifestyle, and racial and gender discrimination. However, the collective standpoint of the Court that evolved in the course of the adjudication was not liberal in a sense that goes beyond the European liberal minimum; therefore, the fundamental rights program of the Court that was in the beginning endorsed emphatically was soon to collapse.

The second dimension is that of welfare protection. Here, the scale extends from a restrained treatment of budgetary issues to daringly intervening in budget affairs. On this scale, the early decisions of the Court were to be found around the extreme of self-restraint, only to swing radically to interventionism after years of preparation. No doubt, the liberal position on this scale is closer to the restrained judicial treatment of budget affairs.[124] Therefore, we find in this sphere, too, that the Court's collective standpoint has become more and more removed from the liberal conception with the passage of time. The privileged significance attributed by the resolutions concerning the stabilization law to family protection and demographic policy also indicates that the shifting consensus of the Court was more and more conceding to considerations that are alien to liberalism.

The moral and political worldview that most closely corresponds to the judicial tendencies of the first Hungarian Constitutional Court is not the liberal or the socialist one but a Christian worldview—to wit, the Catholicism of the period after the Second Vatican Council.[125] The rising to preeminence of this worldview accounts for the decreasing momentum of the protection of fundamental rights after 1993 as well as for the increasing welfare protection.

However, this study does not intend to undertake an exhaustive discussion of the Court's substantive position. We need to address the shifts in conception described here only in so far as they concern the Court's doctrine of constitutional interpretation. Therefore, in relation to the decline of the protection of fundamental rights we need to discuss only whether this tendency was related to the rejection of the critical reading of the constitution by the Court. And we might conclude this question with the negative answer given in the previous section: the rejection of natural law—based adjudication need not lead to giving up the claim to an extension of fundamental rights. The latter must be accounted for by other factors. But the intensification of welfare protection requires further investigations, because it raises the question whether it is compatible with the fundamental principles of constitutional democracy if welfare protection leads to judicial intervention in the budget—and if so, in which cases.

The next section will take a look at this question. I will apply the insights reached in Chapter 3 of "Constitutional Review" to the welfare protection practice of the Court.

1.7. THE PARADOXES
OF WELFARE PROTECTION

Some of the resolutions rejecting the restriction of welfare institutions are based on such reasons that might be assessed without the consideration of budgetary issues. Such was the rejection of imposing social security contribution on authorship fees, which was justified by the Court by pointing out that according to the law, no service would have been given in return for the imposition of the burdens.[126] Such was also the rejection of medical contribution imposed on individual entrepreneurs performing supplementary activities, because this was found to be discriminatory by the Court.[127] I need not address these resolutions here.

The justification of the other welfare-protecting decisions is related either directly or indirectly to the assessment of the budgetary reasons behind the austerity measures. The restriction of child allowances was declared to be unconstitutional on the ground of violating the requirement of sufficient preparatory period; the shifting of the starting date of paying disability allowance to the 26th day of disability was annulled in part because of the lack of sufficient preparatory period and in part because of the *disproportionality* of the incurred burdens; the restriction of subsidized housing loan interest rates were rejected as *unnecessary*. Since, as we have seen, the test of sufficient preparatory period must be applied if the measure in question did not pass the test of necessity/proportionality, we may claim in sum that the assessment of the measures drawn into the investigation depended on whether they in fact violated the requirements involved in this latter test.

It seems, thus, reasonable to begin the analysis of these decisions by examining the way the Court applied the test of necessity/proportionality to the contested cases. The outcome is of some surprise. The rulings that discussed the curbing back of family allowances did not address this issue at all. The Court failed to consult the finance minister responsible for the stabilization program to ask for his reasons for the reduction of allowances; furthermore, it did not even venture to confront the reasons attributable to the government with the norms of the test. It saw it sufficient to declare that "Whether the conditions for such a special intervention obtain must be decided by the Constitutional Court as the ultimate forum."[128] The Court simply left unexplored whether the conditions that may justify an immediate intervention obtained, or whether the stabilization package could really be expected to provide for a sufficient preparatory period for those concerned.

The medical support reduction was first declared unconstitutional by the Court as an immediate measure that allowed no preparatory period;[129] then it was annulled as such a measure that imposed disproportionate burdens on those insured.[130] Thus, the test of necessity/proportionality was taken into account substantively at least in the second ruling. The shifting of the starting date of paying medical support to the 26th day of the illness was claimed to be disproportionate by the resolution on the ground that the average time spent on medical leave is 32 to 33 days, thus the entry into force of the measure would leave 75 percent of the period of illness uncovered. For all practical purposes, this meant the preemption of this provision, the judges claimed.[131] There are three conspicuous problems with this argument. First of all, a burden taken from social security is not equivalent with a burden imposed on the patients: the law made it the obligation of the employers to cover the first 25 days of medical leave.[132] Second, the service provided in return for the medical contribution is not exhausted by the disability allowance paid for the period of illness; it includes contribution to the costs of drug treatment, hospital service, surgeries etc. The reduction of disability allowance paid for the period of illness must be assessed in view of this whole picture, not taken in itself.[133] Finally, in the Court's own conception, the burdens incurred by a government measure may be judged to be proportionate or disproportionate not in themselves but by comparison with the damage the contested measure was intended to avert or mitigate.[134] Therefore, the test of proportionality would have required that the judges measure the burdens imposed on the insured to the adverse consequences of the increasing deficit of the social security, which the judges failed to carry out. Neither did they examine whether the contested measures satisfied the test of necessity; they simply repeated that a decision on this issue belonged to the competence of the Constitutional Court.[135]

The increase of housing loan interest rates from 15 percent specified in 1991 to 25 percent was rejected by the Court by claiming that the measure violated the requirement of necessity. In part, it argued that since market interest rates had barely increased since 1993, the state budget had not suffered significant losses.[136] This would have been a cogent argument, provided that the increase of interest rates was intended merely as a reaction to the change of credit conditions on the market and nothing else. However, the contested measure was part of a comprehensive austerity program and was designed as one of the steps that was expected to block and reverse the increase of the budget deficit.

Therefore, a demonstration that the rise in interest rates did not pass the test of necessity would have required that the judges did not stop at the examination of the changes in market interest rates. They should have demonstrated either that the economic situation did not necessitate any budgetary restriction, or that it did not necessitate this specific restriction, because there were other, much less painful solutions at the government's disposal. By contrast, the resolution did not even bother to take a look at these alternatives; it simply made the totally ungrounded declaration that "The increase of the budget's deficit...is not of such an extraordinary degree that could not have been predicted, or which would exceed the reasonable contractual risks."[137] One is left wondering about the statistics, estimates and calculations that served as the grounds for the strikingly confident judgment of the Court.

To sum up, the resolutions that examined the 1995 stabilization law and the supplementary estimates made the claim of applying the constitutional test of necessity/proportionality on the majority of the measures that cut deeply into the well-being of the citizens, yet they failed to carry out the announced tests. Thus, we are in fact left ignorant about the conditions that should have been met for the judges to declare the contested measures to satisfy the requirements of necessity and proportionality.

But one should notice that the real difficulties would have begun only if the Court in fact had done that which it was committed to do by its own standards. Because these are very strict standards indeed. For when the judges confront various budget measures with the test of necessity/proportionality, they might not rest content with that which is required by the weaker test of reasonable goal; that is, they might not rest content with establishing whether the government's budget conception is coherent in itself, whether there are rational grounds for coming out with an austerity package, whether the basic data are plausible, whether the calculations are accurate, and whether there is a logical correspondence between the goals and the chosen strategy. Beyond this, they must compare the government's conception with other possible conceptions to see, on the one hand, whether there are such solutions that realize the intended goal with less burden (necessity), and on the other hand, whether the failure to realize the goal would imply at least as much burden as that which is imposed on some in the course of the realization (proportionality). And this would mean that whether the contested restrictive measures are accepted as necessary and proportionate or rejected as unnecessary and disproportionate depends on the kind of alternative budgetary conception that the Court would approve as realistic and realizable. In other words, whether the restrictive measures adopted by the legislature could be claimed to be respecting or violating the citizens' legitimate interest in legal security would depend on the kind of budgetary conception the judges agree with. But if this is so, then two budgets would face one another; one adopted by the Parliament, and the other endorsed by the Constitutional Court. The fundamental questions of budget policy would be decided by the Court rather than by the Parliament.

But the stabilization program did not fail at the intervention of the Court! No matter how radical the judicial mitigation of the restriction was, the government did not go bankrupt, the state of the budget improved, the Hungarian economy avoided breaking point. Do not these facts prove that after all the Court was right and the finance minister was wrong when the former declared tens of billions in austerity measures to be unnecessary and blocked them? There are a number of counter-arguments, but we need not go into this dispute here.[138] For the question here is not who was *right* but who had the *authority* to make a decision and consider the risks of budget measures.

The constitution of the Republic of Hungary gives this authority to the legislature.[139] Neither the constitution nor the law on the Constitutional Court gives the Court such an authority. In Hungary, the Constitutional Court unlawfully usurps the constitutionally established authority of the legislative power if it decides about the necessity of budget provisions. Of course, it does not follow from this that the current constitutional arrangement is good. In principle, it is conceivable that the dilemma of constitutional review highlighted here draws attention to a fallacy in the existing scheme of the separation of powers, which should be corrected by constitutional amendment. However, we have seen in the previous study that there are good reasons for retaining the method of separation of powers established by the republican constitution. Budgetary decisions always involve a choice between alternative risks, and practical reasons as well as considerations of principle demand that the decision makers share the risks that are imposed on society by their decision. They must take responsibility for the wrong—either too courageous or too cautious—choice of risks. And then, the ordinary way of sharing these risks is the political responsibility the decision makers must bear: the voters may dismiss them if they are not satisfied. Constitutional adjudication requires, by contrast, out of the nature of the task, that the judges be exempt from political responsibility.

What follows from this with respect to the social provisions of the constitution? There is a simple and a complex answer to this question. The simple answer is that the social rights do not impose any enforceable obligation on the government. These rights are more in the nature of ideals, and the executive as well as the legislature are completely free to decide as to how to realize them. This answer is equivalent to the one given by classical liberal authors to the question of social rights. But let us note that the thesis of total legislative discretion does not follow from the budgetary incompetence of the Court. That thesis also entails a specific conception of political morality, one which, in my view, modern liberals have no reason to endorse. The liberal principle of equal treatment entails certain distributive consequences; it imposes an obligation on the government with regard to those of its citizens whose situation is incompatible with taking themselves to be equal members of the political community. If we accept this, then the social provisions of the constitution must represent some cause for concern for liberals. Likewise, they must represent some cause for concern for socialist or Christian thinkers as well, who attribute social obligations to the government, and at the same time endorse the principles of constitutional democracy.

When I first reached the conclusion summarized in this section, I came to suggest that one should look for such an arrangement in which the Court could, on the one hand, exercise the guardianship over the social obligations of the government without, on the other hand, usurping the authority of the legislature. The Court must be given the opportunity to make a stance on the possible reduction of social allowances, without sliding into making such decisions that—like the resolutions that annulled a good part of the 1995 stabilization law—are based on a revision of the budget. I proposed to develop a certain customary practice to the effect that in the case the executive plans large-scale austerity measures, it submits the draft to the Court, and then makes its final motion to the Parliament by taking into account the standpoint of the judges.[140]

This conception certainly did not cohere well with the direction the Court's practice took over time: after 1991, the justices consistently refused to exercise their right to norm control prior to the submission of bills, or prior to the vote on amendment motions, as was pointed out by many.[141] Another unquestionable weakness of the proposal is that it assumes a great propensity on the part of the executive as well as of the Court to develop and strictly adhere to uncodified customary rules; by contrast, the current political practice in Hungary is characterized by a weakness of this propensity and an absence of respect for customs and self-restraint. In addition, this procedure, provided that it gets off the ground, would have been very complicated; it is hard to expect the executive, which functions in a way very different from the practice of case law, to properly adjust to it.[142]

Therefore, it appears to me now that there is really no other possibility than the Court itself unilaterally developing its own precautionary guidelines. This would of course be necessary even if it were possible to reconcile the judicial protection of social safety and the legislative authority over the budget. I have indicated in the previous study the kind of guidelines I have in mind.

Such a guideline would be for the Court to draw the line between the application of the tests of reasonable goal and of necessity/proportionality in a different manner than it currently does. The received practice of the Court now is to apply the test of necessity/proportionality for the restriction of fundamental rights and for the discrimination regarding fundamental rights, and to assess restrictions and discriminations other than that of fundamental rights according to the test of reasonable goal.[143] It would be reasonable to develop this practice in the following way: budgetary restrictions affecting fundamental rights should be judged by the more demanding test of necessity/proportionality only when the application of this test does not entail the revision of the budget—for instance, when the reduction of allowances is justified by facts other than the state of the budget, e.g. a change in the policy aims of the government. Or if the contested measures are in conflict with such constitutional principles (e.g. the prohibition of discrimination) the violation of which might be established independent of a consideration of costs and benefits. All other cases should belong under the authority of the test of reasonable goal.

In 1995, I thought this to be unacceptably modest. At that time, I wrote that the difficulty lies in that the application of the more demanding test implies the Court's decision about the fundamental facts of the budget, while the application of the weaker test implies the finance minister's decision about the meaning of the social provisions of the constitution. Now I think my claims offered an inaccurate characterization about both horns of the dilemma. On the one hand, there are certain cases where the application of the test of necessity/proportionality does not require budget calculations; only the rest should be left to the test of reasonable goal. On the other hand, the finance minister does not even decide about the constitutionality of the cases subjected to the test of reasonable goal. To be sure, the test of reasonable goal is more efficient if it is applied prior to the legislative decision, because it would entail the nullification of the contested measures only in truly exceptional cases—only a conspicuously incompetent financial apparatus is incapable of justifying the restrictive measures with plausible numbers and demonstrating that they are capable of achieving the intended outcome—but it nevertheless makes possible the expression of constitutional concerns, which are more weighty if voiced prior to the legislature's making the contested decision than after it. But the position of the judges is not wholly inefficient even in the latter cases. True, it leaves the measures in force, but it does not pass unnoticed. It influences the media and political opinion in general, and thus, indirectly, the subsequent decisions of the executive and the legislature, and inevitably affects the shaping of the Court's own doctrine.

All of the above concerns the case where *substantive* objections are being made in relation to the enforcement of the government's social obligations. The objections made against the *procedural* features of the measures that violate social interests must be treated separately. Legislation is bound by a number of procedural rules that are designed to make it more bothersome to arbitrarily alter already established rules. In Hungary, the rules of budget making are not specifically strict but they still do not give complete freedom to the executive and the legislature. Compliance with them may be enforced, and the enforcement does not require the substantive assessment of the budget. This is a characteristic task of the Constitutional Court, and in Hungary, where the formal requirements of the rule of law have such a great role in the doctrine of the Court, it is especially important that the Court fully perform this task. The role of precautionary guidelines begins where procedural adjudication comes to an end.

In a word, if it is the case that the government has social obligations, then the Court can develop its domain of action within which it might confront the decisions of the executive and the legislature with the social provisions of the constitution, without violating the constitutional principles of democracy. But it must not make such resolutions that strike down budget decisions on the grounds of assessing their necessity.

The competing interpretations of classical fundamental rights are all compatible with the conception of constitutional interpretation which was outlined and defended here. Therefore, the shift in the practice of the Court after 1993 does not raise questions about the legitimacy of the doctrine that has finally evolved. Even if one thinks—as I do for my part—that some of the decisions and the underlying principles formulated to justify them are questionable, it might not be doubted that the judges developed their position by exercising their constitutional authority, and that currently this is the official interpretation of the republican constitution.

The case of the social obligations of the government is different. Only the nineteenth-century liberal standpoint is compatible, without further questions, with a defensible conception of the Court's authority to constitutional interpretation. All the other standpoints raise the question of what is and what is not to be resolved by way of the judicial interpretation of the constitution. I have attempted to show in this section that the Court developed a mistaken conception between 1991 and 1994 in this regard, and that it made a series of inadmissible resolutions in 1995 on the basis of this ill-conceived conception. In other words, while its position of principle on the scope of rights adjudication may be regarded as settled, its position on the scope of welfare protection adjudication is in need of a radical correction.

2. Summary and a glance to the future

2.1. THESES

In 1989, at the outset of the third republic, the legal as well as the political community in Hungary were thinking about the new democratic institutions in terms of the traditional conception of parliamentary *Rechtstaat*. This conception allows only for a very limited room for constitutional review. In this view, the Constitutional Court must establish only the straightforward violations of the constitution, those that might not in good faith be questioned. If the Court strikes down a law by relying on such an interpretation that divides the public, then in this conception it inevitably violates the principle of the separation of powers; it usurps either the constituent or the legislative powers (or both) of the elected popular representatives.

The main objective of the last two studies of this volume was to show the narrowness of the traditional conception and to help move on to another conception, one I referred to as parliamentary constitutionalism.

I have tried to show that the same considerations that justify bringing parliamentary sovereignty under the rule of law in fact justify constitutional self-restraint as well. They make it necessary for the community to tie the hand of the Parliament with constitutional provisions, and to appoint a separate body to safeguard the enforcement of constitutional constraints.

Furthermore, I have tried to show that this body is authorized to pass constitutional judgments even in those cases where it cannot avoid making such decisions that might be objected to in good faith, that is, that may be objected to even after seriously considering the evidence in favor of these decisions. In cases when what is at stake is whether some legal provision violates the moral interests of individuals that are protected by the constitution—the principles of treating human persons—the Court in fact not only might, but also must, make such decisions. In cases where the stakes are related to the constitutional rules of governmental organization—the rules of competence and of the separation of powers—the need for decisions that generate controversy depends on how serious the conflict is judged to be, i.e. on judicial consideration. The judges can act in a very broad sphere while performing their duty, without on that account intervening in the activity of the legislature without democratic authorization.

Chapter 2 of the previous study has shown that the substantive interpretation of the constitution is not equivalent with the amendment of the text of the constitution—thus, it does not violate the principle of popular sovereignty. The main task of Chapter 3 was to show that neither does striking down legislation resting on a substantive constitutional interpretation come into conflict with the principle of popular sovereignty. I began to outline a theory of parliamentary constitutionalism in Chapter 2 (Sections 2.1 and 2.11), and then articulated it in Chapter 3 (Sections 3.1 to 3.5). This theory views the constitution and judicial review as one of the democratic procedures, i.e. as means by which the elected representatives make it very difficult for themselves to pass decisions on especially important issues—but only to better realize their own goals.

But the broadness of the framework does not imply that the interpretive competence of the Court has no boundaries. I have tried to introduce and justify three important constraints. First, substantive reading must not slide into critical reading; in other words, an interpretation that is not bound by the text of the constitution or even presumes a revision of the text might not be regarded as an interpretation of the constitution (this consideration was articulated in Section 2.9 of the previous study). Second, as the Court articulates the underlying principles of constitutional provisions while proceeding from case to case, it must act so that each of its decisions determines future decisions only to the smallest degree that is necessary. The fact that a case requires substantive interpretation does not in itself represent a reason for deferring the decision, but the Court must choose that justification of the correct decision among the available alternatives that has the least far-reaching implications (Section 2.8). Third, the Court must proceed with special care in cases that might not be substantively assessed without making such a decision that requires political responsibility, because the primary duty of the Court demands that the judges be exempt from political responsibility (see Sections 3.6 and 3.7 of the previous study). A characteristic example is the substantive revision of the government's budget, to which the Court does not have a legitimate authority.

In the present study, I have tried to apply these insights to the practice of the first Hungarian Constitutional Court.

2.2. MEASURING THE FIRST CONSTITUTIONAL
COURT BY OUR THESES

The first Constitutional Court did not refrain from the substantive reading of the constitution. It ventured courageously to interpret the moral tenets enshrined in the constitution; it inventively explored the principles that underlie the written text, and which justify the explicit provisions and make their interrelations transparent. The explication of the underlying principles of the constitution and the aspiration to order them into a coherent system added enduring values to the common property of the constitution.

This achievement is all the more remarkable because the Court had to exercise its duty in the face of serious reservations and, sometimes, even resistance. Neither constitutional review nor the self-restraint of the democratic community by a written constitution had precedents in Hungary; even some of the ardent proponents of democracy thought that the Court should refrain from striking down legislation in case the decision would have invoked controversial moral convictions.

At the same time, the Court initially tended to endorse the conception that the judges might be authorized—at least in the beginning, when the constitution still bore the traces of ad hoc, contingent and temporary agreements—to critically revise the text. The famous metaphor of the "invisible constitution" might be interpreted to express either of the two conceptions: either that the Court's duty is to develop the underlying principles that articulate and justify the text of the constitution, or that the judges might go as far as to critically revise the text of the constitution by invoking the principles of constitutionalism. This ambiguity made it difficult for the democratic community as well as for the legal profession to endorse that which is right about the metaphor of the "invisible constitution": that the Court has the right and duty to substantively interpret, from case to case, the provisions enshrined in the constitution, and to form a coherent system out of the auxiliary concepts and theses mobilized in the course of this interpretation. Even though it was able to vindicate the authority of its rulings—there was no instance of explicitly resisting the annulling decisions of the Court either by the executive or by the Parliament—it was less successful in vindicating its power to make such decisions that rest on substantive interpretations and the introduction of controversial principles.

By 1992, the claim to critical reading was already a thing of the past. But with this shift the practice of constitutional review was far from being consolidated in Hungary. In the subsequent years, two further tendencies made their appearance in the practice of the Court. First, the current of rulings that sought to raise the level of protection of the fundamental rights came to a standstill. Second, there was an upsurge of welfare protection. The first tendency may be criticized on substantive grounds, but it might not be claimed to break the theoretical boundaries of constitutional review. The second tendency, by contrast, has broken through the barriers, as I have tried to show.

The author of this study shares the position of the first Constitutional Court that the government has constitutional social obligations. At the same time, I hold that the judicial assessment of these obligations must be exercised in a way that respects the legislature's authority over the budget. This is fully possible as long as the judicial review confronts the contested restrictive measures only with the formal, procedural requirements of the legislation. The review of substantive concerns might be carried out, on the other hand, only if the Court develops certain precautionary guidelines for itself, which allow the assessment of the constitutionality of welfare measures in the light of more demanding tests only in those cases in which the application of these tests does not require the Court to judge the necessity of budget decisions. The duty of shaping these indispensable precautionary guidelines awaits the second Constitutional Court.

2.3. FROM "LEGAL REVOLUTION" TO THE "CONSOLIDATION OF THE RULE OF LAW"

The first Constitutional Court started off in the midst of far-reaching changes and as an agent of far-reaching changes. The party state was replaced by a multi-party representative democracy; the legislature submitted itself to constitutional constraints, and not merely to constraints of procedure and competence but also to the constraints represented by observing the moral principles of the acceptable treatment of individuals.

Such a radical transformation is but rarely followed by a rectilinear, smooth progress. The more unusual the new relations are, the more likely they will be met by resistance. In these years, the third Hungarian republic experiences a reaction against the innovations of the transition process. The fundamental ideas of 1989—human rights, separation of powers, the rule of law—are not particularly popular and are under attack from all directions these days. In part, the decline of rights adjudication under the first Constitutional Court may be a reflection of this turn. Be that as it may, it seems likely that the reaction against the constitutional tradition created in 1989 will continue in the years to come. Therefore, if the first Constitutional Court was the depository of the "legal revolution", the second Constitutional Court should become the depository of the "consolidation of the rule of law". It faces the duty of assisting the republican constitution through the years of reaction.

As a part of the reaction, there is an ever stronger pressure on the Court to break with the interpretive practice of its predecessor and to read the constitution as a mere collection of rules rather than as—among other things—a set of moral principles; to refrain from adjudicating such constitutional controversies the settling of which requires the adoption of contested, substantive positions. The statements of the new judges indicate that the Court is not far removed from accommodating these claims. For my part, I see it as a regrettable development that the Court recoils from substantive interpretations. On the other hand, I think this tendency should be assessed in the context of the historical task the Court is to carry out. If it is in fact the case that the second Court should become the Court of the "consolidation of the rule of law", then it might to some extent meet the urges of a more passive judicial practice without thereby betraying its mission.

First of all, the paramount duty of the guardians of the constitution in these years is the protection of the formal requirements of the rule of law. Consolidating the more and more vulnerable rule of the law makes it necessary to carefully guard the constitutional procedural order of legislation and law enforcement, and in this sphere the Court can be very determined and consistent without undertaking the substantive interpretation of controversial constitutional passages. In most of the cases, the enforcement of the standing order, the procedural order of law making does not require more than a rather strict reading of the text.[144]

This is true even about such legislative subjects that fall within the difficult sphere of the government's welfare obligations. At the end of 1999, the Court rejected the motions that attacked those provisions of the budget of the same year that reduced the amount of pension increase.[145] This decision might not be assessed unequivocally. In my view, the majority decided correctly when it refused to establish the unnecessary and disproportionate nature of the amendment, and when it did not apply the test of sufficient preparatory period for the contested measure. If the arguments contained in Sections 3.6 and 3.7 of the previous study are correct, then the judges—as office holders without political responsibility—might not rest their decisions on assessing the risks of budget decisions and whether it is reasonable to take such risks. At the same time, the Court failed to notice the grave procedural flaws made in the course of amending the pension rules. More specifically, the Parliament decided about the amendment in a way that, when establishing the budget for the year 1999, it simply deviated from the longer-term provisions the law. 1997:LXXXI on social security pensions, while leaving the latter in force. This procedure represents serious causes for concern, but there is no indication that the Court so much as considered these concerns, even though it could have done so with its more textual and procedural tools as well.[146]

As far as the classical fundamental rights are concerned, a restrained interpretive practice may be sufficient in a very wide range of cases. First, the task to be carried out by the second Court is the protection and consolidation of the already achieved constitutional state rather than a determined continuation of the transformation. Second, the already achieved constitutional state includes more than the text of the constitution; it contains, among other things, the immense material of case law built up by the first Constitutional Court, a host of precedents, the articulation of underlying principles, and a series of tests to decide whether any one legal provision is compatible with these principles. Many of the questions to which, in the light of the text of the constitution itself, a number of different answers may be given that are mutually exclusive but equally coherent with the text may be answered unequivocally, if one reads the constitution along with the resolutions of the past nine years. In other cases, the answer is not fully determined, but the range of possible decisions is very narrow. If the Court takes it that its resolutions are bound not only by the text of the constitution but also by its own past resolutions, then it can in large part carry out its task even without introducing new principles or new concepts. There are some promising examples that reinforce this possibility.[147]

Yet it makes a lot of difference whether the Court refrains from controversial substantive readings because it thinks that the consolidation of the already achieved constitutional state of affairs does not require them, or because it takes substantive reading to be an illegitimate procedure which is incompatible with democracy. My study tries to show that while the former might be true, the latter is certainly incorrect.

Why is it important to be aware that the Court's mandate to substantive reading is a necessary accompaniment of the constitutional self-restraint of the legislation—that is, that this mandate rests on the requirements of democracy itself? There are two reasons for this.

First of all, if we were compelled to accept that the judges have no right to articulate the underlying principles of the text of the constitution, the next move would be that we were to step by step get rid of the case law legacy inherited from the first Constitutional Court. Illegitimate past rulings might not in the long run bind the Constitutional Court. We would have to retreat from the constitutional tenets and tests developed for the protection of the freedom of speech, personal self-determination, the protection of special data, legal security, the right to privacy, the freedom of conscience and religion, the neutrality of the state, the prohibition of negative discrimination, and so on.

Second, even if it is true that in the period of consolidation the paramount duty of the Court is to solidify the achievements of the past, we might not reasonably think that in the near future the Court will not be faced with issues that require independent, substantive interpretations. No doubt, the typical tasks will be like the ones required by the unconstitutional provisions of the legislation that destroyed the constitutional protection of personal data (such as the Police Act, the law on medical data processing, the law against organized crime, and so on). The restoration of the constitutional norms of data protection would be a highly significant move, one, for that matter, that does not require creative constitutional interpretation. It would suffice to consistently apply the relevant decisions of the first Court. But not all of the tasks will be like this one.

Civil rights against the police are violated not only because the executive and the legislative branches of the government disregard important judicial guidelines, but also because many of the relevant motions—exactly the ones questioning the constitutionality of the Police Act—were never discussed by the first Court. Therefore, there is up to this day no settled judicial doctrine about how the constitutional rights of citizens constrain the activity of the police. This is to be carried out by the second Court.

The tests of the constitutional assessment of discrimination are in many cases highly developed, but as far as the criteria for the two most pressing cases of discrimination in Hungary—racial and gender discrimination—are concerned, these are, as we have seen, completely undeveloped. These are ad hoc examples; the enumeration might be continued.

Thus, the substantive interpretation of the constitution is an indispensable task even in the period of the consolidation of the rule of law. The Court cannot completely retreat behind the rules of strict reading unless it relinquishes its primary duty: the protection of the moral principles of the republican constitution. If this were to happen, the republic would become something other than it was originally designed to be. It would no longer be under the rule of its constitution that "recognizes the fundamental, inviolable and inalienable human rights", and in which "the protection of and respect for these rights is the primary duty of the state.

NOTES

1 I would like to note, nevertheless, that the most controversial structural decisions, interpreting the authority of the president of the republic, satisfy the requirements of the doctrine of constitutional interpretation outlined in the previous study. Therefore, on the question whether these decisions have transgressed the constitutional authority of the Court I share the view of the majority rather than of the dissenting judges. Furthermore, I share the majority's view in substantive terms as well; the analysis I offer in Section 2.5 above of the method of electing the president is very close to that provided by the first decision about the competence of the president. See 48/1991 (IX. 26) (ABH 1991, 189). It is another matter whether the Court must in all instances do what it is permitted to do. The consecutive decisions made many of the observers feel more and more uncomfortable.

2 It was Péter Schmidt and Imre Vörös who authored most of the dissenting opinions that objected to violating the norm of strict textualism. Yet even they voted for decisions relying on interpretations that went far beyond the grammatical and logical analysis of the text on a much larger number of occasions than the number of times they objected to violating the constraints of strict textualism.

3 László Sólyom, "Az alkotmánybíróság önértelmezése", *Jogtudományi Közlöny*, 1992/2, p. 275 (emphasis added).

4 *Ibid.*, p. 275.

5 *Ibid.*, p. 274.

6 *Ibid.*, p. 273.

7 *Ibid.*, p. 274.

8 See the parallel opinion of László Sólyom to 23/1990 (X. 31), ABH 1990, 88, 97.

9 "A 'nehéz eseteknél' a bíró erkölcsi felfogása is szerephez jut. Sólyom Lászlóval, az Alkotmánybíróság elnökével Tóth Gábor Attila beszélget", *Fundamentum*, 1997/1, p. 31. At the same time Sólyom emphasizes that even though the interpretation mobilizes moral convictions, it is always textbound, and thus "the moral rights have been paraphrased in the terminology of constitutional law."

10 Here is an example: Sólyom writes in relation to the judicial interpretation of the right to the protection of personal data, that "in articulating this right, the Constitutional Court *may correct the fault made by the framers,* who adhered to the conservative conception of data protection and ranked it next to the protection of good reputation and secrets, thus divorcing it from its natural counterpart, the freedom of information (which is again falsely ranked next to the freedom of the press by the constitution)." Emphasis added. *Ellenőrzött rendszerváltás*, p. 374.

11 I have argued for this point in detail in Section 2 of the previous study.

12 László Sólyom, "Az emberi jogok és az alkotmánybíráskodás," *A jogállamiság útján–felzárkózás Európához* (Budapest: KOTK, 1992), p. 24 (emphasis added).

13 See n. 22 below.

14 László Sólyom, „Az Alkotmánybíróság önértelmezése", *Jogtudományi Közlöny*, 1992/2, pp. 274–275.

15 I have argued in detail for a possible equivalent though not identical reasoning in my "Az Alkotmánybíróság az élethez való jogról". See János Kis, *Az abortuszról. Érvek és ellenérvek.* (Budapest: Cserépfalvi, 1992) pp. 202–207.

16 23/1990 (X. 31), ABH 1990, 88, 92.

17 *Ibid.*   •

18 ABH 1990, 88, 93.

19 The parallel opinion of László Sólyom attached to 23/1990 (X. 31), ABH 1990, 88, 103.

20 The author of this study tried to show—in opposition to the claims of this ruling— that there are indeed possible degrees of taking life and human dignity, and that even though it were the case that *life* could be taken only fully and definitively, it would not follow that a partial infringement of *the right to life* is a logical impossibility. See my "Az Alkotmánybíróság az élethez való jogról".

21 ABH 1990, 88, 94.

22 It is a plausible assumption that it was the difficulties concerning the interpretation of the right to life offered in the decision that abolished the death penalty that prevented the Court from reaching a decision about the motion made on the issue of euthanasia.

23 This difficulty might have contributed to the fact that the Court never ventured to substantively consider the number of motions made against the law about the police.

24 64/1991 (XII. 17), ABH 1991, 258, 273.

25 See the definition of "supervenient property" in Simon Blackburn's entry "Supervenience" in *The Oxford Dictionary of Philosophy* (Oxford: Oxford University Press, 1996), p. 368. I emphasize that is the primary use because the term "dignity" has another meaning as well, which refers to the property of human beings of behaving in a manner that is worthy of the moral status due to them as humans, and to the duty of everyone else to treat individuals the way that is due to such beings. See R. Nozick, *Philosophical Explanations* (Cambridge, Mass.: Belknap, 1981), pp. 451–473. Shortly I will have to say more about the relation between the primary and secondary uses of this term.

26 ABH 1990, 88, 93.

27 ABH 1991, 258, 268.

28 ABH 1991, 258, 267.

29 ABH 1991, 258, 268.

30 *Ibid.*

31 ABH 1991, 258, 271.

32 *Ibid.*

33 ABH 1991, 258, 270.

34 See J. Rawls, *A Theory of Justice* (Oxford–Melbourne: Oxford University Press 1971), p. 508. Rawls cites the example that all the points that are closer to the center of a circle than its radius are within the circle. The distance from the center is a scalar property, while being in the interior of the circle is a range property, that is, a point is either within the circle or is not within the circle. It is meaningless to speak about a point being more or less within a circle.

35 ABH 1991, 258, 266.

36 *Ibid.*

37 ABH 1991, 258, 266.

38 See Tamás Győrfi, "A tulajdonságok nélküli ember", *Fundamentum*, 1998/3, p. 23.

39 ABH 1991, 258, 266.

40 ABH 1991, 258, 263.

41 ABH 1991, 258, 273. This reasoning is false. It begins with a true claim: the institutions serving the realization of the right to life improve the life chances of fetuses that pregnant women intend to retain. But then this is confused with the false claim that the institutional protection of life might constrain the right to self-determination of pregnant women in favor of the fetuses who do not possess the right to life. The Court's position was somewhat altered in 1998, when making the second abortion decision. Here the judges gave up the reservation that women must be obliged to offer testable reasons but claimed that in the absence of such reasons abortion is acceptable only if it was preceded by substantive counseling directed at retaining the fetus. See 48/1998 (XI. 23), ABH 1998, 333. For a critique of the decision, see Judit Fridli, "Tanácsadás válsághelyzetben", and Gábor Attila Tóth, "A második abortusz-döntés bírálata", *Fundamentum*, 1999/1, p. 92 and, p. 81.

42 There is a further, hidden error in this chain of inference. The conclusion summarized in no. 6 may be drawn from the premises only if the protection of the objective value of life has been appropriately interpreted. Suppose the objective protection of life entails the creation of such conditions under which pregnant women may make a responsible decision that takes into account the respect for the already conceived life—that is, they will not opt for abortion without serious reasons. But this task might be interpreted in two different ways. In one conception, the decision remains the private affair of the women, and the state influences only the circumstances of decision making (through information, offering the possibility of counseling, or reducing the material and social costs of childbearing). In the second conception, the decision is made by some official authority; it is not left to the women's conscience whether they have good reasons for abortion; they must reveal their reasons before the authority granting the permission. The Court opted for the second conception, without, however, outlining the alternatives or offering reasons for its decision.

43 It was only Tamás Lábady who submitted a dissenting opinion, but what he objected to was not that abortion was made dependent upon a permission and that the permission was made dependent on reasons, but that the Court refrained from a constitutional interpretation of the status of fetuses. ABH 1998, 333, 362.

44 The original author of the abortion motions was János Zlinszky. László Sólyom took over the issue only when it became clear that Zlinszky's draft was not capable of commanding a majority.

45 See BvfGE 39, 3, 25.2.1975. The resolution of the Federal Constitutional Court rests on the thesis that pregnancy establishes a special relation between the woman and the fetus. In the typical cases of the application of the right to life, the person protected by this right might continue with his or her life without the cooperation of the other person. By contrast, fetuses might reach the level of development at which they are capable of an independent life only if the women accept to bear them. Therefore, their remaining alive incurs a non-transferable burden on these women. And the resolution establishes that this burden must not be disproportionately severe.

46 In an interview in 1995, László Sólyom reinforced the claim that the Court, if it finds a contradiction in the text of the constitution, must resolve the contradiction. "The Constitutional Court has reinforced a number of times that it takes the constitution to be a closed system, therefore, if it perceives a contradiction, or if others perceive such a contradiction, it has the power to resolve it." Lajos Pogonyi–András Sereg,

"Megmarad-e a fekete gólya?", *Népszabadság,* August 19 1995. To be sure, it never occurred after the death penalty resolution that the Court thought to detect a contradiction in the constitution and that it grounded its decision on resolving it.

47 11/1992 (III.5), ABH 1992, 77, 80.
48 The Court has also addressed two further questions, the property conscription of the legal successors of party-state organizations, and the dismissal of leaders appointed during the party state. But the resolutions made in these issues are unrelated to the judgment to be made about the special circumstances of the transition: in connection with the property conscription, it examined merely whether it is permissible to impose on short notice a prohibition of alienation on the properties brought under control [24/1992 (IV. 21), ABH 1992, 126]. In relation with the dismissal of leaders, the Court rested content with striking down the contested provision on formal grounds [31/1991 (VI. 5), ABH 1991, 118].
49 28/1991 (VI.3), ABH 1991, 80, 85.
50 21/1990 (X. 4), ABH 1990, 73 held a similar view, but it assumed that the property of the cooperatives would be restituted to the original owners by way of disappropriation. Resolution 16/1991 (IV. 20), ABH 1991, 54, 58 ruled that the creation of purchase rights is not equivalent with disappropriation without proper reasons and immediate compensation, which is prohibited by the constitution, because the former amounts only to a restriction rather than a deprivation of property rights. This observation notwithstanding, both this resolution and 28/1991 (VI. 3), ABH 1991, 80 emphasize that it is permissible to create purchase rights against the property of the cooperatives only under the circumstances of the transition, when, as part of adopting a market economy, the transformation of cooperatives is carried out, and in the event the members receive free property.
51 ABH 1991, 80, 85.
52 ABH 1991, 80, 83.
53 Session no. 12 of the Parliament in Fall, 1991, 8 October 1991. See *Országgyűlési Értesítő,* 1990–1994, column no. 10656–10658.
54 ABH 1991, 80, 82.
55 ABH 1991, 80, 81.
56 *Ibid.*
57 *Ibid.*
58 *Ibid.*
59 *Ibid.*
60 *Ibid.*
61 ABH 1991, 80, 85.
62 ABH 1991, 82.
63 László Sólyom, "Az emberi jogok az Alkotmánybíróság újabb gyakorlatában", *Világosság,* 1993/1, p. 18.
64 In an interview already cited above, the term "constitutional positivism" returns, but this time it is brought up by the interviewer, and once again the response associates the so-called "positivist" turn of judicial practice to cooling down the natural law aspirations of political justice. At the same time, Sólyom is anxious to add that "Where fundamental rights adjudication is practiced, positivism is never real but rather *interpreted positivism,* and the interpretation inevitably involves many moral

components" (*Fundamentum*, 1997/1, p. 32.) Therefore, "positivism" means textual relevance here rather than strict textualism.

65 *Ibid.*

66 *Ibid.*

67 ABH 1991, 80, 82.

68 *Fundamentum*, 1997/1, p. 36.

69 As a general rule, the Court approved that the measures suspected of discrimination must meet the strong test of necessity/proportionality in the case of discriminations concerning fundamental rights. In cases when such rights (or other interests that are not protected by rights) are at stake that do not belong to the range of fundamental rights, it is sufficient to apply the weaker test of reasonable goal. However, this is not applicable for many characteristic cases of racial discrimination or discrimination against women. The groups that are subject to systematic discrimination and are identified as a race—in Hungary, the Romas—typically suffer such discriminations that do not concern fundamental rights, and their nature is such that they easily pass the test of reasonable goal. For instance, clubs and bars make service dependent upon complying with such dress codes and rules of conduct that are typically met by members of the majority while not being typically met by members of the minority; or employment is made dependent upon the same kind of requirements. The case of systematic discrimination against women is similar. It is only a test stronger than that of reasonable goal that could detect that the procedure is in fact discriminatory, and in most European constitutional democracies such tests are applied. The first Hungarian Constitutional Court has simply failed to confront this problem.

70 36/1994 (VI. 24), ABH 1994, 219. This resolution applied the landmark ruling of the Federal Supreme Court of the United States in 1964 in the *New York Times* v. *Sullivan* case, 376 US 254.

71 20/1997 (III. 19), ABH 1997, 85. There were two dissenting opinions and two parallel opinions against the majority decision authored by Antal Ádám, although not in the same spirit: Tamás Lábady, László Sólyom (ABH 1997, 85, 96), and Ödön Tyersztyánszky, János Zlinszky (ABH 1997, 85, 98).

72 24/1996 (VI. 25), ABH 1996, 107. The otherwise appropriate resolution rests on the surprising belief that the general freedom of action is due not only to natural persons but to legal persons as well.

73 True, the Court struck down the 1996 law that brought back the criminal prosecution of hate speech, but only in 1999, during the chairmanship of János Németh. Quite interestingly, soon after his departure Sólyom said he saw no chance for striking this law down. See "Búcsú a Donáti utcától. Négyszemközt Sólyom Lászlóval, az Alkotmánybíróság leköszönt elnökével", *Magyar Hírlap*, 28 November, 1998.

74 60/1994 (XII. 24), ABH 1994, 342.

75 The hearing of this petition occurred only in 1999; the second Constitutional Court rejected the motion to declare the separation and differential treatment of the files to be unconstitutional.

76 15/1995 (III. 13), ABH 1995, 88.

77 26/1995 (V. 15), ABH 1995, 123.

78 58/1995 (IX. 15), ABH 1995, 289.

79 6/1998 (III. 11), ABH 1998, 91.

80 21/1994 (IV. 16), ABH 1994, 117.

81 58/1994 (XII. 14), ABH 1994, 334.

82 31/1996 (VII. 3), ABH 1996, 285.

83 22/1995 (III. 31), ABH 1995, 108.

84 23/1995 (IV. 5), ABH 1995, 115.

85 35/1995 (VI. 2), ABH 1995, 163.

86 1/1996 (I. 26), ABH 1996, 29.

87 14/1996 (IV. 24), ABH 1996, 56.

88 31/1997 (V. 16), ABH 1997, 154.

89 58/1997 (XI. 5), ABH 1997, 348.

90 14/1995 (III. 13), ABH 1995, 82.

91 21/1996 (V. 17), ABH 1996, 74. In my study "A Szivárvány-teszt" I have showed in detail that the argumentation of the second resolution is not tenable. See *Beszélő*, 1996/7, p. 26. In fact, the signs of uncertainty were already discernible in the first resolution. When the resolution tries to justify why the argument against discrimination does not extend beyond the institution of partnership, to that of marriage, the best reason it could offer was that marriage and family are traditionally attached to child raising. For my part, I believe there were important prudential considerations in favor of extending the right only to the institution of partnership in the first phase. But these considerations might have found expression in the decision without resorting to the unacceptable reference to the traditional conception. (I owe this latter insight to Zoltán Szente.)

92 The second Constitutional Court made a decision about the former motion in 1999.

93 43/1995 (VI. 30), ABH 1995, 188, 198.

94 48/1998 (XI. 23), ABH 1998, 333.

95 970/B/1994 ABH 1995, 739.

96 I would like to make a remark about the nature of the majority within the Court. Let us call the original position of the judges that which they take on any given question prior to collective discussion, mutual persuasion and (or) bargaining. The collective position is not a mere aggregation of the original positions; in the course of the debates and bargaining, the judges alter the views they have "brought from home". Therefore, what has been written above should not be taken to mean that in the issues left open after 1993, a clear majority of the original (i.e. pre-discussion) positions was against the extension of liberties. My thesis concerns the majority formed after the discussion of cases rather than to the one preceding the discussion. An important consequence of this observation is that the majority formed in the course of the discussions is influenced by, beyond the distribution of original standpoints and the force of arguments, such facts as what are the procedures for discussing an issue, who is the author of the draft, and which positions are favored by the most influential members of the Court. These are important questions; we will not acquire a full picture of the conduct of the Court until we can answer these questions. But any attempt to answer them presupposes vast empirical researches, the experiential basis of which is not limited to the published resolutions.

97 This view is first expressed in László Sólyom's parallel opinion to 31/1990 (XII. 18), ABH 1990, 136, 140, and it returns in a number of later rulings. A very good, analytic summary is offered by Imre Vörös' parallel opinion in ABH 1995, 260, 272. The

same conception was developed by the Court in interpreting the right to "physical and spiritual well-being" (Article 70/D). We need not discuss the bizarre feature of Article 70/D that, on the one hand, it speaks about a right not to the minimum but to the maximum of health services—"the highest level of physical and spiritual well-being"—and, on the other hand, it attributes this right not merely to the citizens of the republic but to the totality of those living within its territory, because the Court, too, failed to discuss it. I take it that the judges understand these articles the same way as they understand Article 70/E on the right to social safety.

98 The calculations are based on the law on supplementary estimates (1995:LXXII), which contains the expected impact of the austerity measures. If we want to find out the total budgetary consequences of the Court's resolutions, we must add 2.6 billion to the 31.4 billion, which was removed by 66/1995 (XI. 26), ABH 1996, 333 from the supplementary estimates by annulling the chapter that raised interest rates on housing loans from 15 percent to 25 percent.

99 Such complaints were in fact made on behalf of the governing coalition; see, for instance, *Népszabadság*, 13 July 1995. Objections were raised by non-partisan observers as well. For instance, Zoltán Szente, "Ki ellenőrzi az Alkotmánybíróságot?" *Népszabadság*, 16 October 1995.

100 After the adopting of the Stabilization Act by the Parliament, the chief justice pronounced in a declaration that should the opposition petition for constitutional review, the Court would delay its summer vacation to get to work immediately. The preparation of the draft was handed over to such a judge (Géza Kilényi) who had voted with the minority in all such cases in the past; the Court did not ask for the opinion of the minister of finance, which it had always done before in cases that concerned the budget.

101 Usually, the Constitutional Court does not publish the distribution of votes on various resolutions. In the absence of such data, one might infer the degree of division from the number of dissenting opinions. Among the resolutions that arbitrated between the president and the prime minister in their conflict of competence, 48/1991 (IX. 26), was approved against the dissenting opinion of Géza Kilényi, Péter Schmidt and Imre Vörös (ABH 1991, 189, 206); 8/1992 (I. 30) was approved against the dissenting opinion of Géza Kilényi and Péter Schmidt (ABH 1992, 51, 57); 36/1992 (VI. 10) was approved against the dissenting opinion of Géza Kilényi (ABH 1992, 207, 220), Péter Schmidt (ABH 1992, 207, 223) and Imre Vörös (ABH 1992, 207, 225). The landmark restitution resolution 28/1991 (VI. 3) was approved against the dissenting opinion of Imre Vörös (ABH 1991, 80, 97); the resolution on the restitution of church real estates, 4/1993 (II. 12), was approved against the dissenting opinion of Péter Schmidt (ABH 1993, 48, 76) and Imre Vörös (ABH 1993, 48, 79). The ruling on the unconstitutionality of the government control of the radio and television, and the deadline for the invalidation of the unconstitutional government statute 17/1993 (III. 19), was approved against the dissenting opinion of Imre Vörös (ABH 1993, 157, 159) resolution 38/1993 on the appointment of judges and leaders of the judiciary was adopted against the dissenting opinion of Antal Ádám (ABH 1993, 272, 278) and Imre Vörös (ABH 1993, 256, 278). The second resolution on the statutes of limitation, 41/1993 (VI. 30), was approved against the dissenting opinion of János Zlinszky (ABH 1993, 292, 296).

102 There was only one dissenting opinion. Ödön Tersztyánszky criticized 54/1995 (IX. 15) in ABH 1995, 245, 251. It is to be noted, however, that this decision struck down one of the provisions of the Stabilization Act on the grounds of discrimination—for tying the security fee of individual entrepreneurs doing supplementary activity to the minimum wage. The objection against discrimination is independent of whether the object of the contested provision is related to the revenues and expenditures of the budget, nor did Tersztyánszky's dissenting opinion concern the fundamental question, i.e. in which cases and to what extent the Court might intervene in the budgetary decisions of the other branches of government. We will see that the shifts occurring in the views of individual judges between 1990 and 1994 had a great impact on the formation of the new consensus, but it seems that the final turn came when the chief justice switched in 1995 to the side of what had been up to that point the minority. For this, see n. 96 on the structure of majorities.

103 Géza Kilényi (ABH 1991, 129, 146) and János Zlinszky (ABH 1991, 129, 147) are attached to 32/1991 (VI. 6).

104 Dissenting opinions by Géza Kilényi (ABH 1991, 196, 204), András Szabó and János Zlinszky (ABH 1991, 196, 208) and Imre Vörös (ABH 1991, 196, 208) attached to 26/1993 (IV. 29).

105 28/1994 (V. 20), ABH 1994, 134, 139, 141. Antal Ádám and Ödön Tersztyánszky attached a dissenting opinion to the ruling (ABH 1994, 134, 145).

106 The dissenting opinion of László Sólyom to resolution 31/1990 (XII. 18), ABH 1990, 136, 140.

107 11/1991 (III. 29), ABH 1991, 33, 34. The resolution struck down Section 2 of Article 57 of Law 1975:II, which declared that the period before 1 January 1929 might not be taken into account in calculating the years of employment.

108 "In the case of all social security services where the insurance component is detectable, the constitutionality of the reduction or abolishing of services is to be determined according to the criteria of the protection of property." 43/1995 (VI. 30), ABH 1995, 188, 195. Cf. 772/B/1990/5: "The system of social security operates partly on the principle of purchased rights..." ABH 1991, 447, 449.

109 For instance: Who should bear the risks of inflation?

110 "The government may constitutionally alter the content of contracts by legal provision only under the same conditions as are required to obtain for a judicial modification of contracts." 32/1991 (VI. 6), ABH 1991, 129, 136.

111 9/1994 (II. 25), ABH 1994, 74.

112 43/1995 (VI. 30), ABH 1995, 188, 191.194

113 This thesis has two additional consequences. On the one hand, the longer the government keeps the promise it made in legal provisions, the more reasonable the expectations with respect to the unaltered maintenance of allowances or benefits will become, and the narrower the government's room in modifying it will be. On the other hand, the longer the terms of the government subsidy in question are, the more likely it will be that after the beginning of the services such changes will occur that make reduction or revocation inevitable—while in the case of short-term supports the likelihood of such occurrences is much smaller. See 43/1995 (VI. 30) on the special protection of "accustomed, well-known and predictable" systems of provision

that have been maintained "for decades". ABH 1995, 188, 191, and the increased protection of "short-term and determinate services", ABH 1995, 188, 194.

114 These types may of course be combined: for instance, the rights acquired through purchase might be reinforced by guarantees promised in legal provision; in the Court's view, this is the case with compulsory social security, where the payments acquire the right to the future services, and the government undertakes a guarantee to perform the service in return for the compulsory contribution. See 43/1995 (VI. 30), ABH 1995, 188.

115 "In the absence of compelling necessity, the restriction or abolition of guarantees that were originally undertaken without time limits may be carried out only if the legislators provide for an extended preparatory period for those concerned between the publication and the entry into force of the modification..." 9/1994 (II. 25), ABH 1994, 74.

116 43/1995 (VI. 30), ABH 1995, 188, 193.

117 "The date of the entry into force of a law must be so determined that there should be sufficient time to prepare for its application". Section 3 of Article 12 of law 1987: XI.

118 "The law must not establish obligations or declare some conduct unlawful with respect to the period that precedes its publication". Section 2 of Article 12 of 1987: XI.

119 34/1991 (VI. 15), ABH 1991, 149; 7/1992 (I. 20), ABH 1992, 45; 25/1992 (IV. 30), ABH 1992, 131 and 28/1992 (IV. 30), ABH 1992, 155. Thus, "the amount of time necessary for the preparation of a given legal provision is a matter of consideration that requires taking into account economic, organizational and technical facts; that is, it is not a constitutional problem". ABH 1992, 155, 158.

120 *Ibid.*

121 9/1994 (II. 25), ABH 1994, 74.

122 ABH 1994, 74, 76.

123 This occurred where the austerity measures transformed the child allowance that was up to that point granted to all families as a right into a need-based allowance: the Court objected to those procedures and criteria that were developed by the stabilization law to determine eligibility. See 52/1995 (IX. 15), ABH 1995, 230, and the related 60/1995 (X. 6), ABH 1995, 304.

124 To be sure, liberals do not always agree as to the principles behind such self-restraint, and as to what it is that the judges should refrain from doing. According to the authors who are close to the classical conception of liberalism, the only obligation the government has is to protect negative liberties, and it is not obliged to provide social allowances. See András Sajó, "Szociális jólét és rossz közérzet", *Beszélő*, 1996/3, p. 26, and András Sajó, "A jogosultságok lehetősége," *Beszélő*, 1997/1, p. 7. Others, as the author of this study, hold that the principle of equal treatment has distributional consequences but think that these implications should not be enforced through judicial intervention in budget decisions. See Chapter 3 of the previous study, and the reasoning of the next section.

125 Csaba Tordai was, as far as I am aware, the first to formulate this characterization. See his "Alkotmánybíráskodás Magyarországon", *Fundamentum*, 1999/2, p. 74.

126 45/1995 (VI. 30), ABH 1995, 210.

127 *Ibid.* and 54/1995 (IX. 15), ABH 1995, 245, and 60/1995 (IX. 15), ABH 1995, 304.

128 43/1995 (VI. 30), ABH 1995, 188, 193, and 56/1995 (IX. 15), ABH 1995, 260, 267.

129 See 44/1995 (VI. 30), ABH 1995, 203 on the amendment of the law on social security (1975: II).

130 See 56/1995 (IX. 15), ABH 1995, 260 on the amendment of the Labor Code and the attached provisions (1992: XXII).

131 ABH 1995, 260, 265.

132 The first relevant resolution, 44/1995 (VI. 30), took this fact explicitly into account: it ordered the postponing of the entry into force of the examined article on the ground that it did not leave sufficient preparatory period for the employers.

133 If viewed from this perspective, not even the total abolition of support for the period of illness is to be judged necessarily as a disproportionate measure, and this is acknowledged by the ruling: "It is a matter of legislation rather than of constitutional review to determine which kind of medical interventions should be supported by the state health insurance, out of the range of all health services."

134 See the judicial definition of the test of proportionality in 20/1990 (X. 4): the requirement of proportionality "demands that the importance of the intended goal be proportionate with the harm to fundamental rights done by the measure made in order to promote this goal". ABH 1990, 69, 71. Cf. 21/1990 (X. 4), ABH 1990, 73, and 16/1991 (IV. 20), ABH 1991, 81.

135 See ABH 1995, 260, 267.

136 66/1995 (XI. 24), ABH 1995, 333, 340.

137 ABH 1995, 333, 341.

138 In the 15 October 1995 issue of *Figyelő*, Tibor Krecz questioned the accuracy of the calculations of the judges in relation to disability allowance reduction: according to resolution 56/1995, the stabilization law revoked 75 percent of the support granted for the period of economic incapacity, which is qualified as disproportionate ("over half") restriction. According to Krecz's alternative calculations, the reduction amounted only to 40 percent, or "less than half". See his article "Tévedett-e az Alkotmánybíróság?" Also noteworthly are some comprehensive economic evaluations of the stabilization. Thus János Kornai in his article "Kiigazítás recesszió nélkül" (*Közgazdasági Szemle*, 43/1996, pp. 55–613) makes the following remarkable claims. First, without the restrictions Hungary could have slid into a financial disaster comparable to that of Mexico. Second, the measures included in the stabilization package prevented the collapse without the significant drop in production and the dramatic increase in unemployment that usually accompany austerity programs. It was this relative advantage that had to be paid for by a considerable drop in living standards and the increase of inflation. In Kornai's reading, the government had to choose between an upsurge of unemployment and a drop in consumption. If this is true, then the Court should have assessed the contested measures from this perspective.

139 According to Section 3 of Article 19 of the constitution, the Parliament establishes the balance of the state finances and approves the budget and its execution.

140 János Kis, "Összekuszálódó hatalmi ágak", *Népszabadság*, 15 July 1995.

141 See László Sólyom's statement in the interview in *Népszabadság* cited above, and Gábor Halmai's article "Alkotmánybíróság és hatalommegosztás", *Népszabadság*, 10 August 1995.

142 See György Márkus, "Illúziók és reáliák", *Beszélő*, 1997/7–8, p. 54.

143 See László Sólyom's summary overview in his parallel opinion attached to 35/1994 (VI. 24), ABH 1994, 197, 215.

144 A promising instance is the re-establishment of the procedural rule that laws approved by a two-thirds majority might be amended only by a two-thirds majority as well; see 1/1999 (II. 24) that declared the law "against organized crime" to be partially unconstitutional. A disquieting instance is the ambiguous treatment of the parliamentary resolution that altered the order of plenary sessions of the Parliament without amending the standing order itself; see 4/1999 (III. 31).

145 1/B/1999.11 (XII. 21).

146 Of course it is conceivable that the judges were prevented from examining the problem of a procedural violation of the constitution by the fact that they more strictly adhere than their predecessors to the requirement that rulings must be bound to the motion; provided that the petitioners did not request to establish the formal violation of the procedural order of the rule of law, the Court could not extend the investigation to this subject.

147 See 12/1999 (V. 21) that struck down the hate speech article reintroduced into the Criminal Code, and 20/1999 (VI. 25), which declared it unconstitutional that the criminal case of "unnatural sexual perversion" is restricted to same sex couples.

Index